This is th

Cultural The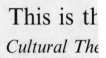

Acknowledgments

The editor gratefully wishes to thank the Consultants of the *NIV Thematic Study Bible*: Alister McGrath, Donald J. Wiseman, J. I. Packer, Stephen Travis, Gordon McConville, and all those who compiled and edited the Thematic Section of the *NIV Thematic Study Bible*, on which this work is based.

THIS IS THE
BIBLE WORLD

Cultural themes
from the Bible

Edited by Martin H. Manser

Hodder & Stoughton
LONDON SYDNEY AUCKLAND

10 9 8 7 6 5 4 3 2 1

A CIP catalogue record for this title is
available from the British Library

ISBN 0 340 65653 0

Typeset by Hewer Text Composition Services, Edinburgh
Printed and bound in Great Britain by
Clays Ltd, St Ives plc

Hodder & Stoughton Ltd
A Division of Hodder Headline PLC
338 Euston Road
London NW1 3BH

Contents

Introduction

The study of Scripture lies at the heart of the Christian faith. It is therefore important that readers of Scripture are given every means of help so that they will derive as much benefit and understanding as possible from reading the Bible. *This is the Bible World* is a selection of some 250 themes from the acclaimed *NIV Thematic Study Bible* published by Hodder and Stoughton.

Thematic study of the Bible is important because it draws together from different parts of the Bible what Scripture says on a particular subject. *This is the Bible World* is a selection of themes relating to the culture and civilisation of life in biblical times. Themes covered include not only general cultural themes such as: animals, languages, occupations, weights and measures, but also religious themes such as: atonement, circumcision, covenant, feasts and festivals, sacrifice, tabernacle.

A thematic study is different from a lexical study in that the former is based on related ideas, the latter on individual words. The difference between them can be appreciated by considering the theme of "poverty". A word-based approach would be limited to identifying biblical passages in which the word "poverty" appears and these are comparatively few (20 in total). A thematic approach, however, goes far beyond this and explores all the various elements of the theme. It identifies its basic concepts, its background and its consequences, in order that the theme in its fulness can be unfolded to the reader. For example the material that deals with poverty covers the causes of poverty (e.g., idleness, debt, oppression, misfortune), attitudes to poverty, the results of poverty and remedies for poverty (e.g., God's concern for the poor, the giving of practical help, the upholding of justice).

In this selection the text of key verses is quoted from the inclusive-language (gender-neutral) NIV Bible text. Many other verse references are also included to provide a wealth of biblical material.

A thorough system of cross-references allows the interrelationship of biblical themes to be understood and explored. For example, from "law" the reader is referred to the following: atonement; clean and unclean; crime; idolatry; justice; offerings; property; ritual law; Sabbath; sacrifice; slavery.

Martin H. Manser
Aylesbury 1998

How to study a theme

Themes in this edition are arranged alphabetically by title. Each theme consists of a precise summary of the nature and importance of the theme, followed by a detailed analysis of its main parts. The text of Scripture for the main references appears in full, and many other scriptural references document each of the theme's aspects. At the end of the themes cross-references are provided to related themes included in this book.

Theme name ──────────── **Holy Spirit, indwelling**
The Holy Spirit dwells within Jesus Christ and his

Introduction gives a concise definition of the theme ──── disciples. Recognisable results in believers' lives
to show its contents and importance include Christlikeness and the fruit of the Spirit.

Major headings set out clearly the key aspects of ──── **The indwelling of the Holy Spirit in the OT**
the theme **Ge 41:38** So Pharaoh asked them [his

Main verse reference printed in bold type ──── officials], "Can we find anyone like this man
(e.g., Ge 41:38) [Joseph], one in whom is the spirit of God?"
Ex 35:31 ". . . and he [the LORD] has filled him
[Bezalel] with the Spirit of God, with skill, ability

Scripture text given for main references ──── and knowledge in all kinds of crafts—" *See
also* **Nu** 27:18; **1Sa** 10:6–7; **Isa** 59:21; **Hag** 2:5

Comment or explanation is in reduced type. If it **The Holy Spirit indwells believers**
relates to a single verse reference it follows it; if **2Ti 1:14** . . . the Holy Spirit who lives in us.
it relates to a group of references it precedes Believers are described as the temple of the Holy Spirit:
them **1Co** 3:16; 6:19

If there are further secondary references after **Eph** 2:22; **1Jn** 2:27; 3:24
such a group, they start on a new line

Parallel passages are preceded by "pp" and are not **Results of the Holy Spirit's indwelling in
in bold type believers**
Preaching and public testimony is aided Mt

Subheadings ──── 10:20 pp Mk 13:11 pp Lk 12:12; **Ac** 4:8–12;
5:29–32
The fruit of the Spirit is displayed

Secondary verses support the main verse, preceded **Gal 5:22–23** . . . the fruit of the Spirit is
by See also. The Bible book name only is love, joy, peace, patience, kindness, goodness,
printed in bold type faithfulness, gentleness and self-control . . .
(e.g., **Ro** 5:5) *See also* **Ro** 5:5; 14:17; 15:13,30

Cross-references to other themes are in italics. **Those without the Holy Spirit's
These enable you to look up related material indwelling are not Christlike**
Gal 5:17; **Jude** 18–19 *See also Christlikeness;
Holy Spirit in life of Jesus Christ; Holy Spirit, filling with;*

Abbreviations

A.D.	since the birth of Jesus Christ	
B.C.	before the birth of Jesus Christ	
c.	about	
fn	footnote	
NT	New Testament	
OT	Old Testament	
pp	parallel passage	

The Old Testament

Genesis	**Ge**	2 Chronicles	**2Ch**	Daniel	**Da**
Exodus	**Ex**	Ezra	**Ezr**	Hosea	**Hos**
Leviticus	**Lev**	Nehemiah	**Ne**	Joel	**Joel**
Numbers	**Nu**	Esther	**Est**	Amos	**Am**
Deuteronomy	**Dt**	Job	**Job**	Obadiah	**Ob**
Joshua	**Jos**	Psalms	**Ps**	Jonah	**Jnh**
Judges	**Jdg**	Proverbs	**Pr**	Micah	**Mic**
Ruth	**Ru**	Ecclesiastes	**Ecc**	Nahum	**Na**
1 Samuel	**1Sa**	Song of Songs	**SS**	Habakkuk	**Hab**
2 Samuel	**2Sa**	Isaiah	**Isa**	Zephaniah	**Zep**
1 Kings	**1Ki**	Jeremiah	**Jer**	Haggai	**Hag**
2 Kings	**2Ki**	Lamentations	**La**	Zechariah	**Zec**
1 Chronicles	**1Ch**	Ezekiel	**Eze**	Malachi	**Mal**

The New Testament

Matthew	**Mt**	Ephesians	**Eph**	Hebrews	**Heb**
Mark	**Mk**	Philippians	**Php**	James	**Jas**
Luke	**Lk**	Colossians	**Col**	1 Peter	**1Pe**
John	**Jn**	1 Thessalonians	**1Th**	2 Peter	**2Pe**
Acts	**Ac**	2 Thessalonians	**2Th**	1 John	**1Jn**
Romans	**Ro**	1 Timothy	**1Ti**	2 John	**2Jn**
1 Corinthians	**1Co**	2 Timothy	**2Ti**	3 John	**3Jn**
2 Corinthians	**2Co**	Titus	**Tit**	Jude	**Jude**
Galatians	**Gal**	Philemon	**Phm**	Revelation	**Rev**

BIBLE THEMES

agriculture

The science of cultivation. The task, given to humanity, of cultivating the land is a reflection of God's own care for his creation.

A major activity for humanity

Ge 2:15 The LORD God took the man and put him in the Garden of Eden to work it and take care of it.   *See also* **Ge** 3:23; 4:2,12; 9:20; 47:19; **Dt** 8:7–8; **1Ki** 19:19; **2Ch** 26:10; **Isa** 37:30

Growth is according to the sovereign will of God

He has established the seasons

Ge 8:22 "As long as the earth endures, seedtime and harvest, cold and heat, summer and winter, day and night will never cease."

Ac 14:17 "Yet he [God] has not left himself without testimony: He has shown kindness by giving you rain from heaven and crops in their seasons; he provides you with plenty of food and fills your hearts with joy."   *See also* **Lev** 26:4; **Jer** 5:24

He provides for the growth of the crops

Ps 65:9 You [LORD] care for the land and water it; you enrich it abundantly. The streams of God are filled with water to provide the people with corn, for so you have ordained it.   *See also* **Ps** 104:14; 107:37–38; 147:8; **Eze** 34:26–27; **Zec** 8:12; **Mt** 6:30; **2Co** 9:10

OT laws for agriculture showed how to co-operate with God

Lev 19:19 " 'Keep my decrees. Do not mate different kinds of animals. Do not plant your field with two kinds of seed . . .' "   *See also* **Lev** 19:23; 25:3–4; **Dt** 22:10

Harvest festivals were for thanking God for his provision

Ex 34:22 "Celebrate the Feast of Weeks with the firstfruits of the wheat harvest, and the Feast of Ingathering at the turn of the year."   *See also* **Lev** 23:10,39–41; **Dt** 16:10,13

Cultivation was affected by the fall

Ge 3:17 To Adam he [God] said, "Because you listened to your wife and ate from the tree about which I commanded you, 'You must not eat of it,' Cursed is the ground because of you; through painful toil you will eat of it all the days of your life."   *See also* **Ge** 3:18–19; 4:12; 5:29; **Ro** 8:20

Agricultural images of God's action among his people

Isa 5:7 The vineyard of the LORD Almighty is the house of Israel, and the people of Judah are the garden of his delight. And he looked for justice, but saw bloodshed; for righteousness, but heard cries of distress.

Mt 9:37 . . . [Jesus] said to his disciples, "The harvest is plentiful but the workers are few."

Jn 12:24 [Jesus said] "I tell you the truth, unless a grain of wheat falls to the ground and dies, it remains only a single seed. But if it dies, it produces many seeds."   *See also* **Isa** 17:5–6; 24:13; **Jer** 8:20; 50:16; 51:33; **Hos** 6:11; **Mt** 13:3–8 pp Mk 4:3–8 pp Lk 8:5–8; **Mt** 13:18–23 pp Mk 4:13–20 pp Lk 8:11–15; **Mt** 13:24–30; **Mk** 4:26–29; **Jn** 4:35–38   *See also* harvest; horticulture; life, animal and plant; ploughing; sowing and reaping; vineyard.

altar

A construction, usually of wood, stone or metal, for the offering of sacrifice. The conflict between true and false religion often focused on altars, which were of key significance in biblical times.

Early altars built to the LORD

Ge 8:20 Then Noah built an altar to the LORD and, taking some of all the clean animals and clean birds, he sacrificed burnt offerings on it.

By Abraham: **Ge** 12:7–8; 13:18; 22:9

Ge 26:25

By Jacob: **Ge** 33:20; 35:7

By Moses: **Ex** 17:15; 24:4

Jos 8:30; **Jdg** 6:24; 21:4; **1Sa** 7:17; 14:35; **2Sa** 24:25 pp 1Ch 21:26

Solomon's temple altar

It was preceded by the tabernacle altar of burnt offering:
Ex 27:1–8; 30:1–10; 37:25–28; 38:1–7; **Heb** 9:3–4

1Ki 8:22; 6:20

OT pagan altars

A symptom of decline in the northern kingdom
1Ki 16:32; **2Ki** 23:15; **Hos** 8:11; 10:1

A symptom of decline in the southern kingdom
2Ki 16:10; 21:3; **Isa** 17:8; **Jer** 11:13; 19:13; **Zep** 1:5

Josiah's reform targeted illicit altars
2Ki 23:12 He [Josiah] pulled down the altars the kings of Judah had erected on the roof near the upper room of Ahaz, and the altars Manasseh had built in the two courts of the temple of the LORD . . . *See also* **Dt** 7:5; 12:8–14; **2Ki** 23:15–20

The altar in the second temple

Ezr 3:2–3 . . . Jeshua son of Jozadak and his fellow priests and Zerubbabel son of Shealtiel and his associates began to build the altar of the God of Israel to sacrifice burnt offerings on it . . . they built the altar on its foundation and sacrificed burnt offerings on it to the LORD . . . *See also* **Ezr** 7:17

Laws concerning the altar of burnt offering

Its construction

Ex 20:24–26 " 'Make an altar of earth for me [the LORD] and sacrifice on it your burnt offerings and fellowship offerings . . . If you make an altar of stones for me, do not build it with dressed stones . . . And do not go up to my altar on steps, lest your nakedness be exposed on it.' " *See also* **Ex** 27:1–8; 38:1–7

Its use for the daily sacrifice

Ex 29:38–39 "This is what you are to offer on the altar regularly each day: two lambs a year old. Offer one in the morning and the other at twilight." *See also* **Ex** 30:28; **Nu** 4:13; 7:10,84

Its use for asylum

1Ki 1:50–51 . . . Then Solomon was told, "Adonijah is afraid of King Solomon and is clinging to the horns of the altar. He says, 'Let King Solomon swear to me today that he will not put his servant to death with the sword.' " *See also* **Ex** 21:14; **1Ki** 2:28; **Am** 3:14

Laws concerning the incense altar

Its construction

Ex 30:1–5 "Make an altar of acacia wood for burning incense . . ." *See also* **Ex** 37:25–28

Its use

Ex 30:7 "Aaron must burn fragrant incense on the altar every morning when he tends the lamps." *See also* **Ex** 30:8–10; **Nu** 4:11

Altars in the NT

The Jerusalem temple altar

Mt 5:23–24 "Therefore, if you are offering your gift at the altar and there remember that your brother or sister has something against you, leave your gift there in front of the altar. First go and be reconciled to them; then come and offer your gift." *See also* **Mt** 23:18–20; **1Co** 9:13; 10:18; **Heb** 7:13; 9:4

Pagan altars

Ac 17:23 "For as I [Paul] walked around and looked carefully at your objects of worship, I even found an altar with this inscription: TO AN UNKNOWN GOD . . ."

The cross as an "altar"

Heb 13:10 We have an altar from which those who minister at the tabernacle have no right to eat.

Altars in heaven

Rev 6:9 When he [the Lamb] opened the fifth seal, I [John] saw under the altar the souls of those who had been slain because of the word of

God and the testimony they had maintained. **Rev 8:3** Another angel, who had a golden censer, came and stood at the altar. He was given much incense to offer, with the prayers of all the saints, on the golden altar before the throne.   *See also* **Rev** 9:13; 11:1; 14:18; 16:7 *See also atonement; blood; offerings; priesthood; sacrifice, in Old Testament; tabernacle; temple.*

animals

A category of living creatures that dwell mainly on the land, distinguished from fishes, birds and insects. Scripture stresses that all animals are created by God and are subordinate to human beings.

animals

As a class within the created order, their variety reflects God's generous giving. He makes human beings their stewards, though they themselves come into the category of creatures.

Animals in their profusion
Ge 1:24–25 And God said, "Let the land produce living creatures according to their kinds: livestock, creatures that move along the ground, and wild animals, each according to its kind." And it was so. God made the wild animals according to their kinds, the livestock according to their kinds, and all the creatures that move along the ground according to their kinds. And God saw that it was good.   *See also* **Ge** 7:1–3,13–16; 8:15–19; **Ps** 50:9–11; 148:7–10; **Isa** 43:20; **Eze** 36:11

Animals as illustrated by their variety
Isa 11:6–8 The wolf will live with the lamb, the leopard will lie down with the goat, the calf and the lion and the yearling together; and a little child will lead them. The cow will feed with the bear, their young will lie down together, and the lion will eat straw like the ox. Infants will play near the hole of the cobra, and children put their hands into the viper's nest.
Ox, donkey Ex 23:12
Goat, sea cow Ex 25:3–5

Rabbit, pig Lev 11:4–7
Weasel, rat Lev 11:29–30
Heifer Nu 19:2
Deer, gazelle, antelope Dt 14:4–5
Sheep, bear, lion 1Sa 17:34–35
Possibly the hippopotamus Job 40:15–24
Possibly the crocodile Job 41:1–34
Snake Ps 58:4
Frog Ps 105:30
Fox SS 2:15
Jackal, wild goat, hyena Isa 13:21–22
Worm Isa 51:8

Human beings within the animal creation
As part of creation
Ge 2:7 the LORD God formed a man from the dust of the ground and breathed into his nostrils the breath of life, and the man became a living being.
Ecc 3:18–21 I also thought, "As for human beings, God tests them so that they may see that they are like the animals. Surely the fate of a human being is like that of an animal; the same fate awaits them both: As one dies, so dies the other. All have the same breath; the human race has no advantage over animals. Everything is meaningless. All go to the same place; all come from dust, and to dust all return. Who knows if the human spirit rises upward and if the spirit of the animal goes down into the earth?"   *See also* **Ps** 49:12
Significantly different from the rest of creation
Ge 1:26–27 Then God said, "Let us make human beings in our image, in our likeness, and let them rule over the fish of the sea and the birds of the air, over the livestock, over all the earth, and over all the creatures that move along the ground." So God created human beings in his own image, in the image of God he created them; male and female he created them.

Human beings as stewards of the animal kingdom
Ps 8:6–8 You [LORD] made them [human beings] rulers over the works of your hands; you put everything under their feet: all flocks and

herds, and the beasts of the field, the birds of the air, and the fish of the sea, all that swim the paths of the seas.   *See also* **Ge** 1:26–28; 2:19–20; 9:1–2; **Heb** 2:6–8; **Jas** 3:7–8

Animals as the objects of divine, and therefore human, care

Ge 9:8–10 Then God said to Noah and to his sons with him: "I now establish my covenant with you and with your descendants after you and with every living creature that was with you—the birds, the livestock and all the wild animals, all those that came out of the ark with you—every living creature on earth."   *See also* **Ge** 8:1; **Ex** 9:4–6; **2Ki** 3:17; **Job** 5:23; 38:39–41; 39:1–30; **Ps** 104:20–21; **Pr** 12:10; 27:23; **Joel** 2:22; **Jnh** 4:11

Animals and Noah's ark

Ge 7:13–23   *See also life, animal and plant.*

animals, religious role

Central to the OT sacrificial system, they were governed by strict laws within the Mosaic code.

Animals as defined by the Law of Moses

Animals for food

Lev 20:25–26 " 'You must therefore make a distinction between clean and unclean animals and between unclean and clean birds. Do not defile yourselves by any animal or bird or anything that moves along the ground—those which I have set apart as unclean for you. You are to be holy to me because I, the LORD, am holy, and I have set you apart from the nations to be my own.' "   *See also* **Ex** 22:31; **Lev** 22:8; **Dt** 12:15–16,21; 14:3–8; **Eze** 4:14; 44:31; **Ac** 10:9–14; 11:6; 15:19–20

Animals dedicated to the LORD

Ex 13:1–2 The LORD said to Moses, "Consecrate to me every firstborn male. The first offspring of every womb among the Israelites belongs to me, whether human or animal."   *See also* **Lev** 27:9–13,26–28,32–33; **Nu** 18:15   **Domestic animals Ex** 21:33–36; 22:10–15; **Lev** 24:18–21

Relationships with animals forbidden Ex 22:19; **Lev** 19:19   **Animal carcasses Lev** 11:39

Animals in the context of Israel's sacrificial system

Used in various sacrifices

Lev 1:1–2 The LORD called to Moses and spoke to him from the Tent of Meeting. He said, "Speak to the Israelites and say to them: 'When you bring an offering to the LORD, bring as your offering an animal from either the herd or the flock.' "

Ps 66:15 I will sacrifice fat animals to you and an offering of rams; I will offer bulls and goats . . .   *See also* **Ge** 8:20; **Lev** 3:1; **Nu** 7:87–88; **Dt** 16:2; **2Ch** 29:32–33; 35:10–13

Animals forbidden as sacrifices

Mal 1:8 "When you bring blind animals for sacrifice, is that not wrong? When you sacrifice crippled or diseased animals, is that not wrong? Try offering them to your governor! Would he be pleased with you? Would he accept you?" says the LORD Almighty.   *See also* **Lev** 22:24–25; **Dt** 15:21; **Mal** 1:13–14

Animals in the context of judgment

Involved in judgment

Zep 1:3 "I will sweep away both people and animals; I will sweep away the birds of the air and the fish of the sea. The wicked will have only heaps of rubble when I cut off people from the face of the earth," declares the LORD.   *See also* **Ge** 6:7; 7:20–23   The plagues of Egypt: **Ex** 9:22–25; 13:15; **Ps** 135:8   **Jer** 9:10; 12:4; 50:3; **Eze** 25:12–13; **Joel** 1:19–20; **Hab** 2:17; **Zec** 14:15

As agents of judgment

Lev 26:21–22 " 'If you [Israelites] remain hostile towards me [the LORD] and refuse to listen to me, I will multiply your afflictions seven times over, as your sins deserve. I will send wild animals against you, and they will rob you of your children, destroy your cattle and make you so few in number that your roads will be deserted.' "   *See also* **Eze** 33:27; 39:4,17–18; **Da** 4:31–32; **Hos** 2:12   *See also blood, Old*

Testament sacrifices; clean and unclean; law; offerings; sacrifice, in Old Testament.

architecture

The design of buildings, for religious or secular use. Building designs were often regarded in Scripture as embodying spiritual truths, and capable of being divinely inspired.

Examples of architecture
The tabernacle
Heb 8:5 They [the High Priests] serve at a sanctuary that is a copy and shadow of what is in heaven. This is why Moses was warned when he was about to build the tabernacle: "See to it that you make everything according to the pattern shown you on the mountain." *See also* **Ex** 25:8–9; 26:1–37
The temple
1Ch 28:11-12 Then David gave his son Solomon the plans for the portico of the temple, its buildings, its storerooms, its upper parts, its inner rooms and the place of atonement. He gave him the plans of all that the Spirit had put in his mind for the courts of the temple of the LORD and all the surrounding rooms, for the treasuries of the temple of God and for the treasuries for the dedicated things. *See also* **1Ki** 6:1–10,15–38; **1Ch** 28:19; **2Ch** 3:1–17; 4:1–22
Altars
Jos 8:31 . . . He [Joshua] built it according to what is written in the Book of the Law of Moses—an altar of uncut stones, on which no iron tool had been used . . . *See also* **Ex** 20:25; **2Ki** 16:10–11
Ordinary dwellings Dt 22:8
Ezekiel's vision of a restored temple Eze 40:1–49; 41:1–26; 42:1–20; 43:10–17
Other structures Ge 11:4; 1Ki 7:1–12; Pr 24:3–4; Jer 22:13–14

Divinely dictated design
The ark Ge 6:14–16

Building design as a spiritual metaphor
The prophecy of the rejected stone Ps 118:22;

Mt 21:42 pp Mk 12:10 pp Lk 20:17; **1Pe** 2:7; **Mt** 7:24–27 pp Lk 6:48–49; **1Co** 3:10–13; **Eph** 2:19–22; **1Pe** 2:4–7; **Isa** 54:11–12; **Heb** 11:10; **Rev** 21:9–22

God as the architect of creation
Job 38:4–5 *See also arts and crafts; building; city; house; palaces; tabernacle, in Old Testament; temple, Solomon's.*

ark of the covenant

A rectangular wooden box, overlaid with gold, measuring 3.75 x 2.25 x 2.25 feet (1.1 x 0.7 x 0.7 metres). It contains the Law tablets and symbolises God's presence with his people.

Descriptions of the ark
Ex 25:22; **Lev** 16:2; **Nu** 10:33; **Jos** 3:6; 4:5,9; **1Sa** 4:11
The construction of the ark Ex 25:10–16; **Dt** 10:1; **Ex** 31:1–7; 35:10–12; 37:1–5; **Dt** 10:3; **Ex** 39:33,35; 40:1–5,20–21
The construction of the atonement cover Ex 25:17–21; 26:34; 30:6; 37:6–9; 39:35; 40:20

The care of the ark
Nu 3:30–32; 4:5; **Dt** 10:8; 31:9

Major events in the history of the ark
The ark is taken to the promised land Jos 3:3,6,15–16; 6:4–16; 8:33
The ark is the focus of the covenant renewal at Mount Ebal Jdg 20:26–28
The ark is captured by the Philistines 1Sa 4:1–11,17–22; 5:1–12
The ark is returned to Israel 1Sa 6:1–3,10–15,19; 7:1–2
The ark is brought to Jerusalem 2Sa 6:1–12 pp 1Ch 13:3–14; **2Sa** 6:17 pp 1Ch 16:1; **1Ch** 15:1; 16:37; **2Sa** 7:2–7 pp 1Ch 17:1–6; **2Sa** 15:24–25,29
The ark is placed in the temple 1Ki 8:1–6 pp 2Ch 5:2–7
The ark in later Israelite history 2Ch 35:3

The function of the ark
To contain the tablets of the Law
Dt 10:5 Then I [Moses] came back down the mountain and put the tablets in the ark I had made, as the LORD commanded me . . .
See also **Ex** 25:16,21; 40:20; **Dt** 31:24–26; **1Ki** 8:9; **Heb** 9:4

As the place where God reveals his commands to Moses
Nu 7:89 . . . Moses . . . heard the voice speaking to him from between the two cherubim above the atonement cover on the ark of the Testimony . . . *See also* **Ex** 25:22; 30:6,36

As a symbol of the presence of God
Lev 16:2 The LORD said to Moses: "Tell your brother Aaron not to come whenever he chooses into the Most Holy Place behind the curtain in front of the atonement cover on the ark, or else he will die, because I appear in the cloud over the atonement cover." *See also* **Nu** 10:33–36; **Jos** 7:6; **Jdg** 20:27; **2Sa** 7:2 pp 1Ch 17:1; **2Ch** 6:41 pp Ps 132:8

Used on the Day of Atonement
Lev 16:13–15 "He [Aaron] is to put the incense on the fire before the LORD, and the smoke of the incense will conceal the atonement cover above the Testimony, so that he will not die. He is to take some of the bull's blood and with his finger sprinkle it on the front of the atonement cover; then he shall sprinkle some of it with his finger seven times before the atonement cover. He shall then slaughter the goat for the sin offering for the people and take its blood behind the curtain and do with it as he did with the bull's blood: He shall sprinkle it on the atonement cover and in front of it."

The ark's holiness and effect
Irreverent treatment of the ark brings judgment
2Sa 6:6–7 When they came to the threshing-floor of Nacon, Uzzah reached out and took hold of the ark of God, because the oxen stumbled. The LORD's anger burned against Uzzah because of his irreverent act; therefore God struck him down and he died there beside the ark of God. pp 1Ch 13:9–10 *See also* **Jos** 3:4; **1Sa** 5:1–4,8–12; 6:19

The presence of the ark brings blessing
2Sa 6:11 The ark of the LORD remained in the house of Obed-Edom the Gittite for three months, and the LORD blessed him and his entire household. pp 1Ch 13:14

A restored Israel in which the ark has no place
Jer 3:16 . . . "people will no longer say, 'The ark of the covenant of the LORD.' It will never enter their minds or be remembered; it will not be missed, nor will another one be made."

The ark in John's revelation
Rev 11:19 Then God's temple in heaven was opened, and within his temple was seen the ark of his covenant . . . *See also Atonement, Day of; law, Ten Commandments; Most Holy Place; tabernacle; temple, Solomon's.*

---

armies
An organised military force for the defence or expansion of national borders. Israel's national life was characterised by many battles with foreign nations such as Egypt, Philistia, Assyria and Babylon and by Roman occupation.

Examples of armies in conflict with Israel
The Egyptian army when Israel left Egypt Ex 14:5–9,23–25
The inhabitants of Canaan when Israel entered the promised land Jos 3:10; 12:1,7; 23:9; **Jdg** 3:1–3
The Philistines, a constant enemy 1Sa 13:5; 14:20–23; 17:1–3; 31:1,7 pp 1Ch 10:7
Assyria, defeating the northern kingdom of Israel 2Ki 15:29; 17:5–6; **Isa** 36:1
Babylon, defeating the southern kingdom of Judah 2Ki 24:1; 25:1; **Jer** 39:1 pp Jer 52:4; **2Ki** 25:10–11 pp 2Ch 36:17

Palestine occupied by the Roman army in NT times
Roman law in force at the time of Jesus Christ Lk 2:1; **Jn** 18:28

Roman military personnel in the life of Jesus
Christ and in the lives of the first Christians
Mt 8:5 pp Lk 7:3; **Mt** 27:54 pp Lk 23:47; **Ac** 10:1;
21:31

Development of Israel's army from the
time of the exodus to the reign of
Solomon

A military census taken after the exodus Nu
1:3; 26:2

Fighting men to secure Israelites' possession
of the promised land Dt 7:1–2; **Jos** 1:10–11;
12:1

The army as a tribal militia assembled in
times of crisis Jdg 4:1–6

Certain tribes gaining reputations for
proficiency in particular forms of combat Jdg
20:16; **1Ch** 12:2,8,24–37

Saul and David having regular contingents of
special forces **1Sa** 13:2; **2Sa** 15:18; 23:8–12 pp
1Ch 11:10–14

Forces divided into twelve battalions, each
serving for a month at a time 1Ch 27:1

Chariot forces hardly known in David's time,
but much used by Solomon 2Sa 8:3–4; **1Ki**
4:26; 10:26

God's sovereignty over the armies of
Israel and over his spiritual armies
Jos 5:13–15; **1Sa** 17:45; **1Ki** 22:19; **2Ki**
6:17

In the final battle between good and evil,
Jesus Christ appearing as the leader of the
armies of heaven Rev 19:14,19

God as the commander of armies
Ps 89:8 O LORD God Almighty, who is like you?
You are mighty, O LORD, and your faithfulness
surrounds you.

The term in Ps 89:8, and in the following verses,
translated as "LORD God Almighty" may also be
translated "LORD God of hosts" or "LORD God of
armies": **1Ki** 19:10; **Jer** 5:14; **Hos** 12:5; **Am**
4:13   *See also armour; warfare; weapons.*

armour
Protective covering worn by soldiers to prevent
injury in battle. However, those who wore it were
not impregnable. Christians are to be equipped
with spiritual armour.

Coat of armour
The breastplate
2Ch 26:14 Uzziah provided shields, spears,
helmets, coats of armour, bows and slingstones
for the entire army.   *See also* **1Sa** 17:5,38; **2Sa**
20:8; **Eph** 6:14
The belt
2Sa 20:8 . . . Joab was wearing his military
tunic, and strapped over it at his waist was a belt
with a dagger in its sheath . . .   *See also* **1Sa**
18:4; **2Sa** 18:11; **Eph** 6:14
The helmet
1Sa 17:5 He [Goliath] had a bronze helmet on
his head . . .   *See also* **1Sa** 17:38; **2Ch** 26:14;
Jer 46:4; **Eze** 38:5
The shield
Jer 46:3 "Prepare your shields, both large and
small, and march out for battle!"   *See also* **2Ch**
11:12; 32:5; **Ne** 4:16; **Eph** 6:16

Armour worn by soldiers
2Ch 26:14 Uzziah provided shields, spears,
helmets, coats of armour, bows and slingstones
for the entire army.   *See also* **Nu** 31:3–5;
32:20–21,27; **Jos** 4:13; **Jer** 46:3–4

Armour-bearers
1Sa 16:21 David came to Saul and entered his
service. Saul liked him very much, and David
became one of his armour-bearers.   *See also* **Jdg**
9:54; **1Sa** 14:1,6–14; 17:7

Those wearing armour were not
impregnable
1Ki 20:11 The king of Israel answered, "Tell
him: 'One who puts on his armour should not
boast like one who takes it off.'"
1Ki 22:34 But someone drew his bow at
random and hit the king of Israel between the
sections of his armour . . . pp 2Ch 18:33

See also **1Sa** 17:48–49; 31:3–4; **Lk** 11:21–22

Christians are to be equipped with spiritual armour

Eph 6:11 Put on the full armour of God so that you can take your stand against the devil's schemes.   *See also* **Eph** 6:13–17; **Ro** 13:12; **2Co** 6:7; **1Th** 5:8   *See also warfare; weapons.*

---

art

Skilful, creative work, carried out using a variety of materials. Purposes included decoration, ornamentation and representation of objects of worship, the last of which Scripture firmly condemns.

Painting

Eze 8:10 . . . I [Ezekiel] went in and looked, and I saw portrayed all over the walls all kinds of crawling things and detestable animals . . . *See also* **Eze** 23:11–15

Decorative panelling

2Ch 3:5–7 He [Solomon] panelled the main hall with pine and covered it with fine gold and decorated it with palm tree and chain designs . . .   *See also* **1Ki** 6:14–15; **Ps** 74:3–6; **Jer** 22:14

Decoration and ornamentation in gold

1Ki 6:21–22 Solomon covered the inside of the temple with pure gold, and he extended gold chains across the front of the inner sanctuary, which was overlaid with gold. So he overlaid the whole interior with gold. He also overlaid with gold the altar that belonged to the inner sanctuary. pp 2Ch 3:4–7   *See also* **1Ki** 6:31–35; 10:14–21 pp 2Ch 9:13–20

Decoration and ornamentation in ivory

SS 5:14 His [the beloved's] arms are rods of gold set with chrysolite. His body is like polished ivory decorated with sapphires.   *See also* **1Ki** 10:18 pp 2Ch 9:17; **1Ki** 22:39; **Ps** 45:8; **Am** 3:15; 6:4

Carving and sculpture

1Ki 6:18 The inside of the temple was cedar, carved with gourds and open flowers. Everything was cedar; no stone was to be seen.   *See also* **1Ki** 6:29–35; **2Ch** 3:7; **Ps** 144:12; **Eze** 41:15–26

Engraving
As an artistic skill

1Ki 7:34–37 . . . He [Huram] engraved cherubim, lions and palm trees on the surfaces of the supports and on the panels, in every available space, with wreaths all around . . .   *See also* **Ex** 28:9–12,15–21,36–38; 39:6–7,8–14,30–31; **1Ki** 7:31,36; **2Ch** 2:5–7,13–14

Metaphorical references to engraving

Job 19:23–24 "Oh, that my [Job's] words were recorded, that they were written on a scroll, that they were inscribed with an iron tool on lead, or engraved in rock for ever!"   *See also* **Isa** 49:16; **Jer** 17:1; **Zec** 3:9

Art in the tabernacle

Ex 26:1 "Make the tabernacle with ten curtains of finely twisted linen and blue, purple and scarlet yarn, with cherubim worked into them by skilled hands."   *See also* **Ex** 25:18–21; 36:8,35–38; 37:7–9

Art in the temple

1Ki 7:48–50 Solomon also made all the furnishings that were in the Lᴏʀᴅ's temple: the golden altar; the golden table on which was the bread of the Presence; the lampstands of pure gold (five on the right and five on the left, in front of the inner sanctuary); the gold floral work and lamps and tongs; the pure gold dishes, wick trimmers, sprinkling bowls, dishes and censers; and the gold sockets for the doors of the innermost room, the Most Holy Place, and also for the doors of the main hall of the temple. pp 2Ch 4:19–22   *See also* **1Ki** 7:13–22,27–37,40–45 pp 2Ch 4:11–16; **2Ch** 3:15–17

Art associated with idolatry
Forbidden

Dt 27:15 "Cursed is anyone who carves an image or casts an idol—a thing detestable to the

LORD, the work of skilled hands—and sets it up in secret." . . .   *See also* **Ex** 20:3–6 pp Dt 5:7–10; **Ex** 20:22–23; 34:10–17; **Lev** 19:4; 26:1; **Dt** 4:16–19,23–24; 29:16–18

Examples of idols and images

2Ki 21:7 He [Manasseh] took the carved Asherah pole he had made and put it in the temple, of which the LORD had said to David and to his son Solomon, "In this temple and in Jerusalem, which I have chosen out of all the tribes of Israel, I will put my Name for ever." pp 2Ch 33:7   *See also* **Ex** 32:1–4; **Jdg** 17:1–6; 18:11–31; **Isa** 46:1–2; **Jer** 50:1–2; **Eze** 8:9–12

Condemned

Hab 2:18 "Of what value is an idol, since someone has carved it? Or an image that teaches lies? For those who make them trust in their own creations; they make idols that cannot speak." *See also* **Ex** 34:10–14; **Nu** 33:51–52; **Dt** 7:25–26; **2Ch** 34:1–4; **Isa** 44:9–20; **Eze** 7:20–22; **Hos** 13:1–3; **Mic** 5:13–14; **Na** 1:14   *See also arts and crafts; idolatry; tabernacle, in Old Testament; temple, Solomon's.*

---

arts and crafts

Artistic skills, usually practised by skilled workers and passed on from generation to generation, of which a wide variety are mentioned in Scripture.

Metalwork

Ex 39:2–3 . . . They hammered out thin sheets of gold and cut strands to be worked into the blue, purple and scarlet yarn and fine linen . . .   *See also* **Ex** 31:1–5 pp Ex 35:30–33; **1Sa** 13:19–21; **1Ki** 7:13–14; **Isa** 41:7; **Jer** 10:9; **Ac** 19:23–41

Stonework

1Ki 5:17–18 . . . The skilled workers of Solomon and Hiram and those from Gebal cut and prepared the timber and stone for the building of the temple.   *See also* **1Ki** 6:36; 7:9–12; **2Ki** 22:3–6 pp 2Ch 34:8–11; **1Ch** 22:2; **2Ch** 2:13–14; **Eze** 40:42

Building

1Co 3:10–15 By the grace God has given me, I [Paul] laid a foundation as an expert builder, and someone else is building on it. But each one should build with care . . .   *See also* **2Ch** 34:11; **Ezr** 3:10; **Isa** 9:8–10; **Am** 5:11; **Heb** 3:3–4

Pottery

Isa 41:25 ". . . He [one from the north] treads on rulers as if they were mortar, as if they were a potter treading the clay."   *See also* **2Sa** 17:27–29; **1Ch** 4:21–23; **Isa** 29:16; 45:9; 64:8; **Jer** 18:1–10; 19:1; **Ro** 9:19–21

Carpentry

Isa 44:13 The carpenter measures with a line and makes an outline with a marker; he roughs it out with chisels and marks it with compasses. He shapes it in human form, human form in all its glory, that it may dwell in a shrine.   *See also* **Ge** 6:14; **2Sa** 5:11 pp 1Ch 14:1; **1Ki** 6:31–33; **2Ki** 12:10–12 pp 2Ch 24:11–12; **Mt** 13:54–55 pp Mk 6:2–3

Engraving

Ex 28:9–12 "Take two onyx stones and engrave on them the names of the sons of Israel in the order of their birth—six names on one stone and the remaining six on the other. Engrave the names of the sons of Israel on the two stones the way a gem cutter engraves a seal . . ." pp Ex 39:6–7   *See also* **Ex** 28:36–37 pp Ex 39:30–31; **1Ki** 7:30–36; **2Ch** 2:13–14

Dyeing

Ex 36:19 Then they made for the tent a covering of ram skins dyed red, and over that a covering of hides of sea cows. pp Ex 26:14 *See also* **Ex** 35:22–23

Weaving and embroidery

Ex 35:34–35 ". . . he [the LORD] has given both him [Bezalel] and Oholiab son of Ahisamach, of the tribe of Dan, the ability to teach others. He has filled them with skill to do all kinds of work as engravers, designers, embroiderers in blue, purple and scarlet yarn and fine linen, and weavers—all of them able to do all kinds of work and design." *See also* **Ex** 28:39–40 pp Ex 39:22–29; **2Ki** 23:7; **1Ch** 4:21; **Isa** 19:9–10; 38:12

Tanning
Ac 9:43 Peter stayed in Joppa for some time with a tanner named Simon. *See also* **Ac** 10:5–6,32–33

Making idols
Lev 26:1 " 'Do not make idols or set up an image or a sacred stone for yourselves, and do not place a carved stone in your land to bow down before it. I am the LORD your God.' "
See also **2Ki** 17:14–16; **Isa** 40:18–20; 41:5–7; 44:9–20 *See also* art; building; idolatry; occupations; potters and pottery.

Atonement, Day of
The most holy day of Israel's year (the tenth day of the seventh month) on which the high priest entered the Most Holy Place to offer sacrifices for the sins of the nation. Hebrews sees this day as symbolic of the achievements of Jesus Christ on the cross.

The priestly rituals on the Day of Atonement
The priest's own preparations Lev 16:4,6,11–14
The preparation of two male goats Lev 16:7–10
The sacrifice atones for the people's sins: **Ex** 30:10; **Lev** 16:15–19
The scapegoat symbolically carries away the people's sins: **Lev** 16:10,20–22
Concluding procedures Lev 16:23–28
Additional offerings on the Day of Atonement Nu 29:8–11

Features unique to the Day of Atonement
The priest entered the Most Holy Place
Heb 9:7 But only the high priest entered the inner room, and that only once a year . . .

See also **Lev** 16:2
Sacrifice was made for all the sins of all the people
Lev 16:30 ". . . on this day atonement will be made for you, to cleanse you. Then, before the LORD, you will be clean from all your sins."
See also **Ex** 30:10; **Lev** 16:16–17,21–22,34
It was a festival requiring humility and fasting
Nu 29:7 " 'On the tenth day of this seventh month hold a sacred assembly. You must deny yourselves and do no work.' " *See also* **Lev** 16:29,31; 23:27–32; **Ac** 27:9

The Day of Atonement is paralleled and contrasted with the achievements of Jesus Christ in his death
Jesus Christ entered the Most Holy Place
Heb 9:24 For Christ did not enter a sanctuary made with human hands that was only a copy of the true one; he entered heaven itself . . .
See also **Heb** 6:19–20; 9:11–12
Jesus Christ's blood was offered in sacrifice
Heb 9:12 He [Christ] did not enter by means of the blood of goats and calves; but he entered the Most Holy Place once for all by his own blood, having obtained eternal redemption.
See also **Ro** 3:25
Jesus Christ's sacrifice was outside the city gates
Heb 13:11–12 The high priest carries the blood of animals into the Most Holy Place as a sin offering, but the bodies are burned outside the camp. And so Jesus also suffered outside the city gate to make the people holy through his own blood.
Jesus Christ's sacrifice was once for all
Heb 9:25–26 Nor did he [Christ] enter heaven to offer himself again and again, the way the high priest enters the Most Holy Place every year with blood that is not his own. Then Christ would have had to suffer many times since the creation of the world. But now he has appeared once for all at the end of the ages to do away with sin by the sacrifice of himself. *See also* **Heb** 10:12
Jesus Christ's sacrifice gives inner rather than ritual cleansing
Heb 9:13–14 The blood of goats and bulls and

the ashes of a heifer sprinkled on those who are ceremonially unclean sanctify them so that they are outwardly clean. How much more, then, will the blood of Christ, who through the eternal Spirit offered himself unblemished to God, cleanse our consciences from acts that lead to death, so that we may serve the living God!   *See also* **Heb** 9:9–10

Jesus Christ's sacrifice gives access to God
Heb 10:19–20 . . . we have confidence to enter the Most Holy Place by the blood of Jesus . . .   *See also* **Lev** 16:17; **Mt** 27:51; **Eph** 2:18; 3:12   *See also atonement; blood; Most Holy Place.*

atonement

Reconciliation; sin has alienated humanity from God and provoked God's anger. God has responded by providing the means of restoring this broken relationship, bringing both sides to a place where they are at one again ("at-one-ment").

atonement, in New Testament

In dying for the sins of the world, Jesus Christ fulfilled and replaced the OT sacrificial system, so that all who believe in him are restored to fellowship with God. Christ is the true high priest, who finally liberates his people from the guilt of sin, by offering himself as the supreme sacrifice.

The atoning purpose of Jesus Christ's death
Jesus Christ's death on behalf of others
Jn 10:11 "I am the good shepherd. The good shepherd lays down his life for the sheep."
See also **Jn** 10:14–18; **2Co** 5:15; **Heb** 2:9; **1Jn** 3:16

Jesus Christ's atoning death for sin
1Co 15:3 . . . that Christ died for our sins according to the Scriptures,   *See also* **Ro** 4:25; 8:3; **Gal** 1:4; **1Pe** 3:18

The atoning significance of Jesus Christ's death is expressed by references to his blood
Ro 5:9 Since we have now been justified by his blood, how much more shall we be saved from God's wrath through him!

Rev 5:9 . . . "You [the Lamb] are worthy to take the scroll and to open its seals, because you were slain, and with your blood you purchased for God members of every tribe and language and people and nation."   *See also* **Eph** 2:13; **1Pe** 1:18–19; **1Jn** 1:7; **Rev** 7:14

Jesus Christ's atoning death is commemorated in the Lord's Supper
1Co 11:23–25 For I [Paul] received from the Lord what I also passed on to you: The Lord Jesus, on the night he was betrayed, took bread, and when he had given thanks, he broke it and said, "This is my body, which is for you; do this in remembrance of me." In the same way, after supper he took the cup, saying, "This cup is the new covenant in my blood; do this, whenever you drink it, in remembrance of me."   *See also* **Mt** 26:26–28 pp Mk 14:22–24 pp Lk 22:19–20

Explanations of the atonement
Jesus Christ's death as an atoning sacrifice
Ro 3:25 God presented him as a sacrifice of atonement, through faith in his blood . . .
See also **1Co** 5:7; **Eph** 5:2; **1Jn** 4:10; **Rev** 5:6
Jesus Christ's atoning death as redemption
Mk 10:45 "For even the Son of Man did not come to be served, but to serve, and to give his life as a ransom for many." pp Mt 20:28   *See also* **Ac** 20:28; **Gal** 3:13–14; **Eph** 1:7; **Col** 1:13–14

The atonement is effective because of Jesus Christ's sinlessness
2Co 5:21 God made him who had no sin to be sin for us, so that in him we might become the righteousness of God.   *See also* **Heb** 4:15; **1Pe** 2:22–24; **1Jn** 3:5

Jesus Christ's death fulfils and replaces the Day of Atonement
Jesus Christ makes atonement as the new high priest Heb 7:26–28
Jesus Christ is the mediator of the new and better covenant Heb 8:6–7; 9:15
Jesus Christ has made atonement in the true heavenly sanctuary Heb 8:1–2; 9:24
Jesus Christ's atoning blood brings effective cleansing Heb 9:12–14

Jesus Christ's single sacrifice replaces the many required under the old covenant Heb 10:11–14

Access to the heavenly sanctuary is now open Heb 10:19–20

By dying with Christ, believers are released from this age into the life of the age to come

Ro 6:1–7 . . . We were therefore buried with him through baptism into death in order that, just as Christ was raised from the dead through the glory of the Father, we too may live a new life . . . *See also* **Ro** 7:4–6; **Gal** 2:19–20; 6:14; **Eph** 2:6–7; **Col** 2:11–13

God the Father and the atoning death of his Son

God's sending of his Son to make atonement 1Jn 4:14 And we have seen and testify that the Father has sent his Son to be the Saviour of the world. *See also* **Jn** 3:16; **Ro** 8:32; **2Co** 5:18; **Gal** 4:4–5

God's grace displayed in making atonement for the ungodly

Eph 2:4–5 But because of his great love for us, God, who is rich in mercy, made us alive with Christ even when we were dead in transgressions—it is by grace you have been saved. *See also* **Ro** 5:6–8; **Eph** 2:8–9; **Tit** 3:4–5

The worldwide scope of Jesus Christ's atoning death

1Jn 2:2 He is the atoning sacrifice for our sins, and not only for ours but also for the sins of the whole world. *See also* **Jn** 1:29; **2Co** 5:19; **1Ti** 2:5

The appropriate response to the atonement

The response of repentance

Ac 3:19 "Repent, then, and turn to God, so that your sins may be wiped out . . ." *See also* **Ac** 2:38; 17:30; 20:21

The response of faith

Ac 10:43 "All the prophets testify about him that everyone who believes in him receives forgiveness of sins through his name." *See also* **Jn** 3:14–15; **Ac** 16:31; **Ro** 3:22; **Gal** 2:16

The response of baptism

Ac 22:16 " 'And now what are you waiting for? Get up, be baptised and wash your sins away, calling on his name.' " *See also* **Ac** 2:38; **1Pe** 3:21 *See also blood; restitution.*

atonement, in Old Testament

The OT laid down complex regulations by which the guilt of sin could be removed through the sacrificial system. Particular emphasis was placed upon the role of the high priest, who was required to make annual atonement for the sins of the people.

The covenantal framework of atonement

As God's covenant partners, the Israelites undertook to keep his laws

Ex 24:3 When Moses went and told the people all the LORD's words and laws, they responded with one voice, "Everything the LORD has said we will do." *See also* **Dt** 26:17; **Jos** 24:24

The sin offering made atonement for unintentional sins under the covenant

Lev 9:7 Moses said to Aaron, "Come to the altar and sacrifice your sin offering and your burnt offering and make atonement for yourself and the people; sacrifice the offering that is for the people and make atonement for them, as the LORD has commanded." *See also* **Lev** 4:13–14; **Nu** 15:22–26

The guilt offering atoned for sins where reparation was required

Lev 19:20–22 " '. . . With the ram of the guilt offering the priest is to make atonement for him before the LORD for the sin he has committed, and his sin will be forgiven.' " *See also* **Lev** 6:1–7

Deliberate flouting of God's law could not be atoned for

Nu 15:30–31 " 'But those who sin defiantly, whether native-born or alien, blaspheme the LORD, and must be cut off from their people. Because they have despised the LORD's word and broken his commands, they must surely be cut off; their guilt remains on them.' " *See also* **Nu** 35:33; **1Sa** 3:14

The Day of Atonement provided for the removal of the nation's sin

Lev 16:34 "This is to be a lasting ordinance for you: Atonement is to be made once a year for all the sins of the Israelites." . . . *See also* **Ex** 30:10; **Lev** 16:1–33; **Heb** 9:7

The atonement cover

Ex 25:17–22 ". . . There, above the cover between the two cherubim that are over the ark of the Testimony, I [the LORD] will meet with you [Moses] and give you all my commands for the Israelites." *See also* **Ex** 30:6; **Lev** 16:2; **Nu** 7:89

Atonement was effected by the blood of the sacrifice

Lev 17:11 " 'For the life of a creature is in the blood, and I have given it to you to make atonement for yourselves on the altar; it is the blood that makes atonement for one's life.' " *See also* **Heb** 9:22

The role of priests in making atonement

Priests were dedicated to God in order to make atonement for others

Ex 29:44 "So I will consecrate the Tent of Meeting and the altar and will consecrate Aaron and his sons to serve me as priests." *See also* **Lev** 8:22–30

The priests had to make atonement for their own sins

Heb 5:1–3 Every high priest . . . has to offer sacrifices for his own sins, as well as for the sins of the people. *See also* **Lev** 9:8–11

The priests represented the people before God to atone for their sin

Heb 5:1 Every high priest is selected from among human beings and is appointed to represent them in matters related to God, to offer gifts and sacrifices for sins. *See also* **Ex** 28:36–38; **Lev** 10:16–17

The people had constant reminders of the need for atonement

Rituals of cleansing included an atoning offering **Lev** 12:7–8; 14:18–22,53; 15:15

Atonement was a feature of Israel's festivals **Nu** 28:22,30; 29:5,11

Abuses of the system of atonement

The sinful conduct of the priests who made atonement

Hos 4:7–8 "The more the priests increased, the more they sinned against me; they exchanged their Glory for something disgraceful. They feed on the sins of my people and relish their wickedness." *See also* **1Sa** 2:12–17; **Jer** 6:13–14; **Eze** 22:26; **Mal** 1:6–8

The sinful conduct of the people who sought atonement without repenting of their sins

Hos 8:11–13 "Though Ephraim built many altars for sin offerings, these have become altars for sinning . . ." *See also* **Isa** 1:10–17; 66:3; **Jer** 7:21–24; **Am** 4:4

The need for repentance for a relationship of atonement

Pr 16:6 Through love and faithfulness sin is atoned for; through the fear of the LORD evil is avoided. *See also* **1Sa** 15:22; **Ps** 51:16–17; **Mic** 6:6–8

The prophets foretold a renewing of God's relationship with Israel, involving atonement for sin

Isaiah's message about the obedient servant **Isa** 53:4–12

Jeremiah's prophecy of a new covenant **Jer** 31:31–34

Ezekiel's vision of a new temple **Eze** 43:18–27 *See also* Atonement, Day of; covenant; priesthood; sacrifice, in Old Testament; sin offering.

banquets

Grand, celebratory meals consisting usually of rich food and flowing wine. Banquets usually accompanied weddings, religious festivals and other celebrations. Prophecies of the Messianic age refer to a banquet to which the righteous will be invited.

Characteristics of banquets
They were usually held in a hall
SS 2:4 He has taken me to the banquet hall, and his banner over me is love. *See also* **Est** 7:8; **Da** 5:10
Honoured guests were given special places
Lk 14:7–11 When he [Jesus] noticed how the guests picked the places of honour at the table, he told them this parable: "When someone invites you to a wedding feast, do not take the place of honour, for a person more distinguished than you may have been invited . . ." *See also* **Pr** 25:6–7; **Mt** 23:6 pp Mk 12:39 pp Lk 20:46
Guests reclined on couches Est 1:6; Mt 26:7 pp Mk 14:3 pp Lk 7:36; Jn 12:2
Invitations were sent out Lk 14:17 pp Mt 22:3

Occasions for holding banquets
To celebrate weddings
Mt 22:2 "The kingdom of heaven is like a king who prepared a wedding banquet for his son." *See also* **Ge** 29:21–22; **Jdg** 14:10; **Est** 2:18; **Mt** 25:10; **Lk** 12:36; **Jn** 2:8–9; **Rev** 19:9
To celebrate birthdays Ge 40:20; Mk 6:21
To celebrate other events Ge 21:8
Jews celebrate their deliverance from Haman in what became the Feast of Purim: **Est** 8:17; 9:17–19 **Lk** 15:23
Religious celebrations
Ps 22:29 All the rich of the earth will feast and worship; all who go down to the dust will kneel before him—those who cannot keep themselves alive. *See also* **2Ch** 30:21–22; 35:13; **Zec** 7:6

Activities at banquets
Good food and drink
Isa 25:6 On this mountain the LORD Almighty will prepare a feast of rich food for all peoples, a banquet of aged wine—the best of meats and the finest of wines. *See also* **Job** 1:4; **Zec** 7:6; **Mt** 22:4; **Lk** 15:23
Drunkenness and revelry
1Sa 25:36 When Abigail went to Nabal, he was in the house holding a banquet like that of a king. He was in high spirits and very drunk . . . *See also* **Est** 1:7–8,10; **Ecc** 10:19; **Jer** 51:39; **Da** 5:3–4

Music and dancing
Isa 5:12 They [people of Israel] have harps and lyres at their banquets, tambourines and flutes and wine, but they have no regard for the deeds of the LORD, no respect for the work of his hands. *See also* **Mt** 14:6 pp Mk 6:22; **Lk** 15:25

Further examples of banquets
Ge 26:30; 43:34; **2Sa** 3:20; **1Ki** 3:15
Xerxes gives a banquet for his nobles and officials: **Est** 1:3,5
Est 1:9
Esther prepares banquets for the king and Haman: **Est** 5:4–5,8
Da 5:1–2; **Lk** 5:29 pp Mt 9:10; **Lk** 14:1

An invitation to a banquet seen as a sign of God's grace
Lk 14:12–14 Then Jesus said to his host, "When you give a luncheon or dinner, do not invite your friends, brothers, sisters, relatives, or your rich neighbours; if you do, they may invite you back and so you will be repaid. But when you give a banquet, invite the poor, the crippled, the lame, the blind . . ." *See also* **2Ki** 6:23; **Mt** 22:8–10 pp Lk 14:21–23

The Messianic banquet
Mt 8:11 "I [Jesus] say to you that many will come from the east and the west, and will take their places at the feast with Abraham, Isaac and Jacob in the kingdom of heaven." *See also* **Lk** 13:29; 14:15 *See also* drinking; eating; feast and festival; food; marriage, customs; wedding.

beggars
People in great need who appeal for help, both from others and from God.

Appeals for material help
2Ki 6:26 As the king of Israel was passing by on the wall, a woman cried to him, "Help me, my lord the king!"
Lk 16:3 "The manager said to himself, 'What shall I do now? My master is taking away my job. I'm not strong enough to dig, and I'm

ashamed to beg—' " *See also* **2Ki** 8:3–5; **Job** 19:16; 24:4–5; 29:11–12; **Ps** 37:25; 109:10; **La** 4:4

Appeals for mercy from others

Est 8:3 Esther again pleaded with the king, falling at his feet and weeping. She begged him to put an end to the evil plan of Haman the Agagite, which he had devised against the Jews. *See also* **1Sa** 15:25; **2Sa** 14:4; **2Ki** 1:13; **Est** 4:8; 7:7; **Job** 30:28; **Mt** 18:26–32

Examples of beggars

Mk 10:46 pp Lk 18:35; **Lk** 16:20–21; **Jn** 9:8; **Ac** 3:2–3

Care for the destitute commended

Isa 58:6–7 "Is not this the kind of fasting I have chosen: to loose the chains of injustice and untie the cords of the yoke, to set the oppressed free and break every yoke? Is it not to share your food with the hungry and to provide the poor wanderer with shelter—when you see the naked, to clothe them, and not to turn away from your own flesh and blood?"

Mt 26:11 "The poor you will always have with you, but you will not always have me." pp Mk 14:7 pp Jn 12:8 *See also* **Dt** 15:11; **Pr** 19:17; 21:13; 22:9; 28:27; 31:9,20; **Zec** 7:10; **Mt** 5:42 pp Lk 6:30; **Mt** 19:21 pp Mk 10:21 pp Lk 18:22; **Lk** 12:33; 14:13

Pleas for God's help
From the Israelites

Ex 2:23 During that long period, the king of Egypt died. The Israelites groaned in their slavery and cried out, and their cry for help because of their slavery went up to God. *See also* **Jos** 24:7; **Jdg** 4:3; 6:6; **2Ch** 14:11; **Am** 7:5

From individuals

Ps 18:6 In my distress I called to the LORD; I cried to my God for help. From his temple he heard my voice; my cry came before him, into his ears. *See also* **2Sa** 24:10 pp 1Ch 21:8; **Ps** 28:2; **Jnh** 2:2; **Hab** 1:2; **Lk** 16:27

People begged Jesus Christ for help

Mt 14:35–36 . . . People brought all their sick to him [Jesus] and begged him to let the sick just touch the edge of his cloak, and all who touched him were healed. pp Mk 6:56 *See also* **Mt** 8:31 pp Mk 5:12 pp Lk 8:32; **Mt** 15:22 pp Mk 7:26; **Mk** 7:32; 10:47; **Lk** 5:12 pp Mk 1:40; **Lk** 8:28; 9:38–40; **Jn** 4:47 *See also famine; poverty.*

---

betrothal

The period of engagement preceding marriage; betrothal was a binding contract established between two families and sealed by the exchange of gifts. During this period the couple did not live together; sexual relations with each other at this stage was regarded as equivalent to adultery. Betrothal describes the relationship between God and his people and between Jesus Christ and the church.

Betrothal and the choice of a spouse
Wives were often chosen by parents for their sons

Ge 21:21 While he [Ishmael] was living in the Desert of Paran, his mother got a wife for him from Egypt. *See also* **Ge** 24:4; 38:6

Suitable husbands were sought by parents for their daughters

Ru 3:1–4 One day Naomi her [Ruth's] mother-in-law said to her, "My daughter, should I not try to find a home for you, where you will be well provided for? . . ." *See also* **Jdg** 1:12–13; **1Sa** 18:17,21

Betrothal following the couple's wishes

Jdg 14:1–4 . . . When he [Samson] returned, he said to his father and mother, "I have seen a Philistine woman in Timnah; now get her for me as my wife." . . . *See also* **Ge** 34:1–4; 24:57–58; 26:34–35

Betrothal preceded marriage

Ge 29:21; **Dt** 20:7; **Mt** 1:24; **1Co** 7:36–38

An exchange of gifts accompanied betrothal
The bride-price

Ge 34:11–12 . . .". . . Make the price for the bride and the gift I [Shechem] am to bring as great as you like, and I'll pay whatever you ask me. Only give me the girl as my wife." *See also* **Ge** 24:53; 29:18,27; **Ex** 22:16–17; **Dt** 22:28–29; **2Sa** 3:14

The dowry

1Ki 9:16 (Pharaoh king of Egypt had attacked and captured Gezer. He had set it on fire. He killed its Canaanite inhabitants, and then gave it as a wedding gift to his daughter, Solomon's wife.)

Servants were given to the bride as a dowry: **Ge** 24:59; 29:24,29

Jdg 1:14–15

Betrothal was treated as marriage

Dt 22:23–24 If a man happens to meet in a town a virgin pledged to be married and he sleeps with her, you shall take both of them to the gate of that town and stone them to death—the woman because she was in a town and did not scream for help, and the man because he violated another man's wife . . . *See also* **Ge** 19:14; **Mt** 1:18–20

Betrothal portrays the relationship between God and his people

Hos 2:19–20 "I [the Lord] will betroth you [Israel] to me for ever; I will betroth you in righteousness and justice, in love and compassion . . ."

2Co 11:2 I [Paul] am jealous for you [the Corinthian Christians] with a godly jealousy. I promised you to one husband, to Christ, so that I might present you as a pure virgin to him. *See also* **Jn** 3:29; **Eph** 5:25–27; **Rev** 19:7–9; 21:2 *See also* bride; bridegroom; husband; marriage; customs; pledges; wedding; wife.

birds

Part of the created world, used for food. In OT times they were also used in sacrifices. In Scripture, birds are used in many metaphors.

Part of creation

Ge 1:21 So God created . . . every winged bird according to its kind. And God saw that it was good.   *See also* **Ge** 1:20–30; 2:20; **1Co** 15:39; **Jas** 3:7

Cared for by God

Lk 12:24 "Consider the ravens: They do not sow or reap . . . yet God feeds them . . ." pp Mt 6:26   *See also* **Job** 38:41; **Ps** 50:11; 147:9

To be cared for by humanity Dt 22:6–7

Specific varieties of bird

Raven Ge 8:7; **1Ki** 17:4; **SS** 5:11

Eagle Ex 19:4; **Job** 39:27; **Pr** 23:5; **Isa** 40:31; **Jer** 49:16; **Eze** 17:3; **Da** 4:33; **Hos** 8:1

Hen Mt 23:37

Cock Pr 30:31; **Mt** 26:74

Ostrich Job 39:13–18; **La** 4:3

Owl Ps 102:6; **Isa** 34:11,15; **Jer** 50:39; **Mic** 1:8; **Zep** 2:14

Quail Ex 16:13; **Nu** 11:31–32; **Ps** 105:40

Sparrow Ps 84:3; **Pr** 26:2; **Mt** 10:29–31

Stork Ps 104:17; **Jer** 8:7; **Zec** 5:9

Vulture Job 15:23; **Pr** 30:17; **Mic** 1:16; **Hab** 1:8; **Mt** 24:28

Birds of prey Dt 28:26; **1Sa** 17:46; **1Ki** 16:4; **Isa** 18:6; **Jer** 12:9; **Rev** 19:17–18

Protected at the flood

Ge 6:20 "Two of every kind of bird, of every kind of animal and of every kind of creature that moves along the ground will come to you to be kept alive."   *See also* **Ge** 8:17–19

Used in sacrifice

Ge 8:20 Then Noah built an altar to the Lord and, taking some of all the clean animals and clean birds, he sacrificed burnt offerings on it. *See also* **Ge** 15:10; **Lev** 1:14; 12:8; 14:3–7,49–53; **Lk** 2:22–24

Used as food

Dt 14:11 You may eat any clean bird. *See also* **Lev** 17:13–14

Some not to be eaten

Lev 20:25 " 'You must therefore make a

distinction between clean and unclean animals and between unclean and clean birds. Do not defile yourselves by any animal or bird or anything that moves along the ground—those which I have set apart as unclean for you.' " *See also* **Lev** 11:13–19 pp Dt 14:12–18

Not to be used as an object of worship
Dt 4:15–17 You saw no form of any kind the day the LORD spoke to you at Horeb out of the fire. Therefore watch yourselves very carefully, so that you do not become corrupt and make for yourselves an idol, an image of any shape, whether formed like a man or a woman, or like any animal on earth or any bird that flies in the air, *See also* **Ro** 1:23

Appearing in dreams and visions
Ge 40:17; **Ac** 11:6; **Rev** 4:7; 12:14

Used metaphorically
Of freedom
Ps 55:6 I said, "Oh, that I had the wings of a dove! I would fly away and be at rest—" *See also* **Ps** 11:1
Of isolation
Ps 102:7 I lie awake; I have become like a bird alone on a roof.
Of powerlessness
Hos 11:11 "They will come trembling like birds from Egypt, like doves from Assyria. I will settle them in their homes," declares the LORD.
Of being trapped
Ps 124:7 We have escaped like a bird out of the fowler's snare; the snare has been broken, and we have escaped. *See also* **Pr** 6:5; 7:23; **Jer** 5:26; **La** 3:52; **Eze** 13:20; **Hos** 7:12; **Am** 3:5
Of cruel invaders
Isa 46:11 "From the east I [the LORD] summon a bird of prey; from a far-off land, a man to fulfil my purpose . . ." *See also* **Dt** 28:49–50
Of an object of hatred
Jer 12:9 "Has not my [the LORD'S] inheritance become to me like a speckled bird of prey that other birds of prey surround and attack? Go and gather all the wild beasts; bring them to

devour." *See also* animals; clean and unclean; idolatry, in Old Testament; sacrifice, in Old Testament.

blood

The symbol of life, which thus plays an especially important role in the sacrificial system of the OT. The shedding of the blood of a sacrificial animal represents the giving up of its life. The "blood of Christ" refers to Jesus Christ's obedient giving of his life, in order to achieve redemption and forgiveness.

blood, basis of life

Scripture treats blood as the basis of life, and regards the shedding of blood as representing the end of life.

Blood symbolises life
Lev 17:10–14 " 'I will set my face against any Israelites or any aliens living among them who eat blood and I will cut them off from their people. For the life of a creature is in the blood, and I have given it to you to make atonement for yourselves on the altar; it is the blood that makes atonement for one's life . . . the life of every creature is its blood. That is why I have said to the Israelites, "You must not eat the blood of any creature, because the life of every creature is its blood; anyone who eats it must be cut off." ' " *See also* **Ge** 9:4–6; **Dt** 12:20–25; **2Sa** 23:15–17; **Ps** 72:14; **Jer** 2:34; **Eze** 33:1–6; **Mt** 27:3–4; **Lk** 11:50–51 pp Mt 23:35–36

Blood indicating violent death
Ge 4:8–11 Now Cain said to his brother Abel, "Let's go out to the field." And while they were in the field, Cain attacked his brother Abel and killed him. Then the LORD said to Cain, "Where is your brother Abel?" "I don't know," he replied. "Am I my brother's keeper?" The LORD said, "What have you done? Listen! Your brother's blood cries out to me from the ground. Now you are under a curse and driven from the ground, which opened its mouth to receive your brother's blood from your hand." *See also* **Ge** 9:6; **Jdg** 9:22–24; **1Ki** 2:5–6,28–34; **2Ki** 9:30–33

Shedding blood as a sin
Ex 20:13 "You shall not murder." pp Dt
5:17   *See also* **Ge** 42:21–22; **Dt** 21:1–9; **2Ki**
21:16; **Pr** 1:10–19; **Isa** 26:21; **Mt** 15:18–19 pp
Mk 7:20–21; **Ro** 1:28–29

The eating of blood forbidden
Lev 3:17 " 'This is a lasting ordinance for the
generations to come, wherever you live: You must
not eat any fat or any blood.' "   *See also* **Lev**
7:26–27; 17:10–14; **Dt** 12:23; **1Sa** 14:31–34; **Ac**
15:19–20,29   *See also life.*

blood, of Jesus Christ
The shedding of the blood of Jesus Christ is seen
as representing the giving of his life as an atoning
sacrifice for the sins of humanity.

The blood of Jesus Christ as part of his
humanity
Jn 19:33–34 But when they came to Jesus
and found that he was already dead, they did not
break his legs. Instead, one of the soldiers pierced
Jesus' side with a spear, bringing a sudden flow
of blood and water.   *See also* **Lk** 22:44; **Ac**
5:28; **1Jn** 5:6

The blood of Jesus Christ as a sacrifice
Heb 9:12–14,23–26; 10:3–14; 13:11–12

The blood of Jesus Christ as a symbol
of atonement
Ro 3:25 God presented him as a sacrifice of
atonement, through faith in his blood. He did this
to demonstrate his justice, because in his
forbearance he had left the sins committed
beforehand unpunished   *See also* **Eph** 1:7; **Rev**
7:14

The effects of the blood of Jesus Christ
The institution of the new covenant
1Co 11:25 In the same way, after supper he
[Jesus] took the cup, saying, "This cup is the
new covenant in my blood; do this, whenever you
drink it, in remembrance of me." pp Mt
26:27–28 pp Mk 14:23–24 pp Lk 22:20
See also **Heb** 9:11–15; 12:24; 13:20

Redemption Ac 20:28; **1Pe** 1:1–2,18–19; **Rev**
5:9–10
Forgiveness and justification
Ro 5:9 Since we have now been justified by his
blood, how much more shall we be saved from
God's wrath through him!   *See also* **Mt** 26:28
pp Mk 14:24 pp Lk 22:20; **Ro** 3:25–26
Victory over evil and Satan Rev 7:14–17;
12:10–11
Liberation from sin Rev 1:5–6
The promise of total restoration Col 1:19–20

The blood of Jesus Christ and believers
Believers are cleansed from all sin Heb 9:14;
10:22; 13:12; **1Jn** 1:6–9
**Believers have a new confidence before God
Eph** 2:13; **Col** 1:19–22; **Heb** 10:19–22

The blood of Jesus Christ and the
Lord's Supper
Invitations to share in the blood of Jesus
Christ
1Co 10:16 Is not the cup of thanksgiving for
which we give thanks a participation in the blood
of Christ? And is not the bread that we break a
participation in the body of Christ?   *See also* **Jn**
6:53–57
Warnings about sinning against the blood of
Jesus Christ
1Co 11:27 Therefore, whoever eats the bread
or drinks the cup of the Lord in an unworthy
manner will be guilty of sinning against the body
and blood of the Lord.   *See also* **Heb**
10:28–31   *See also atonement; covenant, new.*

blood, Old Testament
sacrifices
The pouring out of animals' blood in sacrifice was
God's provision, under the old covenant, for the
atonement of sin.

God's provision of blood sacrifice to
establish the old covenant
Ex 24:4–8 . . . Moses then took the blood,
sprinkled it on the people and said, "This is the
blood of the covenant that the LORD has made
with you in accordance with all these words."

See also **Heb** 9:18–20

God's provision of blood sacrifices within the old covenant
Blood sacrifices and the priesthood Ex 29:10–21 pp Lev 8:14–24; **Lev** 9:8–14; 16:1–14
Blood sacrifices and various offerings Lev 1:1–17; 3:1–17; 4:1–35; 5:14–19; 16:15–22
Blood sacrifices and the Passover
Ex 12:1–14 . . ." . . . On that same night I will pass through Egypt and strike down every firstborn—both people and animals—and I will bring judgment on all the gods of Egypt. I am the LORD. The blood will be a sign for you on the houses where you are; and when I see the blood, I will pass over you . . ." *See also* **2Ch** 30:15–20; 35:1–19; **Ezr** 6:19–21; **Mk** 14:12 pp Lk 22:7–8

Blood sacrifices must come from animals without defect
Lev 22:17–25 . . ." . . .' . . . you must present a male without defect from the cattle, sheep or goats in order that it may be accepted on your behalf. Do not bring anything with a defect, because it will not be accepted on your behalf . . .'" *See also* **Ex** 12:5; **Lev** 1:3; 3:1; 4:3; 5:15; **Nu** 28:9,11; **Dt** 15:21; **Eze** 43:22–27

Blood sacrifices must not come from human beings
2Ki 23:10 He [Josiah] desecrated Topheth, which was in the Valley of Ben Hinnom, so no-one could use it to sacrifice son or daughter in the fire to Molech. *See also* **2Ki** 17:17; 21:1–6; **Eze** 20:25–26; **Mic** 6:7

The limited effect of blood sacrifices
They can become mere external ritual
Isa 1:11–13 "The multitude of your sacrifices—what are they to me?" says the LORD. "I have more than enough of burnt offerings, of rams and the fat of fattened animals; I have no pleasure in the blood of bulls and lambs and goats. When you come to appear before me, who has asked this of you, this trampling of my courts? Stop bringing meaningless offerings! . . ." *See also* **Isa** 66:2–4

They are worthless without obedience to God
Hos 6:6 "For I desire mercy, not sacrifice, and acknowledgment of God rather than burnt offerings." *See also* **1Sa** 15:22–23; **Ps** 40:6–8; **Am** 4:4–5; 5:21–27
They are unable to cleanse the conscience
Heb 9:9–10 This is an illustration for the present time, indicating that the gifts and sacrifices being offered were not able to clear the conscience of the worshipper. They are only a matter of food and drink and various ceremonial washings—external regulations applying until the time of the new order. *See also* **Heb** 10:1–4
See also burnt offering; covenant; fellowship offering; guilt offering; offerings; Passover; sacrifice, in Old Testament; sin offering.

---

blood, symbol of guilt
Blood is often used as an image of people's sin and guilt, and the judgment which follows. Blood-guilt is ascribed to those who are responsible for the shedding of innocent blood.

Blood as an image of sin and guilt
Isa 59:2–3 But your iniquities have separated you from your God; your sins have hidden his face from you, so that he will not hear. For your hands are stained with blood, your fingers with guilt . . . *See also* **Lev** 20:9–13,27; **2Sa** 1:14–16; **Isa** 1:15–18; **Na** 3:1; **Ac** 18:6

Blood as an image of judgment
Isa 34:5–6 My sword has drunk its fill in the heavens; see, it descends in judgment on Edom, the people I have totally destroyed. The sword of the LORD is bathed in blood . . . *See also* **Ex** 7:14–21; **Ps** 78:44; 105:29; **Ac** 2:19–20; **Joel** 2:30–31

Blood as a sign of the end times
Ac 2:19–20 "'I will show wonders in the heaven above and signs on the earth below, blood and fire and billows of smoke. The sun will be turned to darkness and the moon to blood before the coming of the great and glorious day of the Lord.'" *See also* **Joel** 2:30–31; **Rev** 6:12–15; 8:7–9; 16:3–6

Blood-guilt, the result of shedding innocent blood
Examples of blood-guilt
Ge 4:8–11 Now Cain said to his brother Abel, "Let's go out to the field." And while they were in the field, Cain attacked his brother Abel and killed him. Then the LORD said to Cain, "Where is your brother Abel?" "I don't know," he replied. "Am I my brother's keeper?" The LORD said, "What have you done? Listen! Your brother's blood cries out to me from the ground. Now you are under a curse and driven from the ground, which opened its mouth to receive your brother's blood from your hand." *See also* **2Sa** 1:14–16; 4:5–12; **Eze** 35:5–9; **Hab** 2:12; **Mt** 27:3–8,24; **Ac** 5:28
The right to avenge blood-guilt under the law
Dt 19:11–13 But if out of hate someone lies in wait, assaults and kills a neighbour, and then flees to one of these cities, the killer shall be sent for by the town elders, be brought back from the city, and be handed over to the avenger of blood to die. Show no pity. You must purge from Israel the guilt of shedding innocent blood, so that it may go well with you. *See also* **Nu** 35:16–28
Restraint to avoid further blood-guilt
Dt 4:41–42 Then Moses set aside three cities east of the Jordan, to which those who had killed a person could flee if they had unintentionally killed a neighbour without malice aforethought. They could flee into one of these cities and save their lives. *See also* **Ge** 4:15; **Nu** 35:6–34; **Dt** 19:4–10; **Jos** 20:1–9
Blood-guilt cannot be forgotten
Ge 9:5–6 "And for your lifeblood I will surely demand an accounting. I will demand an accounting from every animal. And from each human being, too, I will demand an accounting for the life of another human being. Whoever sheds human blood, by human beings shall their blood be shed; for in the image of God has God made all people." *See also* **Ge** 4:10–16; 42:22; **1Ki** 2:28–33; **Isa** 26:21; **Mt** 23:30–31

book
Used most frequently to refer to a particular book of the Bible being written, another book of the Bible or a source no longer available. It is used occasionally of books in general or metaphorically of God's record of events.

References to books being written
Jer 25:13; 30:2; **Na** 1:1; **Jn** 20:30; **Rev** 22:7,9–10,18–19

References to other books of Scripture
2Ch 35:12; **Ezr** 6:18; **Ne** 13:1; **Mk** 12:26; **Lk** 3:4; 20:42; **Ac** 1:1,20; 7:42; 8:28

References to books no longer available
The Book of the Wars of the LORD Nu 21:14
The Book of Jashar
Jos 10:13 So the sun stood still, and the moon stopped, till the nation avenged itself on its enemies, as it is written in the Book of Jashar. The sun stopped in the middle of the sky and delayed going down about a full day. *See also* **2Sa** 1:18
The book of the annals of the kings of Israel and Judah
2Ch 16:11 The events of Asa's reign, from beginning to end, are written in the book of the kings of Judah and Israel. *See also* **1Ki** 11:41; 14:19,29; **2Ki** 1:18; 8:23; **1Ch** 9:1; 27:24; **2Ch** 24:27; 27:7
The book of the annals Ne 12:23
Similar annals were kept by the Persian kings: **Est** 2:23; 6:1; 10:2

References to books in general
Ecc 12:12 . . . Of making many books there is no end, and much study wearies the body. *See also* **Jn** 21:25; **Ac** 19:19

Books used metaphorically of God's infallible record of events
Rev 20:11–12 Then I [John, the apostle] saw a great white throne and him who was seated on it. Earth and sky fled from his presence, and there was no place for them. And I saw the dead, great and small, standing before the throne, and books were opened. Another book was opened, which is the book of life. The dead were judged

according to what they had done as recorded in the books.   *See also* **Da** 7:10; 10:21; 12:1
See also reading; writing.

bride

A woman who is about to be married or who has just got married. In the NT the church is described as the bride of Christ.

Jewels and ornaments worn by a bride at her wedding

Isa 61:10 I delight greatly in the LORD; my soul rejoices in my God. For he has clothed me with garments of salvation and arrayed me in a robe of righteousness, as a bridegroom adorns his head like a priest, and as a bride adorns herself with her jewels.   *See also* **Ps** 45:9,14; **SS** 4:9; **Isa** 49:18; **Jer** 2:32

Joy and happiness associated with a bride

Jer 33:10–11 "... '... Yet in the towns of Judah and the streets of Jerusalem that are deserted, inhabited by neither people nor animals, there will be heard once more the sounds of joy and gladness, the voices of bride and bridegroom, and the voices of those who bring thank-offerings to the house of the LORD ... '... ."   *See also* **Jer** 7:34; 16:9; 25:10; **Rev** 18:23

The bride as the object of the bridegroom's love and affection

Isa 62:5 As a young man marries a young woman, so will your people marry you; as a bridegroom rejoices over his bride, so will your God rejoice over you.   *See also* **SS** 4:8–15; 5:1

The bridegroom as the object of the bride's love and affection

Jer 2:2–3 "... .'I [the LORD] remember the devotion of your [Israel's] youth, how as a bride you loved me and followed me through the desert, through a land not sown. Israel was holy to the LORD, the firstfruits of his harvest ... .'" ...

Exemptions for a newly married bride

Joel 2:16 Gather the people, consecrate the assembly; bring together the elders, gather the children, those nursing at the breast. Let the bridegroom leave his room and the bride her chamber.   *See also* **Dt** 24:5

The bride price

Ge 34:11–12 Then Shechem said to Dinah's father and brothers, "Let me find favour in your eyes, and I will give you whatever you ask. Make the price for the bride and the gift I am to bring as great as you like, and I'll pay whatever you ask me. Only give me the girl as my wife."
See also **Ge** 29:18–30; **1Sa** 18:20–27

Proof of a bride's virginity was required in certain circumstances
Dt 22:13–21

The church depicted as the bride of Christ

Eph 5:25–27 Husbands, love your wives, just as Christ loved the church and gave himself up for her to make her holy, cleansing her by the washing with water through the word, and to present her to himself as a radiant church, without stain or wrinkle or any other blemish, but holy and blameless.   *See also* **Rev** 19:7–9; 21:1–2, 9–27; 22:17   *See also bridegroom; husband; marriage; wedding; wife.*

bridegroom

A man who is to be married or who has just got married. In the NT Jesus Christ is portrayed as a bridegroom and the church as his bride.

The bridegroom and the wedding ceremony
The bridegroom wore special clothing
Isa 61:10 ... he [the LORD] has clothed me with garments of salvation and arrayed me in a robe of righteousness, as a bridegroom adorns his head like a priest ...
The bridegroom took part in the procession to the bride's home Mt 25:1–12

The bridegroom had a group of companions
Jdg 14:10-11 . . . And Samson made a feast there, as was customary for bridegrooms. When he appeared, he was given thirty companions.
The bridegroom had a special friend as an attendant
Jn 3:29 "The bride belongs to the bridegroom. The friend who attends the bridegroom waits and listens for him, and is full of joy when he hears the bridegroom's voice . . ." *See also* **Jdg** 14:20-15:2; **Jn** 2:7-10
The bridegroom was sometimes responsible for giving the wedding banquet
Jdg 14:10 . . . And Samson made a feast there, as was customary for bridegrooms.
See also **Jn** 2:9-10
The bridegroom led his bride to a specially prepared bridal chamber
Joel 2:16 Gather the people, consecrate the assembly; bring together the elders, gather the children, those nursing at the breast. Let the bridegroom leave his room and the bride her chamber. *See also* **Ps** 19:4-5

Bridegrooms were associated with happiness and rejoicing
Jer 7:34 "'I [the LORD] will bring an end to the sounds of joy and gladness and to the voices of bride and bridegroom in the towns of Judah and the streets of Jerusalem, for the land will become desolate.'" *See also* **Isa** 62:5; **Jer** 16:9; 25:10; 33:11; **Rev** 18:23

Bridegrooms were excused from military service and certain other duties
Dt 24:5 If a man has recently married, he must not be sent to war or have any other duty laid on him. For one year he is to be free to stay at home and bring happiness to the wife he has married. *See also* **Dt** 20:1-7

Jesus Christ is portrayed as a bridegroom
Mt 9:14-15 . . . Jesus answered, "How can the guests of the bridegroom mourn while he is with them? The time will come when the bridegroom will be taken from them; then they

will fast." pp Mk 2:18-20 pp Lk 5:33-35
See also **Eph** 5:22-33

The future coming of Jesus Christ compared to the sudden arrival of the bridegroom
Mt 25:1-10 *See also bride; husband; marriage; wedding; wife.*

building

The construction of something together with the skilled people involved. Scripture also uses the term figuratively.

Building materials
Ge 11:3 They [the people who attempted to build the tower of Babel] said to each other, "Come, let's make bricks and bake them thoroughly." They used brick instead of stone, and bitumen for mortar.
1Ki 5:17 At the king's command they removed from the quarry large blocks of quality stone to provide a foundation of dressed stone for the temple.
Hag 1:8 "Go up into the mountains and bring down timber and build the house, so that I may take pleasure in it and be honoured," says the LORD. *See also* **Ex** 27:1; **1Ki** 6:9; **2Ch** 2:3; **Isa** 54:11

Building skills
1Ki 5:18 The skilled workers of Solomon and Hiram and those from Gebal cut and prepared the timber and stone for the building of the temple. *See also* **Ex** 36:1; **1Ki** 6:7; **2Ki** 12:11; 22:5-6; **1Ch** 22:1-2

The variety of building projects
Towns and cities
1Ki 16:24 He [Omri] bought the hill of Samaria from Shemer for two talents of silver and built a city on the hill, calling it Samaria, after Shemer, the name of the former owner of the hill. *See also* **Ge** 4:17; **Jdg** 1:26; **1Ch** 11:8
Houses
Ecc 2:4 I [the Preacher] undertook great projects:

I built houses for myself and planted vineyards.
See also **Jer** 35:8–9

Temples
Ac 17:24 "The God who made the world and
everything in it is the Lord of heaven and earth
and does not live in temples built by hands."
See also **1Ki** 6:2; 8:13; **Ezr** 3:10

Altars
Jos 8:30–31 Then Joshua built on Mount Ebal
an altar to the LORD, the God of Israel, as Moses
the servant of the LORD had commanded the
Israelites. He built it according to what is written
in the Book of the Law of Moses—an altar of
uncut stones, on which no iron tool had been
used . . .   *See also* **Ge** 8:20; **Ex** 24:4; **2Sa**
24:25

Palaces
2Sa 5:11 Now Hiram king of Tyre sent
messengers to David, along with cedar logs and
carpenters and stonemasons, and they built a
palace for David.   *See also* **1Ki** 3:1; 7:2; **Hos**
8:14

Walls
Ps 51:18 In your [the LORD's] good pleasure
make Zion prosper; build up the walls of
Jerusalem.   *See also* **Ne** 2:17–18; **Mic** 7:11
The tower of Babel Ge 11:4–5

Building used figuratively
Mt 16:18 "And I [Jesus] tell you that you are
Peter, and on this rock I will build my church,
and the gates of Hades will not overcome it."
2Co 5:1 Now we know that if the earthly tent
we live in is destroyed, we have a building from
God, an eternal house in heaven, not built by
human hands.
1Th 5:11 Therefore encourage one another and
build each other up, just as in fact you are doing.
1Pe 2:4–5 As you come to him, the living
Stone—rejected by human beings but chosen by
God and precious to him—you also, like living
stones, are being built into a spiritual house to be a
holy priesthood, offering spiritual sacrifices acceptable
to God through Jesus Christ.   *See also* **1Ki** 11:38
Jesus Christ as the capstone of a building: **Ps** 118:22;
Mt 21:42 pp **Mk** 12:10 pp **Lk** 20:17; **Ac** 4:11; **1Pe**
2:7

Pr 9:1; **Mt** 7:24–26 pp **Lk** 6:48–49; **Ro** 15:20;
1Co 3:9–15; **2Co** 10:8; **Eph** 2:20–22; 4:12,29; **Col**
2:7; **Heb** 3:3–4; 11:10   *See also architecture; arts
and crafts; stones; temple, Solomon's.*

burial

The burying of a dead body, usually in a family
tomb. The lack of a proper burial was regarded as
a great misfortune and disgrace. Burial was usually
accompanied by mourning.

Burial in a family tomb
Ge 49:29–31 Then he [Jacob] gave them
these instructions: "I am about to be gathered to
my people. Bury me with my fathers in the cave
in the field of Ephron the Hittite, the cave in the
field of Machpelah, near Mamre in Canaan, which
Abraham bought as a burial place from Ephron the
Hittite, along with the field. There Abraham and
his wife Sarah were buried, there Isaac and his
wife Rebekah were buried, and there I buried
Leah."   *See also* **Ge** 23:19–20; 25:9–10; 50:13;
Jdg 8:32; 16:31; **1Sa** 25:1; **2Sa** 2:32; 17:23

Other places of burial
Ge 35:8,19–20

Burial of criminals hung on a tree
Dt 21:22–23 If anyone guilty of a capital
offence is put to death and the body is hung on
a tree, you must not leave the body on the tree
overnight. Be sure to bury it that same day,
because anyone who is hung on a tree is under
God's curse . . .   *See also* **Jn** 19:31

**Burial of an executed criminal or
enemy under a heap of stones**
Jos 7:26; 8:29; 10:27; **2Sa** 18:17

Lack of a proper burial
Jer 22:18–19 Therefore this is what the LORD
says about Jehoiakim son of Josiah king of Judah.
". . . He will have the burial of a donkey—
dragged away and thrown outside the gates of
Jerusalem."   *See also* **Dt** 28:26; **2Sa** 21:12–14;
1Ki 13:22; **Ecc** 6:3; **Jer** 7:33; 16:4; 25:33

Common burial-grounds
2Ki 23:6; **Jer** 26:23; **Mt** 27:7

Burial accompanied by mourning
Ac 8:2 Godly men buried Stephen and mourned deeply for him. *See also* Dt 34:5–8

Preparation of Jesus Christ's body for burial
Jn 19:39–40 . . . Taking Jesus' body, the two of them [Joseph of Arimathea and Nicodemus] wrapped it, with the spices, in strips of linen. This was in accordance with Jewish burial customs. *See also* **Mt** 26:12 pp Mk 14:8; **Mk** 16:1 pp Lk 24:1 pp Jn 12:7 *See also mourning.*

---

burnt offering

Probably the earliest and most basic form of sacrifice. It is seen fundamentally as a gift to God, either in thanksgiving for his goodness or for atonement for sin.

Hebrew names for the burnt offering
Dt 33:10 ". . . He [Levi] offers incense before you and whole burnt offerings on your altar." *The rarer Hebrew expression means something whole or complete*
Ps 66:13 I will come to your temple with burnt offerings . . . *The commoner expression in Hebrew means that which "goes up" to God. See also* **1Sa** 7:9; **Ps** 51:19

Early examples of burnt offerings
Ge 8:20 Then Noah built an altar to the LORD and, taking some of all the clean animals and clean birds, he sacrificed burnt offerings on it. *Probably all these examples include an element of propitiation:* Ge 22:2–8,13; Ex 10:25; 18:12; 20:24; 24:5; **Job** 1:5

Regulations concerning the burnt offering
How the offering is to be made Lev 1:1–17; 6:8–13; 7:8; Mal 1:8
Occasions for making the offering
Nu 28:9–10 " 'On the Sabbath day, make an

offering of two lambs a year old without defect . . . This is the burnt offering for every Sabbath . . .' "
As a daily offering: **Ex** 29:38–42; **Ezr** 3:3
Lev 8:18–21
On the Day of Atonement: **Lev** 16:3,24
Nu 28:11–14
At Passover: **Nu** 28:19,23
At Firstfruits and the Feast of Weeks: **Lev** 23:12,18;
Nu 28:27
At the beginning of the seventh month: **Nu** 29:2,6
At the Feast of Tabernacles: **Nu** 29:13
Lk 2:24

Burnt offerings in idolatrous worship
Ex 32:6; **2Ki** 10:25

Warnings about misplaced confidence in the burnt offering
1Sa 15:22 . . . "Does the LORD delight in burnt offerings and sacrifices as much as in obeying the voice of the LORD? . . ." *See also* **Isa** 1:11–15; **Jer** 7:21–22; **Hos** 6:6; **Am** 5:25; **Mic** 6:6–8

NT references to the burnt offering
Jesus Christ endorsed the prophets' teaching
Mk 12:33–34 "To love him [God] with all your heart, with all your understanding and with all your strength, and to love your neighbour as yourself is more important than all burnt offerings and sacrifices." When Jesus saw that he [a teacher of the law] had answered wisely, he said to him, "You are not far from the kingdom of God." . . . *See also* **Mt** 9:13; 12:7
The holy life of Jesus Christ is the perfect burnt offering
Heb 10:5–10 . . . "Sacrifice and offering you did not desire, but a body you prepared for me . . .". . . *See also* **Heb** 10:14 *See also blood, Old Testament sacrifices; Feast of Firstfruits; Feast of Tabernacles; Feast of Weeks; offerings; Passover; sacrifice, in Old Testament.*

---

buying and selling

Buying and selling are an integral part of the everyday life of the world. Scripture makes it clear that God expects moral dealings by his people in this area of life as in every other.

Some biblical transactions
The first recorded transaction
Ge 23:3–4 Then Abraham rose from beside his dead wife and spoke to the Hittites. He said, "I am an alien and a stranger among you. Sell me some property for a burial site here so that I can bury my dead."
Transactions in land Ge 47:20–22; **Ru** 4:3; **Pr** 31:16; **Jer** 32:9–10; **Mt** 27:7; **Lk** 14:18; **Ac** 4:34
Buying animals Lk 14:19
Buying food and drink Ge 41:57; **Dt** 2:28; **Jn** 6:5; 13:29; **Rev** 6:6
Transactions in other goods Rev 18:11–13
Buying of slaves Ge 17:12; **Ex** 21:2; **Lev** 25:44–45; **Hos** 3:1–2
The labour market Lev 25:39–40; **Mt** 20:1–2

God's standards in buying and selling
Fairness Ge 23:5–13; **2Sa** 24:24
Honesty
Lev 19:35–36 " 'Do not use dishonest standards when measuring length, weight or quantity. Use honest scales and honest weights, an honest ephah and an honest hin. I am the LORD your God, who brought you out of Egypt.' " *See also* **Ge** 23:14–16; **Dt** 25:13–16; **Pr** 11:1; 16:11; 20:10,23

Sins to avoid in buying and selling
Dishonesty Pr 20:14; **Am** 8:5; **Mic** 6:10–11
Greed Pr 11:26
Exploitation
Lev 25:14 " 'If you sell land to any of own people or buy any from them, do not take advantage of each other.' " *See also* **La** 5:4; **Am** 8:6
Extravagance Lk 15:13
Desecration of the Sabbath Ne 10:31; 13:15–22; **Am** 8:5
Desecration of the temple
Mt 21:12–13 Jesus entered the temple area and drove out all who were buying and selling there. He overturned the tables of the money-changers and the benches of those selling doves.

"It is written," he said to them, " 'My house will be called a house of prayer,' but you are making it a 'den of robbers'." pp **Mk** 11:15–17 pp **Lk** 19:45–46   *See also* **Jn** 2:14–16
Worldliness Eze 7:12; **1Co** 7:29–31; **Jas** 4:13

Oppression through the control of buying and selling
Rev 13:16–17 He [the Beast] also forced everyone, small and great, rich and poor, free and slave, to receive a mark on their right hands or on their foreheads, so that they could not buy or sell unless they had the mark, which is the name of the beast or the number of his name.

Spiritual transactions
Sinners sold to sin 1Ki 21:20; **Ro** 7:14
Israel sold and redeemed Jdg 2:14; **Ps** 44:12; **Isa** 43:1; 50:1; 52:3
Jesus Christ has bought his people
Ac 20:28 ". . . Be shepherds of the church of God, which he bought with his own blood."
See also **1Co** 6:20; 7:23; **1Pe** 1:18–19; **2Pe** 2:1
Spiritual wealth to be bought
Pr 23:23 Buy the truth and do not sell it; get wisdom, discipline and understanding.   *See also* **Isa** 55:1; **Mt** 13:44–46; 25:9; **Rev** 3:18
Gifts money cannot buy Job 28:12–19; **Ps** 49:7–8; **Mk** 8:37; **Ac** 8:20   *See also market; money; redemption, in life; slavery; trade; wages.*

---

ceremonies
Formal outward practices and rituals symbolising or marking events of importance or spiritual significance. Although they had their place in biblical cultural life, they may become empty and hypocritical, losing their deep spiritual meaning. Ceremonies thus become symbolic of empty legalism which should be rejected.

Ceremonies marking important events
Different stages in life Ge 50:7,10–11; **Ex** 13:2; **Jdg** 14:10; **Jer** 34:5; **Jn** 2:1–2; 20:4
Temple worship
Ne 13:9 I [Nehemiah] gave orders to purify the rooms, and then I put back into them the

equipment of the house of God, with the grain offerings and the incense. *See also* **1Ki** 9:25; **1Ch** 16:40; **2Ch** 8:13; 29:15

Some psalms include excerpts from temple liturgy relating to parts of temple-based worship ceremonies: **Ps** 5:7; 118:19–20; 138:2

Ac 3:1

Appointing leaders

Ac 13:2–3 While they [the church at Antioch] were worshipping the Lord and fasting, the Holy Spirit said, "Set apart for me Barnabas and Saul for the work to which I have called them." So after they had fasted and prayed, they placed their hands on them and sent them off.
See also **Lev** 8:30; **1Sa** 16:13; **1Ki** 1:39; **Ac** 6:5–6; 9:17; **1Ti** 4:14

Historical events

Ru 4:7–8 (Now in earlier times in Israel, for the redemption and transfer of property to become final, one party took off his sandal and gave it to the other. This was the method of legalising transactions in Israel.) . . . *See also* **Ge** 35:14; **Ex** 12:14; 13:9; **Jos** 4:4–9; **1Sa** 7:12; **Lk** 22:19 pp 1Co 11:24–25

Ceremonies as spiritual symbols of God's presence

Mt 18:20 "For where two or three come together in my name, there am I [Jesus] with them." *See also* **Ex** 30:25–29; **Nu** 4:4; 10:35–36; **1Ki** 8:3–6 pp 2Ch 5:4–7; **1Ki** 8:29 pp 2Ch 6:20; **1Ch** 6:49; **Heb** 9:1–7

Initiation ceremonies

Circumcision

Lev 12:3 "'On the eighth day the boy is to be circumcised.'" *See also* **Ge** 17:10; **Jos** 5:2; **Lk** 2:21–24

Baptism

Mt 28:19 ". . . go and make disciples of all nations, baptising them in the name of the Father and of the Son and of the Holy Spirit," *See also* **Ac** 2:38; 16:33–34; **1Pe** 3:21

Ceremonies relating to ritual cleansing

Ex 30:18–20 "Make a bronze basin, with its bronze stand, for washing. Place it between the

Tent of Meeting and the altar, and put water in it. Aaron and his sons are to wash their hands and feet with water from it. Whenever they enter the Tent of Meeting, they shall wash with water so that they will not die . . ." *See also* **Lev** 14:14–18; 16:26; 22:6; **Nu** 19:7; **Heb** 9:10

Ceremonies relating to atonement

Lev 17:11 "'For the life of a creature is in the blood, and I [the Lord] have given it to you [the Israelites] to make atonement for yourselves on the altar; it is the blood that makes atonement for one's life.'" *See also* **Lev** 4:20; 8:30–35; 16:10; **Heb** 5:1

Ceremonies conveying spiritual realities

Passover: a ceremony symbolising salvation history

Lk 22:15–16 And he [Jesus] said to them [the disciples], "I have eagerly desired to eat this Passover with you before I suffer. For I tell you, I will not eat it again until it finds fulfilment in the kingdom of God." *See also* **2Ki** 23:21–22; **Ezr** 6:21–22; **Mt** 26:17 pp Mk 14:12 pp Lk 22:7–9

Baptism: a ceremony symbolising new birth

Jn 3:5 . . ."' . . . no-one can enter the kingdom of God without being born of water and the Spirit." *See also* **Ac** 10:48; 22:16; **Gal** 3:27; **Col** 2:12

Marriage: a ceremony symbolising faithful partnership **Mt** 19:6 pp Mk 10:9; **Eph** 5:25–28; **Heb** 13:4; **Rev** 19:7

Ceremonies which lapsed into hypocrisy

Washing ceremonies without accompanying inner cleanliness

Mt 23:25 "Woe to you, teachers of the law and Pharisees, you hypocrites! You clean the outside of the cup and dish, but inside they are full of greed and self-indulgence." *See also* **Mt** 23:27–28; **Mk** 7:4

Sacrificial ceremonies without inner repentance

Am 5:21–22 ". . . Though you [the Israelites] bring choice fellowship offerings, I [the Lord] will have no regard for them." *See also* **1Sa** 15:22; **Ps** 51:16–17; **Isa** 1:11–17; **Hos** 8:11–13; **Mal** 1:8

Initiation ceremonies without real commitment
1Co 7:19 Circumcision is nothing and
uncircumcision is nothing. Keeping God's
commands is what counts.   *See also* **Ac**
15:1,8–10; **Ro** 2:28–29; **Gal** 5:6

Jesus Christ brings freedom from meaningless ceremonies

Gal 5:1 It is for freedom that Christ has set us
free. Stand firm, then, and do not let yourselves
be burdened again by a yoke of slavery.
See also **Gal** 4:8–10; **Eph** 2:14–18; **Col** 2:13–23;
Heb 7:18–19   *See also ritual; sacraments; wedding.*

chief priests

A group of individuals in charge of temple worship
in Jerusalem, and regarded as leading
representatives of the Jewish people, who came
into conflict with Jesus Christ and plotted his
death.

OT references to the chief priest
2Ch 19:11 "Amariah the chief priest will be
over you in any matter concerning the LORD, and
Zebadiah son of Ishmael, the leader of the tribe
of Judah, will be over you in any matter
concerning the king, and the Levites will serve as
officials before you . . ."   *See also* **2Ki** 25:18
pp Jer 52:24
Jehoiada: **2Ch** 24:6,11
2Ch 31:10; **Ezr** 7:5

The chief priests were in charge of temple worship in Jerusalem
Mt 2:4; 21:15

Jesus Christ predicted his suffering at the hands of the chief priests and elders
Mt 16:21 From that time on Jesus began to
explain to his disciples that he must go to
Jerusalem and suffer many things at the hands of
the elders, chief priests and teachers of the law,
and that he must be killed and on the third day
be raised to life. pp Mk 8:31 pp Lk 9:22
See also **Mt** 20:18 pp Mk 10:33

The response of the chief priests to Jesus Christ
They were puzzled by Jesus Christ's teaching
Mt 21:23 Jesus entered the temple courts, and,
while he was teaching, the chief priests and the
elders of the people came to him. "By what
authority are you doing these things?" they
asked. "And who gave you this authority?" pp
Mk 11:27–28 pp Lk 20:1–2   *See also* **Mt**
21:45–46 pp Lk 20:19; **Jn** 7:32,45; 11:47
They and the elders plotted Jesus Christ's
death
Mt 26:3–5 Then the chief priests and the
elders of the people assembled in the palace of
the high priest, whose name was Caiaphas, and
they plotted to arrest Jesus in some sly way and
kill him . . . pp Mk 14:1   *See also* **Mt** 26:59
pp Mk 14:55; **Mt** 27:1
They collaborated with Judas Mt 26:14 pp Mk
14:10 pp Lk 22:4; **Mt** 26:47 pp Mk 14:43 pp Lk
22:52 pp Jn 18:3; **Mt** 27:3–6

The role of the chief priests in the trial of Jesus Christ
They made accusations against Jesus Christ Mt
27:12 pp Mk 15:3; **Lk** 22:66; 23:10
They persuaded the crowd against Jesus Christ
Mt 27:20; **Lk** 23:4,13; **Jn** 19:6
They mocked Jesus Christ Mt 27:41 pp Mk
15:31
They handed Jesus Christ over to Pilate Mk
15:10; **Lk** 24:20; **Jn** 18:35
They persuaded Pilate to have the tomb
guarded Mt 27:62–66
They bribed the soldiers Mt 28:11–15
They rejected Jesus Christ as king Jn 19:15,21

The chief priests' attempt to prevent the preaching of the gospel
By silencing the apostles Ac 4:23; 5:24
By authorising Paul to arrest believers Ac
9:14,21; 26:10,12

The involvement of the chief priests in the arrest and trial of Paul
Ac 22:30; 23:14; 25:2,15   *See also temple,*
Herod's.

children

Scripture indicates that children are a gift from God and are to be loved, disciplined and cared for. The term "children of God" is used to describe Christian believers, who must grow up in the faith which they have accepted.

children, attitudes to

Christians must welcome children as Jesus Christ did. They are used by Christ as an example of how believers should receive the kingdom, and as an example of immaturity by Paul.

Children as a gift from God

Ps 113:9 He settles the barren woman in her home as a happy mother of children. Praise the LORD.

Ps 127:3 Children are a heritage from the LORD, offspring a reward from him. *See also* **Ge** 33:5; 48:9; **Jos** 24:3

Jesus Christ welcomes children

Mt 19:13–14 Then little children were brought to Jesus for him to place his hands on them and pray for them. But the disciples rebuked those who brought them. Jesus said, "Let the little children come to me, and do not hinder them, for the kingdom of heaven belongs to such as these." pp Mk 10:13–16 pp Lk 18:15–17

Those who enter the kingdom must be like children

God's truth is revealed to the childlike

Mt 11:25 At that time Jesus said, "I praise you, Father, Lord of heaven and earth, because you have hidden these things from the wise and learned, and revealed them to little children." pp Lk 10:21 *See also* **1Co** 1:26–29

Children as people welcomed by Jesus Christ

Mt 18:2–5 He [Jesus] called a little child whom he placed among them. And he said: "I tell you the truth, unless you change and become like little children, you will never enter the kingdom of heaven. Therefore, those who humble themselves like this child are the greatest in the kingdom of heaven. And whoever welcomes a little child like this in my name welcomes me." pp Mk 9:36–37 pp Lk 9:47–48 *See also* **Mt** 10:40–42 pp Mk 9:41; **Mt** 18:10,14

Children as a picture of immature Christians

1Co 14:20 Brothers and sisters, stop thinking like children. In regard to evil be infants, but in your thinking be adults.

1Pe 2:2–3 Like newborn babies, crave pure spiritual milk, so that by it you may grow up in your salvation, now that you have tasted that the Lord is good. *See also* **1Co** 13:11; **Heb** 5:13

Promises to children

Dt 5:16 "Honour your father and your mother, as the LORD your God has commanded you, so that you may live long and that it may go well with you in the land the LORD your God is giving you."

Ac 2:39 "The promise [of the Holy Spirit] is for you and your children and for all who are far off—for all whom the Lord our God will call." *See also* **Pr** 8:32; **Eph** 6:2–3

Warnings relating to children

Warnings to those who cause children to stumble

Mt 18:6 "But if any of you causes one of these little ones who believe in me to sin, it would be better for you to have a large millstone hung around your neck and to be drowned in the depths of the sea." pp Mk 9:42

Warnings to Israel, the disobedient child

Isa 30:1 "Woe to the obstinate children," declares the LORD, "to those who carry out plans that are not mine, forming an alliance, but not by my Spirit, heaping sin upon sin;" *See also* **Isa** 30:9

children, needs

Children need love, affection, discipline and guidance from their parents. This is shown through teaching, training, discipline, the meeting of material needs and the provision of a personal example of faith.

Teaching children
Dt 6:6–7 These commandments that I give you today are to be upon your hearts. Impress them on your children . . .   *See also* **Ex** 10:2; 12:26–27; **Dt** 4:9; **Ex** 13:14–15; **Dt** 6:20–21; 11:19; **Pr** 1:8; **Isa** 38:19; **Joel** 1:3

Training children
Pr 22:6 Train children in the way they should go, and when they are old they will not turn from it.
Eph 6:4 Fathers, do not exasperate your children; instead, bring them up in the training and instruction of the Lord.   *See also* **Dt** 31:12–13; **Jos** 8:35; **2Ki** 12:2; **Ps** 34:11; 78:5; **Pr** 3:1

Disciplining children
Pr 13:24 Those who spare the rod hate their children, but those who love them are careful to discipline them.
Heb 12:7–11 Endure hardship as discipline; God is treating you as children. For what children are not disciplined by their parents? . . .   *See also* **Pr** 19:18; 22:15; 23:13; 29:15,17; **1Ti** 3:4,12
Lack of discipline   1Sa 3:13; **1Ki** 1:6

Good examples set for children by parents
David: **1Ki** 9:4; **2Ch** 17:3
2Ch 26:4
Lois and Eunice: **2Ti** 1:5; 3:15

Bad examples set for children by parents
Ahab and Jezebel: **1Ki** 22:52; **2Ch** 22:3; **Jer** 9:14
Mt 14:8

Provision and care for children
Mt 7:9–11 ". . . If you, then, though you are evil, know how to give good gifts to your children, how much more will your Father in heaven give good gifts to those who ask him!" pp **Lk** 11:11–13   *See also* **1Sa** 2:19; **Pr** 31:15,21; **2Co** 12:14

Love for children
Tit 2:4 . . . they [the older women] can train the younger women to love their husbands and children,   *See also* **Ge** 37:3
Jacob's love for Benjamin: **Ge** 44:20,29–31
2Sa 18:33; **Lk** 15:20

children, responsibilities to God
The responsibilities of children to God as their heavenly Father include honouring and obeying him.

The responsibilities of children to their heavenly Father
To honour and obey him in reverent fear
Ps 34:11 Come, my children, listen to me; I will teach you the fear of the LORD.   *See also* **Pr** 2:5; 9:10
To seek wisdom
Pr 4:5–7 Get wisdom, get understanding; do not forget my words or swerve from them . . .   *See also* **Pr** 1:1–4; 8:32–33; 10:1
To listen and learn
Pr 1:8–9 Listen, my son, to your father's instruction and do not forsake your mother's teaching. They will be a garland to grace your head and a chain to adorn your neck.   *See also* **Pr** 4:1–4; 23:22
To praise God
Ps 8:2 From the lips of children and infants you have ordained praise . . .   *See also* **Mt** 21:15–16
To join in worship
Ne 12:43 And on that day they offered great sacrifices, rejoicing because God had given them great joy. The women and children also rejoiced. The sound of rejoicing in Jerusalem could be heard far away.   *See also* **Jos** 8:35

Relationship to Jesus Christ transcends the child-parent relationship
Lk 18:29–30 "I tell you the truth," Jesus said to them, "no-one who has left home or wife or brothers or sisters or parents or children for the sake of the kingdom of God will fail to receive many times as much in this age and, in the age

to come, eternal life." pp Mt 19:29 pp Mk 10:29–30

children, responsibilities to parents

Children owe their parents certain important responsibilities, including the duty to honour and obey them.

The duties of children towards their parents

They are to honour their parents
Ex 20:12 "Honour your father and your mother, so that you may live long in the land the LORD your God is giving you." pp Dt 5:16   *See also* **Pr** 17:6; **Mk** 7:10; **Eph** 6:1–3

They are to obey their parents
Col 3:20–21 Children, obey your parents in everything, for this pleases the Lord. Fathers, do not embitter your children, or they will become discouraged.   *See also* **Eph** 6:1

They are to behave well
Pr 20:11 Even children are known by their actions, by whether their conduct is pure and right.

Children as a blessing and source of joy to their parents

Ps 127:4–5 Like arrows in the hands of a warrior are children born in one's youth. Blessed are those whose quivers are full of them . . .
Pr 23:24 The father of a righteous child has great joy; whoever has a wise son delights in him.   *See also* **Ps** 128:3; **Pr** 15:20; 27:11; 29:3; **Lk** 15:23–24

Children born to barren mothers bring special joy

Sarah: **Ge** 18:11; 21:2
Rachel: **Ge** 29:31; 30:22
Manoah's wife: **Jdg** 13:2,24
Hannah: **1Sa** 1:5,20
Elizabeth: **Lk** 1:7,24,57

Children as a source of grief and disappointment to their parents

Pr 17:25 Foolish children bring grief to their fathers and bitterness to those who bore them.
See also **1Sa** 8:3; **Pr** 17:21; 19:13,26; 28:7; 29:15

The punishment of children

The punishment of wicked children **Ex** 21:15; **Lev** 20:9; **Dt** 21:18–21; **Pr** 30:17; **2Ti** 3:2

The punishment of children for the sins of their fathers

Ex 20:5–6; **Nu** 14:18; **Jer** 31:29–30; 32:18   *See also* **fathers, responsibilities**; **mothers, responsibilities.**

circumcision

The practice of cutting away the foreskin of male children, usually within a short time of birth. In the OT, the practice is seen as a sign of membership of the people of God. The NT makes it clear that Christians are under no obligation to be circumcised.

circumcision, physical

In the OT, circumcision is seen as an outward sign of membership of Israel, the people of God.

The significance of circumcision in God's covenant with Abraham

Ge 17:10–14 "This is my covenant with you and your descendants after you, the covenant you are to keep: Every male among you shall be circumcised. You are to undergo circumcision, and it will be the sign of the covenant between me and you. For the generations to come every male among you who is eight days old must be circumcised, including those born in your household or bought with money from a foreigner—those who are not your offspring. Whether born in your household or bought with your money, they must be circumcised. My covenant in your flesh is to be an everlasting covenant. Any uncircumcised male, who has not been circumcised in the flesh, will be cut off from his people; he has broken my covenant."   *See also* **Ac** 7:8

Circumcision is also for Abraham's descendants
Ge 17:7

Circumcision as a sign of national identity
Dinah's brothers and the Shechemites: **Ge** 34:8–9,14–17
Ex 4:24–26; **Jos** 5:4–8

Circumcision is integrated into the Mosaic law
Lev 12:3; **Jn** 7:22

Circumcision as an important Passover restriction
Ex 12:44,48–49; **Jdg** 14:3

Circumcision was not necessarily a sign of consecration to God
Jer 9:25–26

NT accounts of circumcision practised in obedience to the law
Lk 1:59; 2:21; **Jn** 7:23; **Php** 3:5; **Ac** 16:3

The subject of circumcision debated by the first Christians
Ac 10:45; 11:2; 15:5; **Gal** 2:3; **Eph** 2:11; **Col** 3:11; **Tit** 1:10   *See also covenant, with Abraham; law, Old Testament; ritual; sacraments.*

---

circumcision, spiritual
On its own, the physical sign of circumcision is no guarantee of finding favour in the sight of God. It was intended to be the outward sign of inward consecration and should be accompanied by repentance, faith and obedience. Paul stresses that circumcision confers no special privileges upon individuals; it is faith in God, rather than any outward sign, that ensures that believers stand in a right relationship to God.

Physical circumcision has no value without the obedience of the heart
Dt 30:6 The LORD your God will circumcise your hearts and the hearts of your descendants, so that you may love him with all your heart and with all your soul, and live.   *See also* **Dt** 10:14–16; **Jer** 4:4
Ro 2:28–29 A person is not a Jew who is only one outwardly, nor is circumcision merely outward and physical. No, a person is a Jew who is one inwardly; and circumcision is circumcision of the heart, by the Spirit, not by the written code. Such a person's praise is not from others, but from God.   *See also* **Ro** 2:25–27; **1Co** 7:19

Circumcision and faith
Gal 5:6 For in Christ Jesus neither circumcision nor uncircumcision has any value. The only thing that counts is faith expressing itself through love.   *See also* **Ro** 3:30
Abraham's righteousness depended on his faith, not on the covenant of circumcision Gal 3:6; **Ge** 15:6; **Ro** 4:9–12
Paul values the law as part of God's plan Ro 3:1–2

The sharp debate about circumcision for Christians
The Council of Jerusalem Ac 15:1–19
Jewish Christians in Jerusalem criticise Peter for accepting hospitality from Cornelius and his (uncircumcised) friends Ac 11:1–3
God's acceptance of uncircumcised Gentiles is clear from the outpouring of the Holy Spirit upon them
Ac 10:44–46 . . . The circumcised believers who had come with Peter were astonished that the gift of the Holy Spirit had been poured out even on the Gentiles. For they heard them speaking in tongues and praising God . . .
See also **Ac** 10:34
Peter's misgivings about Gentile believers and the law Gal 2:11–16

Imposing circumcision upon Gentile Christians denies the freedom of the gospel
Gal 5:1–6 It is for freedom that Christ has set us free. Stand firm, then, and do not let yourselves be burdened again by a yoke of slavery . . .   *See also* **Gal** 2:3–5; 3:14

"Judaisers" should be resisted
Gal 5:7–12; 6:12–13,15; **Php** 3:2–3; **Tit** 1:10–11

To be "in Christ" is to be spiritually circumcised
Col 2:11–12 In him you were also circumcised, in the putting off of the sinful nature, not with a circumcision done by human hands but with the circumcision done by Christ . . .   *See also* **Col** 3:11

Paul's confidence in Jesus Christ
Php 3:4–9

The relationship between baptism and circumcision in the NT
Col 2:11–13; **Ro** 4:11; **2Co** 1:21–22; **Eph** 1:13

---

city

A large walled centre of population providing security for its inhabitants. The OT often uses the term as a symbol of the security of heaven.

Types of city
Ancient cities Ge 4:17; 10:10–12
Fortified cities Nu 32:34–36; **Dt** 9:1; **Jos** 10:20; 14:12
Royal cities Jos 10:2; **1Sa** 27:5; **1Ch** 11:7
Cities of refuge Dt 4:41–43; 19:1–13

Cities were frequently large
Dt 1:28 ". . .'. . . the cities are large, with walls up to the sky . . .'"
Jnh 3:2–3 "Go to the great city of Nineveh and proclaim to it the message I give you." Jonah obeyed the word of the LORD and went to Nineveh. Now Nineveh was a very important city—a visit required three days.   *See also* **Dt** 6:10; 9:1; **Ne** 7:4; **Jnh** 4:11

Cities were surrounded by walls
Dt 3:5 All these cities were fortified with high walls and with gates and bars, and there were also a great many unwalled villages.
Ezr 4:12 The king should know that the Jews who came up to us from you have gone to Jerusalem and are rebuilding that rebellious and wicked city. They are restoring the walls and repairing the foundations.

2Co 11:32–33 In Damascus the governor under King Aretas had the city of the Damascenes guarded in order to arrest me [Paul]. But I was lowered in a basket from a window in the wall and slipped through his hands.   *See also* **Dt** 28:52; **Jos** 2:15; **1Ki** 3:1; 4:13; **2Ch** 33:14

Cities were places of security
Nu 32:17 ". . . our women and children will live in fortified cities, for protection from the inhabitants of the land."   *See also* **Jos** 10:20; **2Ch** 11:5–12; 14:6; 17:2; **Jer** 4:5

Cities could fall
2Sa 5:7 Nevertheless, David captured the fortress of Zion, the City of David.
Ne 1:3 . . .". . . The wall of Jerusalem is broken down, and its gates have been burned with fire."
Jer 51:58 This is what the LORD Almighty says: "Babylon's thick wall will be levelled and her high gates set on fire; the peoples exhaust themselves for nothing, the nations' labour is only fuel for the flames."   *See also* **Dt** 20:12,19–20; **1Ki** 16:17–18; **2Ki** 25:1–4; **Isa** 13:19; **Jer** 32:24–25; **Am** 5:9

The holy city
Ps 48:1–2 Great is the LORD, and most worthy of praise, in the city of our God, his holy mountain. It is beautiful in its loftiness, the joy of the whole earth. Like the utmost heights of Zaphon is Mount Zion, the city of the Great King.   *See also* **1Ki** 11:36; 14:21; **1Ch** 11:7; **Ne** 11:1; **Isa** 52:1; **Jer** 25:29; **Da** 9:16; **Mt** 5:35

City law
Lev 25:29–30

The city as a symbol
Of strength
Jer 1:18 "Today I [the LORD] have made you [Jeremiah] a fortified city, an iron pillar and a bronze wall to stand against the whole land— against the kings of Judah, its officials, its priests and the people of the land."

Of heaven

Heb 11:10 For he [Abraham] was looking forward to the city with foundations, whose architect and builder is God.   *See also* **Heb** 11:16; 12:22; 13:14; **Rev** 21:2,20–27; 22:1–5

clean and unclean

The distinction between things which were ritually acceptable and unacceptable to God. Animals were classified as either clean or unclean, denoting their suitability or unsuitability for sacrifice and food. The motives and intentions of the heart were also sometimes judged to be clean or unclean, as uncleanness was often linked with sin.

The OT distinction between clean and unclean

The command to distinguish between clean and unclean

Lev 15:31 " 'You [Moses and Aaron] must keep the Israelites separate from things that make them unclean, so they will not die in their uncleanness for defiling my dwelling-place, which is among them.' "   *See also* **Lev** 10:8–11; 20:22–26; **Eze** 22:26; 44:23

The distinction between clean and unclean animals

Ge 7:2 Take with you [Noah] seven of every kind of clean animal, a male and its mate, and two of every kind of unclean animal, a male and its mate,   *See also* **Ge** 7:8–9; 8:20; **Lev** 11:1–47 pp Dt 14:3–20; **Lev** 27:11–13

The NT attitude to clean and unclean animals
Mk 7:14–23 pp Mt 15:10–20; **Ac** 10:11–15; 11:5–9

Places and inanimate objects could be clean or unclean

Lev 10:14 "But you [priests] and your sons and your daughters may eat the breast that was waved and the thigh that was presented. Eat them in a ceremonially clean place; they have been given to you and your children as your share of the Israelites' fellowship offerings."   *See also* **Lev** 4:12; 6:11; 11:32–38; 14:33–57; **2Ch** 13:11

Causes of uncleanness

Physical contact with anything unclean

Lev 5:2–3 " '. . . if anyone touches anything ceremonially unclean—whether the carcasses of unclean wild animals or of unclean livestock or of unclean creatures that move along the ground—even though they are unaware of it, they have become unclean and are guilty. Or if they touch human uncleanness—anything that would make them unclean—even though they are unaware of it, when they learn of it they will be guilty.' "   *See also* **Lev** 7:19; **Hos** 9:3–4; **Hag** 2:10–14

Contact with corpses
Nu 19:11 "Whoever touches the dead body of anyone will be unclean for seven days."   *See also* **Lev** 21:1–4,10–12; **Nu** 6:5–8

Infectious skin diseases
Lev 13:1–46 . . ." '. . . The priest is to examine the sore on the skin, and if the hair in the sore has turned white and the sore appears to be more than skin deep, it is an infectious skin disease. When the priest examines them, he shall pronounce them ceremonially unclean . . .' "   *See also* **Lev** 14:1–32; **Mt** 8:2–4 pp Mk 1:40–44 pp Lk 5:12–14

Certain bodily functions
Lev 12:2 " '. . . 'A woman who becomes pregnant and gives birth to a son will be ceremonially unclean for seven days, just as she is unclean during her monthly period.' "   *See also* **Lev** 12:5; 15:1–33

Consequences of uncleanness
Exclusion from worship
Lev 22:3–5 ". . . 'For the generations to come, if any of your descendants is ceremonially unclean and yet comes near the sacred offerings that the Israelites consecrate to the LORD, that person must be cut off from my presence. I am the LORD . . .' "   *See also* **Lev** 12:4; **Nu** 9:6–12; **1Sa** 20:24–26; **2Ch** 23:19; 30:17

Isolation from God's people
Nu 5:2 "Command the Israelites to send away from the camp anyone who has an infectious skin disease or a discharge of any kind, or who is ceremonially unclean because of a dead body."   *See also* **Lev** 7:20–21; **Dt** 23:10–11

Cleansing from uncleanness

Lev 16:29–30 ". . . on this day atonement will be made for you, to cleanse you. Then, before the LORD, you will be clean from all your sins." *See also* **Lev** 12:6–8; 16:15–16; 22:4–7; **Nu** 6:9–12; 19:1–22; 31:21–24; **Heb** 9:13

Inner, spiritual cleanness and uncleanness

Job 33:9 "'I [Job] am pure and without sin; I am clean and free from guilt.'"

Ps 51:7 Cleanse me with hyssop, and I shall be clean; wash me, and I shall be whiter than snow. *See also* **Ge** 20:5; **Ps** 24:3–4; **Pr** 20:9; **Isa** 1:15–16; 64:6; **La** 1:8; **Eze** 36:25; **Mt** 15:10–20 pp Mk 7:14–23; **Mt** 23:25–28; **Ac** 10:28 *See also disease; food; ritual law; ritual washing; washing.*

cloth

A woven material from which garments or coverings were made. Different kinds of material are associated with different ranks and social positions.

Cloth for daily wear

Pr 31:22 She [the good wife] makes coverings for her bed; she is clothed in fine linen and purple. *See also* **Nu** 15:38; **Jdg** 5:30; 14:12; **2Sa** 1:24; **1Ch** 15:27; **Ps** 45:14; **Eze** 16:10,13; **Mt** 9:16; **Jn** 19:23; **Ac** 9:39

Cloth for general coverings

1Sa 21:9 The priest replied, "The sword of Goliath the Philistine, whom you killed in the Valley of Elah, is here; it is wrapped in a cloth behind the ephod. If you want it, take it; there is no sword here but that one." David said, "There is none like it; give it to me." *See also* **2Sa** 17:19; **Pr** 7:16

Cloth for special uses
For religious garments

Ex 28:6 "Make the ephod of gold, and of blue, purple and scarlet yarn, and of finely twisted linen—the work of skilled hands." *See also*

Ex 28:8,31,39,42; 35:19; 39:1,5,22,41
For the tabernacle

Ex 26:1 "Make the tabernacle with ten curtains of finely twisted linen and blue, purple and scarlet yarn, with cherubim worked into them by skilled hands." *See also* **Ex** 26:4; 36:8; **2Ch** 3:14
To cover religious objects Nu 4:5–13
Sackcloth as a sign of mourning

Ge 37:34 Then Jacob tore his clothes, put on sackcloth and mourned for his son many days. *See also* **2Sa** 3:31; **1Ki** 21:27; **2Ki** 19:1; **Ne** 9:1; **Ps** 35:13; **Isa** 3:24; **Jer** 4:8; **Joel** 1:13
For burials

Mt 27:59 Joseph took the body, wrapped it in a clean linen cloth, pp Mk 15:46 pp Lk 23:53 *See also* **Jn** 11:44; 20:7
To wrap babies in

Eze 16:4 "'On the day you were born your cord was not cut, nor were you washed with water to make you clean, nor were you rubbed with salt or wrapped in cloths.'" *See also* **Lk** 2:7,12

Rules relating to cloth

Lev 13:47–49; 19:19 *See also arts and crafts; burial; clothing; colours; tabernacle, in Old Testament; tents.*

clothing

Garments were originally provided by God for Adam and Eve. Kings and priests were given special garments. God's people should neither be unduly anxious about how they dress, nor judge others by what they wear. Inner clothing is more important than outer adornment.

The origin of clothing

Ge 3:21 The LORD God made garments of skin for Adam and his wife and clothed them.

Various regulations regarding clothing

Lev 15:1–27; **Dt** 22:5,11–12

Special clothing for priests

Ex 28:1–5; 29:5–6; 39:1; **Lev** 8:7–9; **Eze** 44:17–19

Rich clothing a sign of wealth or status
Ge 41:42; **2Sa** 13:18; **Est** 6:8–9; 8:15; **Ps**
45:13–14; **Da** 5:7; **Lk** 16:19; **Ac** 12:21

The Israelites' clothing did not wear out in the desert wanderings
Dt 8:4; 29:5; **Ne** 9:21

Clothing as a symbol of fragility and perishability
Isa 51:8 "For the moth will eat them up like a garment . . ."   *See also* **Isa** 50:9

Symbolic actions involving clothing
The hem or corner of a garment Ru 3:9
Touching or taking hold of the corner of a garment indicates putting oneself under the control or domination of another: **Zec** 8:23; **Mt** 9:20 pp Lk 8:44; **Jn** 20:17
Cutting or tearing off the corner of someone else's garment indicates rebellion or a desire to break away from their control or authority: **1Sa** 15:27; 24:4–5
Tearing one's own garments is a sign of mourning or distress: **Ge** 37:29,34; 44:13; **Lev** 10:6
2Sa 3:31 Then David said to Joab and all the people with him, "Tear your clothes and put on sackcloth and walk in mourning in front of Abner." . . .

Provision of rich clothing a picture of God's love
Eze 16:10–13; **Lk** 15:22

Examples of unusual clothing
Joseph's richly ornamented robe Ge 37:3,23,32
The dress of Elijah and John the Baptist 2Ki
1:8; **Mt** 3:4 pp Mk 1:6
Isaiah's lack of clothing a prophetic sign Isa
20:2–4
The mock robing of Jesus Christ Mt 27:28 pp
Mk 15:17 pp Jn 19:2; **Lk** 23:11
Gambling at the cross for Jesus Christ's clothing Mt 27:35 pp Mk 15:24 pp Lk 23:34 pp Jn
19:23–24; **Ps** 22:18

Women and clothing
Women praised for making clothing Pr
31:21,24; **Ac** 9:39

Women urged to dress modestly
1Ti 2:9 I [Paul] also want women to dress modestly, with decency and propriety, not with braided hair or gold or pearls or expensive clothes,   *See also* **1Pe** 3:3

Believers not to be unduly anxious about clothing
Mt 6:28–30 pp Lk 12:27–28

Believers not to discriminate because of clothing
Jas 2:1–4 . . . If you [believers] show special attention to the one wearing fine clothes and say, "Here's a good seat for you," but say to the one who is poor, "You stand there" or "Sit on the floor by my feet," have you not discriminated among yourselves and become judges with evil thoughts?

Inner clothing more important than outer adornment
1Pe 3:3–4 Your [believing women's] beauty should not come from outward adornment, such as braided hair and the wearing of gold jewellery and fine clothes. Instead, it should be that of your inner self, the unfading beauty of a gentle and quiet spirit, which is of great worth in God's sight.   *See also* **1Sa** 16:7; **Pr** 31:25; **Isa** 52:1;
61:3; **Col** 3:12; **1Ti** 2:9–10; **1Pe** 5:5

The robe of righteousness
Isa 61:10 I delight greatly in the LORD; my soul rejoices in my God. For he has clothed me with garments of salvation and arrayed me in a robe of righteousness, as a bridegroom adorns his head like a priest, and as a bride adorns herself with her jewels.   *See also* **Job** 29:14; **Ps** 132:9,16;
Zec 3:3–5; **Mt** 22:1–14; **2Co** 5:2–4; **Rev**
3:17–18; 19:8

White clothing, the clothing of heaven
The transfiguration of Jesus Christ
Mt 17:2 There he [Jesus] was transfigured before them [Peter, James and John]. His face shone like the sun, and his clothes became as white as the light. pp Mk 9:3 pp Lk 9:29

The angels at the tomb Mt 28:3 pp Mk 16:5 pp Lk 24:4; **Jn** 20:12

The vision of the redeemed

Rev 3:4–5 "Yet you have a few people in Sardis who have not soiled their clothes. They will walk with me, dressed in white, for they are worthy. Those who overcome will, like them, be dressed in white . . ."   *See also* **Rev** 3:18; 4:4; 6:11; 7:9

The vision of the exalted Christ Rev 1:13; 19:13   *See also cloth; colours; ornaments; washing.*

---

coinage

Coinage was not used until the late 7th century B.C. Weights of silver and gold were earlier used as "currency". By the later exile a variety of minted coinage, made from gold, silver, bronze or copper, gradually replaced the method of reckoning currency by weighing out precious metals. Israelite, Persian, Greek and Roman coins are mentioned in Scripture.

The talent
A unit of weight

1Ki 10:14 The weight of the gold that Solomon received yearly was 666 talents, pp 2Ch 9:13   *See also* **Ex** 38:25,29; **1Ki** 9:28 pp 2Ch 8:18; **1Ki** 10:10 pp 2Ch 9:9; **1Ch** 22:14

A weight for precious metals used as currency

1Ki 20:39 As the king [Ahab] passed by, the prophet called out to him, "Your servant went into the thick of the battle, and someone came to me with a captive and said, 'Guard this man. If he is missing, it will be your life for his life, or you must pay a talent of silver.'"   *See also* **1Ki** 9:14; 16:24; **2Ki** 5:5,22–23; 15:19; 18:14; 23:33 pp 2Ch 36:3; **1Ch** 19:6; **2Ch** 25:6,9; 27:5; **Est** 3:9

Adopted as the name of a coin

Mt 18:23–35 ". . . the kingdom of heaven is like a king who wanted to settle accounts with his servants. As he began the settlement, a man who owed him ten thousand talents was brought to him . . ."   *See also* **Mt** 25:14–30

The shekel
Its value

Eze 45:10–12 "'. . . The shekel is to consist of twenty gerahs. Twenty shekels plus twenty-five shekels plus fifteen shekels equal one mina.'"   *See also* **Ex** 30:13; 38:25–26; **Lev** 27:25; **Nu** 3:46–47; 18:16

Used as currency

Isa 7:23 In that day, in every place where there were a thousand vines worth a thousand silver shekels, there will be only briers and thorns.   *See also* **Ex** 30:15; **Lev** 27:1–8; **Dt** 22:19,29; **Jdg** 9:4; 16:5; 17:10; **1Sa** 13:21; **2Sa** 18:12; **2Ki** 6:25; 7:1,16,18; **1Ch** 21:25; **2Ch** 1:17; **Ne** 5:15; 10:32; **Jer** 32:9; **Hos** 3:2

The denarius
Referred to in Jesus Christ's parables

Mt 20:1–16 "For the kingdom of heaven is like a landowner who went out early in the morning to hire workers for his vineyard. He agreed to pay them a denarius for the day and sent them into his vineyard . . ."   *See also* **Mt** 18:21–35; **Lk** 7:41–47

As the unit for the payment of taxes to Rome

Mt 22:15–21 . . . Jesus, knowing their evil intent, said, "You hypocrites, why are you trying to trap me? Show me the coin used for paying the tax." They [the Pharisees] brought him a denarius, and he asked them, "Whose portrait is this? And whose inscription?" "Caesar's," they replied. Then he said to them, "Give to Caesar what is Caesar's, and to God what is God's." pp Mk 12:13–17 pp Lk 20:20–26

The penny

Mt 10:29 "Are not two sparrows sold for a penny? Yet not one of them will fall to the ground apart from the will of your Father." pp Lk 12:6   *The "penny" was not a coin in use in biblical times, but the term is employed in the NIV for two different copper coins, the "assarion" and the "quadrans", which were of relatively little value.*   *See also* **Mt** 5:25–26 pp Lk 12:58–59; **Mk** 12:42

The gerah
Lev 27:25 " 'Every value is to be set according to the sanctuary shekel, twenty gerahs to the shekel.' " *See also* **Ex** 30:13; **Nu** 3:47; 18:16; **Eze** 45:12

The drachma
Ac 19:19 A number who had practised sorcery brought their scrolls together and burned them publicly. When they calculated the value of the scrolls, the total came to fifty thousand drachmas. *See also* **Ezr** 2:69; **Ne** 7:70–72

The four-drachma coin
Mt 17:24–27 . . ." . . . go to the lake and throw out your line. Take the first fish you [Peter] catch; open its mouth and you will find a four-drachma coin. Take it and give it to them [the tax collectors] for my [Jesus'] tax and yours."

The daric
1Ch 29:7 They [the people] gave towards the work on the temple of God five thousand talents and ten thousand darics of gold, ten thousand talents of silver, eighteen thousand talents of bronze and a hundred thousand talents of iron. *See also* **Ezr** 8:27

Unnamed coins
General references to coins
Jn 2:13–16 . . . So he [Jesus] made a whip out of cords, and drove all from the temple area, both sheep and cattle; he scattered the coins of the money changers and overturned their tables . . . *See also* **Mt** 27:6
Silver coins
Mt 26:14–15 Then one of the Twelve—the one called Judas Iscariot—went to the chief priests and asked, "What are you willing to give me if I hand him over to you?" So they counted out for him thirty silver coins. *See also* **Mt** 27:3–10; **Zec** 11:12–13; **Lk** 10:30–35; 15:8–10 *Although translated simply as "silver coins", it is the "drachma" which is referred to here.*
Copper coins
Mk 12:41–42 . . . a poor widow came and put in two very small copper coins, worth only a

fraction of a penny. pp Lk 21:1–2 *The Greek coin "lepton" is translated as "copper coin" in these passages.* *See also metals; money; taxation; weights.*

---

colours
A wide range of colours are mentioned in Scripture, some being used symbolically.

Colours mentioned in Scripture
White
Ge 49:12 ". . . his [Judah's] teeth [will be] whiter than milk."
2Ki 5:27 . . . he [Gehazi] was leprous, as white as snow.
Blue
Est 1:6 The garden had hangings of white and blue linen . . .
Eze 27:24 " 'In your [Tyre's] market-place they traded with you beautiful garments, blue fabric, embroidered work and multicoloured rugs with cords twisted and tightly knotted.' " *See also* **Ex** 26:1; 39:22
Yellow
Rev 9:17 . . . yellow as sulphur . . . *See also* **Lev** 13:30
Green
Mk 6:39 Then Jesus directed them [the disciples] to have all the people sit down in groups on the green grass. All the references are to plants or foliage: **Ge** 1:30; **Ps** 23:2; **Jer** 17:8; **Rev** 8:7
Red
2Ki 3:22 . . . To the Moabites across the way, the water looked red—like blood.
Mt 16:2 He [Jesus] replied, "When evening comes, you say, 'It will be fair weather, for the sky is red . . .' " *See also* **Ge** 25:30; **Ex** 36:19; **Rev** 12:3
Purple
Mk 15:17 They [the soldiers] put a purple robe on him [Jesus], then twisted together a crown of thorns and set it on him. All the references are to rich or royal cloth: **Nu** 4:13; **Pr** 31:22; **Da** 5:7; **Ac** 16:14

Scarlet

Isa 1:18 "Come now, let us reason together," says the LORD. "Though your sins are like scarlet, they shall be as white as snow; though they are red as crimson, they shall be like wool."
See also **Ge** 38:28; **Ex** 35:23; **Nu** 4:8; **SS** 4:3; **Mt** 27:28; **Rev** 17:4

Crimson

Isa 63:1 Who is this coming from Edom, from Bozrah, with his garments stained crimson? . . . *See also* **2Ch** 2:7

Black

SS 5:11 . . . his hair is wavy and black as a raven. *See also* **Rev** 6:12

The whole spectrum

Eze 1:28 Like the appearance of a rainbow in the clouds on a rainy day, so was the radiance around him. This was the appearance of the likeness of the glory of the LORD . . . *See also* **Rev** 4:3; 10:1

Colours used symbolically

Rev 6:2 I looked, and there before me was a white horse! Its rider held a bow, and he was given a crown, and he rode out as a conqueror bent on conquest. *White here symbolises conquest*

Rev 17:3 Then the angel carried me away in the Spirit into a desert. There I saw a woman sitting on a scarlet beast that was covered with blasphemous names and had seven heads and ten horns. *See also* **Rev** 6:4 *bloodshed and war;* **Rev** 6:8 *death*
Blessedness and purity: **Rev** 7:9; 19:14,11
Rev 20:11 *holiness*

---

cooking

Scripture contains much evidence of methods of cooking and types of food cooked in biblical times. Cooking was an essential part of sacrificial worship, as well as being a domestic necessity.

Cooks

1Sa 8:10–13 . . . ". . . He [the king] will take your daughters to be perfumers and cooks and bakers." *See also* **1Sa** 9:23–24

Cooking utensils

1Sa 2:13–14 Now it was the practice of the priests with the people that whenever anyone offered a sacrifice and while the meat was being boiled, the servant of the priest would come with a three-pronged fork in his hand. He would plunge it into the pan or kettle or cauldron or pot, and the priest would take for himself whatever the fork brought up . . . *See also* **Lev** 2:7; 6:28; 7:9; 11:35; **Nu** 11:8; **Eze** 11:3; **Zec** 14:20–21

Cooking methods

Baking Ge 19:3; **Ex** 16:23; **Lev** 26:26; **1Sa** 28:24; **Eze** 46:20

Boiling
Ex 16:23 He [Moses] said to them [the Israelites], "This is what the LORD commanded: 'Tomorrow is to be a day of rest, a holy Sabbath to the LORD. So bake what you want to bake and boil what you want to boil. Save whatever is left and keep it until morning.'" *See also* **Nu** 6:19; **1Sa** 2:13

Roasting
1Sa 2:15 . . . even before the fat was burned, the servant of the priest would come and say to those who were sacrificing, "Give the priest some meat to roast; he won't accept boiled meat from you, but only raw." *See also* **Ex** 12:8–9; **Dt** 16:5–7; **Pr** 12:27; **Isa** 44:16,19

Food cooked

Meat
Eze 24:10 "'. . . heap on the wood and kindle the fire. Cook the meat well, mixing in the spices; and let the bones be charred.'" *See also* **Ge** 27:3–19; **Ex** 29:31; **Lev** 8:31; **1Ki** 17:6; **Mic** 3:3
Injunctions against cooking a goat in its mother's milk: **Ex** 23:19; 34:26; **Dt** 14:21

Grain
1Sa 17:17 Now Jesse said to his son David, "Take this ephah of roasted grain and these ten loaves of bread for your brothers and hurry to their camp." *See also* **Jos** 5:11; **Ru** 2:14; **1Sa** 25:18; **2Sa** 17:27–28; **1Ki** 17:10–16

Stew
Ge 25:29 Once when Jacob was cooking some

stew, Esau came in from the open country,
famished.   *See also* **2Ki** 4:38–41
Human flesh
La 4:10 With their own hands compassionate
women have cooked their own children, who
became their food when my people were
destroyed.   *See also* **2Ki** 6:26–29

Cooked offerings
Lev 2:7 " 'If your grain offering is cooked in a
pan, it is to be made of fine flour and oil.' "
See also **Lev** 2:14; 7:9; 8:31; **2Ch** 35:13; **Eze**
46:20,24   *See also clean and unclean; food; herbs
and spices; meat; offerings; water.*

---

covenant

God's commitment to, and requirement of, his
people expressed in promise, law, judgment,
faithfulness and mercy. Also used of commitment
within human relationships based upon
agreements.

---

covenant, at Sinai

God's faithful commitment, made in pursuance of
his promises to Abraham, to acknowledge the
newly-redeemed Israel as his own special people.
Israel's required response to the grace of God in
election was to be holiness and obedience to the
law.

The occasion of the covenant
**The covenant fulfilled God's promises to
Abraham**
Dt 29:12–13 You [the Israelites] are standing
here in order to enter into a covenant with the
LORD your God, a covenant the LORD is making
with you this day and sealing with an oath, to
confirm you this day as his people, that he may
be your God as he promised you and as he
swore to your fathers, Abraham, Isaac and
Jacob.   *See also* **Ex** 2:24; 6:4–8; **Dt** 7:8
**The covenant followed Israel's redemption
from slavery**
Jer 34:13 "This is what the LORD, the God of
Israel, says: I made a covenant with your
ancestors when I brought them out of Egypt, out

of the land of slavery . . ."   *See also* **Ex** 20:2
pp Dt 5:6; **Lev** 26:45
The covenant was mediated through Moses Ex
34:27; **Lev** 26:46; **Dt** 29:1; **Jn** 1:17
**The covenant was accompanied by signs of
God's presence Ex** 19:18–19; 20:18–19; 24:16;
Ps 68:8

Sealing the covenant
Sharing a meal Ex 24:11
Offering a sacrifice Ex 24:5–8; **Ps** 50:5
God's oath Dt 28:9; 29:14; **Eze** 16:8
Israel's promise Ex 19:8; 24:3,7

The covenant relationship
Israel as God's people
Dt 7:6 For you [Israel] are a people holy to the
LORD your God. The LORD your God has chosen
you out of all the peoples on the face of the
earth to be his people, his treasured
possession.   *See also* **Ex** 19:5–6; **Lev** 26:12; **Dt**
14:2; **Jer** 13:11
Israel adopted into God's family
Hos 11:1 "When Israel was a child, I [the
LORD] loved him, and out of Egypt I called my
son."   *See also* **Dt** 1:30–31; 8:5; **Isa** 63:16;
Mal 2:10
Israel as God's bride
Jer 2:2 ". . .'I [the LORD] remember the
devotion of your [Israel's] youth, how as a bride
you loved me and followed me through the
desert, through a land not sown.' "   *See also*
Isa 54:5–8; **Jer** 31:32; **Eze** 16:8; **Hos** 2:14–16

The blessings of the covenant
Inheriting God's promises Dt 6:3; 26:18–19;
28:9; **Jos** 23:5
Provision and protection Lev 26:3–13; **Dt**
28:1–14

The requirements of the covenant
Obedience to the law
Ex 24:7 Then he [Moses] took the Book of the
Covenant and read it to the people [Israel]. They
responded, "We will do everything the LORD has
said; we will obey."
Ex 34:27–28 Then the LORD said to Moses,

"Write down these words, for in accordance with these words I have made a covenant with you and with Israel." . . . And he wrote on the tablets the words of the covenant—the Ten Commandments.   *See also* **Dt** 4:13; **Jos** 8:31; **Ne** 8:1

Holiness
Dt 14:2 for you [Israel] are a people holy to the LORD your God. Out of all the peoples on the face of the earth, the LORD has chosen you to be his treasured possession.
Lev 11:45 " 'I am the LORD who brought you [the people of Israel] up out of Egypt to be your God; therefore be holy, because I am holy.' "
See also **Lev** 20:26

Wholehearted devotion
Ex 34:14 "Do not worship any other god, for the LORD, whose name is Jealous, is a jealous God."
Dt 10:12 And now, O Israel, what does the LORD your God ask of you but to fear the LORD your God, to walk in all his ways, to love him, to serve the LORD your God with all your heart and with all your soul,   *See also* **Ex** 23:32; **Dt** 4:23; 6:5; 10:20; **Jos** 24:14–15

Breaking the covenant
The consequences of breaking the covenant
Disease: **Lev** 26:15–16; **Dt** 28:21–22
Drought and crop failure: **Lev** 26:19–20; **Dt** 28:23–24
Defeat by enemies: **Lev** 26:17,25; **Dt** 28:25
Exile from the land: **Lev** 26:32–33; **Dt** 28:36–37; **Jos** 23:16; **Eze** 17:19–20

Israel's unfaithfulness to the covenant
Ps 78:37 their [the people of Israel's] hearts were not loyal to him [God], they were not faithful to his covenant.   *See also* **2Ki** 18:12; **1Ch** 5:25; **Jer** 3:8; 11:10; **Eze** 16:32; **Hos** 6:7

God's commitment to the covenant
God's covenant of love
Dt 7:9 Know therefore that the LORD your God is God; he is the faithful God, keeping his covenant of love to a thousand generations of those who love him and keep his commands.
See also **Ne** 1:5; **Da** 9:4

The everlasting covenant
Eze 16:60 " 'Yet I [the LORD] will remember

the covenant I made with you [Israel] in the days of your youth, and I will establish an everlasting covenant with you.' "   *See also* **Isa** 61:8; **Jer** 32:40

Renewing the covenant
Lev 26:40–45; **Dt** 29:1; **Jos** 24:22–25; **2Ki** 23:3 pp 2Ch 34:31   *See also law, Ten Commandments.*

---

covenant, nature of

A solemn agreement or promise, sometimes confirmed by sacrifice or by sharing in a meal, by which two or more parties commit themselves to the rights and responsibilities demanded by their relationship and their agreed course of action, and accept the serious consequences of breaking faith.

Kinds of covenant relationship
The relationship between king and people
2Sa 5:3 When all the elders of Israel had come to King David at Hebron, the king made a compact with them at Hebron before the LORD, and they anointed David king over Israel. pp 1Ch 11:3   *See also* **2Sa** 3:21; **2Ki** 11:17; **2Ch** 23:3
Terms for peace granted to a weaker party
Jos 9:15 Then Joshua made a treaty of peace with them [the Gibeonites] to let them live, and the leaders of the assembly ratified it by oath.
See also **1Sa** 11:1; **1Ki** 15:19–20; 20:34; **Eze** 17:13–14
A mutual commitment to peaceful relations
1Ki 5:12 The LORD gave Solomon wisdom, just as he had promised him. There were peaceful relations between Hiram and Solomon, and the two of them made a treaty.   *See also* **Ge** 21:27; 26:28–29; 31:44; **Am** 1:9
An agreement on a common course of action
Jer 34:8 The word came to Jeremiah from the LORD after King Zedekiah had made a covenant with all the people in Jerusalem to proclaim freedom for the slaves.   *See also* **2Ki** 11:4 pp 2Ch 23:1; **Ezr** 10:3; **Ne** 9:38; **Ps** 83:5
The relationship between husband and wife Pr 2:17; **Mal** 2:14
God's covenant with Israel is likened to a marriage: **Jer** 2:2; **Eze** 16:8

An expression of friendship
1Sa 18:3 And Jonathan made a covenant with David because he loved him as himself.   *See also* **1Sa** 20:16–17

Sealing a covenant
By sharing a meal Ge 26:30; 31:53–54
The meal Jesus Christ shared with his disciples is an important part of the institution of the new covenant: **Mt** 26:26–29 pp Mk 14:22–25 pp Lk 22:17–20; **1Co** 11:23–25
By offering a sacrifice Ge 15:9–18; **Ex** 24:4–8; **Ps** 50:5; **Jer** 34:18–19; **Heb** 12:24
By making an oath Ge 21:31; 26:31; **Jos** 9:15; **2Ki** 11:4; **Ne** 10:28–29

The obligations of a covenant
Covenant responsibilities must be honoured
Nu 30:2 "When a man makes a vow to the LORD or takes an oath to bind himself by a pledge, he must not break his word but must do everything he said."
1Sa 20:8 "As for you [Jonathan], show kindness to your servant [David], for you have brought him into a covenant with you before the LORD . . ."   *See also* **Jos** 9:18; **Mt** 5:33–37; **Gal** 3:15
Covenant obligations are watched over by God
1Sa 20:42 Jonathan said to David, "Go in peace, for we have sworn friendship with each other in the name of the LORD, saying, 'The LORD is witness between you and me, and between your descendants and my descendants for ever.'" . . .   *See also* **Ge** 31:48–54; **Jos** 9:19; **Jer** 34:15–16; **Mal** 2:14–16
The consequences of breaking covenant faith
Jos 9:20 "This is what we [Israel's leaders] will do to them [the Gibeonites]: We will let them live, so that wrath will not fall on us for breaking the oath we swore to them."   *See also* **Jer** 34:18–22; **Eze** 17:16–18; **Am** 1:9

Covenants with other nations are forbidden
Ex 34:12 "Be careful not to make a treaty with those who live in the land where you are going, or they will be a snare among you

[Israel]."   *See also* **Dt** 23:6; **Jos** 9:7
Covenants with other nations lead to a commitment to foreign gods Ex 23:32–33; 34:15–16; **Dt** 7:2–4
Covenants with other nations lead to a denial of faith in God Isa 28:15,18; 30:1–2; 31:1; **Hos** 12:1   *See also* idolatry; marriage; treaty.

---

covenant, new

The fulfilment of God's purposes of salvation expressed in the covenants of the OT, mediated by Jesus Christ and sealed in his blood. It is a covenant of grace, the benefits of which include forgiveness, a renewed relationship with God and, through the Holy Spirit, an inward transformation that enables obedience to its demands and so ensures that it will not again be broken.
Jer 31:31 "The time is coming," declares the LORD, "when I will make a new covenant with the house of Israel and with the house of Judah."   *See also* **Heb** 8:8

The new covenant fulfils the OT covenants
God's covenant with Noah Isa 54:9–10; **Hos** 2:18
God's covenant with Abraham Lk 1:72–73; **Ac** 3:25–26; **Gal** 3:14–16
God's covenant at Sinai Eze 16:60,62; 20:37
God's covenant with David Isa 55:3; **Eze** 34:24–26; 37:25–26; **Lk** 1:69

Jesus Christ, the mediator of the new covenant
The new covenant fulfilled in the Messiah
Mal 3:1 ". . . suddenly the Lord you are seeking will come to his temple; the messenger of the covenant, whom you desire, will come," says the Lord Almighty.   *See also* **Isa** 42:6; 49:8
The new covenant effected through Jesus Christ's death
Heb 9:15 For this reason Christ is the mediator of a new covenant, that those who are called may receive the promised eternal inheritance— now that he has died as a ransom to set them free from the sins committed under the first covenant.   *See also* **Heb** 9:16–17

The new covenant sealed in Jesus Christ's blood

Lk 22:20 In the same way, after the supper he [Jesus] took the cup, saying, "This cup is the new covenant in my blood, which is poured out for you." pp Mt 26:28 pp Mk 14:24   *See also* **Ex** 24:8; **Jn** 6:54; **1Co** 10:16; 11:25; **Heb** 10:29

The ministry of the Holy Spirit

2Co 3:6 He [God] has made us competent as ministers of a new covenant—not of the letter but of the Spirit; for the letter kills, but the Spirit gives life.

2Co 3:18 And we, who with unveiled faces all reflect the Lord's glory, are being transformed into his likeness with ever-increasing glory, which comes from the Lord, who is the Spirit.   *See also* **Isa** 59:21; **Eze** 36:26–27; **Ro** 8:2–4; **2Co** 3:8

The superior blessings of the new covenant

God's grace and mercy

Heb 12:24 to Jesus the mediator of a new covenant, and to the sprinkled blood that speaks a better word than the blood of Abel.

A complete forgiveness

Heb 8:12 "For I [the Lord] will forgive their wickedness and will remember their sins no more."   *See also* **Jer** 31:34; **Ro** 11:27; **Heb** 10:17

Release from the law's condemnation 2Co 3:9; **Gal** 3:13–14

An inward enabling to obey God's laws

Jer 31:32–33 "It [the new covenant] will not be like the covenant I made with their ancestors when I took them by the hand to lead them out of Egypt, because they broke my covenant, though I was a husband to them," declares the LORD. "This is the covenant that I will make with the house of Israel after that time," declares the LORD. "I will put my law in their minds and write it on their hearts. I will be their God, and they will be my people."   *See also* **Jer** 32:38–40; **Eze** 11:19–20; **2Co** 3:3; **Heb** 8:9–10; 9:14; 10:16

A new knowledge of God

Heb 8:11 "No longer will they teach their neighbours, or say to one another, 'Know the LORD,' because they will all know me, from the least of them to the greatest."   *See also* **Jer** 31:34; **2Co** 3:15–16

A renewed relationship with God

Eze 37:26–27 " 'I [the LORD] will make a covenant of peace with them [a re-united Israel]; it will be an everlasting covenant . . . I will put my sanctuary among them for ever. My dwelling-place will be with them; I will be their God, and they will be my people.' "   *See also* **Jer** 24:7; 31:1; **Eze** 34:30–31; **Hos** 2:19–23

A superior priesthood

Heb 8:6 But the ministry Jesus has received is as superior to theirs [the OT priests] as the covenant of which he is mediator is superior to the old one, and it is founded on better promises.   *See also* **Heb** 7:22; 9:24–25

A superior sacrifice

Heb 9:14 How much more, then, will the blood of Christ, who through the eternal Spirit offered himself unblemished to God, cleanse our consciences from acts that lead to death, so that we may serve the living God!   *See also* **Heb** 9:20–23,26–28; 10:4,8–14

A lasting covenant

Isa 61:8 "For I, the LORD, love justice; I hate robbery and iniquity. In my faithfulness I will reward them and make an everlasting covenant with them."

2Co 3:11 And if what was fading away came with glory, how much greater is the glory of that which lasts!   *See also* **Jer** 50:5; **Heb** 8:7,13; 13:20   *See also* blood, of Jesus Christ; sacrifice; New Testament fulfilment.

covenant, with Abraham

God's gracious promise made to Abraham, and repeated to his descendants, to bless both them and, through them, the whole world. In response God calls for faithful obedience, expressed particularly in the outward sign of circumcision.

Features of the Abrahamic covenant

The covenant is based upon God's gracious promise

Gal 3:18 For if the inheritance depends on the law, then it no longer depends on a promise; but

God in his grace gave it to Abraham through a promise. *See also* **Ge** 15:4–7; 17:4–8; 18:10,14; **Heb** 6:13–15

The covenant was confirmed by sacrifice Ge 15:9–18

The covenant was given in perpetuity
Ge 17:7 "I [God] will establish my covenant as an everlasting covenant between me and you [Abraham] and your descendants after you for the generations to come . . ." *See also* **Ge** 17:13,19; **1Ch** 16:15–17 pp Ps 105:8–10; **Jer** 33:23–25

God's promises to Abraham

Ge 12:2–3 "I [the LORD] will make you [Abraham] into a great nation and I will bless you; I will make your name great, and you will be a blessing. I will bless those who bless you, and whoever curses you I will curse; and all peoples on earth will be blessed through you."

God promised the land of Canaan
Ge 17:8 "The whole land of Canaan, where you [Abraham] are now an alien, I [God] will give as an everlasting possession to you and your descendants after you . . ." *See also* **Ge** 12:7; 15:18–21; **Ex** 6:4; **Jos** 1:3; **Ne** 9:8; **Ac** 7:5

God promised that Abraham would be the father of a nation
Ge 15:5 He [God] took him [Abraham] outside and said, "Look up at the heavens and count the stars—if indeed you can count them." Then he said to him, "So shall your offspring be." *See also* **Ge** 12:2; 17:4–6,16; 22:17; **Heb** 11:11–12

God promised a relationship with himself
Ge 17:8 ". . . I will be their God." *See also* **Ge** 26:24; **Dt** 29:13; **Mt** 22:32 pp Mk 12:26; **Ex** 3:6; **Ac** 7:32

The requirements of the covenant
Obedience

Ge 17:9–14 Then God said to Abraham, "As for you, you must keep my covenant, you and your descendants after you for the generations to come . . ."

Ge 22:18 ". . . through your offspring all nations on earth will be blessed, because you [Abraham] have obeyed me [the LORD]."

See also **Ge** 26:5; **Heb** 11:8,17–19
Faith

Ge 15:6 Abram believed the LORD, and he credited it to him as righteousness.
Ne 9:8 "You [God] found his [Abraham's] heart faithful to you, and you made a covenant with him to give to his descendants the land of the Canaanites, Hittites, Amorites, Perizzites, Jebusites and Girgashites . . ." *See also* **Ro** 4:3,11–12,18; **Gal** 3:6–7; **Heb** 11:8–12; **Jas** 2:23

God's faithfulness to the covenant
God remembers his promise

Ps 105:42 For he [the LORD] remembered his holy promise given to his servant Abraham. *See also* **Ge** 21:2; 50:24; **Ex** 33:1; **Ac** 7:17; **Heb** 6:15

God shows compassion for his people

2Ki 13:23 But the LORD was gracious to them [Israel] and had compassion and showed concern for them because of his covenant with Abraham, Isaac and Jacob. To this day he has been unwilling to destroy them or banish them from his presence. *See also* **Ex** 2:24–25; 32:13–14; **Dt** 9:27; **Lk** 1:72–73

The scope of the covenant
The covenant continued through Isaac, not Ishmael

Ge 17:19–21 . . ." . . . your wife Sarah will bear you a son, and you [Abraham] will call him Isaac. I [God] will establish my covenant with him as an everlasting covenant for his descendants after him . . ." *See also* **Ge** 21:12; **Ro** 9:7–8; **Gal** 4:28

The covenant confirmed through Abraham, Isaac and Jacob

Lev 26:42 "I [the LORD] will remember my covenant with Jacob and my covenant with Isaac and my covenant with Abraham, and I will remember the land.'" *See also* **Ge** 26:24 Jacob: **Ge** 28:13–14; 32:12 **Ex** 3:6; **Dt** 1:8; **Ac** 7:8

The people of Israel are heirs to the covenant

Dt 29:12–13 You [the people of Israel] are standing here in order to enter into a covenant with the LORD your God, a covenant the LORD is making with you this day and sealing with an oath, to confirm you this day as his people, that he may be your God as he promised you and as he swore to your fathers, Abraham, Isaac and Jacob. *See also* **Ac** 3:25

All nations will be blessed through Abraham
Ge 18:18 "Abraham will surely become a great and powerful nation, and all nations on earth will be blessed through him." *See also* **Ge** 26:4; **Ac** 3:25; **Gal** 3:8–9,14,29 *See also circumcision.*

---

covenant, with David

God's promise to establish David and his descendants on Israel's throne for ever. It provided Israel with a basis for the hope of deliverance and restoration, and became a focus for the Messianic expectation which was fulfilled, ultimately, in Jesus Christ.

God's promise to establish David's line
God's election of David
Ps 78:70 He [the Lord] chose David his servant and took him from the sheep pens; *See also* **2Sa** 6:21; **1Ki** 8:16 pp 2Ch 6:6
God's covenant is everlasting
Ps 89:3–4 You [the LORD] said, "I have made a covenant with my chosen one, I have sworn to David my servant, 'I will establish your line for ever and make your throne firm through all generations.'" . . . *See also* **2Sa** 7:11–16; 23:5; **1Ki** 2:45; **2Ch** 13:5; **Ps** 18:50; 89:28–29,35–37; **Jer** 33:17
God's covenant is inherited through obedience
Ps 132:11–12 The LORD swore an oath to David, a sure oath that he will not revoke: "One of your own descendants I will place on your throne—if your sons keep my covenant and the statutes I teach them, then their sons shall sit on your throne for ever and ever." *See also* **1Ki** 8:25–26 pp 2Ch 6:16–17; **1Ki** 9:4–5 pp 2Ch 7:17–18
God's covenant blessings are forfeited through disobedience
Jer 22:4–5 " 'For if you [the king and leaders of Judah] are careful to carry out these commands, then kings who sit on David's throne will come through the gates of this palace, riding

in chariots and on horses, accompanied by their officials and their people. But if you do not obey these commands, declares the LORD, I swear by myself that this palace will become a ruin.' "
See also **1Ki** 9:6–9 pp 2Ch 7:19–22; **1Ki** 11:11–13,31–33; **Jer** 7:24–26; 22:6–9; 36:30–31
God's promise is fulfilled by grace
2Ch 21:7 Nevertheless, because of the covenant the LORD had made with David, the LORD was not willing to destroy the house of David. He had promised to maintain a lamp for him and his descendants for ever. pp 2Ki 8:19 *See also* **1Ki** 11:34–36,39; 15:4; **Ps** 89:30–34

The Davidic covenant as a basis for hope
God's election of Jerusalem
2Ki 21:7 . . . the LORD had said to David and to his son Solomon, "In this temple and in Jerusalem, which I have chosen out of all the tribes of Israel, I will put my Name for ever." pp 2Ch 33:7 *See also* **1Ki** 8:20–21 pp 2Ch 6:10–11; **1Ki** 11:32,36; **1Ch** 23:25; **2Ch** 6:41–42 pp Ps 132:8–10
God's promise to defend Jerusalem
Isa 37:35 "I [the LORD] will defend this city [Jerusalem] and save it, for my sake and for the sake of David my servant!" pp 2Ki 19:34
See also **2Ki** 19:20; **Zec** 12:7–9
God's promise to restore David's house
Am 9:11 "In that day I [the LORD] will restore David's fallen tent. I will repair its broken places, restore its ruins, and build it as it used to be," *See also* **Ac** 15:16; **Jer** 33:25–26

Hopes expressed in the Davidic covenant are focused in the Messiah
The Messiah fulfils the Davidic hope
Jer 23:5–6 "The days are coming," declares the LORD, "when I will raise up to David a righteous Branch, a King who will reign wisely and do what is just and right in the land. In his days Judah will be saved and Israel will live in safety. This is the name by which he will be called: The LORD Our Righteousness." *See also* **Ps** 110:1–2; **Isa** 9:7; 11:1–2; 16:5; 55:3; **Eze** 34:23–25; **Zec** 3:8; **Jn** 7:42

God's promise to David fulfilled in Jesus Christ

Lk 1:32-33 "He [Jesus] will be great and will be called the Son of the Most High. The Lord God will give him the throne of his father David, and he will reign over the house of Jacob for ever; his kingdom will never end."

Rev 22:16 "I, Jesus, have sent my angel to give you [John] this testimony for the churches. I am the Root and the Offspring of David, and the bright Morning Star." *See also* **Mt** 1:1; 22:41–46 pp Mk 12:35–37 pp Lk 20:41–44

Many Jews in Jesus Christ's day were expecting a literal fulfilment of God's promise to restore the Davidic empire. The true hope expressed in the Davidic covenant and fulfilled in Christ is the coming of the kingdom of God: **Mk** 11:10 pp Mt 21:9; **Lk** 24:21; **Ac** 1:6

Ac 2:29–31; 13:34; **Ro** 1:3; **2Ti** 2:8

---

covenant, with Noah

God's confirmation of, and commitment to maintain, his relationship with the natural order— implicit in the act of creation—whereby he promised never again to destroy the earth with a flood. This divine pledge, given unconditionally to Noah and to every living creature on earth, was accompanied by the sign of the rainbow.

The occasion of the covenant
The flood as divine judgment

Ge 6:17 "I [God] am going to bring floodwaters on the earth to destroy all life under the heavens, every creature that has the breath of life in it. Everything on earth will perish."
See also **Ge** 6:5–7,11–13; **2Pe** 2:5

God's promise of salvation to Noah and his family

Ge 6:18 "But I [God] will establish my covenant with you [Noah], and you will enter the ark—you and your sons and your wife and your sons' wives with you." *See also* **Ge** 7:23; 8:1,15–17; **Heb** 11:7; **1Pe** 3:20

God's promise never again to destroy the earth with a flood

Ge 9:11 "I [God] establish my covenant with you [Noah and his sons]: Never again will all life be cut off by the waters of a flood; never again

will there be a flood to destroy the earth."
See also **Ge** 8:21; **Isa** 54:9

The sign of the covenant

Ge 9:13 "I [God] have set my rainbow in the clouds, and it will be the sign of the covenant between me and the earth." *See also* **Ge** 9:14–17

A universal covenant
God's relationship with every living creature

Ge 9:8-10 Then God said to Noah and to his sons with him: "I now establish my covenant with you and with your descendants after you and with every living creature that was with you—the birds, the livestock and all the wild animals, all those that came out of the ark with you—every living creature on earth." *See also* **Ge** 7:1–3; **Eze** 34:25; **Hos** 2:18; **Zec** 11:10

God's relationship with the natural order

Ge 8:22 "As long as the earth endures, seedtime and harvest, cold and heat, summer and winter, day and night will never cease."

Jer 33:25-26 "This is what the LORD says: 'If I have not established my covenant with day and night and the fixed laws of heaven and earth, then I will reject the descendants of Jacob and David my servant and will not choose one of his sons to rule over the descendants of Abraham, Isaac and Jacob. For I will restore their fortunes and have compassion on them.'" *See also* **Ge** 1:14,31–2:1; **Ps** 74:16–17; **Jer** 5:24; 33:20–21

An everlasting covenant

Ge 9:16 "Whenever the rainbow appears in the clouds, I [God] will see it and remember the everlasting covenant between God and all living creatures of every kind on the earth." *See also* **Ge** 9:12

Isa 24:5 The earth is defiled by its people; they have disobeyed the laws, violated the statutes and broken the everlasting covenant. *See also* **Ge** 9:6; **Nu** 35:33; **Isa** 26:21

---

crime

An offence against the established laws of society including murder, adultery, theft, perjury and treason. Scripture contains both warnings and teaching to help young people avoid a life of crime.

Crime in Israel
Dt 6:1–2 These are the commands, decrees and laws the LORD your God directed me to teach you to observe in the land that you are crossing the Jordan to possess, so that you, your children and their children after them may fear the LORD your God as long as you live by keeping all his decrees and commands that I give you, and so that you may enjoy long life. *Crime in Israel was the breaking of laws given by God.*

Examples of crimes covered by Israel's laws
Ex 20:13 *murder;* **Ex** 20:14 *adultery;* **Ex** 20:15 *theft;* **Ex** 20:16 *perjury*
Treason: **Jos** 1:16–18; **2Sa** 15:7–10; **1Ki** 16:15–18; **2Ki** 11:1–3 pp 2Ch 22:10–12

Examples of crime in the NT
Murder Mt 2:16; **Ac** 7:58
Adultery Jn 8:3–4; **1Co** 5:1
Theft Jn 12:6
Perjury Mt 26:59–60 pp Mk 14:55–56; **Ac** 6:13; 25:7

Scripture warns young people that temptation may lead to crime
Violence Pr 1:10–19
Sexual immorality Pr 5:1–23; 6:20–29; 7:6–27

Scripture teaches parents to discipline their children
Pr 13:24; 19:18; 22:6,15; 23:13 *See also law.*

---

cures
The removing of illness or other disorder, either mental or physical. Scripture describes the curing of various diseases and conditions. It also points to humanity's area of spiritual need, its sinful condition, declaring Jesus Christ to be the only effective cure.

God's curing of illness
Job 5:17–18 "Blessed are those whom God corrects; so do not despise the discipline of the Almighty. For he wounds, but he also binds up; he injures, but his hands also heal." *See also* **Ps** 30:2; 103:2–5; 147:3; **Jer** 33:6

Illnesses and conditions cured by Jesus Christ
Mt 11:4–5 Jesus replied, "Go back and report to John what you hear and see: The blind receive sight, the lame walk, those who have leprosy are cured, the deaf hear, the dead are raised, and the good news is preached to the poor." pp Lk 7:21–22 *See also* **Isa** 35:5–6
Demon-possession Mt 15:22–28; **Mk** 5:1–20 pp Lk 8:26–39
Deafness and muteness Mt 12:22 pp Lk 11:14; **Mk** 7:31–37
Paralysis and lameness Mt 9:2–8 pp Mk 2:3–12 pp Lk 5:18–26; **Jn** 5:1–14
Bleeding Mk 5:25–34
Blindness Mk 8:22–26; **Jn** 9:1–7
Leprosy Mt 8:2–4 pp Mk 1:40–44 pp Lk 5:12–14; **Lk** 17:11–19

Death itself is cured by Jesus Christ
Jn 11:1–44 . . . Jesus called in a loud voice, "Lazarus, come out!" The dead man came out, his hands and feet wrapped with strips of linen, and a cloth around his face. Jesus said to them, "Take off the grave clothes and let him go." *See also* **Mk** 5:35–43; **Lk** 7:11–16

Illnesses and conditions cured by the apostles
Ac 5:12–16 The apostles performed many miraculous signs and wonders among the people. And all the believers used to meet together in Solomon's Colonnade. No-one else dared join them, even though they were highly regarded by the people. Nevertheless, more and more men and women believed in the Lord and were added to their number. As a result, people brought the sick into the streets and laid them on beds and mats so that at least Peter's shadow might fall on some of them as he passed by. Crowds gathered

also from the towns around Jerusalem, bringing their sick and those tormented by evil spirits, and all of them were healed.   *See also* **Ac** 3:1–10; 19:11–12

Illnesses cured by the grace of God
Php 2:26–27; **Jas** 5:15–16

Illnesses cured in the name of Jesus Christ
Mk 9:39; **Ac** 3:6,16; 4:10,30

Humanity's sinfulness cured by Jesus Christ
Sinfulness affects all humanity Ro 3:23
Prophecy of healing through Jesus Christ's death
Isa 53:5 But he [the Messiah] was pierced for our transgressions, he was crushed for our iniquities; the punishment that brought us peace was upon him, and by his wounds we are healed.
Jesus Christ's mission to cure humanity
Mt 9:12–13 On hearing this, Jesus said, "It is not the healthy who need a doctor, but the sick. But go and learn what this means: 'I desire mercy, not sacrifice.' For I have not come to call the righteous, but sinners." pp Mk 2:17 pp Lk 5:31   *See also* **Lk** 19:10   *See also healing; medicine.*

curtain
Mentioned chiefly in relation to the construction of the tabernacle. The curtain which separated off the Most Holy Place symbolised the separation between God and humanity. The tearing of the curtain when Jesus Christ was crucified symbolised the end of this separation and gave access into God's presence for believers.

Curtains for the construction of the tabernacle
Ex 26:1–6 "Make the tabernacle with ten curtains of finely twisted linen and blue, purple and scarlet yarn, with cherubim worked into them by skilled hands . . ."   *See also* **Ex** 36:8–13
Ex 26:7–13 "Make curtains of goat hair for the tent over the tabernacle—eleven altogether . . ."   *See also* **Ex** 36:14–18
Ex 26:36–37 "For the entrance to the tent make a curtain of blue, purple and scarlet yarn and finely twisted linen—the work of an embroiderer . . ."   *See also* **Ex** 36:37–38
Ex 27:9–18 "Make a courtyard for the tabernacle. The south side shall be a hundred cubits long and is to have curtains of finely twisted linen . . . For the entrance to the courtyard, provide a curtain twenty cubits long, of blue, purple and scarlet yarn and finely twisted linen—the work of an embroiderer—with four posts and four bases . . ."   *See also* **Ex** 38:9–19; 35:10–17 pp Ex 39:33–40; **Nu** 3:25–26

The curtain in the Most Holy Place
The Most Holy Place shielded with a curtain
Heb 9:2–4 . . . Behind the second curtain was a room called the Most Holy Place . . .   *See also* **Ex** 26:31–33; 40:2–3,21; **Nu** 4:5; **2Ch** 3:14
The curtain symbolises separation from God
Lev 16:2 The LORD said to Moses: "Tell your brother Aaron not to come whenever he chooses into the Most Holy Place behind the curtain in front of the atonement cover on the ark, or else he will die, because I appear in the cloud over the atonement cover."   *See also* **Nu** 18:7; **Heb** 9:6–9
The curtain indicates the hiddenness of God
Ps 18:11 He [the LORD] made darkness his covering, his canopy around him—the dark rain clouds of the sky. pp 2Sa 22:12   *See also* **Ex** 20:21; **Dt** 4:11; **Job** 22:14; **Ps** 97:2; **1Ti** 6:16
The torn curtain symbolises access to God
Mt 27:51 At that moment [of Jesus' death] the curtain of the temple was torn in two from top to bottom . . . pp Mk 15:38 pp Lk 23:45
Heb 10:19–20 Therefore, brothers and sisters . . . we have confidence to enter the Most Holy Place by the blood of Jesus, by a new and living way opened for us through the curtain, that is, his body,   *See also* **Heb** 6:19–20

Other examples of tent curtains
SS 1:5; **Isa** 54:2   *See also art; Most Holy Place; tabernacle, in Old Testament; temple, Herod's; temple, Solomon's; tents.*

custom

An established way or rule (often unwritten) of behaviour, either for an individual or in a society.

Examples of the customs of individuals
1Sa 27:11; **Job** 1:5; **Mk** 10:1; **Lk** 4:16; **Ac** 17:2

Examples of group customs
1Sa 2:13; **1Ki** 18:28; **Lk** 1:9; **Ac** 16:20–21

Examples of social customs
Ge 29:26; **Jdg** 8:24; 14:10; **Ru** 4:7; **1Sa** 20:25
Court customs: **2Ki** 11:14; **Est** 1:13
Mourning customs: **Eze** 24:17,22
Mt 27:15 pp Mk 15:6 pp Jn 18:39
Mary and Joseph obey the customs of the law: **Lk** 2:27,42
Jn 19:40; **Ac** 25:16

A custom can commemorate a particular event
Jdg 11:39–40; **Est** 9:27

God's people are not to follow improper customs
Lev 18:30 " 'Keep my requirements and do not follow any of the detestable customs that were practised before you came and do not defile yourselves with them. I am the LORD your God.' " *See also* **Lev** 20:23; **2Ki** 17:7–8,19,33,40–41; **Est** 3:8; **Ps** 106:34–35,40–41; **Jer** 10:2–3

The issue of whether or not Gentile Christians should follow Jewish customs
Gal 2:14–16 When I [Paul] saw that they [Peter, Barnabas and certain other Jewish Christians] were not acting in line with the truth of the gospel, I said to Peter in front of them all, "You are a Jew, yet you live like a Gentile and not like a Jew. How is it, then, that you force Gentiles to follow Jewish customs? . . ."
See also **Ac** 6:11–14; 15:1–2,28–29; 21:21,24; 28:17; **Gal** 4:9–10; **Col** 2:8   *See also ceremonies; marriage, customs; ritual.*

desert

The desert as a harsh place
Jer 2:6 "They [the Israelites] did not ask, 'Where is the LORD, who brought us up out of Egypt and led us through the barren wilderness, through a land of deserts and rifts, a land of drought and darkness, a land where no-one travels and no-one lives?' "   *See also* **Isa** 25:4–5; 49:10; **Jer** 4:26; 22:6; **Hos** 13:5

The desert as a place of human activity
Living in the desert
Ge 21:21 While he [Ishmael] was living in the Desert of Paran, his mother got a wife for him from Egypt.   *See also* **Jdg** 1:16; **Pr** 21:19; **Jer** 25:24; **Eze** 34:25; **Lk** 1:80

Grazing livestock in the desert
Ex 3:1 Now Moses was tending the flock of Jethro his father-in-law, the priest of Midian, and he led the flock to the far side of the desert and came to Horeb, the mountain of God.   *See also* **Ge** 36:24; **1Ch** 5:9; **Job** 24:5

Hiding in the desert
1Sa 23:14–15 David stayed in the desert strongholds and in the hills of the Desert of Ziph. Day after day Saul searched for him, but God did not give David into his hands. While David was at Horesh in the Desert of Ziph, he learned that Saul had come out to take his life.   *See also* **1Sa** 23:25

Dying in the desert
Ex 14:11–12 They [the Israelites] said to Moses, "Was it because there were no graves in Egypt that you brought us to the desert to die? What have you done to us by bringing us out of Egypt? Didn't we say to you in Egypt, 'Leave us alone; let us serve the Egyptians'? It would have been better for us to serve the Egyptians than to die in the desert!"

Jn 6:49 "Your ancestors ate the manna in the desert, yet they died."   *See also* **Ex** 16:3; **Nu** 3:4; 14:29; 32:13; **1Co** 10:5; **Heb** 3:17

God leading and caring for his people in the desert

Dt 2:7 The LORD your God has blessed you [Israelites] in all the work of your hands. He has watched over your journey through this vast desert. These forty years the LORD your God has been with you, and you have not lacked anything.

Ne 9:19–21 "Because of your [the LORD's] great compassion you did not abandon them in the desert. By day the pillar of cloud did not cease to guide them on their path, nor the pillar of fire by night to shine on the way they were to take. You gave your good Spirit to instruct them. You did not withhold your manna from their mouths, and you gave them water for their thirst. For forty years you sustained them in the desert; they lacked nothing, their clothes did not wear out nor did their feet become swollen."

Ps 78:52 But he [the LORD] brought his people out like a flock; he led them like sheep through the desert.   *See also* **Ex** 13:18; 17:1,5–6; **Dt** 1:19; 8:2; 29:5; 32:10; **Jos** 24:7; **Ps** 136:16; **Am** 2:10; **Ac** 7:36; 13:18

John the Baptist in the desert

Mk 1:4 And so John came, baptising in the desert region and preaching a baptism of repentance for the forgiveness of sins.   *See also* **Mt** 3:3 pp Mk 1:2–3 pp Lk 3:4; **Isa** 40:3

Jesus Christ in the desert

Mt 4:1 Then Jesus was led by the Spirit into the desert to be tempted by the devil. pp Mk 1:12–13 pp Lk 4:1

Specific deserts

Ge 21:14; **Ex** 15:22; 16:1; 19:1–2; **Nu** 12:16; 13:21; 33:8; **Dt** 2:26; **Jos** 18:12; **1Sa** 23:24; 24:1; 26:2; **1Ki** 19:15; **2Ki** 3:8; **2Ch** 20:16,20; **Ps** 29:8; 63:1 Title; **Mt** 3:1; **Ac** 8:26

Deserts used figuratively

Jer 2:31 "You of this generation, consider the word of the LORD: Have I been a desert to Israel or a land of great darkness? Why do my people say, 'We are free to roam; we will come to you

no more'?"   *See also* **Isa** 35:6; 40:3; **Jer** 50:12; **La** 4:3; **Hos** 2:3

---

disease

An illness or other condition which prevents people or animals from achieving their full potential or adversely affects their abilities.

General and specific examples of disease

General references

Mt 8:17 This was to fulfil what was spoken through the prophet Isaiah: "He took up our infirmities and carried our diseases."

Mk 3:10 For he had healed many, so that those with diseases were pushing forward to touch him.   *See also* **Ex** 15:26; **Dt** 7:15; **2Ch** 16:12; **Jn** 5:3; **Ac** 28:9

Blindness Jn 9:1

Boils and sores Ex 9:9; **Job** 2:7; **Isa** 38:21; **Lk** 16:20

Depression

Pr 13:12 Hope deferred makes the heart sick, but a longing fulfilled is a tree of life.

Dropsy Lk 14:2

Dysentery Ac 28:8

Epilepsy

Mt 17:15 "Lord, have mercy on my son," he said. "He has seizures and is suffering greatly. He often falls into the fire or into the water." *See also* **Mt** 4:24; **Mk** 9:17–18

Fever

Job 30:30 "My skin grows black and peels; my body burns with fever."   *See also* **Mt** 8:14 pp Mk 1:30 pp Lk 4:38; **Ac** 28:8

Haemorrhaging Mt 9:20 pp Mk 5:25 pp Lk 8:43

Inflammation Dt 28:22

Insanity 1Sa 21:13; **Da** 4:33–35

Leprosy Nu 12:10; **2Ch** 26:21; **Mt** 11:5; **Lk** 17:11–19

Paralysis Mt 4:24; 8:6; 9:2 pp Mk 2:3 pp Lk 5:18; **Lk** 13:11; **Ac** 3:2; 8:7; 9:33

Sunstroke 2Ki 4:18–19; **Ps** 121:5–6; **Isa** 49:10; **Jnh** 4:8

Tumours Dt 28:27; **1Sa** 5:6

Voluntary starvation 1Sa 1:7; 28:20; **Ps** 102:4; 107:18

Wasting Lev 26:16; **Dt** 28:22

Even the righteous suffer disease

Job 2:3 Then the LORD said to Satan, "Have you considered my servant Job? There is no-one on earth like him; he is blameless and upright, a man who fears God and shuns evil. And he still maintains his integrity, though you incited me against him to ruin him without any reason."

Job 2:7 So Satan went out from the presence of the LORD and afflicted Job with painful sores from the soles of his feet to the top of his head. *See also* **Ps** 38:2–3; 41:7–8

Examples of the righteous suffering 2Ki 20:1 pp 2Ch 32:24; **Da** 8:27; **Lk** 7:2; **Jn** 11:1; **Ac** 9:36–37; **Gal** 4:13; **Php** 2:25–27; **1Ti** 5:23; **2Ti** 4:20

Causes of disease

Jn 9:2 His disciples asked him, "Rabbi, who sinned, this man or his parents, that he was born blind?"

Original sin

Ge 3:16–17 To the woman he said, "I will greatly increase your pains in childbearing; with pain you will give birth to children . . ." To Adam he said, ". . . Cursed is the ground because of you; through painful toil you will eat of it all the days of your life."

Accident 2Ki 4:39–40

Judgment

Ps 107:17–18 Some became fools through their rebellious ways and suffered affliction because of their iniquities. They loathed all food and drew near the gates of death. *See also* **Ex** 9:8–10; **Lev** 26:14–16; **Nu** 16:41–49; **2Ki** 5:27; **Jer** 14:12; **1Co** 11:29–30

Testing

Job 2:5 "But now stretch out your hand and strike his flesh and bones, and he will surely curse you to your face."

Response to sickness and disease
The compassion of God

Mk 1:32–34 That evening after sunset the people brought to Jesus all the sick and demon-possessed. The whole town gathered at the door, and Jesus healed many who had various diseases. He also drove out many demons, but he would not let the demons speak because they knew who he was. *See also* **Ps** 41:3; **Mt** 8:17

Compassion Eze 34:4; **Mt** 25:36; **Lk** 9:2; 10:30–37

Humble submission

Job 13:15 "Though he slay me, yet will I hope in him; I will surely defend my ways to his face." *See also* **2Co** 12:8–10

Prayer

Jas 5:14 Is any one of you sick? Call the elders of the church to pray over you and anoint you with oil in the name of the Lord. *See also* **Ge** 20:17; **2Co** 12:8

Spiritual disease

Isa 1:5–6 Why should you be beaten any more? Why do you persist in rebellion? Your whole head is injured, your whole heart afflicted. From the sole of your foot to the top of your head there is no soundness—only wounds and bruises and open sores, not cleansed or bandaged or soothed with oil. *See also* **Jer** 8:22; 30:12; **Mic** 1:9; **Mt** 9:12–13 pp Lk 5:31–32

Salvation and healing from disease
Salvation achieved through the cross of Jesus Christ

Isa 53:4–5 Surely he took up our infirmities and carried our sorrows, yet we considered him stricken by God, smitten by him, and afflicted. But he was pierced for our transgressions, he was crushed for our iniquities; the punishment that brought us peace was upon him, and by his wounds we are healed.

Salvation made perfect in heaven

Rev 22:1–3 . . . On each side of the river stood the tree of life, bearing twelve crops of fruit, yielding its fruit every month. And the leaves of the tree are for the healing of the nations. No longer will there be any curse . . . *See also* **Eze** 47:12; **Rev** 7:17; 21:1–4 *See also cures; healing; medicine; plague; suffering, causes.*

divorce

The legal dissolution of a marriage. Though not part of God's original intention for marriage, divorce is permitted under certain circumstances, especially marital unfaithfulness. In general, properly divorced parties are free to remarry.

divorce, among believers

Jesus Christ challenged the liberal approach to divorce taken by some rabbis of his day, and upheld the idea of marriage as a lifelong commitment. Remarriage after divorce is generally classed as adultery and, where possible, divorced parties should seek reconciliation. There are circumstances, however, where remarriage is permissible.

The liberal attitude to divorce

Mt 19:3 Some Pharisees came to him [Jesus] to test him. They asked, "Is it lawful for a man to divorce his wife for any and every reason?" *See also* **Dt** 21:14; 24:1

The undesirability of divorce
God's plan for marriage

Mt 19:4-6 . . ."'. . . at the beginning the Creator 'made them male and female', and said, 'For this reason a man will leave his father and mother and be united to his wife, and the two will become one flesh'? So they are no longer two, but one. Therefore what God has joined together, let no-one separate." pp Mk 10:6–9 *See also* **Ge** 1:27; 2:24; **Mal** 2:15; **Eph** 5:31

Divorce is permitted because of human sinfulness

Mt 19:8 Jesus replied, "Moses permitted you to divorce your wives because your hearts were hard. But it was not this way from the beginning." pp Mk 10:5

Christians should not seek divorce

1Co 7:10 To the married I [Paul] give this command (not I, but the Lord): A wife must not separate from her husband.   *See also* **1Co** 7:12–14

Remarriage after divorce
Believers should seek reconciliation

1Co 7:11 But if she does [separate], she must remain unmarried or else be reconciled to her husband. And a husband must not divorce his wife.   *See also* **Dt** 24:2–4   *Marriage to another after divorce prevents reconciliation.*

Remarriage after divorce is classed as adultery

Lk 16:18 "Anyone who divorces his wife and marries another woman commits adultery, and the man who marries a divorced woman commits adultery." pp Mk 10:11–12   *This is a general rule, though there may be exceptions (see below).   See also* **Ro** 7:2–3; **1Co** 7:39

Remarriage may be permissible 1Co 7:27–28   *"unmarried" means literally "freed from a wife" and thus may be applied to those widowed or properly divorced. It is no sin for them to (re)marry.*

Possible grounds for divorce and remarriage

Mt 19:9 "I [Jesus] tell you that anyone who divorces his wife, except for marital unfaithfulness, and marries another woman commits adultery."

1Co 7:15 But if the unbeliever leaves, let it be so. A believing man or woman is not bound in such circumstances; God has called us to live in peace.   *See also* **Jer** 3:8; **Mt** 1:18–19; 5:32

divorce, in Old Testament

Usually initiated by the husband who issued his wife with a certificate of divorce and sent her from his home, divorce broke the marriage bond and allowed parties to remarry. It was not part of God's original purpose for marriage, and is permitted only because of human sinfulness. God is depicted as taking divorce proceedings against adulterous Israel.

The nature of divorce
Divorce dissolves a marriage

Mk 10:4 They said, "Moses permitted a man to write a certificate of divorce and send her away." pp Mt 19:7   *See also* **Lev** 22:12–13; **Nu** 30:9   *Following divorce a husband is no longer responsible for his wife;* **Dt** 24:1–2   *Divorce properly entered into allows the parties to remarry;* **Hos** 2:2; **Mt** 5:31

Divorce was not God's original intention
Mal 2:10–16 . . . "I hate divorce," says the LORD God of Israel . . . So guard yourself in your spirit, and do not break faith.
Mt 19:4–8 . . . Jesus replied, "Moses permitted you to divorce your wives because your hearts were hard. But it was not this way from the beginning." pp Mk 10:5–9 *See also* **Ge** 1:27; 2:24

Circumstances permitting divorce
Displeasure
Dt 24:1 If a man marries a woman who becomes displeasing to him because he finds something indecent about her, and he writes her a certificate of divorce, gives it to her and sends her from his house, *See also* **Dt** 21:13–14; **Mt** 19:3
Returning exiles were required to divorce their foreign wives
Ezr 10:10–11 . . ." . . . Now make confession to the LORD, the God of your ancestors, and do his will. Separate yourselves from the peoples around you and from your foreign wives."
See also **Ezr** 10:2–3

Circumstances where divorce was not allowed
Dt 22:13–19 *where a husband makes false accusations about his wife's virginity;* **Dt** 22:28–29 *where the marriage is contracted following the rape of a virgin*

Restrictions on remarriage after divorce
Former partners who marry others
Dt 24:3–4 . . . her first husband, who divorced her, is not allowed to marry her again after she has been defiled . . . *See also* **Jer** 3:1
Priests could not marry divorcees Lev 21:7,14; **Eze** 44:22

The divorce between God and Israel
It was due to Israel's unfaithfulness
Jer 3:6–10 . . ." . . . I [the LORD] gave faithless Israel her certificate of divorce and sent her away because of all her adulteries . . ." . . . *See also* **Isa** 50:1; **Jer** 31:32

God's desire for reconciliation
Isa 54:4–8 " . . . The LORD will call you [Israel] back as if you were a wife deserted and distressed in spirit—a wife who married young, only to be rejected," says your God . . .
See also **Isa** 62:4–5; **Eze** 16:60–63; **Hos** 2:14–16 *See also law; marriage.*

drink offering

A sacrificial offering of wine poured out at the foot of the altar, to accompany a burnt, fellowship or grain offering.

The drink offering was an ancient custom
Ge 35:14 Jacob set up a stone pillar at the place where God had talked with him, and he poured out a drink offering on it; he also poured oil on it.

Drink offerings were proportionate to the size of animal sacrificed
Nu 15:5,7,10

Drink offerings were required on feasts and sacred days
As part of the daily offerings: **Ex** 29:41; **Nu** 28:7–8
Lev 23:13
Feast of Weeks: **Lev** 23:18; **Nu** 28:31
Feast of Tabernacles: **Lev** 23:37; **Nu** 29:30–31;
Nu 28:9–10,14,24; 29:6,11

Occasions for making a drink offering
To accompany sacrifices for unintentional sins
Nu 15:24
To mark special occasions Nu 6:17; **1Ch** 29:21;
2Ch 29:35; **Eze** 45:17

God's displeasure when drink offerings were poured out to idols
Jer 7:18 " . . . They pour out drink offerings to other gods to provoke me to anger." *See also* **Isa** 57:6; **Jer** 19:13; 32:29; 44:17–19,25; **Eze** 20:28

Drink offerings as a symbol
Of restoration after a locust plague Joel
2:13–14
Of devotion and sacrifice
Php 2:17 But even if I am being poured out like a drink offering on the sacrifice and service coming from your faith, I am glad and rejoice with all of you.   *See also* **2Sa** 23:15–17; **2Ti** 4:6–8   *See also altar; burnt offering; fellowship offering; grain offering; wine.*

drinking
Scripture lays down no general prohibition of the consumption of alcohol, but warns against its abuse.

drinking

Wine as a gift of God
A sign of his blessing
Dt 7:13 He [the LORD] will love you and bless you and increase your numbers. He will bless the fruit of your womb, the crops of your land—your grain, new wine and oil . . .   *See also* **Ge** 27:28; **Dt** 33:28; **Pr** 3:9–10; **Joel** 2:18–19,22–24; 3:18; **Am** 9:13–14
Drinking wine has God's approval
Dt 14:26 Use the silver to buy whatever you like: cattle, sheep, wine or other fermented drink, or anything you wish . . .   *See also* **Jn** 2:1–10; **1Ti** 5:23   *approval is implicit in the advice given*

Withdrawal of wine is evidence of divine judgment
Isa 24:6–7 Therefore a curse consumes the earth; its people must bear their guilt. Therefore earth's inhabitants are burned up, and very few are left. The new wine dries up and the vine withers . . .   *See also* **Jer** 48:32–33

Drinking used extensively as a metaphor
Of suffering God's judgment Job 21:20; **Ps** 75:8; **Isa** 29:9; **Jer** 25:15–17; **Eze** 23:31–34; **Hab** 2:16; **Rev** 18:3
Of love Pr 7:18

Of Jesus Christ's destiny of suffering
Mt 26:42 . . . "My Father, if it is not possible for this cup to be taken away unless I drink it, may your will be done."   *See also* **Mt** 26:39 pp Mk 14:36 pp Lk 22:42; **Mt** 20:22–23 pp Mk 10:38–39; **Jn** 18:11
Of spiritual satisfaction Jn 4:13–14
Of the Christian experience of the Holy Spirit
Jn 7:37 . . . "Let anyone who is thirsty come to me and drink."

Jesus Christ's symbolic use of wine
Mt 26:27–29 . . . "Drink from it, all of you. This is my blood of the covenant, which is poured out for many for the forgiveness of sins . . ." pp Mk 14:23–25 pp Lk 22:17–18 pp Lk 22:20
See also **Jn** 6:53–56   *See also drink offering; water; wine.*

drinking, abstention
Scripture indicates that the abuse of drinking, such as drunkenness, is unacceptable. It also indicates the advantages of abstention from drinking in certain situations.

For some, at certain times, total abstinence is right
Lev 10:8–9; **Eze** 44:21; **Nu** 6:1–4,20; **Jdg** 13:2–5,7,13–14; **Pr** 31:4–5; **Isa** 22:12–13; **Jer** 35:1–14; **Da** 1:5–16
John the Baptist: **Mt** 11:18; **Lk** 1:15
Mt 27:34; **Ro** 14:21

Warnings against the abuse of alcohol
Isa 5:11 Woe to those who rise early in the morning to run after their drinks, who stay up late at night till they are inflamed with wine.
See also **Pr** 20:1; **Isa** 5:22; **Hab** 2:15; **Lk** 21:34; **Ro** 13:13; **1Co** 6:9–10; 11:20–21; **Gal** 5:19–21; **Eph** 5:18; **1Th** 5:7–8; **Tit** 2:3

Christian leaders are to be sober
1Ti 3:2–3 Now the overseer must be above reproach, the husband of but one wife, temperate, self-controlled, respectable, hospitable, able to teach, not given to drunkenness . . .   *See also* **1Ti** 3:8; **Tit** 1:7

Examples of drunkenness
Ge 9:20–21; 19:30–35; **1Sa** 25:36; **2Sa** 11:12–13; **1Ki** 16:9; 20:16; **Est** 1:10; **Isa** 28:7; 56:10–12; **Mt** 24:49 pp Lk 12:45

Some accusations of drunkenness were unfounded
1Sa 1:13–15; **Mt** 11:19 pp Lk 7:34; **Ac** 2:13–15

eating
The consumption of food, necessary for survival. Scripture cites enjoyment of eating as a gift of God but emphasises that it is not the main priority in life, for God will provide abundantly for his children.

Eating for survival
Ne 5:1–2 . . . Some were saying, "We and our sons and daughters are numerous; in order for us to eat and stay alive, we must get grain." *See also* **Ge** 28:20–22; **1Ki** 17:12; 19:3–8; **2Ki** 25:3

Eating as a sign of life and health
Dt 4:28 . . . gods of wood and stone made by human hands, which cannot see or hear or eat or smell. *See also* **2Sa** 13:5–10; **Ps** 102:4; **Mk** 5:35–43 pp Lk 8:49–56; **Lk** 24:36–43; **Jn** 6:48–58

Enjoyment of eating as a gift of God
Ecc 3:13 That each of them may eat and drink, and find satisfaction in all their toil—this is the gift of God. *See also* **Ge** 27:1–25; **Ecc** 2:24–25; 5:18; 8:15; 9:7

God blesses his people with sufficient food
Ps 37:25 I [David] was young and now I am old, yet I have never seen the righteous forsaken or their children begging bread. *See also* **Lev** 26:3–5,23–26; **Dt** 8:16; 11:15; 12:7; **Jos** 24:11–13; **Ps** 22:26; 78:23–29; 127:2; 128:1–2; **Pr** 13:25; **Isa** 1:19; 7:22; 65:13,21–22; **Joel** 2:26; **Am** 9:14; **Mic** 6:9–16; **Hag** 1:5–11

Eating should not be one's chief priority
Mt 4:1–4 . . . The tempter came to him [Jesus] and said, "If you are the Son of God, tell these stones to become bread." Jesus answered, "It is written: 'People do not live on bread alone, but on every word that comes from the mouth of God.'" pp Lk 4:1–4 *See also* **Dt** 8:3; **Nu** 11:4–34; **Mt** 6:25–34 pp Lk 12:22–31; **Lk** 12:16–20; **Col** 2:13–17

Eating as a religious observance
Sacrificial meals
Ex 18:12 Then Jethro, Moses' father-in-law, brought a burnt offering and other sacrifices to God, and Aaron came with all the elders of Israel to eat bread with Moses' father-in-law in the presence of God. *See also* **Ex** 29:32–33; 32:6; **Lev** 6:14—7:10; 8:31; 21:21–23; **Nu** 18:8–13; **Dt** 15:19–20; **1Sa** 1:1–5; 9:11–13; 20:24–29; **Eze** 44:3; **Hos** 8:13; **Heb** 13:9–10
Sacrificial meals for pagan gods
Ex 34:15 "Be careful not to make a treaty with those who live in the land; for when they prostitute themselves to their gods and sacrifice to them, they will invite you [Israelites] and you will eat their sacrifices." *See also* **Eze** 18:5–6,14–15; 22:9; **1Co** 8:4–13; 10:23–28
The Passover and Feast of Unleavened Bread
Ex 12:1–11 . . ."... Tell the whole community of Israel that on the tenth day of this month each man is to take a lamb for his family, one for each household . . . they are to eat the meat roasted over the fire, along with bitter herbs, and bread made without yeast . . ." *See also* **Ex** 12:14–20; **Lev** 23:4–8; **Nu** 28:16–25; **Dt** 16:1–8; **Mt** 26:17–19 pp Mk 14:12–16 pp Lk 22:7–13

The Lord's Supper
Mt 26:26–29 While they [the disciples] were eating, Jesus took bread, gave thanks and broke it, and gave it to his disciples, saying, "Take and eat; this is my body." Then he took the cup, gave thanks and offered it to them, saying, "Drink from it, all of you. This is my blood of the covenant, which is poured out for many for the forgiveness of sins . . ." pp Mk 14:22–25

pp Lk 22:17–20   *See also* **1Co** 11:23–34

Restrictions on eating

Ge 9:1–4 . . .". . . you must not eat meat that has its lifeblood still in it." *See also* **Ge** 2:15–17; 3:1–7,22; 32:22–32; 43:32; **Ex** 22:31; **Lev** 7:19,22–27; 11:1–47 pp Dt 14:3–20; **Lev** 22:4–8; 23:6; **Nu** 6:1–4; **Dt** 12:23–25; **Eze** 44:31; **Mk** 7:14–19; **Ro** 14:1–3,19–21

Eating and hospitality
Eating at a royal court

1Ki 2:7 ". . . show kindness to the sons of Barzillai of Gilead and let them be among those who eat at your [Solomon's] table. They stood by me when I fled from your brother Absalom." *See also* **2Sa** 9:1–13; **1Ki** 18:19; **Da** 11:26

Eating as a guest in another's home

Ge 18:3–5 He [Abraham] said, "If I have found favour in your eyes, my lord, do not pass your servant by. Let a little water be brought, and then you [Abraham's visitors] may all wash your feet and rest under this tree. Let me get you something to eat, so you can be refreshed and then go on your way—now that you have come to your servant." "Very well," they answered, "do as you say." *See also* **Ge** 19:3; 43:16; **Ex** 2:18–20; **Jdg** 19:5–9; **2Ki** 4:8; **Pr** 23:6–7; **Mt** 9:9–13 pp Mk 2:14–17 pp Lk 5:27–32; **Mt** 26:6–7 pp Mk 14:3; **Lk** 14:1–14

Fasting

Est 4:16 "Go, gather together all the Jews who are in Susa, and fast for me [Esther]. Do not eat or drink for three days, night or day. I and my attendants will fast as you do. When this is done, I will go to the king, even though it is against the law. And if I perish, I perish." *See also* **2Sa** 3:35; **Mt** 4:1–2 pp Lk 4:1–2

Cannibalism

Dt 28:53 Because of the suffering that your enemy will inflict on you [Israel] during the siege, you will eat the fruit of the womb, the flesh of the sons and daughters the LORD your God has given you. *See also* **2Ki** 6:24–29; **Jer** 19:9

Metaphorical references to eating

Jn 6:50 "But here is the bread that comes down from heaven, which people may eat and not die."

Rev 3:20 "Here I am! I stand at the door and knock. If anyone hears my voice and opens the door, I will come in and eat with them, and they with me." *See also* **Ps** 14:4 pp Ps 53:4; **Ps** 141:4; **Pr** 1:29–31; 4:17; 18:21; 31:27; **SS** 5:1; **Isa** 55:1–2; **Eze** 3:1–3; **Mic** 3:1–3; **Rev** 2:7; 10:9; 17:16; 19:17–19   *See also banquets; feast and festival; feasting; food; meals; Passover; sacrifice, in Old Testament; water.*

education

The imparting of spiritual, intellectual, moral and social instruction, the basis for which is the fear of the LORD. People continue learning throughout the whole of life. The education of children in the OT was centred on the home and synagogue and was largely of a religious and ethical nature. In the NT, children were included in the community of the church, but the home was still the main sphere of their education.

The fear of the LORD is the basis for all education

Ps 111:10 The fear of the LORD is the beginning of wisdom; all who follow his precepts have good understanding . . .   *See also* **2Ch** 26:5; **Ps** 25:12; **Pr** 1:7; 2:1–8; 9:10; 15:33; **Isa** 11:1–3

Faith is an essential element of Christian education

Heb 11:3 By faith we understand that the universe was formed at God's command, so that what is seen was not made out of what was visible. *See also* **2Ti** 3:15

Education should not oppose the truth about God

2Co 10:5 We demolish arguments and every pretension that sets itself up against the knowledge of God, and we take captive every thought to make it obedient to Christ. *See also* **Mt** 18:6; **1Ti** 6:20–21

Education should emphasise that the world has a richness and coherence derived from God

Ps 24:1 The earth is the LORD's, and everything in it, the world, and all who live in it;

Jn 1:3 Through him [the Word] all things were made; without him nothing was made that has been made.   *See also* **Job** 12:7–10; **Ps** 104:5–26; **1Co** 10:26; **Col** 1:17; **Heb** 1:3

Education in the home
Through parental instruction
Dt 6:4–9 Hear, O Israel: The LORD our God, the LORD is one. Love the LORD your God with all your heart and with all your soul and with all your strength. These commandments that I give you today are to be upon your hearts. Impress them on your children. Talk about them when you sit at home and when you walk along the road, when you lie down and when you get up. Tie them as symbols on your hands and bind them on your foreheads. Write them on the door-frames of your houses and on your gates.

Ps 78:4–6 We [God's people] will not hide them from their children; we will tell the next generation the praiseworthy deeds of the LORD, his power, and the wonders he has done. He decreed statutes for Jacob and established the law in Israel, which he commanded our ancestors to teach their children, so that the next generation would know them, even the children yet to be born, and they in turn would tell their children.
See also **Dt** 4:9–10; 6:20–25; 11:18–21; **Pr** 22:6; **Isa** 38:19; **Eph** 6:4; **Col** 3:21

Examples of parents teaching their children Ge 18:19; **Pr** 31:1–9; **2Ti** 3:14–15

Through parental example
2Ti 1:5 I [Paul] have been reminded of your sincere faith, which first lived in your grandmother Lois and in your mother Eunice and, I am persuaded, now lives in you also.   *See also* **2Ch** 20:31–32; 26:3–4

Through discipline
Pr 29:15 The rod of correction imparts wisdom, but children left to themselves disgrace their mothers.   *See also* **Pr** 1:7; **2Ti** 4:2; **Tit** 1:13

Education through religious worship
Jos 8:34–35 Afterwards, Joshua read all the words of the law—the blessings and the curses—just as it is written in the Book of the Law. There was not a word of all that Moses had commanded that Joshua did not read to the whole assembly of Israel, including the women and children, and the aliens who lived among them.   *See also* **2Ch** 20:13; **Ezr** 8:21; **Ne** 12:43; **Mt** 21:15–16

Education through religious festivals
Dt 31:9–13 So Moses wrote down this law and gave it to the priests, the sons of Levi, who carried the ark of the covenant of the LORD, and to all the elders of Israel. Then Moses commanded them: "At the end of every seven years, in the year for cancelling debts, during the Feast of Tabernacles, when all Israel comes to appear before the LORD your God at the place he will choose, you shall read this law before them in their hearing. Assemble the people—men, women and children, and the aliens living in your towns—so that they can listen and learn to fear the LORD your God and follow carefully all the words of this law. Their children, who do not know this law, must hear it and learn to fear the LORD your God as long as you live in the land you are crossing the Jordan to possess."
See also **Ex** 12:24–27; 13:6–8   *See also children; fathers, responsibilities; feast and festival.*

famine

A severe long-term absence of food, leading to disaster for the people affected in this way. Scripture provides examples of such famines, while also indicating the possibility and dangers of spiritual famine arising through disobedience or lack of faith.

famine, physical

A serious shortage of food caused by drought, war or natural disasters. Famine is seen as a sign of God's judgment on Israel.

Examples of famines
In the days of Abraham
Ge 12:10 Now there was a famine in the land, and Abram went down to Egypt to live there for a while because the famine was severe.
See also **Ge** 26:1
In the days of Joseph Ge 41:53–57; Ac 7:11
In the days of Ruth Ru 1:1
In the days of David 2Sa 21:1
In the days of Elijah 1Ki 18:1–5; Lk 4:25
In the days of Elisha 2Ki 4:38; 6:25
In the days of the prophets Isa 51:19; Jer 44:13; Eze 7:15; Joel 1:10–12
In the days of Claudius Ac 11:28
In the last days
Mt 24:7 "Nation will rise against nation, and kingdom against kingdom. There will be famines and earthquakes in various places." pp Mk 13:8 pp Lk 21:11

Natural causes of famine
Dt 28:22
Drought: **1Ki** 18:1–2; **Jer** 14:1–6
War: **2Ki** 6:24–25; 25:1–3
Joel 1:4

Spiritual causes of famine
The disobedience of God's people
Dt 28:15–18 However, if you do not obey the LORD your God and do not carefully follow all his commands and decrees I am giving you today, all these curses will come upon you and overtake you . . . Your basket and your kneading trough will be cursed. The fruit of your womb will be cursed, and the crops of your land, and the calves of your herds and the lambs of your flocks.
See also **Dt** 28:22–24,38–40,42,51,53; 32:24; **Jdg** 6:1–5; **2Sa** 21:1; 24:13 pp 1Ch 21:11–12; **Isa** 51:19–20; **Jer** 5:17; 11:22; 14:11–18; 18:21; 29:17–18; 32:24; **Eze** 5:16–17; 6:11–12; 14:13
God's judgment on the ungodly Ge 41:28–30; **Isa** 14:29–30; **Rev** 6:8; 18:8

The effects of famine
Desperation and death
La 4:9 Those killed by the sword are better off than those who die of famine; racked with

hunger, they waste away for lack of food from the field. *See also* **Ge** 47:13,20; **Dt** 28:53; **2Ki** 7:3–4; **Ne** 5:3; **Jer** 52:6; **Lk** 15:14–16; 23:28–29
God's people seek him and return to him
Jdg 6:6 Midian so impoverished the Israelites that they cried out to the LORD for help.
See also **2Sa** 21:1; **Lk** 15:17–18

God's provision in famine
He gives warnings beforehand Ge 41:25–27; 1Ki 17:1; 2Ki 8:1; Ac 11:28
He gives wisdom to men Ge 41:33–36; 42:1–2; 45:11; 47:4; Ps 105:16–22; Ac 7:10–11
He provides for his people
Job 5:20 "In famine he will ransom you from death . . ." *See also* **Ge** 26:1–3; **1Ki** 17:2–16; **Ps** 33:18–19; 37:19; **Eze** 34:29; 36:29–30
He sends deliverance 2Ki 7:1–9,16; Jer 32:36–37

Responses to famine
Accepting God's chastisements Jer 27:12–13; 38:2–3; 42:13–17; 44:27
Caring for one's family Ge 45:11; Ru 1:1; 2Ki 8:1–2
Helping those in need Ac 11:29–30
Praying 1Ki 8:35–40 pp 2Ch 6:26–31
Trusting in the Lord
Ro 8:35–37 Who shall separate us from the love of Christ? Shall trouble or hardship or persecution or famine or nakedness or danger or sword? . . . No, in all these things we are more than conquerors through him who loved us.
See also harvest; warfare.

fathers
The male parent of children. Scripture indicates the role and responsibilities of fathers, and shows how God can be thought of as a loving father, who directs and guides his children.

fathers, examples
The ideal father, from a biblical perspective, is one who loves God, is obedient to him and reflects this in his daily living and in the care and upbringing of his children.

Fathers who followed divine principles within their families

Abraham

Ge 18:19 "For I [the Lord] have chosen him [Abraham], so that he will direct his children and his household after him to keep the way of the Lord by doing what is right and just, so that the Lord will bring about for Abraham what he has promised him." *See also* **Ge** 17:1–7; 21:1–5; 17:18–20; 21:8–13; 22:1–18

Zechariah

Lk 1:5–20 In the time of Herod king of Judea there was a priest named Zechariah, who belonged to the priestly division of Abijah; his wife Elizabeth was also a descendant of Aaron. Both of them were upright in the sight of God, observing all the Lord's commandments and regulations blamelessly . . . *See also* **Lk** 1:62–80

The father of the prodigal Lk 15:11–31

Fathers who acted wrongly

Through favouritism

Ge 37:3–4 Now Israel loved Joseph more than any of his other sons, because he had been born to him in his old age; and he made a richly ornamented robe for him. When his brothers saw that their father loved him more than any of them, they hated him and could not speak a kind word to him. *See also* **Ge** 25:28

Through lack of discipline

1Sa 2:22–25 Now Eli, who was very old, heard about everything his sons were doing to all Israel and how they slept with the women who served at the entrance to the Tent of Meeting. So he said to them, "Why do you do such things? . . ." His sons, however, did not listen to their father's rebuke, for it was the Lord's will to put them to death. *See also* **1Sa** 2:27–36; 3:11–18

The intercession of fathers for their children

Abraham

Ge 17:18–22 And Abraham said to God, "If only Ishmael might live under your blessing!" . . .

David

1Ch 29:10–19 . . ." . . . And give my son Solomon the wholehearted devotion to keep your commands, requirements and decrees and to do everything to build the palatial structure for which I have provided." *See also* **2Sa** 12:15–23

Job

Job 1:4–5 . . . Early in the morning he [Job] would sacrifice a burnt offering for each of them [his children], thinking, "Perhaps my children have sinned and cursed God in their hearts." This was Job's regular custom.

The father of the demoniac

Mt 17:14–15 When they came to the crowd, a man approached Jesus and knelt before him. "Lord, have mercy on my son," he said. "He has seizures and is suffering greatly. He often falls into the fire or into the water." pp Mk 9:17–18 pp Lk 9:38–39

The royal official

Jn 4:46–49 . . . When this man heard that Jesus had arrived in Galilee from Judea, he went to him and begged him to come and heal his son, who was close to death . . . The royal official said, "Sir, come down before my child dies." *See also mothers.*

fathers, responsibilities

Fathers have a responsibility to love, instruct and discipline their children in the ways of the Lord. In return they are to be honoured and obeyed by their children.

The role of fathers

To love and care for their children

Ps 103:13 As a father has compassion on his children, so the Lord has compassion on those who fear him; *See also* **Dt** 1:31; **Job** 1:4–5; **Mt** 7:9–11 pp Lk 11:11–13; **Col** 3:21

To discipline their children

Pr 13:24 Those who spare the rod hate their children, but those who love them are careful to discipline them. *See also* **Dt** 8:5; 21:18–21; **Pr** 3:11–12; 15:5; 19:18; 22:15; 23:13; 29:15; **1Ti** 3:2–5,12; **Heb** 12:7–11

To instruct their children

Ps 78:2–8 . . . We will not hide them from

their children; we will tell the next generation the praiseworthy deeds of the LORD, his power, and the wonders he has done. He decreed statutes for Jacob and established the law in Israel, which he commanded our ancestors to teach their children, so that the next generation would know them, even the children yet to be born, and they in turn would tell their children. Then they would put their trust in God and would not forget his deeds but would keep his commands . . .   *See also* **Dt** 4:9; 6:6–7,20–24; 11:18–21; 31:13; **Pr** 13:1; 22:6; **Eph** 6:4

The rights of fathers

To be honoured by their children

Ex 20:12 "Honour your father and your mother, so that you may live long in the land the LORD your God is giving you." pp Dt 5:16   *See also* **Lev** 19:3; **Mt** 15:4 pp Mk 7:10; **Ex** 21:17; **Mt** 19:17–19 pp Mk 10:18–19 pp Lk 18:19–20; **Eph** 6:2–3

To be obeyed by their children

Col 3:20 Children, obey your parents in everything, for this pleases the Lord.   *See also* **Dt** 21:18–21; **Pr** 6:20; 8:32; **Lk** 2:51; **Eph** 6:1

To be heeded by their children

Pr 23:22 Listen to your father, who gave you life, and do not despise your mother when she is old.   *See also* **Pr** 1:8; 4:1,10; 13:1

The joy of fathers

Pr 23:24 The father of a righteous child has great joy; whoever has a wise son delights in him.   *See also* **Ps** 127:3–5; 128:3–4; **Pr** 10:1; 28:7; 29:3

The sorrow of fathers

Pr 17:21 To have a fool for a child brings grief; there is no joy for the parent of a fool. *See also* **Pr** 10:1; 17:25; 19:13

The roles of fathers-in-law

Ge 29:21–23; 31:39–42; **Ex** 3:1; 18:14–27; **Jdg** 19:3–9; **1Sa** 4:19–21; **Jn** 18:13

Children's responsibility to honour their parents

Ex 20:12 "Honour your father and your mother, so that you may live long in the land the LORD your God is giving you." pp Dt 5:16   *See also* **Lev** 19:3; **Mt** 19:19 pp Mk 10:19 pp Lk 18:20; **Eph** 6:1–3

Penalties for disobeying parents

Ex 21:15,17; **Dt** 21:18–21; **Pr** 20:20; **Mt** 15:4–6; **Mk** 7:10–13

The ministry of Jesus Christ may produce conflict within families

Lk 12:53 "They will be divided, father against son and son against father, mother against daughter and daughter against mother, mother-in-law against daughter-in-law and daughter-in-law against mother-in-law." pp Mt 10:35–36

Following Jesus Christ involves a commitment to him even deeper than love of one's parents

Mt 10:37 "Anyone who loves father or mother more than me is not worthy of me . . ." *See also* **Lk** 14:26   *See also children; husband.*

---

feast and festival

Israel's feasts and festivals were to be times of religious and community celebration. Ordained by God, they were to be the outward expression of a right spiritual attitude. The OT makes reference to a number of feasts and festivals, which generally commemorate an event in Israel's history (e.g., the Feast of Passover) or some season of the year (e.g., the Feast of Weeks). In the NT, some of these festivals are given new meanings, such as Pentecost, which was originally a harvest festival, but which came to celebrate the coming of the Holy Spirit.

Feasts and festivals were appointed by God

Ex 5:1 Afterwards Moses and Aaron went to Pharaoh and said, "This is what the LORD, the God of Israel, says: 'Let my people go, so that they may hold a festival to me in the desert.'" *See also* **Ex** 10:9; **Hos** 9:5

Israel's three annual festivals
The three pilgrim festivals
Ex 23:14–19 "Three times a year you are to celebrate a festival to me . . ."
2Ch 8:12–13 . . . the three annual feasts—the Feast of Unleavened Bread, the Feast of Weeks and the Feast of Tabernacles.
The Feast of Unleavened Bread/Passover: **Ex** 12:14; **Nu** 28:17
The Feast of Weeks/Harvest: **Lev** 23:15–21; **Nu** 28:26
The Feast of Tabernacles/Ingathering: **Lev** 23:39–41; **Nu** 29:12; **Jdg** 21:19; **1Ki** 8:65 pp 2Ch 7:8
They were a joyful response to God's blessings
Zec 8:19 This is what the Lord Almighty says: "The fasts of the fourth, fifth, seventh and tenth months will become joyful and glad occasions and happy festivals for Judah . . ." *See also* **Na** 1:15
They were celebrated with sacrifices and offerings Nu 29:39; **Eze** 46:11

Israel's other festivals
New Moon festivals: **Nu** 10:10; **1Sa** 20:18; **1Ch** 23:31; **Hos** 2:11
Unlawful festivals: **Ex** 32:5; **1Ki** 12:32–33

Festivals should be the outward expression of a right spiritual attitude
Isa 1:14; 29:1; **Hos** 5:7; **Mal** 2:3; **1Co** 5:8

OT festivals find their fulfilment in Jesus Christ
Col 2:16–17 *See also feasting; idolatry; Passover; sacrifice, in Old Testament.*

Feast of Dedication
This feast began on 25th Kislev (November/December) and lasted seven days. It celebrated the cleansing of the temple and altar by Judas Maccabeus after they had been defiled by Antiochus Epiphanes.

Jesus Christ was challenged to declare his messiahship at the Feast of Dedication
Jn 10:22–24

Feast of Firstfruits
The date of the offering of firstfruits, a celebration of God's gift of the harvest, is not clear; it was probably held on 16th Abib.

Offerings made at the celebration of the firstfruits
A burnt offering and a grain offering Lev 23:12–13
Other offerings Lev 23:19–20 *See also burnt offering; firstfruits; grain offering; harvest; wave offering.*

Feast of Tabernacles
This feast began on 15th Tishri (September/October) and lasted seven days. It celebrated the first gathering of the fruit and grain harvests and also God's provision for his people during their wilderness journey from Egypt to the promised land.

Instructions for celebrating the Feast of Tabernacles
Ex 23:16 "Celebrate the Feast of Harvest with the firstfruits of the crops you sow in your field. Celebrate the Feast of Ingathering at the end of the year, when you gather in your crops from the field." *See also* **Ex** 23:14; 34:22–23; **Lev** 23:33–34,39; **Nu** 29:12; **Dt** 16:14,13,16

People lived in booths for the duration of the Feast of Tabernacles
Lev 23:40,42–43

The offerings to be made on each day of the Feast of Tabernacles
Lev 23:37; **Nu** 29:13–38

The Feast of Tabernacles was celebrated throughout Israel's history
2Ch 8:12–13
After the return from exile: **Ezr** 3:4; **Ne** 8:17–18
In NT times: **Jn** 7:2–3,37–38 *See also burnt offering; grain offering; sin offering.*

Feast of Trumpets

This feast, which is not specifically mentioned as such in the OT, took place at the observance of the new moon in the month of Tishri (September/October). It signalled the end of the agricultural year.

It was to be a day of rest, commemorated with the sounding of trumpets
Lev 23:24–25; **Nu** 29:1

Offerings were made to God
Lev 23:25; **Nu** 29:2–5

Celebrated after the exile
Ne 8:2–6 *See also agriculture.*

Feast of Unleavened Bread

The feast was kept from 15th–21st Abib (March/April), to commemorate the haste with which the Israelites left Egypt. It was always celebrated in the calendar of feasts with the Feast of Passover.

Celebrating the Feast of Unleavened Bread
Ex 12:15–20 ". . . Celebrate the Feast of Unleavened Bread, because it was on this very day that I brought your divisions out of Egypt . . ." *See also* **Ex** 12:39; 23:15; **Lev** 23:6; **Nu** 28:17; **Dt** 16:3

All use of yeast was forbidden during the Feast of Unleavened Bread
All leaven was to be removed from the home before the feast began Ex 12:19; 13:7; **Dt** 16:4
No yeast was to be used in the preparation of food Ex 12:18–20; 13:6–7; 23:15

Sacrifices made at the Feast of Unleavened Bread
Lev 23:8; **Nu** 28:19–24

The Feast of Unleavened Bread in NT times
Mk 14:1,12; **Ac** 12:3; **1Co** 5:6–8 *See also food; offerings; Passover.*

Feast of Weeks

This feast, which took place seven weeks after Passover in Sivan (May/June), was also known as the Feast of Pentecost. It expressed joy and thankfulness to God for the harvest.

The Feast of Weeks was one of three compulsory feasts
Ex 23:16; 34:22

Offerings made at the Feast of Weeks
The firstfruits of the wheat harvest were offered to God Nu 28:26; **Dt** 16:10
Two loaves of bread were also offered Lev 23:17
Burnt offerings and sin offerings were made Lev 23:18–20 pp Nu 28:27–30

The Feast of Weeks (Pentecost) in the NT
Ac 2:1–4 When the day of Pentecost came, they were all together in one place. Suddenly a sound like the blowing of a violent wind came from heaven and filled the whole house where they were sitting. They saw what seemed to be tongues of fire that separated and came to rest on each of them. All of them were filled with the Holy Spirit and began to speak in other tongues as the Spirit enabled them. *See also burnt offering; firstfruits; harvest; offerings; Pentecost; sin offering.*

feasting

Taking part in festive meals that were often a feature of Israel's celebrations of religious festivals.

Feasting on special occasions
To mark a covenant
Ge 31:54 He [Jacob] offered a sacrifice there in the hill country and invited his relatives to a meal. After they had eaten, they spent the night there. *See also* **Ge** 26:28–31; **Ex** 24:11; **1Co** 11:25–26
Weddings
Jdg 14:10 . . . And Samson made a feast there, as was customary for bridegrooms.

See also **Ge** 29:22; **Est** 2:18; **Mt** 22:2; **Jn** 2:1–10; **Rev** 19:9

Family celebrations

Ge 21:8 . . . and on the day Isaac was weaned Abraham held a great feast. *See also* **Lk** 15:23–24

National celebrations

1Ki 1:25 "Today he [Adonijah] has gone down and sacrificed great numbers of cattle, fattened calves, and sheep. He has invited all the king's sons, the commanders of the army and Abiathar the priest. Right now they are eating and drinking with him and saying, 'Long live King Adonijah!' " *See also* **Est** 9:17

Israel's religious feasts

Passover (or the Feast of Unleavened Bread) to celebrate the exodus Ex 23:15; **Dt** 16:1–3; **Lev** 23:4–6; **2Ch** 35:17; **Mt** 26:17; **Lk** 2:41

Pentecost, to celebrate the early harvest

Ex 34:22 "Celebrate the Feast of Weeks with the firstfruits of the wheat harvest . . ." *See also* **Ex** 23:16; **Nu** 28:26

The Feast of Tabernacles, to celebrate the autumn harvest

Ex 23:16 ". . . Celebrate the Feast of Ingathering at the end of the year, when you gather in your crops from the field." *See also* **Lev** 23:34; **Dt** 16:13; **Ezr** 3:4; **Ne** 8:14; **Zec** 14:16

The Feast of Dedication, to celebrate the rededication of the temple

Jn 10:22 Then came the Feast of Dedication at Jerusalem . . .

The Feast of Purim, to celebrate deliverance

Est 9:17 . . . on the fourteenth they rested and made it a day of feasting and joy. *See also* **Est** 9:22,26

Feasting amongst God's people

Ne 8:10 Nehemiah said, "Go and enjoy choice food and sweet drinks, and send some to those who have nothing prepared. This day is sacred to our Lord. Do not grieve, for the joy of the LORD is your strength."

Ac 2:46 . . . They [the believers] broke bread in their homes and ate together with glad and sincere hearts, *See also* **1Ki** 3:15; **Est** 8:17; 9:17; **Job** 1:4

Feasting amongst the heathen

Examples of pagan feasts 1Sa 30:16; **Da** 5:1; **Mk** 6:21–28

Warnings and instructions to Christians regarding pagan feasts 1Co 10:27–28; **1Pe** 4:3–4

Feasting as an occasion to sin

1Co 10:7 Do not be idolaters, as some of them were; as it is written: "The people sat down to eat and drink and got up to indulge in pagan revelry." *See also* **Ex** 32:6; **1Sa** 25:36; **2Sa** 13:28; **Hab** 2:15; **1Co** 10:28

Feasting as an evangelistic occasion

Lk 5:29 Then Levi held a great banquet for Jesus at his house, and a large crowd of tax collectors and others were eating with them. *See also* **Mk** 2:16–17; **Lk** 15:2

Feasting defended by Jesus Christ

Mt 11:19 "The Son of Man came eating and drinking, and they say, 'Here is a glutton and a drunkard, a friend of tax collectors and "sinners".' But wisdom is proved right by her actions." pp Lk 7:34–35 *See also* **Mt** 9:14–15 pp Mk 2:18–20 pp Lk 5:33–35

Feasting as a symbol of spiritual blessings

Mt 22:2 "The kingdom of heaven is like a king who prepared a wedding banquet for his son." *See also* **Pr** 9:1–6; **Isa** 25:6; 55:1–2; **Lk** 14:15; **Rev** 3:20

Feasting in heaven

Rev 19:9 Then the angel said to me [John], "Write: 'Blessed are those who are invited to the wedding supper of the Lamb!' " . . . *See also* **Mt** 8:11 *See also banquets; marriage, customs; Passover; Pentecost.*

fellowship offering

Sacrificial meals shared by offerer, people and priests. The name of these offerings is related to the Hebrew "shalom", meaning "wholeness" or "peace", and they are therefore also known as "peace offerings".

Fellowship offerings were required by God
Ex 20:24
Their purpose was thanksgiving, vow fulfilment or freewill offering Lev 7:11–18

Regulations for making a fellowship offering
The animal Lev 3:1,6,12
Its slaughter Lev 3:2,8,13; 17:5–6
All requirements must be fulfilled for the offering to be acceptable Lev 19:5; 22:21; **Jos** 22:29
A right attitude: **Am** 5:22,24

The fellowship offering was shared
God received the best Lev 3:3–5,9–11,14–16
The priests received their share as food Lev 7:29–34
The people ate the rest Lev 10:14

Fellowship offerings affirmed the covenant relationship
The Sinai covenant with Israel: **Ex** 20:24; 24:4–6; **Jos** 8:31–32
God's covenant with the king: **1Sa** 10:8; 11:15; **1Ki** 9:25

The celebration of fellowship offerings
At seasonal festivals Lev 23:19; **Nu** 29:39
On other religious and national occasions
At the completion of the time of separation of a Nazirite: **Nu** 6:14,17–18
Nu 10:10
Numbers chapter 7 contains many examples of the offerings made at the dedication of the tabernacle: **Nu** 7:17,23,29
On entering the promised land: **Nu** 15:8; **Dt** 27:7
2Sa 6:17–18; 24:25
1Ki 8:63–64 pp 2Ch 7:7
Re-establishing the ordinances of the temple: **2Ch** 29:35; 30:22; 31:2; 33:16
Pr 7:14
Ezekiel's vision of the restored temple includes the re-establishing of offerings: **Eze** 45:15,17; 46:2,12

Fellowship offerings in idolatrous worship
Ex 32:6   *See also altar; animals; freewill offering; sacrifice, in Old Testament; tabernacle, in Old Testament; thank-offering; vows; wave offering.*

---

firstborn
The firstborn male in a family; as in many cultures, in an Israelite family the eldest son had unique privileges, including the right of inheritance. The title "firstborn" was therefore a title of honour.

The privileges of the firstborn
The place of honour in the family
Ge 10:15 Canaan was the father of Sidon his firstborn . . .
Ge 43:33 The men had been seated before him in the order of their ages, from the firstborn to the youngest . . .   *See also* **Ge** 22:21; 25:13; 35:23; 36:15; 46:8; **Dt** 33:17
The right of inheritance Dt 21:15–17; **2Ch** 21:3
The right to a blessing Ge 27:19,30–39
The sin of despising these privileges
Ge 25:31–34 . . . So Esau despised his birthright.   *See also* **Heb** 12:16–17
These privileges could be transferred
Ge 48:14 But Israel reached out his right hand and put it on Ephraim's head, though he was the younger, and crossing his arms, he put his left hand on Manasseh's head, even though Manasseh was the firstborn.   *See also* **Ge** 48:18–19; 49:3–4; **1Ch** 2:3; 5:1–2; 26:10

The death of the firstborn a great tragedy
Ex 4:23 "'. . . I told you, "Let my son go, so that he may worship me." But you refused to let him go; so I will kill your firstborn son.'"
See also **Ex** 11:4–6; 12:12,29; **Nu** 33:4; **Jos** 6:26; **1Ki** 16:34; **Ps** 78:51; 105:36; 135:8; 136:10; **Heb** 11:28
Repentance likened to grief over the death of a firstborn Zec 12:10

God's claim upon the firstborn
In ancient times
Ge 4:4 But Abel brought fat portions from some of the firstborn of his flock . . . *See also* **Ge** 22:1–2,12
After the exodus
Ex 13:1–2 The LORD said to Moses, "Consecrate to me every firstborn male. The first offspring of every womb among the Israelites belongs to me, whether human or animal." *See also* **Ex** 13:11–15; 22:29; 34:19–20; **Nu** 18:15,17; **Dt** 14:23; 15:19; **Ne** 10:36
The Levites consecrated in place of the firstborn Nu 3:11–13,39–51; 8:15–18
The offering of a firstborn insufficient to redeem from the consequences of sin Mic 6:7

Heathen sacrifice of the firstborn 2Ch 28:3; **Eze** 20:26

Jesus Christ the "firstborn"
The firstborn of Mary Lk 2:7,22–23
The firstborn of God
Ro 8:29 . . . that he might be the firstborn among many brothers and sisters. *"firstborn" here means that Jesus Christ is above creation, rather than part of it. The title "firstborn" has strong Messianic associations*
Col 1:15 He is the image of the invisible God, the firstborn over all creation.
Heb 1:6 And again, when God brings his firstborn into the world, he says, "Let all God's angels worship him."
The "firstborn from the dead"
Col 1:18 . . . the firstborn from among the dead, so that in everything he might have the supremacy. *See also* **Rev** 1:5

God's people honoured as his "firstborn"
Israel
Ex 4:22 ". . . 'This is what the LORD says: Israel is my firstborn son . . .' "
David Ps 89:27
Ephraim Jer 31:9
The church
Heb 12:23 to the church of the firstborn, whose names are written in heaven. You have come to God, the judge of all people, to the spirits of the righteous made perfect, *See also* *firstfruits.*

---

firstfruits
Offerings of the produce of the land, being the first and best of the crops, given in acknowledgment of God's abundant blessings. The term is also used metaphorically to indicate the first of a much larger group that is to follow, such as those who will be raised from the dead.

Offering firstfruits
Ex 23:19 "Bring the best of the firstfruits of your soil to the house of the LORD your God . . ." *See also* **Ex** 34:26; **Lev** 2:11–16; **Dt** 26:1–11; **Ne** 10:35–39; 13:31; **Pr** 3:9–10; **Ro** 11:16

Firstfruits given to priests and Levites
Nu 18:8–13 . . . ". . . I [the LORD] give you all the finest olive oil and all the finest new wine and grain they give to the LORD as the firstfruits of their harvest. All the land's firstfruits that they bring to the LORD will be yours. Everyone in your household who is ceremonially clean may eat it." *See also* **Dt** 18:1–5; **2Ch** 31:2–5; **Ne** 12:44–47; **Eze** 44:28–30

Firstfruits offered at feasts
The Feast of Firstfruits
Lev 23:9–14 . . . ". . . 'When you [the Israelites] enter the land I [the LORD] am going to give you and you reap its harvest, bring to the priest a sheaf of the first grain you harvest . . .' "
The Feast of Weeks (Harvest) Ex 23:16; 34:22; **Lev** 23:15–20; **Nu** 28:26

Firstborn of human beings and animals regarded as firstfruits
Ps 78:51 He [the LORD] struck down all the firstborn of Egypt, the firstfruits of manhood in the tents of Ham. *See also* **Ex** 13:1–2,11–16; **Nu** 18:14–19; **Ps** 105:36

Metaphorical use of firstfruits
Firstfruits of God's harvest
Jer 2:1–3 . . .". . .'I [the LORD] remember the
devotion of your youth, how as a bride you loved
me and followed me through the desert, through
a land not sown. Israel was holy to the LORD, the
firstfruits of his harvest; all who devoured her
were held guilty, and disaster overtook them,'"
declares the LORD.
Jesus Christ the firstfruits of the resurrection
1Co 15:20–28 . . . Christ has indeed been
raised from the dead, the firstfruits of those who
have fallen asleep . . . For as in Adam all die, so
in Christ all will be made alive. But in this order:
Christ, the firstfruits; then, when he comes, those
who belong to him . . .   *See also* **Ac** 26:22–23
Firstfruits of salvation
Jas 1:18 He [the Father] chose to give us
[believers] birth through the word of truth, that
we might be a kind of firstfruits of all he
created.   *See also* **Ro** 8:23; **2Th** 2:13 fn; **Rev**
14:1–5   *See also Feast of Firstfruits; firstborn;
offerings; tithing; wine.*

---

fish
A basic ingredient of diet in biblical times. Fishing
was regarded as a trade rather than a recreation.

Fish as part of God's creation
Ge 1:20–22 And God said, "Let the water
teem with living creatures . . ." So God created
the great creatures of the sea and every living
and moving thing with which the water teems,
according to their kinds . . . And God saw that it
was good. God blessed them and said, "Be
fruitful and increase in number and fill the water
in the seas . . ."   *See also* **Ge** 1:26; 9:2; **1Ki**
4:33; **Ps** 8:8; **1Co** 15:39

Fish as food
Mt 7:9–10 "Which of you, if your children ask
for bread, will give them a stone? Or if they ask
for a fish, will give them a snake?" pp Lk 11:11
Mt 14:17 "We have here only five loaves of
bread and two fish," they [the disciples]
answered [Jesus]. pp Mk 6:38 pp Lk 9:16 pp

Jn 6:9   *See also* **Nu** 11:5; **Ne** 13:16; **Mt** 15:34
pp Mk 8:7; **Lk** 24:42; **Jn** 21:13

Rules about eating fish
Lev 11:9–12; **Dt** 14:9–10

Fish related to judgment
Ex 7:18 "'The fish in the Nile will die, and the
river will stink; the Egyptians will not be able to
drink its water.'"
Isa 19:8 Those who fish will groan and lament,
all who cast hooks into the Nile; those who throw
nets on the water will pine away.   *See also* **Ps**
105:29; **Isa** 50:2; **Hos** 4:3; **Zep** 1:3

Fish as the object of pagan worship
Dt 4:15–18 . . . Therefore watch yourselves
very carefully, so that you do not become corrupt
and make for yourselves an idol, an image of any
shape, whether formed like a man or a
woman . . . or any fish in the waters below.
See also **Jdg** 16:23   *Dagon was the fish god.*

Fish involved in miracles
Jnh 1:17 . . . the LORD provided a great fish to
swallow Jonah, and Jonah was inside the fish
three days and three nights.
Lk 5:4–7 When he [Jesus] had finished
speaking, he said to Simon, "Put out into deep
water, and let down the nets for a catch." Simon
answered, "Master, we've worked hard all night
and haven't caught anything. But because you say
so, I will let down the nets." When they had
done so, they caught such a large number of fish
that their nets began to break. So they signalled
to their partners in the other boat to come and
help them, and they came and filled both boats
so full that they began to sink.   *See also* **Mt**
14:19–21 pp Mk 6:39–44 pp Lk 9:14–17 pp Jn
6:10–13; **Mt** 15:35–38 pp Mk 8:7–9; **Mt**
17:24–27; **Jn** 21:5–6

Figurative uses of fish
Fish as a symbol of entrapment
Ecc 9:12 Moreover, people do not know when
their hour will come: As fish are caught in a cruel
net, or birds are taken in a snare, so people are

trapped by evil times that fall unexpectedly upon them.   *See also* **Eze** 29:4–5; **Hab** 1:14–17

Fish as a symbol of the kingdom of God
Mt 13:47–48 "Once again, the kingdom of heaven is like a net that was let down into the lake and caught all kinds of fish. When it was full, the fishermen pulled it up on the shore. Then they sat down and collected the good fish in baskets, but threw the bad away."   *See also* **Eze** 47:10

Fish as a symbol of the resurrection
Mt 12:40 "For as Jonah was three days and three nights in the belly of a huge fish, so the Son of Man will be three days and three nights in the heart of the earth."

Fishermen as the first disciples
Mt 4:18 As Jesus was walking beside the Sea of Galilee, he saw two brothers, Simon called Peter and his brother Andrew. They were casting a net into the lake, for they were fishermen. pp Mk 1:16

Figurative use of fishers
Jer 16:16 "But now I will send for many fishers," declares the LORD, "and they will catch them. After that I will send for many hunters, and they will hunt them down on every mountain and hill and from the crevices of the rocks."
Mt 4:19 "Come, follow me," Jesus said, "and I will make you fishers of men and women."
See also occupations.

---

flowers
The blossoming part of plants and trees, from which the seeds or fruit develop. Often admired for their beauty, Scripture uses their fleeting existence as an illustration of the transience of human life.

Carvings of flowers
In the tabernacle
Ex 25:31–36 ". . . Six branches are to extend from the sides of the lampstand—three on one side and three on the other. Three cups shaped like almond flowers with buds and blossoms are to be on one branch, three on the next branch,

and the same for all six branches extending from the lampstand . . ." pp **Ex** 37:17–22
In the temple
1Ki 6:18 The inside of the temple was cedar, carved with gourds and open flowers. Everything was cedar; no stone was to be seen.   *See also* **1Ki** 6:29,31–35; 7:15–22,25–26 pp 2Ch 4:4–5

Metaphorical depictions of people as flowers
Isa 28:1–6 Woe to that wreath, the pride of Ephraim's drunkards, to the fading flower, his glorious beauty, set on the head of a fertile valley—to that city, the pride of those laid low by wine! . . .   *See also* **Isa** 5:18–25

Human existence is likened to the short life cycle of flowers
1Pe 1:24–25 For, "All human beings are like grass, and all their glory is like the flowers of the field; the grass withers and the flowers fall, but the word of the Lord stands for ever.". . .
See also **Isa** 40:6–8; **Job** 14:1–2; **Ps** 103:13–18; **Jas** 1:9–11

Flowers and the changing seasons
SS 2:11–13 "See! The winter is past; the rains are over and gone. Flowers appear on the earth; the season of singing has come . . ."
See also **Isa** 18:5–6

The lily
Its beauty
Lk 12:27–28 "Consider how the lilies grow. They do not labour or spin. Yet I tell you, not even Solomon in all his splendour was dressed like one of these . . ." pp **Mt** 6:28–30
See also **SS** 2:1–2; **Hos** 14:4–7
Lilies in psalm titles
Ps 45 Title For the director of music. To (the tune of) "Lilies". Of the Sons of Korah. A maskil. A wedding song.   *See also* **Ps** 60:1 Title; 69:1 Title; 80:1 Title
Their metaphorical use
SS 4:5 Your two breasts are like two fawns, like twin fawns of a gazelle that browse among the lilies.   *See also* **SS** 2:16; 5:13; 6:2–3; 7:2

The crocus
Isa 35:1–2 The desert and the parched land will be glad; the wilderness will rejoice and blossom. Like the crocus, it will burst into bloom; it will rejoice greatly and shout for joy. The glory of Lebanon will be given to it, the splendour of Carmel and Sharon; they will see the glory of the LORD, the splendour of our God.

The rose
SS 2:1 I am a rose of Sharon, a lily of the valleys.   *See also herbs and spices; horticulture; plants; tabernacle, in Old Testament; temple, Solomon's.*

---

food
Scripture contains references to varied foodstuffs, which comprised the diet of the people of the Near East in biblical times.

God made provision for food in creation
Ge 1:29–30 Then God said, "I give you every seed-bearing plant on the face of the whole earth and every tree that has fruit with seed in it. They will be yours for food. And to all the beasts of the earth and all the birds of the air and all the creatures that move on the ground—everything that has the breath of life in it—I give every green plant for food." And it was so.

Flour
Flour the main ingredient in bread
Ge 18:6 . . . Abraham hurried into the tent to Sarah. "Quick," he said, "get three seahs of fine flour and knead it and bake some bread."
See also **Ex** 29:2; **Jdg** 6:19; **1Sa** 28:24; **Mt** 13:33 pp Lk 13:21
Flour figured largely in the staple diet
1Ki 17:12–16 "As surely as the LORD your God lives," she [the widow at Zarephath] replied, "I don't have any bread—only a handful of flour in a jar and a little oil in a jug. I am gathering a few sticks to take home and make a meal for myself and my son, that we may eat it—and die." . . .   *See also* **2Sa** 17:27–29; **1Ki** 4:22–23; **2Ki** 4:41; 7:1,16; **1Ch** 12:40

Fine flour more refined and more expensive than the common variety
Eze 16:13 " 'So you [Jerusalem] were adorned with gold and silver; your clothes were of fine linen and costly fabric and embroidered cloth. Your food was fine flour, honey and olive oil. You became very beautiful and rose to be a queen.
See also **Eze** 16:19; **Rev** 18:11–13
Flour in grain offerings
Lev 2:1–10 " 'When any of you bring a grain offering to the LORD, your offering is to be of fine flour. You are to pour oil on it, put incense on it and take it to Aaron's sons the priests. The priest shall take a handful of the fine flour and oil, together with all the incense, and burn this as a memorial portion on the altar, an offering made by fire, an aroma pleasing to the LORD . . .' "
See also **Lev** 6:14–23; 14:8–11; **Nu** 5:11–15; 6:13–15; 15:1–4; 28:9; 29:7–11; **1Ch** 23:29; **Eze** 46:14
Flour in other offerings
Lev 5:11 " 'If, however, they [the worshippers] cannot afford two doves or two young pigeons, they are each to bring as an offering for their sin a tenth of an ephah of fine flour for a sin offering. They must not put oil or incense on it, because it is a sin offering.' "   *See also* **Ex** 29:1–3,22–25; **Lev** 7:12; 8:25–28; 23:15–17

Honey
Honey a sweet delicacy
Ge 43:11 . . . their father Israel said to them [Joseph's brothers], "If it must be, then do this: Put some of the best products of the land in your bags and take them down to the man as a gift—a little balm and a little honey, some spices and myrrh, some pistachio nuts and almonds."
See also **Ex** 16:31; **Dt** 32:13; **Jdg** 14:8–9; **1Sa** 14:25–26; **2Sa** 17:27–29; **1Ki** 14:1–3; **2Ki** 18:31–32
Honey's sweetness and the sweetness of God's law: **Ps** 19:10; 119:103
Ps 81:13–16; **SS** 4:11; 5:1; **Isa** 7:22; **Jer** 41:8; **Eze** 16:13
The promised land described as flowing with milk and honey
Ex 3:7–8 The LORD said, "I have indeed seen

the misery of my people in Egypt. I have heard them crying out because of their slave drivers, and I am concerned about their suffering. So I have come down to rescue them from the hand of the Egyptians and to bring them up out of that land into a good and spacious land, a land flowing with milk and honey . . ." *See also* **Ex** 3:17; 13:5; 33:3; **Lev** 20:24

The spies confirm the goodness of the promised land: **Nu** 13:27; 14:8

Nu 16:12–14; **Dt** 6:3; 11:8–9; 26:9; 31:20; **Jos** 5:6; **Jer** 32:22; **Eze** 20:6,15

Prohibition against burning honey on the altar
Lev 2:11 " 'Every grain offering you bring to the Lord must be made without yeast, for you are not to burn any yeast or honey in an offering made to the Lord by fire.' "

Raisins

2Sa 16:1 When David had gone a short distance beyond the summit, there was Ziba, the steward of Mephibosheth, waiting to meet him. He had a string of donkeys saddled and loaded with two hundred loaves of bread, a hundred cakes of raisins, a hundred cakes of figs and a skin of wine. *See also* **Nu** 6:1–4; **1Sa** 25:18; 30:11–12; **2Sa** 6:19 pp 1Ch 16:3; **1Ch** 12:40; **SS** 2:5; **Hos** 3:1

Lentils

Ge 25:29–34 . . . Jacob gave Esau some bread and some lentil stew. He ate and drank, and then got up and left. So Esau despised his birthright. *See also* **2Sa** 17:27–29; 23:11–12; **Eze** 4:1–10

Cheese

1Sa 17:17–18 Now Jesse said to his son David, "Take this ephah of roasted grain and these ten loaves of bread for your brothers and hurry to their camp. Take along these ten cheeses to the commander of their unit . . ." *See also* **2Sa** 17:27–29; **Job** 10:8–11

Believers should not eat food offered to idols

Ac 15:19–20 "It is my judgment, therefore,

that we should not make it difficult for the Gentiles who are turning to God. Instead we should write to them, telling them to abstain from food polluted by idols, from sexual immorality, from the meat of strangled animals and from blood." *See also* **Ac** 21:25; **1Co** 8:1–13; **Rev** 2:14 *See also birds; eating; fish; fruit; idolatry, in New Testament; meals; meat; offerings.*

---

forests

Forests the source of timber

Ne 2:8 "And may I [Nehemiah] have a letter to Asaph, keeper of the king's [Artaxerxes'] forest, so he will give me timber to make beams for the gates of the citadel by the temple and for the city wall and for the residence I will occupy?" . . . *See also* **Dt** 19:5; **Isa** 44:13–14; **Jer** 10:3; **Eze** 39:10

Forests the habitat of wild animals

Ps 50:9–11 ". . . every animal of the forest is mine [the Lord's], and the cattle on a thousand hills . . ." *See also* **Ps** 80:13; 104:20–22; **Isa** 56:9; **Jer** 5:6; 12:8; **Eze** 34:25; **Mic** 5:8; 7:14

Destruction of forests
As punishment

Jer 21:14 " 'I [the Lord] will punish you as your deeds deserve, declares the Lord. I will kindle a fire in your forests that will consume everything around you.' " *See also* **Isa** 10:18–19,33–34; **Zec** 11:1–3

As a demonstration of power

Jer 46:23 "They [the Babylonians] will chop down her [Egypt's] forest," declares the Lord, "dense though it be. They are more numerous than locusts, they cannot be counted." *See also* **2Ki** 19:22–24 pp Isa 37:23–25; **Eze** 20:46–48

To render land suitable for human habitation
Jos 17:14–18

Forest fires

Jas 3:5 . . . the tongue is a small part of the body, but it makes great boasts. Consider what a great forest is set on fire by a small spark.

See also **Ps** 83:14–15; **Isa** 9:18; **Jer** 21:14

The Palace of the Forest of Lebanon
1Ki 7:2 He [Solomon] built the Palace of the
Forest of Lebanon a hundred cubits long, fifty
wide and thirty high, with four rows of cedar
columns supporting trimmed cedar beams.
See also **1Ki** 10:17 pp 2Ch 9:16; **1Ki** 10:21 pp 2Ch
9:20

Location of forests
1Sa 22:5 But the prophet Gad said to David,
"Do not stay in the stronghold. Go into the land
of Judah." So David left and went to the forest
of Hereth.   *See also* **2Sa** 18:6–17; **Eze**
20:46–48

Poetic references to forests
SS 2:3 Like an apple tree among the trees of
the forest is my lover among the young men. I
delight to sit in his shade, and his fruit is sweet
to my taste.   *See also* **1Ch** 16:33; **Ps** 29:9;
96:12; **Isa** 7:2; 44:23   *See also animals.*

---

freewill offering

An offering that in some ways resembled the
thank-offering or peace offering. It was completely
voluntary, prompted by an occasion of celebration
or spiritual significance. The animal offered was
eaten at a festive banquet.

**Instructions for presenting a freewill
offering**
The animal to be offered Lev 22:17–22,23
Eating the offering Lev 7:16

**Freewill offerings were associated with
joy and celebration**
Ps 54:6–7 I will sacrifice a freewill offering to
you; I will praise your name, O Lord, for it is
good. For he has delivered me from all my
troubles . . .   *See also* **Dt** 16:9–12

Occasions for making freewill offerings
**In maintaining public worship and at times of
religious renewal**
Ex 35:20–29 . . . all who were willing and
whose hearts moved them came and brought an
offering to the Lord for the work on the Tent of
Meeting, for all its service, and for the sacred
garments . . . All the Israelite men and women
who were willing brought to the Lord freewill
offerings for all the work the Lord through Moses
had commanded them to do.   *See also* **2Ch**
31:14

The return from exile: **Ezr** 1:4–6; 2:68; 7:16; 8:28;
Ne 7:70–72

Eze 46:11–12

As an additional offering at certain festivals
Nu 29:39

The offering had to be made at the sanctuary to be
acceptable: **Dt** 12:5–6,17–18

**Prophetic criticism of bragging over
freewill offerings**
Am 4:5 "Burn leavened bread as a thank-
offering and brag about your freewill offerings—
boast about them, you Israelites, for this is what
you love to do," . . .   *See also animals, religious
role; fellowship offering; offerings; sacrifice, in Old
Testament; thank-offering; tithing.*

---

fruit

Edible produce of trees, usually sweet and
pleasant-tasting. The climate of the Near East is
particularly suitable for a wide range of fruit and
several varieties are mentioned in Scripture.

Apples
Sweet, pleasant-tasting fruit
SS 2:3 Like an apple tree among the trees of
the forest is my lover among the young men. I
delight to sit in his shade, and his fruit is sweet
to my taste.   *See also* **Pr** 25:11; **SS** 2:5; 7:8
Apple trees
Joel 1:12 The vine is dried up and the fig-tree
is withered; the pomegranate, the palm and the
apple tree—all the trees of the field—are dried
up. Surely the people's joy is withered away.
See also **SS** 2:3; 8:5

Figurative use: the apple of the eye: **Dt** 32:10; **Ps**
17:8; **Pr** 7:2; **Zec** 2:8

Dates

2Sa 6:19 Then he gave a loaf of bread, a cake of dates and a cake of raisins to each person in the whole crowd of Israelites, both men and women. And all the people went to their homes. pp 1Ch 16:3

Figs

Nu 13:23 When they [the Israelite spies] reached the Valley of Eshcol, they cut off a branch bearing a single cluster of grapes. Two of them carried it on a pole between them, along with some pomegranates and figs.   *See also* **Nu** 20:5; **1Sa** 25:18–20; 30:11–12; **2Sa** 16:1; **1Ch** 12:40; **Mk** 11:13

Grapes

Dt 32:3–14 . . . He [the Lord] nourished him [Israel] with honey from the rock, and with oil from the flinty crag, with curds and milk from herd and flock and with fattened lambs and goats, with choice rams of Bashan and the finest grains of wheat. You drank the foaming blood of the grape.   *See also* **Ge** 40:9–11; **Nu** 13:23–24; 20:5

Melons

Nu 11:5 We [Israelites] remember the fish we ate in Egypt at no cost—also the cucumbers, melons, leeks, onions and garlic.   *See also* **Isa** 1:8; **Jer** 10:5

Pomegranates

Pleasant-tasting fruit

Dt 8:7–8 . . . the Lord your God is bringing you [Israel] into a good land—a land with streams and pools of water, with springs flowing in the valleys and hills; a land with wheat and barley, vines and fig-trees, pomegranates, olive oil and honey;   *See also* **Nu** 13:23; 20:5; **SS** 6:11; 7:12; 8:2

Pomegranate trees

1Sa 14:2 Saul was staying on the outskirts of Gibeah under a pomegranate tree in Migron . . .   *See also* **Joel** 1:12; **Hag** 2:19 Use in similes: **SS** 4:3,13; 6:7

Representations of pomegranates in the tabernacle and temple

2Ki 25:16–17 The bronze from the two pillars, the Sea and the movable stands, which Solomon had made for the temple of the Lord, was more than could be weighed. Each pillar was twenty-seven feet high. The bronze capital on top of one pillar was four and a half feet high and was decorated with a network and pomegranates of bronze all around. The other pillar, with its network, was similar. pp Jer 52:20–23   *See also* **Ex** 28:31–35 pp Ex 39:22–26; **1Ki** 7:15–20,40–42 pp 2Ch 4:11–13; **2Ch** 3:16

Fruit and the fall

Ge 3:12 The man said, "The woman you [Lord God] put here with me—she gave me some fruit from the tree, and I ate it."   *See also* **Ge** 3:1–7

General references to fruit

Am 8:1–2 This is what the Sovereign Lord showed me: a basket of ripe fruit. "What do you see, Amos?" he asked. "A basket of ripe fruit," I answered. Then the Lord said to me, "The time is ripe for my people Israel; I will spare them no longer."   *See also* **Ge** 1:11–12,29; **Lev** 19:23–25; **Ecc** 2:5; **Eze** 47:12; **Mic** 7:1; **Rev** 22:1–2

Fruit as a symbol of spiritual growth

Mt 3:10; 12:33   *See also* food; plants; vine.

---

gate

A point of entry to a walled city or walled-off area, such as the temple. It was a place where business was transacted and where justice and punishment were dispensed. It is used figuratively of the entry to death and also of the starting-point of the Christian life.

The purpose of gates as defended points of entry

Dt 3:5 All these cities were fortified with high walls and with gates and bars . . . The gates of Jericho: **Jos** 2:5,7

Jdg 5:8; **1Sa** 23:7; **2Ch** 8:5; 14:7; **Ps** 107:16;
147:13; **Isa** 22:7; 45:1–2
The destruction of Babylon's gates foretold: **Jer**
51:30,58
Eze 38:11; 46:9; **Hos** 11:6; **Lk** 7:12; **Ac** 9:24;
12:10; 16:13
The new Jerusalem: **Rev** 21:25; 22:14

Examples of gates
The gates of Jerusalem
Ne 2:13–15 By night I [Nehemiah] went out
through the Valley Gate towards the Jackal Well
and the Dung Gate, examining the walls of
Jerusalem, which had been broken down, and its
gates, which had been destroyed by fire . . .
See also **2Ki** 14:13 pp 2Ch 25:23; **Ne** 1:3; 2:3,8
The Sheep Gate: **Ne** 3:1,32; **Jn** 5:2
Ne 3:3,6,13–15,26,28–29,31; 6:1; 7:3; 11:19;
12:39; **Ps** 122:2; **Isa** 60:11; **Jer** 1:15
The gates of the temple
Ac 3:2 Now a man crippled from birth was
being carried to the temple gate called Beautiful,
where he was put every day to beg from those
going into the temple courts. *See also* **2Ch**
23:19; 24:8; 31:2; **Jer** 20:2; **Eze** 44:11; **Ac** 3:10
Other examples of gates
Jos 6:26 At that time Joshua pronounced this
solemn oath: "Cursed before the LORD are any
who undertake to rebuild this city, Jericho: At the
cost of their firstborn son will they lay its
foundations; at the cost of their youngest will they
set up its gates." *See also* **Ge** 28:17; **1Sa**
17:52; **1Ki** 16:34; **Mt** 16:18; **Jn** 10:1–3; **Ac** 10:17

Uses of the area around the gate
A place of (sometimes false) worship
2Ch 31:2 Hezekiah assigned the priests and
Levites to divisions—each of them according to
their duties as priests or Levites—to offer burnt
offerings and fellowship offerings, to minister, to
give thanks and to sing praises at the gates of
the LORD's dwelling. *See also* **2Ki** 23:8; **Ps**
9:14; 118:19–20; **Eze** 46:2; **Ac** 14:13
A place of business
Ge 23:10–11 Ephron the Hittite was sitting
among his people and he replied to Abraham in
the hearing of all the Hittites who had come to

the gate of his city. "No, my lord," he said.
"Listen to me; I give you the field, and I give
you the cave that is in it. I give it to you in the
presence of my people. Bury your dead."
See also **Ru** 4:1,11; **2Ki** 7:1,18; **Ne** 13:19–22
A place where decisions are made and justice dispensed
Ge 34:19–20 The young man, who was the
most honoured of all his father's family, lost no
time in doing what they said, because he was
delighted with Jacob's daughter. So Hamor and
his son Shechem went to the gate of their city to
speak to the men of their city. *See also* **Dt**
21:19; 22:13–19; 25:7–10; **Jos** 20:4; **2Sa** 15:2;
1Ki 22:10; **Est** 2:19,21; 3:2–3
A place of punishment, banishment and begging
Dt 17:5 take the man or woman who has done
this evil deed to your city gate and stone that
person to death. *See also* **Dt** 22:23–24; **Jos**
8:29; **2Ki** 7:3; **Jer** 20:2; **Eze** 21:15; **Lk** 16:20; **Heb**
13:12; **Rev** 22:14–15
A place of counsel **Pr** 1:20–21; 8:1–3

Figurative use of the gate
Coming to worship **Ps** 24:7–10; 100:4
The entrance to death
Isa 38:10 I said, "In the prime of my life must
I go through the gates of death and be robbed of
the rest of my years?" *See also* **Job** 17:16;
38:17; **Ps** 9:13; 107:18
The entrance to the Christian life
Mt 7:13–14 "Enter through the narrow gate.
For wide is the gate and broad is the road that
leads to destruction, and many enter through it.
But small is the gate and narrow the road that
leads to life, and only a few find it." *See also*
Jn 10:7–10
The entry to the heavenly city of God
Rev 22:14 "Blessed are those who wash their
robes, that they may have the right to the tree of
life and may go through the gates into the
city." *See also* **Eze** 48:30–34; **Rev**
21:12–15,21,25 *See also* **city**.

gestures

Significant acts, bodily movements or signals which carry meaning, evoke responses or convey positive or negative feelings. They may or may not be accompanied by words or other communications.

Gestures are part of human communication

They give weight to a contract

Ru 4:7 (Now in earlier times in Israel, for the redemption and transfer of property to become final, one party took off his sandal and gave it to the other. This was the method of legalising transactions in Israel.) *See also* **2Sa** 24:22–24 pp 1Ch 21:23–24; **Jer** 32:10–12

They add force to words

1Sa 11:7 He [Saul] took a pair of oxen, cut them into pieces, and sent the pieces by messengers throughout Israel, proclaiming, "This is what will be done to the oxen of anyone who does not follow Saul and Samuel." Then the terror of the LORD fell on the people, and they turned out as one. *See also* **Jos** 7:25–26; **1Sa** 15:27–28; **2Sa** 12:16; **Mt** 21:12–13 pp Mk 11:15–17 pp Lk 19:45–46 pp Jn 2:15–16

Gestures often convey more than words

Gestures of joy

2Sa 6:14 David, wearing a linen ephod, danced before the LORD with all his might,
There is a spontaneous and unpremeditated element in many gestures: **Ge** 21:6; **Lev** 9:24; **Ac** 3:8

Gestures of love

1Sa 1:5 . . . to Hannah he [Elkanah] gave a double portion because he loved her . . .
See also **Ge** 37:3; **1Sa** 2:19; **Lk** 7:46–47; 10:34; 15:20; **Jn** 15:13; **Ro** 5:8

Gestures of mercy

Isa 6:6–7 Then one of the seraphs flew to me [Isaiah] with a live coal in his hand, which he had taken with tongs from the altar. With it he touched my mouth and said, "See, this has touched your lips; your guilt is taken away and your sin atoned for." *See also* **1Sa** 24:10–11; **2Sa** 9:1,7; **Mt** 18:27

Gestures of worship and reverence

Ex 3:5 "Do not come any closer," God said. "Take off your sandals, for the place where you are standing is holy ground." *See also* **Ex** 3:6; **Jos** 5:14; **Ne** 8:6; **Ps** 63:4; 134:2; **Mt** 2:11; **Lk** 5:8; **Jn** 11:32; **Rev** 1:17

Gestures of repentance

Job 42:6 "Therefore I [Job] despise myself and repent in dust and ashes." *See also* **1Ki** 21:27; **Ezr** 10:1; **Isa** 22:12; **Joel** 2:12; **Jnh** 3:6–8; **Mt** 11:21 pp Lk 10:13; **Mt** 27:3–5

Gestures of sorrow and mourning

2Sa 3:31 Then David said to Joab and all the people with him, "Tear your clothes and put on sackcloth and walk in mourning in front of Abner." King David himself walked behind the bier. *See also* **2Sa** 19:4; **Est** 4:1; **Ps** 137:1; **Joel** 1:13; **Am** 5:16

Gestures of dedication

Ac 22:16 " 'And now what are you [Paul] waiting for? Get up, be baptised and wash your sins away, calling on his name.' " *See also* **Ge** 17:10; **Ex** 21:6; **1Sa** 20:41–42; **Ne** 10:35–37

Gestures of anger

Lk 15:28 "The older brother became angry and refused to go in . . ." *See also* **Ex** 32:19; **Nu** 22:27; **1Sa** 20:33–34; **Mt** 26:65 pp Mk 14:63; **Ac** 7:54,57; **Rev** 3:16

Gestures of treachery

Lk 22:47–48 . . . Jesus asked him, "Judas, are you betraying the Son of Man with a kiss?" pp Mt 26:47–49 pp Mk 14:43–45 *See also* **2Sa** 3:27; 20:9–10

Gestures of contempt

Shaking of the head: **Ps** 22:7; 64:8; **Mt** 27:39 pp Mk 15:29
Spitting: **Mt** 26:67 pp Mk 14:65; **Rev** 3:16

Other examples of gestures

The gesture of washing hands

Mt 27:24 When Pilate saw that he was getting nowhere, but that instead an uproar was starting, he took water and washed his hands in front of the crowd. "I am innocent of this man's blood," he said. "It is your responsibility!" *See also* **Dt** 21:6–7; **Ps** 26:6; 73:13

The gesture of shaking dust from the feet
Mt 10:14 "If anyone will not welcome you or listen to your words, shake the dust off your feet when you leave that home or town." pp Mk 6:11 pp Lk 9:5   *See also* **Lk** 10:11; **Ac** 13:51
Jesus Christ's gesture of washing the disciples' feet Jn 13:4–5,12–15   *See also covenant.*

---

government

God's gracious rule over the nations, particularly Israel. Also, the divinely established ruling of people by God's appointed authorities for the good of society and to prevent anarchy.

God governs the nations
Ps 22:28 for dominion belongs to the Lord and he rules over the nations.   *See also* **1Ch** 29:12; **2Ch** 20:6; **Ps** 9:7–8; 47:2,7–8; 66:7; 67:4; 103:19; **Da** 4:32,35; **1Ti** 6:15

Jesus Christ also governs the nations
Isa 9:6 . . . the government will be on his [the Messiah's] shoulders . . .   *See also* **Ps** 72:8–11; 110:2; **Zec** 6:13; 9:10; **Rev** 2:27; **Ps** 2:9; **Rev** 12:5; 19:15

The manner of God's government of Israel was unique
Jdg 8:23 But Gideon told them, "I will not rule over you, nor will my son rule over you. The Lord will rule over you."   *See also* **1Sa** 8:7

God governs individuals
1Sa 12:12
Pr 21:1 The king's heart is in the hand of the Lord; he directs it like a watercourse wherever he pleases.   *See also* **Pr** 16:1,9; 19:21; 20:24; **Jer** 10:23; **La** 3:37; **Da** 5:23; **Ac** 17:26; **Jas** 4:13–15

God has established human agencies for the government of people
Ro 13:1 Let everyone be subject to the governing authorities, for there is no authority except that which God has established. The authorities that exist have been established by God.   *See also* **Ge** 9:5–6; **Pr** 8:15–16; **Da** 2:37–38; 4:17,32; 5:21; **Mt** 22:17–21; **Jn** 19:11; **1Ti** 2:2–3; **1Pe** 2:13

Government is for the good of society
Ro 13:4 For the one in authority is God's servant to do you good. But if you do wrong, be afraid, for rulers do not bear the sword for nothing. They are God's servants, agents of wrath to bring punishment on the wrongdoer.   *See also* **Ps** 72:12–14; 82:3–4

Government is established to prevent anarchy
Ro 13:2–3 . . . whoever rebels against the authority is rebelling against what God has instituted, and those who do so will bring judgment on themselves. For rulers hold no terror for those who do right, but for those who do wrong . . .   *See also* **Ge** 9:6; **Ezr** 7:26; **Pr** 21:15; 28:2; 29:4; **Ac** 25:11; **Ro** 13:4; **1Pe** 2:14
See also law.

---

grain offering

An offering that was usually offered as an accompaniment to animal sacrifices, but in special circumstances was presented alone. It could be cooked in various ways or presented uncooked. The offering could be made for a variety of purposes, depending on the sacrifice it accompanied.

The Hebrew word for "grain offering" can also mean simply "gift"
Ge 4:4; 32:13; **1Sa** 2:17; **1Ki** 4:21; **Mk** 7:11

The ingredients of the grain offering
Flour, oil and incense
Lev 2:1–2 " 'When any of you bring a grain offering to the Lord, your offering is to be of fine flour. You are to pour oil on it, put incense on it . . .' "
Salt Lev 2:13
No yeast or honey Lev 2:11
Roasted ears of corn Lev 2:14–16

The preparation of the grain offering
Lev 2:4–6

The presentation of the grain offering
By fire
Lev 2:2 "'. . . The priest shall take a handful of the fine flour and oil, together with all the incense, and burn this as a memorial portion on the altar, an offering made by fire . . .'"
See also **Lev** 2:3
Accompanying vow fulfilment or freewill offerings Nu 15:1–10
With an animal sacrifice
Nu 15:6 "'With a ram prepare a grain offering of two-tenths of an ephah of fine flour mixed with a third of a hin of oil,'"   *See also* **Nu** 15:8–9
With the two daily offerings Ex 29:38–41
Circumstances under which the grain offering was presented alone Lev 6:19–23
In the ritual for a jealous husband: **Nu** 5:15,25

The character of the grain offering
It is most holy
Lev 6:17 "'. . . Like the sin offering and the guilt offering, it is most holy.'"
It is an aroma pleasing to the Lord Lev 2:2,9   *See also sacrifice, in Old Testament.*

guilt offering
An offering that resembled the sin offering, but was offered especially in cases where restitution could be made for an unintentional sin.

Circumstances for making the guilt offering
Unintentional sin against God
Lev 5:17 "'If anyone sins and does what is forbidden in any of the Lord's commands, even though they do not know it, they are guilty and will be held responsible."   *See also* **Lev** 5:15
Sin against a neighbour where restitution can be made Lev 5:16; 6:1–5; **Nu** 5:5–8

The nature of the guilt offering
A ram without defect
Lev 5:18 "They [the people who sin] are each to bring to the priest as a guilt offering a ram from the flock, one without defect and of the

proper value. In this way the priest will make atonement for them for the wrong they have committed unintentionally, and they will be forgiven."
Regulations governing the offering Lev 7:1–6; **Nu** 18:9

Other situations requiring a guilt offering
Lev 14:12–14; 19:20–22; **Nu** 6:12; **Ezr** 10:19

Guilt offerings in Ezekiel's vision of the temple
Eze 40:38–39; 42:13; 44:29; 46:20

The death of the "suffering servant" is interpreted as a guilt offering
Isa 53:10 Yet it was the Lord's will to crush him and cause him to suffer, and though the Lord makes his life a guilt offering . . .
See also offerings; restitution; sin offering.

harvest
The gathering of mature crops from the land. The successful culmination of the agricultural year was evidence of God's goodness and consequently marked with festivity. Harvest is also used widely in a metaphorical sense.

The harvest is evidence of God's goodness
Ge 8:22 "As long as the earth endures, seedtime and harvest, cold and heat, summer and winter, day and night will never cease."
2Co 9:10 Now he who supplies seed to the sower and bread for food will also supply and increase your store of seed and will enlarge the harvest of your righteousness.   *See also* **Lev** 26:5,9–10; **Ps** 67:6; 85:12; 107:37; **Isa** 62:8–9; **Jer** 5:24

Laws relating to the harvest
Ex 23:10–11; 34:21; **Lev** 19:9,23–25; 23:22; 25:4–5,11–12,18–27; **Nu** 18:12–13; **Dt** 24:19–21

Harvest festivals
Ex 23:16; 34:22; **Lev** 23:10–16,33–43; **Dt** 16:13–15

Harvest marked times of the year
Ru 1:22 So Naomi returned from Moab accompanied by Ruth the Moabite, her daughter-in-law, arriving in Bethlehem as the barley harvest was beginning.   *See also* **Jos** 3:15; **Jdg** 15:1; **1Sa** 6:13; 12:17; **2Sa** 21:9–10; 23:13; **Jer** 8:20

Characteristics of harvest
Rejoicing
Isa 9:3 You have enlarged the nation and increased their joy; they rejoice before you as people rejoice at the harvest, as soldiers rejoice when dividing the plunder.   *See also* **Ps** 126:5–6; **Isa** 16:9
Hard work
Pr 10:5 He who gathers crops in summer is a wise son, but he who sleeps during harvest is a disgraceful son.   *See also* **Pr** 14:4; 20:4

Failed harvests are a sign of God's judgment
Poor harvests
Jer 12:13 "They will sow wheat but reap thorns; they will wear themselves out but gain nothing. So bear the shame of your harvest because of the LORD's fierce anger."   *See also* **Isa** 17:10–11; 32:10; **Jer** 8:13; **Joel** 1:11; **Am** 4:7; **Mic** 6:15; **Hag** 1:6
Others eating the harvest
Jer 5:17 "They [the invaders] will devour your harvests and food, devour your sons and daughters; they will devour your flocks and herds, devour your vines and fig-trees. With the sword they will destroy the fortified cities in which you trust."   *See also* **Ne** 9:37; **Job** 5:5; 31:12

The metaphorical use of harvest
Joel 3:13 "Swing the sickle, for the harvest is ripe. Come, trample the grapes, for the winepress is full and the vats overflow—so great is their wickedness!"
Mt 9:37–38 Then he [Jesus] said to his disciples, "The harvest is plentiful but the workers

are few. Ask the Lord of the harvest, therefore, to send out workers into his harvest field."
Gal 6:9 Let us not become weary in doing good, for at the proper time we will reap a harvest if we do not give up.
Rev 14:15–16 Then another angel came out of the temple and called in a loud voice to him who was sitting on the cloud, "Take your sickle and reap, because the time to reap has come, for the harvest of the earth is ripe." So he who was seated on the cloud swung his sickle over the earth, and the earth was harvested.   *See also* **Pr** 18:20; 25:13; 26:1; **Isa** 17:5; 18:4–5; 24:13; 28:4; 33:4; **Jer** 2:3; 51:33; **Hos** 6:11
The parable of the weeds and its explanation: **Mt** 13:30,39
Mt 25:24; **Mk** 4:29; 12:1–9; **Lk** 10:2; **Jn** 4:35–36; **Ro** 1:13; **1Co** 9:10–11; **Heb** 12:11; **Jas** 3:18
See also agriculture; Feast of Firstfruits; Feast of Tabernacles; Feast of Weeks; offerings; sowing and reaping.

healing

The bringing about of a state of physical or spiritual health. Scripture recognises a close link between physical and spiritual health, with healing often being seen as an image of salvation in Christ.

God as the author of healing
Ex 15:26 He [the LORD] said, "If you listen carefully to the voice of the LORD your God and do what is right in his eyes, if you pay attention to his commands and keep all his decrees, I will not bring on you any of the diseases I brought on the Egyptians, for I am the LORD, who heals you."
Ps 103:2–3 Praise the LORD . . . who forgives all your sins and heals all your diseases,
See also **Lk** 5:15

General aspects of healing
Requests for healing
2Ki 20:1–11 In those days Hezekiah became ill and was at the point of death. The prophet Isaiah son of Amoz went to him and said, "This

is what the LORD says: Put your house in order, because you are going to die; you will not recover." Hezekiah turned his face to the wall and prayed to the LORD . . . pp 2Ch 32:24–26 pp Isa 38:1–8   *See also* **2Ki** 1:2; **Jas** 5:14

Quarantine regulations Lev 12:1–4; 13:4,26,46; 14:8; **Nu** 5:2; 31:19; **2Ki** 15:5; **Lk** 17:12

Healing results in discipleship
Mk 10:52 "Go," said Jesus, "your faith has healed you." Immediately he received his sight and followed Jesus along the road.   *See also* **Jn** 6:2

Healing results in praise
Ac 3:8–9 He [the crippled beggar] jumped to his feet and began to walk. Then he went with them [Peter and John] into the temple courts, walking and jumping, and praising God . . .
See also **Mk** 2:12; **Jn** 9:30–33,38

Miraculous healing
By Jesus Christ
Mt 8:2–3 A man with leprosy came and knelt before him [Jesus] and said, "Lord, if you are willing, you can make me clean." Jesus reached out his hand and touched the man. "I am willing," he said. "Be clean!" Immediately he was cured of his leprosy.

Lk 4:18 "The Spirit of the Lord is on me, because he has anointed me to preach good news to the poor. He has sent me to proclaim freedom for the prisoners and recovery of sight for the blind, to release the oppressed."   *See also* **Mt** 9:27–30; 14:34–36 pp Mk 6:53–56; **Mt** 15:21–28 pp Mk 7:24–30; **Mk** 1:32–34 pp Lk 4:40; **Lk** 6:17–19; 8:48; 9:11; 17:19

Through the prophets 1Ki 17:17–24; **2Ki** 4:29–37; 5:10–14

Through the apostles Mt 10:1 pp Lk 9:1–2; **Ac** 3:6–8; 5:15–16; 9:34; 14:8–10; 19:11–12; 28:8–9

In the church
1Co 12:8–9 To one there is given . . . gifts of healing by that one Spirit,   *See also* **Mk** 16:17–18; **1Co** 12:28,30

Healing of fever
Mt 8:15 pp Mk 1:31 pp Lk 4:39; **Jn** 4:46–54

Healing of demon-possession
Mt 9:32–33; 12:22; **Mk** 5:1–20; 9:17–27 pp Lk 9:38–43; **Ac** 16:16–19; 19:11–12

Healing withheld
2Co 12:8–9; **2Ti** 4:20

Medical treatments to bring healing
Consulting doctors
2Ch 16:12 . . . Though his [Asa's] disease was severe, even in his illness he did not seek help from the LORD, but only from the physicians.

Mt 9:12 . . . Jesus said, "It is not the healthy who need a doctor, but the sick."   *See also* **Jer** 8:22; **Col** 4:14

Taking medicine 1Ti 5:23
Disinfecting the house Lev 14:41–42
Using splints Eze 30:21
Using bandages and oil
Isa 1:6 From the sole of your foot to the top of your head there is no soundness—only wounds and bruises and open sores, not cleansed or bandaged or soothed with oil.   *See also* **Lk** 10:34

The spiritual significance of healing
As an image of salvation Ps 41:4; 103:2–5; 147:3; **Jer** 3:22; 14:19; 17:14; **Eze** 47:12; **Hos** 6:1; **Mal** 4:2; **Mt** 8:17; **Isa** 53:4–5

Heaven is the place of ultimate healing
Rev 21:4 "He [God] will wipe every tear from their eyes. There will be no more death or mourning or crying or pain, for the old order of things has passed away."   *See also* **Ro** 8:18; **Rev** 22:2   *See also disease; medicine.*

herbs and spices
Plants whose leaves or seeds are used as food or flavourings and sometimes for medicine. The rich variety of such plants in the Near East results in numerous references in Scripture.

Aloes
Jn 19:39–40 He [Joseph of Arimathea] was accompanied by Nicodemus, the man who earlier had visited Jesus at night. Nicodemus brought a

mixture of myrrh and aloes, about seventy-five pounds. Taking Jesus' body, the two of them wrapped it, with the spices, in strips of linen. This was in accordance with Jewish burial customs.
See also **Nu** 24:5–6; **Ps** 45:6–8; **Pr** 7:17–18; **SS** 4:12–14

Balm
Ge 43:11 . . . their father Israel said to them [Joseph's brothers], "If it must be, then do this: Put some of the best products of the land in your bags and take them down to the man as a gift—a little balm and a little honey, some spices and myrrh, some pistachio nuts and almonds."
See also **Ge** 37:25; **Jer** 8:22

Bitter herbs
Ex 12:5–8 ". . . they [the Israelites] are to eat the meat roasted over the fire, along with bitter herbs, and bread made without yeast."
See also **Nu** 9:9–11; **La** 3:15

Caraway
Isa 28:27 Caraway is not threshed with a sledge, nor is a cartwheel rolled over cummin; caraway is beaten out with a rod, and cummin with a stick. *See also* **Isa** 28:25

Cassia
Ps 45:8 All your robes are fragrant with myrrh and aloes and cassia . . . *See also* **Ex** 30:22–25; **Eze** 27:19

Cinnamon
Rev 18:11–13 "The merchants of the earth will weep and mourn over her [Babylon the Great] because no-one buys their cargoes any more . . . cargoes of cinnamon and spice, of incense, myrrh and frankincense, of wine and olive oil, of fine flour and wheat; cattle and sheep; horses and carriages; and slaves—human beings!" *See also* **Ex** 30:22–25; **Pr** 7:17–18; **SS** 4:12–14

Coriander
Ex 16:31 The people of Israel called the bread manna. It was white like coriander seed and tasted like wafers made with honey. *See also* **Nu** 11:7

Cummin
Isa 28:25,27; **Mt** 23:23

Dill
Mt 23:23 "Woe to you, teachers of the law and Pharisees, you hypocrites! You give a tenth of your spices—mint, dill and cummin. But you have neglected the more important matters of the law—justice, mercy and faithfulness. You should have practised the latter, without neglecting the former."

Henna
SS 1:14 My lover is to me a cluster of henna blossoms from the vineyards of En Gedi.
See also **SS** 4:13

Mint
Mt 23:23 pp Lk 11:42

Myrrh
Est 2:12 Before a young woman's turn came to go in to King Xerxes, she had to complete twelve months of beauty treatments prescribed for the women, six months with oil of myrrh and six with perfumes and cosmetics. *See also* **SS** 1:13; **Mt** 2:11; **Jn** 19:38–39

Rue
Lk 11:42 "Woe to you Pharisees, because you give God a tenth of your mint, rue and all other kinds of garden herbs, but you neglect justice and the love of God. You should have practised the latter without leaving the former undone."

Saffron
SS 4:13–14 Your [the lover's] plants are an orchard of pomegranates with choice fruits, with henna and nard, nard and saffron, calamus and cinnamon, with every kind of incense tree, with myrrh and aloes and all the finest spices.

Salt herbs
Job 30:1–5 ". . . In the brush they gathered

salt herbs, and their food was the root of the broom tree . . ."

Other spices
Given as gifts or as tribute
1Ki 10:10 . . . she gave the king 120 talents of gold, large quantities of spices, and precious stones. Never again were so many spices brought in as those the queen of Sheba gave to King Solomon. pp 2Ch 9:9   *See also* **1Ki** 10:1–2 pp 2Ch 9:1; **1Ki** 10:25 pp 2Ch 9:24

Traded between countries
Ge 37:25 As they [Joseph's brothers] sat down to eat their meal, they looked up and saw a caravan of Ishmaelites coming from Gilead. Their camels were loaded with spices, balm and myrrh, and they were on their way to take them down to Egypt.   *See also* **Eze** 27:22; **Rev** 18:11–13

Used in burial customs
2Ch 16:14 They [the people] buried him [Asa] in the tomb that he had cut out for himself in the City of David. They laid him on a bier covered with spices and various blended perfumes, and they made a huge fire in his honour.   *See also* **Mk** 16:1 pp Lk 23:56—24:1; **Jn** 19:40

Used for perfume or flavouring
Ex 30:34–35 Then the Lord said to Moses, "Take fragrant spices—gum resin, onycha and galbanum—and pure frankincense, all in equal amounts, and make a fragrant blend of incense, the work of a perfumer . . ."   *See also* **Ps** 75:8; **SS** 4:10; **Eze** 24:10

Stores of spices
2Ch 32:27 Hezekiah had very great riches and honour, and he made treasuries for his silver and gold and for his precious stones, spices, shields and all kinds of valuables.   *See also* **2Ki** 20:13 pp Isa 39:2; **1Ch** 9:29–30   *See also burial; Passover; plants; trade.*

---

horticulture
The art of garden cultivation, first practised in the Garden of Eden.

Horticulture in the Garden of Eden
The man and woman tended the garden
Ge 2:15–23 The Lord God took the man and put him in the Garden of Eden to work it and take care of it . . .

The fall brought about a change in human priorities from horticulture to agriculture
Ge 3:17–19 To Adam he [the Lord God] said, "Because you listened to your wife and ate from the tree about which I commanded you, 'You must not eat of it,' Cursed is the ground because of you; through painful toil you will eat of it all the days of your life. It will produce thorns and thistles for you, and you will eat the plants of the field. By the sweat of your brow you will eat your food until you return to the ground, since from it you were taken; for dust you are and to dust you will return."   *See also* **Ge** 4:2

Egyptian agriculture is likened to horticulture
Dt 11:10–11 The land you are entering to take over is not like the land of Egypt, from which you have come, where you planted your seed and irrigated it by foot as in a vegetable garden . . .

Horticulture is totally dependent on good irrigation
Isa 58:11 "The Lord will guide you [Israel] always; he will satisfy your needs in a sun-scorched land and will strengthen your frame. You will be like a well-watered garden, like a spring whose waters never fail."   *See also* **Ge** 2:4–14; 13:10; **Nu** 24:5–7; **Job** 8:16; **SS** 4:12,15; **Isa** 51:3; **Jer** 31:12

Those who practised horticulture
Kings
Ecc 2:5–6 I [the Teacher] made gardens and parks and planted all kinds of fruit trees in them . . .   *See also* **1Ki** 21:2; **2Ki** 21:18,26; 25:4 pp Jer 39:4 pp Jer 52:7; **Ne** 3:15; **Est** 1:5–6; 7:7–8; **SS** 8:13

Common people
Jer 29:28 " 'He [Jeremiah] has sent this message to us [the exiles] in Babylon: It will be a long time. Therefore build houses and settle down; plant gardens and eat what they

produce.'"   *See also* **Jer** 29:1–7; **Jn** 19:41

Gardeners

Jn 20:15 "Woman," he [Jesus] said, "why are you crying? Who is it you are looking for?" Thinking he was the gardener, she [Mary] said, "Sir, if you have carried him away, tell me where you have put him, and I will get him."   *See also* **Isa** 5:7; **Jn** 15:1

Kinds of horticulture
Vegetable gardens
1Ki 21:2 Ahab said to Naboth, "Let me have your vineyard to use for a vegetable garden, since it is close to my palace. In exchange I will give you a better vineyard or, if you prefer, I will pay you whatever it is worth."

Fruit gardens
Am 9:14 "I [the Lord] will bring back my exiled people Israel; they will rebuild the ruined cities and live in them. They will plant vineyards and drink their wine; they will make gardens and eat their fruit."   *See also* **Ge** 2:16–17; 3:1–3

Herb gardens
Lk 11:42 "Woe to you Pharisees, because you give God a tenth of your mint, rue and all other kinds of garden herbs, but you neglect justice and the love of God . . ."   *See also* **SS** 6:2; **Mt** 13:31–32 pp Mk 4:31–32 pp Lk 13:19

Horticultural diseases and pestilence
Am 4:9 "Many times I struck your gardens and vineyards, I struck them with blight and mildew. Locusts devoured your fig and olive trees, yet you have not returned to me," declares the Lord. *See also agriculture; fruit; herbs and spices; vineyard.*

---

hospitality, examples
Scripture provides many examples of friendship and generosity towards strangers, and encourages believers to be hospitable in turn.

Examples of hospitality in the OT
Ge 18:2–5 Abraham looked up and saw three men standing nearby. When he saw them, he hurried from the entrance of his tent to meet them and bowed low to the ground. He said, "If

I have found favour in your eyes, my lord, do not pass your servant by. Let a little water be brought, and then you may all wash your feet and rest under this tree. Let me get you something to eat, so you can be refreshed and then go on your way—now that you have come to your servant." . . .   *See also* **Ge** 19:1–3; 24:22–25; **Ex** 2:20; **Jdg** 13:15

Shelter is given to a Levite: **Jdg** 19:1–4,20–21

2Sa 17:27–29; **1Ki** 17:7–16; **2Ki** 4:8–10; **Ne** 5:17

Hospitality shown to Jesus Christ
Mt 9:10 While Jesus was having dinner at Matthew's house, many tax collectors and "sinners" came and ate with him and his disciples. pp Mk 2:15 pp Lk 5:29   *See also* **Mt** 8:14–15 pp Mk 1:29–31 pp Lk 4:38–39

Jesus Christ anointed at Bethany: **Mt** 26:6–7 pp Mk 14:3; **Jn** 12:1–3

Lk 7:36; 10:38; 14:1; 19:5–7; 24:29; **Jn** 2:2

Hospitality assisted the mission of the apostles
Hospitality shown to the disciples
Mt 10:11–12 "Whatever town or village you enter, search for some worthy person there and stay at that house until you leave. As you enter the home, give it your greeting." pp Mk 6:10 pp Lk 9:4   *See also* **Lk** 10:5–7

Hospitality shown to Peter Ac 10:32,48

Hospitality shown to Paul and his companions **Ac** 16:15,34; 18:2–3; 21:8,16; 28:2,7; **Ro** 16:23; **Phm** 22

Christians opened their homes for gatherings of believers
1Co 16:19 . . . Aquila and Priscilla greet you warmly in the Lord, and so does the church that meets at their house.   *See also* **Ac** 2:46; **Ro** 16:3–5; **Col** 4:15; **Phm** 2

Examples of inhospitable behaviour
1Sa 25:10–11 Nabal answered David's servants, "Who is this David? Who is this son of Jesse? . . . Why should I take my bread and water, and the meat I have slaughtered for my

shearers, and give it to people coming from who knows where?'' *See also* **Nu** 20:18; 21:21–23; **Dt** 23:3–4; **Jdg** 19:15; **Lk** 9:52–53 *See also eating; meals.*

---

house

The place where someone lives. Its extended use includes a household and dynasty and its figurative use includes the house of God and heaven.

The construction of houses
Foundations 1Ki 5:17; **Ezr** 6:3–4; **Jer** 51:26; **Eze** 41:8

Building materials Ge 11:3–4; **Ex** 1:11–14; **Lev** 14:40–45; **1Ki** 5:18; 7:9–12; **SS** 1:17; **Isa** 9:10

Rooms and decoration Ge 43:30; **Jdg** 3:20,23–25; **1Ki** 7:6; 17:19; 22:25; **2Ki** 1:2; 4:10; **Ne** 8:16; **Jer** 22:14; **Eze** 8:10; **Da** 5:5; **Am** 3:15; **Ac** 20:8–9

Roofs Jos 2:6; **1Sa** 9:25–26; **Mk** 2:4 pp Lk 5:19

Regulations regarding houses
Lev 14:33–53; 25:29–34; 27:14–15; **Dt** 22:8

Various uses for houses
House arrest
Jer 37:15 They were angry with Jeremiah and had him beaten and imprisoned in the house of Jonathan the secretary, which they had made into a prison. *See also* **Ge** 40:2–3; **2Sa** 20:3; **Ac** 28:16,30–31

Church gatherings
Col 4:15 Give my [Paul's] greetings to the brothers and sisters at Laodicea, and to Nympha and the church in her house. *See also* **Ac** 1:13–14; 2:1–2; 5:42; 12:12; **Ro** 16:5; **1Co** 16:19; **Phm** 1–2

Parables and proverbs about houses
Pr 21:20 In the house of the wise are stores of choice food and oil, but fools devour all they have. *See also* **Pr** 9:1–4,13–18; 14:1; 17:13; 21:9; 24:27; 25:17; **Ecc** 10:18; **SS** 8:7; **Mt** 12:29 pp Mk 3:27 pp Lk 11:21–22; **Mt** 12:43–45 pp Lk 11:24–26; **Mt** 13:52; 24:42–51 pp Lk 12:39–46

The house of God
God's heavenly dwelling
Isa 66:1–2 This is what the LORD says: ''Heaven is my throne, and the earth is my footstool. Where is the house you will build for me? Where will my resting place be? Has not my hand made all these things, and so they came into being?'' declares the LORD. ''These are the ones I esteem: those who are humble and contrite in spirit, and tremble at my word.'' *See also* **1Ki** 8:30 pp 2Ch 6:21; **1Ki** 8:39 pp 2Ch 6:30; **1Ki** 8:43 pp 2Ch 6:33; **1Ki** 8:49–50 pp 2Ch 6:39; **Isa** 57:15; **Jn** 14:2

The earthly tabernacle and temple
Ex 25:8 ''Then have them make a sanctuary for me [the LORD], and I will dwell among them.'' *See also* **Ex** 15:17; 29:44–46; **Dt** 12:5,11; **2Sa** 7:1–7 pp 1Ch 17:1–6; **Ezr** 5:13–16; **Ps** 23:6; 26:8; 27:4; 84:1–4,10; **Hag** 1:2–3,8–9,14

The household
Household affairs
2Sa 17:23 When Ahithophel saw that his advice had not been followed, he saddled his donkey and set out for his house in his home town. He put his house in order and then hanged himself. So he died and was buried in his father's tomb. *See also* **2Ki** 20:1 pp Isa 38:1; **Pr** 31:21,27; **1Ti** 3:4–5,12

Examples of how God relates to households
Ge 17:12–14,23–27; **Lev** 16:6,11,17; **Nu** 16:31–33; **Jn** 4:53; **Ac** 16:15,31–34; **1Co** 16:15

The church as God's household
Eph 2:19–22 Consequently, you are no longer foreigners and aliens, but fellow-citizens with God's people and members of God's household . . . *See also* **Nu** 12:7; **1Ti** 3:14–15; **Heb** 3:1–6; **1Pe** 2:4–5

House in the sense of a dynasty
2Sa 7:16 '' 'Your [David's] house and your kingdom shall endure for ever before me [the LORD]; your throne shall be established for ever.' '' pp **1Ch** 17:14 *See also* **Ex** 40:38; **Jos** 21:43–45
The house of Eli: **1Sa** 2:27–36; 3:11–14
The house of Saul: **2Sa** 3:1; 9:1

2Sa 3:28–29

The house of David: **2Sa** 7:25–29 pp 1Ch 17:23–27; **1Ki** 2:31–33

1Ki 21:21–22,28–29; **Zec** 12:10–14   *See also building; property, houses; tabernacle, in Old Testament; temple, Solomon's.*

husband

The male partner in a marriage relationship. The origin of this God-ordained institution is traced back in the Bible to the Garden of Eden. Scripture stresses that marriage is a God-ordained institution, within which the husband is pledged to love and care for his wife. Scripture contains many examples, both good and bad, of how husbands behaved. The ultimate examples of a good husband in Scripture are God as the husband of Israel and Jesus Christ as the bridegroom of the church.

God's pattern for marriage
Husband and wife are one flesh
Ge 1:27 So God created human beings in his own image, in the image of God he created them; male and female he created them.
See also **Ge** 2:23–24; **Mal** 2:15; **Mt** 19:4–6 pp Mk 10:6–9
The husband is head of the wife
Eph 5:23 For the husband is the head of the wife as Christ is the head of the church, his body, of which he is the Saviour.   *See also* **1Co** 11:3

Duties of a husband
To leave his parents and be united to his wife
Mt 19:5 ". . . 'For this reason a man will leave his father and mother and be united to his wife, and the two will become one flesh'?" pp Mk 10:7–8   *See also* **Ge** 2:24
To love his wife
Eph 5:25 Husbands, love your wives, just as Christ loved the church and gave himself up for her   *See also* **Dt** 24:5; **Pr** 5:18; **Ecc** 9:9; **Eph** 5:28–33; **Col** 3:19; **1Pe** 3:7
To fulfil his marital duty
1Co 7:3–5 The husband should fulfil his marital duty to his wife . . . Do not deprive each other except by mutual consent and for a time, so that you may devote yourselves to prayer. Then come together again so that Satan will not tempt you because of your lack of self-control.   *See also* **Ex** 21:10–11
To be faithful to his wife
Ex 20:14 "You shall not commit adultery." pp Dt 5:18   *See also* **Lev** 20:10; **Dt** 22:22; **Mal** 2:14; **Mt** 5:27–28; **1Co** 7:14–16

Adam, the first husband
Ge 2:20–24 . . . The man said, "This is now bone of my bones and flesh of my flesh; she shall be called 'woman', for she was taken out of man." . . .

Behaviour which is commended in husbands
1Sa 1:3–8 . . . to Hannah he [Elkanah] gave a double portion because he loved her, and the Lord had closed her womb . . . Elkanah her husband would say to her, "Hannah, why are you weeping? Why don't you eat? Why are you downhearted? Don't I mean more to you than ten sons?"   *See also* **Ge** 24:67; 29:20; **Ru** 3:7—4:11; **Est** 5:1–3; **Hos** 3:1–3; **Mt** 1:18–25

Behaviour which is condemned in husbands
2Sa 12:7–10 . . .". . .'. . . I [the Lord] gave your master's house to you [David], and your master's wives into your arms. I gave you the house of Israel and Judah. And if all this had been too little, I would have given you even more . . . Now, therefore, the sword shall never depart from your house, because you despised me and took the wife of Uriah the Hittite to be your own.'"   *See also* **Ge** 29:30–31; 38:8–10; **Jdg** 19:16–29; **Mal** 2:13–16

God as a husband
Isa 54:5 "For your Maker is your husband— the Lord Almighty is his name—the Holy One of Israel is your Redeemer; he is called the God of all the earth."   *See also* **Jer** 3:14; 31:32; **Eze** 16:8

Jesus Christ as a bridegroom

Eph 5:25–27 Husbands, love your wives, just as Christ loved the church and gave himself up for her to make her holy, cleansing her by the washing with water through the word, and to present her to himself as a radiant church, without stain or wrinkle or any other blemish, but holy and blameless. *See also* **Mt** 9:14–15 pp Mk 2:18–20 pp Lk 5:33–35; **2Co** 11:2; **Rev** 21:2 *See also bridegroom; divorce; marriage; wife.*

idolatry

The worship or adoration of anyone or anything other than the LORD God. Idolatry includes the worship of other gods, such as those of the nations surrounding Israel, images or idols and the creation itself.

idolatry, in New Testament

The NT world included many religions which promoted the worship of idols. Idolatry was thus of continuing importance to NT writers, especially Paul.

Idolatry in the Gentile world

Ac 17:16 While Paul was waiting for them [Silas and Timothy] in Athens, he was greatly distressed to see that the city was full of idols. *See also* **Ac** 14:11–13; 17:22–23; 19:24; **1Co** 8:5; **Gal** 4:8

Criticism of idolatry

Idolatry leads to other sinful behaviour
Ro 1:24 Therefore God gave them over in the sinful desires of their hearts to sexual impurity for the degrading of their bodies with one another.
Idolatry is an offence against the doctrine of creation
Ro 1:20 For since the creation of the world God's invisible qualities—his eternal power and divine nature—have been clearly seen, being understood from what has been made, so that they are without excuse. *See also* **Ac** 17:24–29
Idols are futile and degrading
Ro 1:22–23 Although they claimed to be wise, they became fools and exchanged the glory of the

immortal God for images made to look like mortal human beings and birds and animals and reptiles. *See also* **1Co** 8:4; 10:19; 12:2
Idolatrous worship of human beings
Ac 12:22 They [the people of Tyre and Sidon to Herod] shouted, "This is the voice of a god, not of a mere mortal." *See also* **Lk** 20:24–25; **Ac** 28:6
Demonic powers are involved with idolatry
1Co 10:20 No, but the sacrifices of pagans are offered to demons, not to God, and I do not want you to be participants with demons. *See also* **Rev** 9:20; 13:4
Food sacrificed to idols
Ac 15:20 "Instead we [apostles and elders] should write to them [Gentiles], telling them to abstain from food polluted by idols, from sexual immorality, from the meat of strangled animals and from blood." *See also* **Ro** 14:2–3,6; **1Co** 8:4–13; 10:14–31
Encounters with idolatrous practice
Ac 19:28 When they [the silversmiths and other skilled workers] heard this, they were furious and began shouting: "Great is Artemis of the Ephesians!" *See also* **Ac** 14:11–18; 17:18–31

Spiritual idolatry

1Jn 5:21 Dear children, keep yourselves from idols.

The temptations of Jesus Christ present three main kinds of spiritual idolatry

Possessions
Mt 4:3 . . ."If you are the Son of God, tell these stones to become bread." pp Lk 4:3
See also **Mt** 6:24 pp Lk 16:13; **Lk** 18:23; **Php** 3:19; **Col** 3:5; **1Ti** 6:10
Prestige and self-esteem
Mt 4:6 "If you are the Son of God," he said, "throw yourself down . . ." pp Lk 4:9 *See also* **Lk** 3:8; 10:29; 18:11–12,21; **Ro** 2:19
Power
Mt 4:8–9 Again, the devil took him to a very high mountain and showed him all the kingdoms of the world and their splendour. "All this I will give you," he said, "if you will bow down and worship me." pp Lk 4:6–7 *See also*

Lk 9:54–55; 23:39; **Jn** 18:10–11; 19:10; **Php** 2:6;
Jas 4:6,10

idolatry, in Old Testament

Scripture provides illustrations of idolatry from
various periods in the history of the people of
God. Idolatry is seen as a constant temptation for
believers, especially in times of national or
personal stress.

Idolatry among the Gentiles
Jdg 11:24; 16:23–24; **2Ki** 5:18; **Isa**
36:18–20; 37:38; 46:1; **Eze** 8:14; **Ac**
14:11–13; **1Co** 8:5

Idolatry among God's people
In patriarchal times
Jos 24:2 . . . " . . . '. . . your ancestors,
including Terah the father of Abraham and Nahor,
lived beyond the River and worshipped other
gods.'" *See also* **Ge** 31:30,34; 35:2
In the Mosaic period
Ex 32:4 He [Aaron] took what they [the people
of Israel] handed him and made it into an idol
cast in the shape of a calf, fashioning it with a
tool. Then they said, "These are your gods, O
Israel, who brought you up out of Egypt."
In the period of the judges
Jdg 17:5 Now this man Micah had a shrine,
and he made an ephod and some idols and
installed one of his sons as his priest. *See also*
Jdg 10:6
In the early monarchy
1Ki 11:10 Although he had forbidden Solomon
to follow other gods, Solomon did not keep the
LORD's command. *See also* **1Ki** 12:28
In the middle monarchy
1Ki 16:33 Ahab also made an Asherah pole
and did more to provoke the LORD, the God of
Israel, to anger than did all the kings of Israel
before him. *See also* **1Ki** 11:7–8; 16:32
In the late monarchy
2Ki 21:2–6 . . . He [Manasseh] rebuilt the
high places his father Hezekiah had destroyed; he
also erected altars to Baal and made an Asherah
pole, as Ahab king of Israel had done. He bowed
down to all the starry hosts and worshipped

them . . . In both courts of the temple of the
LORD, he built altars to all the starry hosts. He
sacrificed his own son in the fire, practised sorcery
and divination, and consulted mediums and
spiritists . . .
After the fall of Jerusalem
Eze 8:10 So I [Ezekiel] went in and looked,
and I saw portrayed all over the walls all kinds of
crawling things and detestable animals and all the
idols of the house of Israel. *See also* **Eze**
8:3,14,16

Objects of false worship
The sun, moon and stars
Dt 4:19 And when you look up to the sky and
see the sun, the moon and the stars—all the
heavenly array—do not be enticed into bowing
down to them and worshipping things the LORD
your God has apportioned to all the nations under
heaven. *See also* **Dt** 17:3; **Job** 31:26
Other objects of worship
Dt 4:28 There you [people of Israel] will
worship gods of wood and stone made by human
hands, which cannot see or hear or eat or
smell. *See also* **Dt** 16:22; **1Ki** 12:31; **Isa** 1:29

Practices associated with idolatry
The burning of children
2Ki 23:10 He [Josiah] desecrated Topheth,
which was in the Valley of Ben Hinnom, so no-
one could use it to sacrifice son or daughter in
the fire to Molech.
The superstitious use of religious symbols
2Ki 18:4 . . . He [Hezekiah] broke into pieces
the bronze snake Moses had made, for up to that
time the Israelites had been burning incense to
it . . . *See also* **Jdg** 8:27
Sexual deviance
Dt 23:17 No Israelite man or woman is to
become a shrine-prostitute. *See also* **1Ki** 14:24;
Hos 4:14

idolatry, objections

Scripture presents idolatry as absurd and irrational,
offensive to God and a source of spiritual and
moral danger.

Idolatry is disparaged
The absurdity of making idols
Hab 2:18 "Of what value is an idol, since someone has carved it? Or an image that teaches lies? For those who make them trust in their own creations; they make idols that cannot speak." *See also* **Dt** 4:28; **Isa** 40:18–20; 41:6–7; **Jer** 10:3–9; **Hos** 10:6; **Hab** 2:19

Idols represent falsehood and fraud
Ps 40:4 Blessed are those who make the LORD their trust, who do not look to the proud, to those who turn aside to false gods.   *See also* **Jer** 2:5; 10:14; 16:19; 51:17–18; **Hos** 12:1; **Am** 2:4

Bowing down to idols is inappropriate
Ps 135:17–18 they [the idols of the nations] have ears, but cannot hear, nor is there breath in their mouths. Those who make them will be like them, and so will all who trust in them. pp Ps 115:5–8   *See also* **Isa** 2:8; 44:15–17; 46:6; **Jer** 1:16; **Mic** 5:13

Idols contrasted with the LORD
Isa 46:5 "To whom will you compare me or count me equal? To whom will you liken me that we may be compared?"   *See also* **Isa** 40:25–26; **Jer** 5:24; 10:10; **Hos** 2:8; **Ac** 17:24–25

Idolatry is forbidden by God
Ex 20:3–4 "You shall have no other gods before me. You shall not make for yourself an idol in the form of anything in heaven above or on the earth beneath or in the waters below." pp Dt 5:7–8

Idolatry incurs severe penalties
Zep 1:4 "I will stretch out my hand against Judah and against all who live in Jerusalem. I will cut off from this place every remnant of Baal, the names of the pagan and the idolatrous priests—"   *See also* **Dt** 13:1–9,12–15; **Isa** 66:4; **Am** 5:27; **Na** 1:14

God abominates idols
Eze 7:20 "They were proud of their beautiful jewellery and used it to make their detestable idols and vile images . . ."   *See also* **Dt** 7:25; **2Ki** 23:24; **Eze** 5:9,11; 6:4

Pressure to worship idols must be resisted and idols abandoned
Da 3:18 "But even if he [God] does not [rescue us], we [Shadrach, Meshach and Abednego] want you to know, O king, that we will not serve your gods or worship the image of gold you have set up."   *See also* **Isa** 2:20; 30:22; 31:7

The dangers of idolatry
Blindness
Isa 44:18 They [idol-worshippers] know nothing, they understand nothing; their eyes are plastered over so that they cannot see, and their minds closed so that they cannot understand.

Becoming like idols
Ps 115:8 Those who make them [idols] will be like them, and so will all who trust in them. *See also* **Jer** 2:5; **Hos** 9:10

Spiritual adultery
Dt 31:16 . . . ". . . these people will soon prostitute themselves to the foreign gods of the land they are entering. They will forsake me and break the covenant I made with them." *See also* **Jdg** 8:33; **Isa** 1:21; **Jer** 13:27; **Hos** 1:2; 2:7; 8:9

Injustice
Am 5:7 You who turn justice into bitterness and cast righteousness to the ground

invasions
A hostile incursion into the territory of another tribe or nation, often with the object of its permanent annexation.

The Israelites' invasion of Canaan
Their success had been preordained
Dt 7:22 The LORD your God will drive out those nations before you, little by little . . .
Lev 20:23–24 "'You must not live according to the customs of the nations I am going to drive out before you. Because they did all these things, I abhorred them. But I said to you, "You will possess their land; I will give it to you as an inheritance, a land flowing with milk and honey." I am the LORD your God, who has set you apart

from the nations.' "   *See also* **Ex** 12:25; **Lev** 14:34; 23:10; **Dt** 6:10–12; 7:17–24

Moses gave instructions on how to proceed Dt 7:1–5; 20:10–20

Joshua followed Moses in leading the invasion Jos 11:23 So Joshua took the entire land, just as the LORD had directed Moses, and he gave it as an inheritance to Israel according to their tribal divisions. Then the land had rest from war.
See also **Jos** 6:20; 8:18–19; 10:29–43

The invasion continued under other leaders Jdg 1:4; 4:23–24; 11:21–22,32–33; **2Ki** 3:24; **1Ch** 4:41–43

Invasion of the Israelites' land
By the Philistines Jdg 10:6–10; **1Ch** 14:9; **2Ch** 21:16–17

By other nations
Jdg 6:3–5 Whenever the Israelites planted their crops, the Midianites, Amalekites and other eastern peoples invaded the country. They camped on the land and ruined the crops all the way to Gaza and did not spare a living thing for Israel, neither sheep nor cattle nor donkeys. They came up with their livestock and their tents like swarms of locusts. It was impossible to count them or their camels; they invaded the land to ravage it.
See also **Jdg** 2:14; **2Ki** 13:20; **2Ch** 20:1; 24:23

Israel taken into captivity by Assyrian invaders
2Ki 17:5–6 The king of Assyria invaded the entire land, marched against Samaria and laid siege to it for three years. In the ninth year of Hoshea, the king of Assyria captured Samaria and deported the Israelites to Assyria. He settled them in Halah, in Gozan on the Habor River and in the towns of the Medes. pp 2Ki 18:9–11

Judah taken into captivity by Babylonian invaders
2Ki 25:1 So in the ninth year of Zedekiah's reign, on the tenth day of the tenth month, Nebuchadnezzar king of Babylon marched against Jerusalem with his whole army. He encamped outside the city and built siege works all around it. pp Jer 39:1

2Ki 25:10–11 The whole Babylonian army, under the commander of the imperial guard, broke down the walls around Jerusalem. Nebuzaradan the commander of the guard carried into exile the people who remained in the city, along with the rest of the populace and those who had gone over to the king of Babylon. pp Jer 39:8–9 pp Jer 52:4

Invasion of the promised land was a cause of great sadness
Ps 79:1 O God, the nations have invaded your inheritance; they have defiled your holy temple, they have reduced Jerusalem to rubble.   *See also* **Ne** 1:1–4; **La** 1:1–3; **Da** 9:4–6

Examples of non-human invasion
By locusts
Ex 10:14 they [the locusts] invaded all Egypt and settled down in every area of the country in great numbers. Never before had there been such a plague of locusts, nor will there ever be again.

By evil spiritual forces
Mt 12:43–45 "When an evil spirit comes out of anyone, it goes through arid places seeking rest and does not find it. Then it says, 'I will return to the house I left.' When it arrives, it finds the house unoccupied, swept clean and put in order. Then it goes and takes with it seven other spirits more wicked than itself, and they go in and live there. And the final condition of that person is worse than the first . . ." pp Lk 11:24–26

Lk 22:3 Then Satan entered Judas, called Iscariot, one of the Twelve.   *See also* **Mk** 9:17–18 pp Mt 17:14–16 pp Lk 9:38–40; **Ro** 5:12–14; **Eph** 6:12   *See also* plague; warfare.

---

justice
A concern to act rightly, and to be seen by others to act rightly. Divine justice embraces every aspect of the right ordering of human society according to the will of God, its creator.

justice, human
God created the world in justice, and expects that his creatures will deal fairly and justly with one another as a result. Sin brings injustice into the world, by disrupting the justice established by God

at creation. As a result, human justice often falls short of God's standards.

God shows his concern for human justice
By commanding it
Isa 56:1 This is what the LORD says: "Maintain justice and do what is right . . ."
Mic 6:8 He has showed you, O people, what is good. And what does the LORD require of you? To act justly and to love mercy and to walk humbly with your God. *See also* **Ex** 23:1–9; **Dt** 24:17; **Ps** 82:3; **Pr** 21:3; **Hos** 12:6; **Ro** 13:7
By commending its maintenance
Ps 106:3 Blessed are those who maintain justice, who constantly do what is right. *See also* **Ge** 20:5–6; **1Ki** 3:11–12,28; **Job** 1:8; **Ps** 37:37; 112:5
By condemning its neglect
Mal 3:5 "So I will come near to you for judgment. I will be quick to testify against sorcerers, adulterers and perjurers, against those who defraud labourers of their wages, who oppress the widows and the fatherless, and deprive aliens of justice, but do not fear me," says the LORD Almighty. *See also* **Dt** 27:19; **Job** 31:13–14; **Isa** 3:14,15; 10:1; **Jer** 7:5–8,14; **Eze** 22:29–31

Justice in relationships within the family
Parents and children
Ex 20:12 "Honour your father and your mother, so that you may live long in the land the LORD your God is giving you." pp **Dt** 5:16 *See also* **Mt** 15:4; **Eph** 6:1–3; **Col** 3:20–21; **1Ti** 3:4
Brothers and sisters Ge 4:9–10
Husband and wife Mal 2:14; **1Co** 7:4–5; **Col** 3:18–19

Justice in the community
Pr 29:7 The righteous care about justice for the poor, but the wicked have no such concern.
Jas 1:27 Religion that God our Father accepts as pure and faultless is this: to look after orphans and widows in their distress . . . *See also* **Job** 29:16; **Ps** 82:3; **Pr** 29:14; 31:8–9; **Isa** 1:17; **Jer** 22:16

Justice in the business world
Col 4:1 Masters, provide your slaves with what is right and fair, because you know that you also have a Master in heaven. *See also* **Lev** 19:35–36; **Dt** 25:15; **Eph** 6:9; **Jas** 5:1–4

Justice in courts of law
Ex 23:6–8 "Do not deny justice to your poor people in their lawsuits. Have nothing to do with a false charge and do not put an innocent or honest person to death, for I will not acquit the guilty. Do not accept a bribe, for a bribe blinds those who see and twists the words of the righteous." *See also* **Lev** 19:15; **Dt** 1:16; 16:18–20; 17:6; 25:1–3; 27:25; **2Ch** 19:5–7
Partiality condemned: **Pr** 12:17; 18:5; 24:23–25; 28:21

Pr 18:17; **Jn** 18:23; **Ac** 23:3

Justice in rulers and governments
Pr 8:15 "By me [Wisdom] kings reign and rulers make laws that are just; *See also* **1Ki** 10:9; **1Ch** 18:14; **Pr** 16:12–13; 29:26–27; 31:8–9; **Jer** 22:13–16; **Eze** 45:9; **Ro** 13:1–4; **1Pe** 2:13–14,17

Justice in the community of faith
Am 5:21–24 "I [God] hate, I despise your [Israel's] religious feasts; I cannot stand your assemblies . . . But let justice roll on like a river, righteousness like a never-failing stream!"
Lk 11:42 "Woe to you Pharisees, because you give God a tenth of your mint, rue and all other kinds of garden herbs, but you neglect justice and the love of God . . ." *See also* **Isa** 58:6–7; **Hos** 6:6; 12:6; **Mt** 23:23; **1Co** 6:1–8; **Jas** 2:1–4,12–13

Justice in a believer's life
Mic 6:8 He has showed you, O people, what is good. And what does the LORD require of you? To act justly and to love mercy and to walk humbly with your God. *See also* **Pr** 21:3; **Php** 4:8; **Tit** 2:12; **1Pe** 3:16 *See also* law; poverty; servants; widows.

justice, of God

The moral righteousness of God is revealed in his laws and expressed in his judicial acts. God's commands and judgments meet perfect standards of justice, and his apportioning of punishments and rewards is also perfectly just. God's justice is impartial. Special praise is his for vindicating the penitent and the needy who have no human champions. Ultimately, all God's ways will be seen as just and equitable.

God's justice declared
God the Father

Ps 92:15 . . . "The LORD is upright; he is my Rock, and there is no wickedness in him."

1Pe 1:17 Since you call on a Father who judges each person's work impartially, live your lives as strangers here in reverent fear.   *See also* **Ge** 18:25; **Job** 36:3; **Ps** 11:7; 25:8; 33:5; 51:4; **Isa** 61:8; **Jer** 9:24; **Zep** 3:5; **Rev** 15:3

God the Son

1Jn 2:1 My [John's] dear children, I write this to you so that you will not sin. But if anybody does sin, we have one who speaks to the Father in our defence—Jesus Christ, the Righteous One.   *See also* **Ps** 45:6; **Heb** 1:8–9; **Ps** 72:1–4
The righteousness of the coming Messiah: **Isa** 9:7; 11:3–5; 42:1,3; **Mal** 3:1–3
Ac 3:14; **1Co** 1:30; **Rev** 19:11

God the Spirit

Jn 16:8–11 "When he [the Counsellor] comes, he will convict the world of guilt in regard to sin and righteousness and judgment . . ."   *See also* **Ac** 5:3,9; **Eph** 4:1,28,30

God's justice described
As impartial

1Pe 1:17 . . . a Father who judges each person's work impartially . . .   *See also* **Dt** 10:17; **2Ch** 19:7; **Job** 34:19; **Da** 5:27; **Ac** 10:34; **Ro** 2:5,11; **Gal** 2:6; **Eph** 6:9; **Col** 3:25

As inescapable

Ro 2:3 So when you, a mere human being, pass judgment on them and yet do the same things, do you think you will escape God's judgment?   *See also* **Ps** 68:21–23; **Jer** 11:11; 16:16–18; 51:53; **La** 2:22; **Am** 9:1–4; **Ob** 4; **Heb** 2:2–3

As infallible

Heb 4:13 Nothing in all creation is hidden from God's sight. Everything is uncovered and laid bare before the eyes of him to whom we must give account.   *See also* **1Sa** 2:3; **1Ch** 28:9; **Pr** 16:2; 21:2; 24:12; **Lk** 16:15; **Ro** 2:2,16

God's justice desired
By the oppressed

Ps 9:19 Arise, O LORD, let not mortals triumph; let the nations be judged in your presence.
See also **Jdg** 3:9; **Ps** 7:6; 10:12–14

By those who are misrepresented

Ps 26:1 Vindicate me [David] O LORD, for I have led a blameless life . . .   *See also* **1Sa** 24:15; **Ps** 35:23–24

God's justice doubted

Mal 2:17 You [Judah] have wearied the LORD with your words. "How have we wearied him?" you ask. By saying, "All who do evil are good in the eyes of the LORD, and he is pleased with them" or "Where is the God of justice?"
See also **Job** 6:29; 27:2; 34:5; **Ps** 73:2–14; **Ecc** 8:11,14; **Isa** 40:27; **Ro** 9:14,19–20

God's justice demonstrated
In his demands for social justice

Mic 6:8 He has showed you, O people, what is good. And what does the LORD require of you? To act justly and to love mercy and to walk humbly with your God.   *See also* **Dt** 16:18,20; **Isa** 1:16–17; **Am** 5:21–24; **Mal** 3:5; **Mt** 23:23; **Lk** 20:46–47

In his defence of the oppressed

Ps 103:6 The LORD works righteousness and justice for all the oppressed.   *See also* **Ps** 72:2; 140:12; **Pr** 22:22–23; **Isa** 11:4; **Eze** 34:16; **Lk** 18:7–8

In his vindication of the righteous

Ro 8:33 Who will bring any charge against those whom God has chosen? It is God who justifies.   *See also* **Ps** 17:1–2; 24:5; **Isa** 50:8–9; 54:17; 61:8

In the cross
Ro 3:25–26 God presented him [Jesus] as a sacrifice of atonement . . . to demonstrate his justice at the present time, so as to be just and the one who justifies those who have faith in Jesus. *See also* **2Co** 5:21; **Gal** 3:13

In the resurrection
Ac 17:31 "For he has set a day when he will judge the world with justice by the man he has appointed. He has given proof of this to everyone by raising him from the dead."

On the day of judgment
Ro 2:5 . . . for the day of God's wrath, when his righteous judgment will be revealed. *See also* **Ps** 9:8; **Ac** 17:31; **Rev** 16:5,7; 19:2 *See also atonement.*

---

king

The ruler or monarch of a country or realm. God is king of all the earth and human kings are called to rule in accordance with his will. The failure of kings in Israel and Judah after David led to the expectation of a coming king like David. This was fulfilled in Jesus Christ: the true King of Israel and all the world.

God is king of his people and of all the earth
Ps 47:8 God reigns over the nations; God is seated on his holy throne.

1Ti 6:15–16 . . . God, the blessed and only Ruler, the King of kings and Lord of lords, who alone is immortal and who lives in unapproachable light, whom no-one has seen or can see. To him be honour and might for ever. Amen. *See also* **Ex** 15:18; **1Sa** 12:12; **2Ch** 20:6; **Ps** 24:10; 47:2,6–7; 93:1; 96:10; 97:1; 99:1; **Isa** 6:5; 44:6; **1Ti** 1:17; **Rev** 15:3; 19:6

Significant kings
Melchizedek, king of Salem Ge 14:18; **Heb** 5:6,10; 6:20—7:17; **Ps** 110:4

The Pharaohs, the kings of Egypt Ge 12:14–20; 41:39–40; **Ex** 12:30–32; 14:4; **1Ki** 3:1; **2Ki** 23:29,33–34; **Eze** 32:1–10; **Ro** 9:17

Saul
Israel's demand for a king is seen as a rejection of God's rule: **1Sa** 8:4–9,19–22; 10:17–19; 12:12–15
The king is seen as a gracious gift from God: **1Sa** 9:1–2; 10:1,24; 11:14–15; 13:1,11–14; 15:17,26
Saul's death: **1Sa** 31:1–4 pp 1Ch 10:1–4; **1Ch** 10:13–14

David
1Ch 29:26–28 David son of Jesse was king over all Israel. He ruled over Israel for forty years—seven in Hebron and thirty-three in Jerusalem . . . pp 1Ki 2:10–12 *See also* **1Sa** 16:13; **2Sa** 5:3–5 pp 1Ch 11:3; **2Sa** 8:1–14 pp 1Ch 18:1–13; **1Ki** 11:38; **Ps** 18:50; 78:70–72
God's covenant with David: **2Sa** 7:8–16 pp 1Ch 17:7–14; **1Ki** 9:4–5; **2Ch** 7:17–18; **Ps** 132:11–12
Solomon **2Sa** 12:24–25; **1Ki** 2:12 pp 2Ch 1:1; **1Ki** 4:29–34; 6:1 pp 2Ch 3:1; **1Ki** 10:23–25 pp 2Ch 9:22–24; **1Ki** 11:1,4,42–43 pp 2Ch 9:30–31

Nebuchadnezzar, king of Babylon 2Ki 24:1 pp 2Ch 36:6–7
Nebuchadnezzar laid siege to Jerusalem in 588 B.C.: **2Ki** 25:1 pp 2Ch 36:17 pp Jer 39:1 pp Jer 52:4; **Da** 1:1
Jer 21:7; 27:6,8; **Eze** 29:18–19; **Da** 2:1,46–47; 3:1,28–29; 4:28–37

Cyrus, king of Persia 2Ch 36:22–23 pp Ezr 1:1–4; **Ezr** 5:13–6:5; **Isa** 44:28—45:1,13; **Da** 6:28

The Herods, rulers in Palestine
Herod the Great: **Mt** 2:1–3,16
Herod Antipas: **Mt** 14:1–2 pp Mk 6:14–16 pp Lk 9:7–9; **Mk** 8:15; **Lk** 3:19–20; 13:31; 23:7–12; **Ac** 4:27
Herod Agrippa I: **Ac** 12:1–4,19–23

The kings of the united kingdom
Saul 1Sa 10:20–24; 11:12–15
David 1Sa 16:13; **2Sa** 2:1–4; 5:1–5; **1Ki** 2:11; **1Ch** 11:1—29:30
Solomon 1Ki 1:39; **2Ch** 1:1—9:31

The kings of Israel, the northern kingdom
Jeroboam I 1Ki 12:20,25—14:20
Nadab 1Ki 15:25–31
Baasha 1Ki 15:32—16:7
Elah 1Ki 16:8–14

Zimri 1Ki 16:15–20
Tibni 1Ki 16:21–22
Omri 1Ki 16:23–28
Ahab 1Ki 16:29—22:40
Ahaziah 1Ki 22:51–53; **2Ki** 1:1–18
Joram (Jehoram) 2Ki 3:1—8:15
Jehu 2Ki 9:3—10:36
Jehoahaz 2Ki 13:1–9
Jehoash (Joash) 2Ki 13:10–25; 14:8–16
Jeroboam II 2Ki 14:23–29
Zechariah 2Ki 15:8–12
Shallum 2Ki 15:13–15
Menahem 2Ki 15:16–22
Pekahiah 2Ki 15:23–26
Pekah 2Ki 15:27–31
Hoshea 2Ki 17:1–6

The kings and queen of Judah, the southern kingdom

Rehoboam 1Ki 12:1–24 pp 2Ch 10:1—11:4; **2Ch** 11:5—12:8; **1Ki** 14:21–31 pp 2Ch 12:9–16
Abijah 1Ki 15:1–8 pp 2Ch 13:1—14:1
Asa 1Ki 15:9–24 pp 2Ch 14:2—16:14
Jehoshaphat 1Ki 22:41–50 pp 2Ch 20:31—21:1; **2Ch** 17:1—21:3
Jehoram (Joram) 2Ki 8:16–24 pp 2Ch 21:4–20
Ahaziah 2Ki 8:25–29 pp 2Ch 22:1–6; **2Ki** 9:21–29 pp 2Ch 22:7–9
Queen Athaliah 2Ki 11:1–21 pp 2Ch 22:10—23:21
Joash (Jehoash) 2Ki 11:2—12:21 pp 2Ch 22:10—24:27
Amaziah 2Ki 14:1–22 pp 2Ch 25:1–28
Azariah (= Uzziah) 2Ki 14:21–22; 15:1–7 pp 2Ch 26:1–23
Jotham 2Ki 15:32–38 pp 2Ch 27:1–9
Ahaz 2Ki 16:1–20 pp 2Ch 28:1–27
Hezekiah 2Ki 18:1—20:21 pp 2Ch 29:1—32:33 pp Isa 36:1—39:8
Manasseh 2Ki 21:1–18 pp 2Ch 33:1–20
Amon 2Ki 21:19–26 pp 2Ch 33:21–25
Josiah 2Ki 22:1—23:30 pp 2Ch 34:1—35:27
Jehoahaz 2Ki 23:31–34 pp 2Ch 36:2–4
Jehoiakim 2Ki 23:36—24:6 pp 2Ch 36:5–8
Jehoiachin 2Ki 24:8–17 pp 2Ch 36:9–10
Zedekiah (= Mattaniah) 2Ki 24:18—25:7 pp 2Ch 36:11–21 pp Jer 52:1–11

The expectation of a future king like David

Jer 23:5–6 "The days are coming," declares the LORD, "when I will raise up to David a righteous Branch, a King who will reign wisely and do what is just and right in the land . . ."
See also **Isa** 9:6–7; 11:1–5; 16:5; **Jer** 30:8–9; 33:15; **Eze** 34:23–24; 37:24–25; **Am** 9:11; **Mic** 5:2–5; **Hag** 2:20–23

The duties of the king
To fear God

2Sa 23:3–4 "The God of Israel spoke, the Rock of Israel said to me: 'When one rules over people in righteousness, when he rules in the fear of God, he is like the light of morning at sunrise on a cloudless morning, like the brightness after rain that brings the grass from the earth.'"

Pr 20:28 Love and faithfulness keep a king safe; through love his throne is made secure.
See also **Dt** 17:14–20; **1Sa** 10:25; **Ps** 2:10–11

To maintain righteousness and administer justice

Pr 29:4 By justice a king gives a country stability, but one who is greedy for bribes tears it down.

Pr 29:14 If a king judges the poor with fairness, his throne will always be secure.
See also **1Ki** 3:28; **Ps** 72:1–4; **Pr** 16:12–13; 20:8,26; 31:4–5,8–9; **Isa** 11:4; **Jer** 33:15; **Ro** 13:4

To read the law of God and ensure it was obeyed

Dt 17:18–20 When he [the king the LORD chooses] takes the throne of his kingdom, he is to write for himself on a scroll a copy of this law, taken from that of the priests, who are Levites. It is to be with him, and he is to read it all the days of his life so that he may learn to revere the LORD his God and follow carefully all the words of this law and these decrees and not consider himself better than his people and turn from the law to the right or to the left. Then he and his descendants will reign a long time over his kingdom in Israel.   *See also* **1Ki** 2:1–4; 9:4–5; **2Ki** 11:12

The coronation of the king
His anointing by the prophet of God 1Sa 10:1; 16:1–13
His proclamation as king before the people
2Ki 11:12 Jehoiada [the priest] brought out the king's son and put the crown on him; he presented him with a copy of the covenant and proclaimed him king. They anointed him, and the people clapped their hands and shouted, "Long live the king!" pp 2Ch 23:11   *See also* **1Sa** 10:17–25; 11:15; **2Sa** 2:4; 5:1–3 pp 1Ch 11:1–3; **2Sa** 15:10; **1Ki** 1:28–40; 12:1 pp 2Ch 10:1; **1Ki** 12:20
Royal Psalms
These Psalms, although used in honour of the king of the day, possibly at his coronation, share the expectation of a greater king. The NT regards them as fulfilled in Jesus Christ: **Ps** 2:6–9; 45:1; 72:1; 110:1; 132:10

Jesus Christ is the true King of Israel and of the world
Mt 27:37 Above his head they placed the written charge against him: THIS IS JESUS, THE KING OF THE JEWS. pp Mk 15:26 pp Lk 23:38
Jn 1:49 Then Nathanael declared, "Rabbi, you are the Son of God; you are the King of Israel."   *See also* **Mt** 21:5; **Mk** 15:2 pp Mt 27:11 pp Lk 23:3; **Jn** 18:36–37; **Ac** 17:7; **1Co** 15:25; **Heb** 1:8; **Ps** 45:6; **Rev** 17:14; 19:16

Jesus Christ fulfils the expectation of a son of David who will be a king like David
Lk 1:32–33 "He [Jesus] will be great and will be called the Son of the Most High. The Lord God will give him the throne of his father David, and he will reign over the house of Jacob for ever; his kingdom will never end."   *See also* **Lk** 1:69; **Ac** 13:22–23; **Ro** 1:3; **2Ti** 2:8; **Rev** 5:5; 22:16
See also queen.

---

land
Areas of territory, the possession of which was regarded as a sign of security and prosperity. The land of Israel was regarded as the land promised by God to his people and a sign of his covenant faithfulness.

---

land, divine gift
God's gift of the land of Israel is fundamental to the covenant promises made to Abraham and his descendants.

Land as part of God's creation
Ge 1:9–10

The land (Canaan) promised to Abraham
Ge 12:7 The Lord appeared to Abram and said, "To your offspring I will give this land." . . .
See also **Ge** 12:1; 13:15–17; 17:8; 24:7

The boundaries of the promised land
Ge 15:18–21 On that day the Lord made a covenant with Abram and said, "To your descendants I give this land, from the river of Egypt to the great river, the Euphrates—the land of the Kenites, Kenizzites, Kadmonites, Hittites, Perizzites, Rephaites, Amorites, Canaanites, Girgashites and Jebusites."   *See also* **Ex** 23:31; **Nu** 34:1–12

God's promise and its gradual fulfilment
The promise made to the patriarchs
Ge 26:3–4 "Stay in this land for a while, and I will be with you and will bless you. For to you and your descendants I will give all these lands and will confirm the oath I swore to your father Abraham. I will make your descendants as numerous as the stars in the sky and will give them all these lands, and through your offspring all nations on earth will be blessed,"   *See also* **Ge** 23:17–20; 28:13; 35:12; 48:3–4; 50:24–25
The promise confirmed during the wilderness wanderings
Ex 3:7–8 The Lord said, "I have indeed seen the misery of my people in Egypt. I have heard them crying out because of their slave drivers, and I am concerned about their suffering. So I have come down to rescue them from the hand of the Egyptians and to bring them up out of that land into a good and spacious land, a land flowing with milk and honey . . ."   *See also* **Ex** 6:4,8;

13:5,11; 32:11–14; 33:1–3; **Nu** 11:10–12

Exploration of the promised land

Nu 13:1–2 The LORD said to Moses, "Send
some men to explore the land of Canaan, which I
am giving to the Israelites. From each ancestral
tribe send one of its leaders."   *See also* **Nu**
13:21–25

Entry delayed because of unbelief and rebellion

Nu 13:27–33 . . . Then Caleb silenced the
people before Moses and said, "We should go up
and take possession of the land, for we can
certainly do it." But the men who had gone up
with him said, "We can't attack those people;
they are stronger than we are." And they spread
among the Israelites a bad report about the land
they had explored. They said, "The land we
explored devours those living in it. All the people
we saw there are of great size. We saw the
Nephilim there (the descendants of Anak come
from the Nephilim). We seemed like grasshoppers
in our own eyes, and we looked the same to
them."   *See also* **Nu** 14:1–4,26–35,40–45

**Critical importance of obedience in the
promised land**

Dt 5:32–33 . . . Walk in all the way that the
LORD your God has commanded you, so that you
may live and prosper and prolong your days in
the land that you will possess.   *See also* **Dt**
6:10–12

Invasion of the land

Jos 1:2 "Moses my servant is dead. Now then,
you [Joshua] and all these people, get ready to
cross the Jordan River into the land I am about
to give to them—to the Israelites."   *See also*
Jos 2:1

Gradual conquest of the land

Jos 13:1 When Joshua was old and well
advanced in years, the LORD said to him, "You
are very old, and there are still very large areas
of land to be taken over."   *See also* **Jos** 7:2;
8:1; 9:1–2; 10:29–30; 13:2–6; 14:12; 17:12–18

The promise fulfilled

Jos 21:43–45 So the LORD gave Israel all the
land he had sworn to give their ancestors, and
they took possession of it and settled there. The
LORD gave them rest on every side, just as he
had sworn to their ancestors. Not one of their

enemies withstood them; the LORD handed all their
enemies over to them. Not one of all the LORD's
good promises to the house of Israel failed; every
one was fulfilled.

Division of the land

Jos 23:4–5 "Remember how I have allotted as
an inheritance for your tribes all the land of the
nations that remain—the nations I conquered—
between the Jordan and the Great Sea in the
west. The LORD your God himself will drive them
out of your way. He will push them out before
you, and you will take possession of their land,
as the LORD your God promised you."

Conflict with the Philistines over the land

1Sa 7:7–14 When the Philistines heard that
Israel had assembled at Mizpah, the rulers of the
Philistines came up to attack them. And when the
Israelites heard of it, they were afraid because of
the Philistines . . . So the Philistines were
subdued and did not invade Israelite territory
again. Throughout Samuel's lifetime, the hand of
the LORD was against the Philistines . . .
See also **Jdg** 2:21–22; 13:1; 15:11; **1Sa** 4:10–11;
13:17–19; 17:1–2; 31:1,7

Jerusalem captured by David 2Sa 5:6–7

The land at rest and prosperous

Under David

2Sa 7:1 . . . the king [David] was settled in
his palace and the LORD had given him rest from
all his enemies around him,   *See also* **2Sa**
8:1–6,14; 10:15–19

Under Solomon

1Ki 5:4 "But now the LORD my [Solomon's]
God has given me rest on every side, and there
is no adversary or disaster."   *See also* **1Ki**
4:20–21

The exile and subsequent return to the land

Losing the land

Lev 26:14 " 'But if you will not listen to me
and carry out all these commands,' "

Lev 26:32–33 " 'I will lay waste the land, so
that your enemies who live there will be appalled.
I will scatter you among the nations and will
draw out my sword and pursue you. Your land

will be laid waste, and your cities will lie in ruins.' " *See also* **Dt** 28:63–65; **Jer** 16:13; 17:4; 25:11; 44:22; **La** 5:2

Return to the land

Jer 23:7–8 "So then, the days are coming," declares the LORD, "when people will no longer say, 'As surely as the LORD lives, who brought the Israelites up out of Egypt,' but they will say, 'As surely as the LORD lives, who brought the descendants of Israel up out of the land of the north and out of all the countries where he had banished them.' Then they will live in their own land." *See also* **Isa** 14:1; 35:10; 43:5–6; **Eze** 20:41–42; 34:11–13; **Am** 9:14–15 *See also covenant, with Abraham; property, land; warfare.*

---

land, divine responsibility

Israel's land is a gift from God, though ultimately it remains under divine ownership. Life in the land is therefore characterised by both privilege and responsibility.

The land is a gift from God

Dt 26:5–9 . . . ". . . He [The LORD] brought us to this place and gave us this land, a land flowing with milk and honey;"

It is Israel's inheritance

Dt 26:1 When you have entered the land that the LORD your God is giving you as an inheritance . . . *See also* **Ex** 32:13; **Dt** 4:21,38; 15:4; 19:10

Eleven full tribes share the inheritance

Nu 26:52–55 The LORD said to Moses, "The land is to be allotted to them as an inheritance based on the number of names. To a larger group give a larger inheritance, and to a smaller group a smaller one; each is to receive its inheritance according to the number of those listed . . ."

Inherited land east of Jordan allotted by Moses

Nu 32:33 Then Moses gave to the Gadites, the Reubenites and the half-tribe of Manasseh son of Joseph the kingdom of Sihon king of the Amorites and the kingdom of Og king of Bashan—the whole land with its cities and the territory around them. *See also* **Jos** 12:6; 13:8,15,24,29

Inherited land west of Jordan allotted by Joshua and others

Nu 34:17–29 ". . . the men who are to assign the land for you as an inheritance: Eleazar the priest and Joshua son of Nun. And appoint one leader from each tribe to help assign the land . . ." . . . *See also* **Jos** 14:1,13; 15:1,20; 16:4; 18:11; 19:1,10,17,24,32,40,51

Levi receives no inheritance of land Nu 26:62; **Dt** 18:1; **Jos** 13:14,33

Israelite households to hold their inheritance in perpetuity

Nu 36:7–9 "No inheritance in Israel is to pass from tribe to tribe, for each of the Israelites shall keep the tribal land inherited from their ancestors . . ." *See also* **1Ki** 21:3; **Eze** 46:18

The land remains under divine ownership

Lev 25:23 " 'The land must not be sold permanently, because the land is mine and you are but aliens and my tenants.' "

Responsibility to God for the land

Mt 21:33–46

The tithe

Lev 27:30 " 'A tithe of everything from the land, whether grain from the soil or fruit from the trees, belongs to the LORD; it is holy to the LORD.' "

Harvest festivals

Ex 23:16 "Celebrate the Feast of Harvest with the firstfruits of the crops you sow in your field. Celebrate the Feast of Ingathering at the end of the year, when you gather in your crops from the field." *See also* **Lev** 23:15–21,33–43

Sabbath rest

Lev 25:1–7 . . . ". . . in the seventh year the land is to have a sabbath of rest, a sabbath to the LORD. Do not sow your fields or prune your vineyards. Do not reap what grows of itself or harvest the grapes of your untended vines. The land is to have a year of rest . . ."

The Year of Jubilee

Lev 25:8–13 " '. . . The fiftieth year shall be a jubilee for you; do not sow and do not reap what grows of itself or harvest the untended vines. For it is a jubilee and is to be holy for you; eat only what is taken directly from the fields. In this Year of Jubilee all of you are to return to your own property.' "

Responsibility to fellow Israelites in the land
Individual property rights to be respected
Dt 19:14 Do not move your neighbour's boundary stone set up by your predecessors in the inheritance you receive in the land the LORD your God is giving you to possess.   *See also* **Dt** 27:17; **Pr** 15:25; 22:28; 23:10; **Hos** 5:10
Violation of these rights severely condemned
Isa 5:8 Woe to you who add house to house and join field to field till no space is left and you live alone in the land.   *See also* **1Ki** 21:17–19; **Job** 20:19; **Eze** 45:8–9; **Mic** 2:2,9

Responsibility to the poor in the land
The fallow (sabbath) year
Ex 23:10–11 "For six years you are to sow your fields and harvest the crops, but during the seventh year let the land lie unploughed and unused. Then the poor among your people may get food from it, and the wild animals may eat what they leave. Do the same with your vineyard and your olive grove."   *See also* **Lev** 25:6–7; **Dt** 15:1–3
The Year of Jubilee Lev 25:8–13
Harvesting conventions
Lev 19:9–10 " 'When you reap the harvest of your land, do not reap to the very edges of your field or gather the gleanings of your harvest. Do not go over your vineyard a second time or pick up the grapes that have fallen. Leave them for the poor and the alien. I am the LORD your God.' "   *See also* **Lev** 23:22; **Dt** 24:19–22; **Ru** 2:2–3

The land reflects God's blessing and curse
Blessing
Dt 28:1–6 If you fully obey the LORD your God and carefully follow all his commands that I give you today, the LORD your God will set you high above all the nations on earth . . .

Dt 28:11–12 The LORD will grant you abundant prosperity—in the fruit of your womb, the young of your livestock and the crops of your ground—in the land he swore to your ancestors to give you. The LORD will open the heavens, the storehouse of his bounty, to send rain on your land in season and to bless all the work of your hands. You will lend to many nations but will borrow from none.   *See also* **Lev** 25:18–19; **Dt** 11:13–15; **Ps** 65:9–13; 67:5–6
Curse
Dt 28:15 However, if you do not obey the LORD your God and do not carefully follow all his commands and decrees I am giving you today, all these curses will come upon you and overtake you:
Dt 28:18 The fruit of your womb will be cursed, and the crops of your land, and the calves of your herds and the lambs of your flocks.
Dt 28:21 The LORD will plague you with diseases until he has destroyed you from the land you are entering to possess.   *See also* **Lev** 18:24–28; 20:22–24; 26:42–45; **1Ki** 17:1
See also feast and festival; harvest; poverty; Sabbath, in Old Testament; tithing.

languages
The means of communication shared in common by groups of people. Scripture teaches that the diversity of languages in the world is a result of sin, but the outpouring of the Holy Spirit in Acts broke down the barriers of language and nationality.

The origin of different languages
Ge 11:1–9 Now the whole world had one language and a common speech . . . The LORD said, "If as one people speaking the same language they have begun to do this, then nothing they plan to do will be impossible for them. Come, let us go down and confuse their language so they will not understand each other." So the LORD scattered them from there over all the earth, and they stopped building the city. That is why it was called Babel—because there the LORD confused the language of the whole world.

From there the LORD scattered them over the face of the whole earth. *See also* **Ge** 10:2–5,20,30–31

The close relationship between language and national identity
Isa 19:18 In that day five cities in Egypt will speak the language of Canaan and swear allegiance to the LORD Almighty. One of them will be called the City of Destruction. *See also* **Ne** 13:23–27; **Zec** 8:23; **Rev** 5:9; 7:9; 10:11; 11:9; 13:7; 14:6; 17:15

Language barriers
Ne 13:23–24 . . . in those days I [Nehemiah] saw men of Judah who had married women from Ashdod, Ammon and Moab. Half of their children spoke the language of Ashdod or the language of one of the other peoples, and did not know how to speak the language of Judah. *See also* **Dt** 28:49–50; **Ps** 81:5; **Jer** 5:15; **Eze** 3:5–6; **Da** 1:4; **1Co** 14:10–11

The diversity of languages in the Persian empire
Est 8:9 At once the royal secretaries were summoned—on the twenty-third day of the third month, the month of Sivan. They wrote out all Mordecai's orders to the Jews, and to the satraps, governors and nobles of the 127 provinces stretching from India to Cush. These orders were written in the script of each province and the language of each people and also to the Jews in their own script and language. *See also* **Ezr** 4:7; **Est** 1:22; 3:12

God's revelation not limited to any single language
Ac 2:1–11 . . . All of them [disciples] were filled with the Holy Spirit and began to speak in other tongues as the Spirit enabled them. Now there were staying in Jerusalem God-fearing Jews from every nation under heaven . . . Utterly amazed, they asked: "Are not all these who are speaking Galileans? Then how is it that each of us hears them in our own native language? . . ." *See also* **Ps** 19:1–4; **Ac** 10:44–48

Aramaic
Aramaic in the OT
2Ki 18:26 . . . Eliakim son of Hilkiah, and Shebna and Joah said to the field commander, "Please speak to your servants in Aramaic, since we understand it. Don't speak to us in Hebrew in the hearing of the people on the wall." pp Isa 36:11 *Aramaic is a language related to Hebrew, known from Assyrian times. Under the influence of the Persian empire Aramaic was the diplomatic language in later OT times. In Palestine, by the time of the NT, it was spoken widely, having largely displaced Hebrew as the everyday language of the Jews. See also* **Ezr** 4:7 *The text of Ezr 4:8—6:18 and 7:12–26 is in Aramaic;* **Jer** 10:11 *The text of Jer 10:11 is in Aramaic;* **Da** 2:4 *The text of Da 2:4—7:28 is in Aramaic.*

By NT times Aramaic had become the common language of Palestinian Jews
Jn 20:16 Jesus said to her, "Mary." She turned towards him and cried out in Aramaic, "Rabboni!" (which means Teacher). *See also* **Jn** 5:2; 19:13,17,20; **Ac** 21:40—22:2; 26:14

Aramaic expressions found in the NT
Mt 27:46 About the ninth hour Jesus cried out in a loud voice, *"Eloi, Eloi, lama sabachthani?"*—which means, "My God, my God, why have you forsaken me?" pp Mk 15:34 *See also* **Mt** 5:22; **Mk** 5:41; 7:34; 14:36; **Jn** 20:16; **Ro** 8:15; **1Co** 16:22 fn; **Gal** 4:6

Hebrew
2Ki 18:26 Then Eliakim son of Hilkiah and Shebna and Joah said to the field commander, "Please speak to your servants in Aramaic, since we understand it. Don't speak to us in Hebrew in the hearing of the people on the wall." pp Isa 36:11 *Hebrew was the language of Israel in the period of the OT. By the time of the NT, it had been partially displaced in everyday use by Aramaic. See also* **2Ki** 18:28 pp 2Ch 32:18 pp Isa 36:13; **Rev** 9:11; 16:16

Greek
Jn 19:20 Many of the Jews read this sign, for the place where Jesus was crucified was near the city, and the sign was written in Aramaic, Latin

and Greek. *Greek was the major cultural and commercial language of the eastern Mediterranean world. The NT was written in this language, ensuring the rapid spread of the gospel in this region.* See also **Ac** 21:37–39; **Rev** 9:11

law

The God-given regulation of the life of the people of God in relationship with him. As the command of God, it enables and gives shape to the relationship between God and human beings on the one hand, and between fellow human beings on the other.

law, Old Testament

OT laws and legal traditions govern every aspect of the life of the covenant people of God.

Kinds of OT law
Criminal law
Ex 21:12–14 "Anyone who strikes someone a fatal blow shall surely be put to death. However, if it is not done intentionally, but God lets it happen, that person is to flee to a place I will designate. But if anyone schemes and kills someone deliberately, that person shall be taken from my altar and put to death."
Civil law
Dt 16:18–20 Appoint judges and officials for each of your tribes in every town the LORD your God is giving you, and they shall judge the people fairly. Do not pervert justice or show partiality. Do not accept a bribe, for a bribe blinds the eyes of the wise and twists the words of the righteous. Follow justice and justice alone, so that you may live and possess the land the LORD your God is giving you.   See also **Dt** 15:12–18
Social law
Ex 22:21–22 "Do not ill-treat or oppress an alien, for you were aliens in Egypt. Do not take advantage of a widow or an orphan."   See also **Dt** 24:19–22
Cultic law
Cultic law deals explicitly with the ritual or religious life of the people of God. Leviticus chapters 1—7 are

totally devoted to this kind of law: **Lev** 1:10–13; 4:13–21; 7:11–18

Examples of OT law
Conditions for freeing servants
Ex 21:2–6 "If you buy a Hebrew servant, he is to serve you for six years. But in the seventh year, he shall go free, without paying anything . . ." pp Dt 15:12–18   See also **Ex** 21:3–11; **Lev** 25:39–55
Dealing with injuries
Ex 21:23–25 "But if there is serious injury, you are to take life for life, eye for eye, tooth for tooth, hand for hand, foot for foot, burn for burn, wound for wound, bruise for bruise."   See also **Mt** 5:38
Property is to be protected
Ex 22:1 "Whoever steals an ox or a sheep and slaughters it or sells it must pay back five head of cattle for the ox and four sheep for the sheep."   See also **Lev** 6:1–7; **Lk** 19:8
The rights of aliens must be respected
Ex 22:21 "Do not ill-treat or oppress an alien, for you were aliens in Egypt."   See also **Lev** 19:33; **Dt** 10:19
Justice must be universally respected
Ex 23:2–3 ". . . When you give testimony in a lawsuit, do not pervert justice by siding with the crowd, and do not show favouritism to the poor in a lawsuit."   See also **Lev** 19:15
The Sabbath must be observed by all
Ex 23:12 "Six days do your work, but on the seventh day do not work, so that your ox and your donkey may rest and the slave born in your household, and the alien as well, may be refreshed."   See also **Ex** 20:8–11
Three annual festivals are to be celebrated
Ex 23:15–16 "Celebrate the Feast of Unleavened Bread . . . Celebrate the Feast of Harvest with the firstfruits of the crops you sow in your field. Celebrate the Feast of Ingathering at the end of the year . . ."   See also **Ex** 12:17; **Dt** 16:16
Worship must be in accordance with God's will and must be kept pure **Dt** 12:1–7; 13:6–8
Certain foods are declared to be unclean **Lev** 11:1–23 pp Dt 14:3–20

A tenth of all produce must be given to God

Dt 14:22 Be sure to set aside a tenth of all that your fields produce each year. *See also* **Lev** 27:30

Cultic laws are grounded in the holiness of God

Lev 11:44 " 'I am the LORD your God; consecrate yourselves and be holy, because I am holy . . . ' "

Lev 19:1-2 The LORD said to Moses, "Speak to the entire assembly of Israel and say to them: 'Be holy because I, the LORD your God, am holy.' " *See also* **1Pe** 1:16

Full details were given for each type of offering: burnt, grain, fellowship, sin and guilt offerings. Only perfect animals were to be offered: **Lev** 1:3; 2:1–2; 3:1–2; 4:27–28; 5:17–18

Rules governing infectious or contagious diseases

Lev 13:2 "When anyone has a swelling or a rash or a bright spot on the skin that may become an infectious skin disease, they must be brought to Aaron the priest or to one of his sons who is a priest."

Lev 15:13 " 'When people are cleansed from their discharge, they are to count off seven days for their ceremonial cleansing; they must wash their clothes and bathe themselves with fresh water, and they will be clean.' "

There must not be unlawful sexual relations

Lev 18:6 " 'No-one is to approach any close relative to have sexual relations. I am the LORD.' "

A Day of Atonement must be held **Lev** 23:26–32 pp Lev 16:2–34 pp Nu 29:7–11 *See also atonement; clean and unclean; offerings; property; ritual law; sacrifice; slavery; tithing.*

---

law, purpose

The law covers and regulates every area of life of the covenant people of God in accordance with the commands of God. Although the laws may be divided into categories of civil, criminal, social and cultic (or ritual) law, these distinctions are not clear-cut, and occasionally overlap with one another.

The origins of the law
Law as God's command is found in the story of creation

Ge 2:16-17 And the LORD God commanded the man, "You are free to eat from any tree in the garden; but you must not eat from the tree of the knowledge of good and evil, for when you eat of it you will surely die."

The law expresses the covenant relation between God and his people

Dt 4:44-45 This is the law Moses set before the Israelites. These are the stipulations, decrees and laws Moses gave them when they came out of Egypt . . .

Dt 5:1 Moses summoned all Israel and said: Hear, O Israel, the decrees and the laws I declare in your hearing today. Learn them and be sure to follow them. *See also* **Ex** 20:1–17 pp Dt 5:6–21; **Dt** 10:12–13; 30:1–16

The purpose of the law
The law shows the proper response to the holiness of God

Lev 19:2 "Speak to the entire assembly of Israel and say to them: 'Be holy because I, the LORD your God, am holy.' "

The law ensures that the people continue to receive the blessings of the covenant promises

Dt 6:24-25 "The LORD commanded us to obey all these decrees and to fear the LORD our God, so that we might always prosper and be kept alive, as is the case today. And if we are careful to obey all this law before the LORD our God, as he has commanded us, that will be our righteousness." *See also* **Ge** 22:17–18; **Ex** 20:12; **Dt** 6:3–7

Breaking the law leads to forfeiting the covenant blessings

Jer 11:9-11 Then the LORD said to me [Jeremiah], "There is a conspiracy among the people of Judah and those who live in Jerusalem. They have returned to the sins of their ancestors who refused to listen to my words. They have followed other gods to serve them. Both the house of Israel and the house of Judah have broken the covenant I made with their ancestors. Therefore this is what the LORD says: 'I will bring on them a disaster they cannot escape. Although they cry out to me, I will not listen to them.'" *See also* **Ex** 32:1–4

The law deepens the believer's knowledge of God through meditation

Ps 1:1–2 Blessed are those who does not walk in the counsel of the wicked or stand in the way of sinners or sit in the seat of mockers. But their delight is in the law of the LORD, and on his law they meditate day and night. *See also* **Dt** 6:2; **Ps** 19:7–14; 119:25–32,105–120

The law will finally be written on believers' hearts

Jer 31:33 . . . "I will put my law in their minds and write it on their hearts. I will be their God, and they will be my people." *See also* **Eze** 11:19–20

The general principles underlying the law

Justice

Dt 16:20 Follow justice and justice alone, so that you may live and possess the land the LORD your God is giving you.

Righteousness

Dt 16:18 Appoint judges and officials for each of your tribes in every town the LORD your God is giving you, and they shall judge the people fairly.

Holiness

Lev 19:2 ". . . 'Be holy because I, the LORD your God, am holy.'"

Love

Lev 19:18–19 "'Do not seek revenge or bear a grudge against one of your people, but love your neighbour as yourself. I am the LORD. Keep my decrees. Do not mate different kinds of animals. Do not plant your field with two kinds of seed. Do not wear clothing woven of two kinds of material.'" *See also covenant; crime; justice.*

---

law, Ten Commandments

The basic laws given to Israel through Moses following the exodus from Egypt (Ex 20:1–17; Dt 5:6–21). The first four commandments safeguard Israel's special relation to God; the remaining six protect individuals within the community and promote their well-being.

The Ten Commandments are to govern the life of Israel as the people of God

Israel should obey God alone

Ex 20:2–3 "I am the LORD your God, who brought you out of Egypt, out of the land of slavery. You shall have no other gods before me." pp **Dt** 5:6–7 *See also* **Dt** 6:13–15

Idolatry forbidden

Ex 20:4–6 "You shall not make for yourself an idol in the form of anything in heaven above or on the earth beneath or in the waters below. You shall not bow down to them or worship them . . ." pp **Dt** 5:8–10 *See also* **Ex** 32:1–8; **Lev** 19:4; **1Co** 10:7

God's name should not be misused

Ex 20:7 "You shall not misuse the name of the LORD your God, for the LORD will not hold anyone guiltless who misuses his name." pp **Dt** 5:11 *See also* **Mt** 7:21

A day of rest is commanded

Ex 20:8–11 "Remember the Sabbath day by keeping it holy. Six days you shall labour and do all your work, but the seventh day is a Sabbath to the LORD your God. On it you shall not do any work, neither you, nor your son or daughter, nor your male or female servant, nor your animals, nor the alien within your gates. For in six days the LORD made the heavens and the earth, the sea, and all that is in them, but he rested on the seventh day. Therefore the LORD blessed the Sabbath day and made it holy." pp **Dt** 5:12–15 *See also* **Ex** 16:23; **Lev** 19:3; **Isa** 56:2; **Jer** 17:21–22

Parents are to be honoured

Ex 20:12 "Honour your father and your mother, so that you may live long in the land the LORD your God is giving you." pp **Dt** 5:16 *See also* **Mt** 15:4; **Eph** 6:1–3

Murder is forbidden

Ex 20:13 "You shall not murder." pp **Dt** 5:17 *See also* **Ge** 4:8–16; **Mt** 5:21

Adultery is forbidden

Ex 20:14 "You shall not commit adultery." pp **Dt** 5:18 *See also* **Lev** 18:20; **2Sa** 11:2–5; **Mt** 5:27; **Heb** 13:4

Stealing is forbidden

Ex 20:15 "You shall not steal." pp **Dt** 5:19

See also **Lev** 19:11,13
False witness is forbidden
Ex 20:16 "You shall not give false testimony
against your neighbour." pp Dt 5:20   *See also*
Lev 19:11
Coveting is forbidden
Ex 20:17 "You shall not covet your neighbour's
house. You shall not covet your neighbour's wife,
or his male or female servant, his ox or donkey,
or anything that belongs to your neighbour." pp
Dt 5:21   *See also* **Lev** 19:17–18; **Job** 31:9–12;
Ro 7:7

**The circumstances surrounding the
giving of the Ten Commandments**
The Ten Commandments written on stone tablets
Ex 24:12 The LORD said to Moses, "Come up
to me on the mountain and stay here, and I will
give you the tablets of stone, with the law and
commands I have written for their instruction."
See also **Dt** 4:13; 9:9–10
The stone tablets broken
Ex 32:19 When Moses approached the camp
and saw the calf and the dancing, his anger
burned and he threw the tablets out of his hands,
breaking them to pieces at the foot of the
mountain.   *See also* **Dt** 9:16–17
A second set of stone tablets made
Ex 34:1 The LORD said to Moses, "Chisel out
two stone tablets like the first ones, and I will
write on them the words that were on the first
tablets, which you broke."
Ex 34:28 Moses was there with the LORD forty
days and forty nights without eating bread or
drinking water. And he wrote on the tablets the
words of the covenant—the Ten
Commandments.   *See also* **Dt** 10:1–2
**The second set of stone tablets put in the ark
of the covenant**
Ex 40:20 He took the Testimony and placed it
in the ark . . .   *See also* **Dt** 10:1–2   *See also*
idolatry; Sabbath.

leaders, political

Since God is the ultimate ruler of all things,
earthly authority derives from him. Although

political leadership was exercised in various ways
in Israel, there was always some overlap between
political and spiritual leadership.

Israel had a variety of political leaders
Judges Jdg 2:16; 4:4
Kings 1Sa 8:1–21; 10:1; 16:1–13; **2Sa** 7:12; **1Ki**
1:28–40
Tribal elders and judges Ex 19:7; **Dt** 21:1–2; **Ru**
4:1–2; **Job** 29:7–12
Foreign powers imposed rulers on Israel Lk 3:1

**Examples of those who were both
political and spiritual leaders**
1Sa 7:15 Samuel continued as judge over Israel
all the days of his life.
Moses: **Ex** 34:1,27–28
Jdg 6:25–27; **2Ki** 18:4 pp 2Ch 31:1; **1Ch** 6:31

**Political leaders, like spiritual ones,
were called by God**
1Ki 11:31 . . . ". . . 'See, I [the LORD] am
going to tear the kingdom out of Solomon's hand
and give you [Jeroboam] ten tribes.' "   *See also*
Ex 3:10; **Jdg** 6:14
David: **1Sa** 16:1,6–12
Isa 45:1–2

**To reject God's leadership is to reject
God**
1Sa 8:6–8 . . . ". . . it is not you [Samuel]
they have rejected, but they have rejected me
[the LORD] as their king . . ."   *See also* **1Sa**
8:5,19–20

Responsibilities of leaders
To protect the weak Ps 72:12–14
To administer justice Ps 72:2; **Pr** 20:8; 29:4,14;
Isa 9:7; 11:3–4
To shepherd the people Ps 78:70–72; **Eze**
34:2–6

Attributes required in leaders
Being anointed by the Spirit of God
Isa 11:1–2 . . . The Spirit of the LORD will rest
on him [God's chosen king]—the Spirit of
wisdom and of understanding, the Spirit of counsel

and of power, the Spirit of knowledge and of the fear of the LORD—

Reverence Dt 17:18–20; **Isa** 11:3
Trustworthiness Isa 11:5
Wisdom Pr 8:15–16

The failure of leaders
Through exploiting their subjects
Mt 20:25 . . . ". . . the rulers of the Gentiles lord it over them, and their high officials exercise authority over them." *See also* **Dt** 17:16–17; **1Sa** 8:11–17; **1Ki** 12:4; **Jer** 22:13
Through usurping religious authority 1Sa 13:8–13; **2Ch** 26:16–18
Through apostasy 1Ki 11:7–8; **2Ki** 21:1–6
Through trusting in alliances with heathen powers
Isa 31:1 Woe to those who go down to Egypt for help, who rely on horses, who trust in the multitude of their chariots and in the great strength of their horsemen, but do not look to the Holy One of Israel, or seek help from the LORD. *See also* **2Ki** 20:12,17–18; **Isa** 30:1–2; **Hos** 7:11

Godless leadership is evil
Lk 13:32 . . . "Go tell that fox [Herod], 'I [Jesus] will drive out demons and heal people today and tomorrow, and on the third day I will reach my goal.'" *See also* **Da** 7:1–7; **Rev** 13:1–3

People must have a right attitude to political leaders
They are to be obeyed
Ro 13:1 Let everyone be subject to the governing authorities, for there is no authority except that which God has established . . .
See also **Ro** 13:5; **1Pe** 2:13–17
But obedience to God must come first
Ac 5:29 Peter and the other apostles replied: "We must obey God rather than human beings!" *See also* **Da** 3:18; 6:13
Prayers are to be made for them 1Ti 2:1–2
See also king.

life
The state of being alive, characterised by vitality, growth and development.

life, animal and plant
All living creatures and plants were made by God and are sustained by him.

Animal life
Animals were created by God
Ge 2:19 Now the LORD God had formed out of the ground all the beasts of the field and all the birds of the air . . .
Ps 104:24 How many are your works, O LORD! In wisdom you made them all; the earth is full of your creatures. *See also* **Ge** 1:20–25
Animals are cared for by God
Ps 145:15–16 The eyes of all look to you, and you give them their food at the proper time. You open your hand and satisfy the desires of every living thing.
Mt 6:26 "Look at the birds of the air; they do not sow or reap or store away in barns, and yet your heavenly Father feeds them . . ." pp Lk 12:24 *See also* **Dt** 22:7; **Ps** 104:10–12,14,17–18,21,27; 136:25; 147:9; **Jnh** 4:11; **Mt** 10:29
Animal life is controlled by God
Da 6:22 "My God sent his angel, and he shut the mouths of the lions . . ." *See also* **Nu** 22:28; **Jnh** 1:17; **Heb** 11:33
Animal life has been placed under human care
Ge 1:26 Then God said, "Let us make human beings in our image, in our likeness, and let them rule over the fish of the sea and the birds of the air, over the livestock, over all the earth, and over all the creatures that move along the ground."
See also **Ge** 1:28; 2:19; 9:2; **Ps** 8:6–8; **Da** 2:38; **Heb** 2:8; **Jas** 3:7
Animals serve human needs Ge 3:21; **Mt** 21:1–3 pp Mk 11:1–3 pp Lk 19:29–31
Animal life saved by Noah from the flood Ge 6:19–22
Animals subsequently given to humanity for food Ge 9:3–4; **Dt** 12:20–25
Clean and unclean animals Ge 7:2–3; **Lev** 11:47

Animals used in sacrifice

Ge 4:4 But Abel brought fat portions from some of the firstborn of his flock. The LORD looked with favour on Abel and his offering,   *See also* **Ge** 8:20; **Lev** 17:11; **Heb** 9:22

Animal life glorifies God Ps 148:7; 150:6

Plant life
Plants were created by God

Ge 1:11–12 Then God said, "Let the land produce vegetation: seed-bearing plants and trees on the land that bear fruit with seed in it, according to their various kinds." And it was so. The land produced vegetation: plants bearing seed according to their kinds and trees bearing fruit with seed in it according to their kinds. And God saw that it was good.

Plant life is often short-lived

Mt 6:30 "If that is how God clothes the grass of the field, which is here today and tomorrow is thrown into the fire, will he not much more clothe you, O you of little faith?" pp Lk 12:28
See also **Ps** 90:5–6; 103:15–16; **Isa** 37:27; 51:12; **1Pe** 1:24; **Isa** 40:6–8

Plants are provided for food

Ge 1:29–30 Then God said, "I give you every seed-bearing plant on the face of the whole earth and every tree that has fruit with seed in it. They will be yours for food. And to all the beasts of the earth and all the birds of the air and all the creatures that move on the ground—everything that has the breath of life in it—I give every green plant for food." And it was so.   *See also* **Ge** 2:16–17; 3:2; 9:3; **1Ki** 18:5; **Job** 28:5; **Ps** 104:14; 147:8–9; **Da** 4:32; **Joel** 2:22

Plant life glorifies God Ps 96:12–13   *See also* animals; atonement; blood; food; law; plants.

---

life, human

Seen by Scripture as the climax of the work of creation, life is a gift of God and is to be treated with reverence and respect.

Life is from God

Ge 2:7 the LORD God formed a man from the dust of the ground and breathed into his nostrils the breath of life, and the man became a living being.

Ac 3:15 "You [the Jews] killed the author of life . . ."

Ac 17:25 ". . . he himself gives all life and breath and everything else."   *See also* **1Sa** 2:6; **Job** 33:4; **Ps** 139:13; **Da** 5:23; **Ac** 17:28; **Jas** 4:14–15

The ultimate duration of life is unknown to people

Ps 39:4 "Show me, O LORD, my life's end and the number of my days; let me know how fleeting is my life."   *See also* **Ge** 27:2; **Jas** 4:13–14

Life is precious

Mt 10:31 "So don't be afraid; you are worth more than many sparrows."   *See also* **Ge** 1:26–27; 9:5–6; **Ps** 49:7–9; 139:14; **Mt** 16:26 pp Lk 9:25

God's presence in life

Dt 30:16 For I [the LORD] command you [his people] today to love the LORD your God, to walk in his ways, and to keep his commands, decrees and laws . . .

Ps 23:6 Surely goodness and love will follow me all the days of my life, and I will dwell in the house of the LORD for ever.   *See also* **Ps** 71:5–6,9

Life is to be lived for God

Ecc 12:13; **Jer** 10:23; **Mic** 6:8; **Mt** 10:39; **Php** 1:21

The span of human life

Ecc 11:8—12:8 However many years people may live, let them enjoy them all. But let them remember the days of darkness, for there will be many. Everything to come is meaningless . . .
See also **Ps** 90:10

Life is temporary

2Co 5:1 Now we know that if the earthly tent we live in is destroyed, we have a building from God, an eternal house in heaven, not built by human hands.   *See also* **Ps** 49:12; 103:15–16; **Isa** 38:12; **2Pe** 1:13–14

Life is short

1Ch 29:15 "We are aliens and strangers in your sight, as were all our ancestors. Our days on earth are like a shadow, without hope."

Job 14:1 "Mortals, born of woman, are of few days and full of trouble."

Jas 4:14 Why, you do not even know what will happen tomorrow. What is your life? You are a mist that appears for a little while and then vanishes.   *See also* **Job** 7:6–7; 8:9; 9:25; 14:2; **Ps** 39:4–6; 89:47; 90:12; 102:11; 144:4; **Ecc** 6:12; **Isa** 40:6–8

The termination of life by death is due to sin

Ro 5:12 Therefore, just as sin entered the world through one man, and death through sin, and in this way death came to all people, because all sinned-   *See also* **Ge** 2:17; **1Co** 15:22

Examples of long life Ge 5:3–32; 9:29; 11:10–32

A full span of years

Pr 3:16 Long life is in her [wisdom's] right hand . . .   *See also* **Ex** 20:12 pp Dt 5:16; **Ex** 23:25–26; **1Ki** 3:14; **Job** 5:26; **Pr** 3:2; 9:11; 10:27

Attitudes to life
Life loved

1Pe 3:10 For, "Whoever among you would love life and see good days must keep your tongue from evil and your lips from deceitful speech."   *See also* **Ps** 34:12–13; **Job** 8:21; **Ps** 91:16

Life despised

Ecc 2:22–23 What do people get for all the toil and anxious striving with which they labour under the sun? All their days their work is pain and grief; even at night their minds do not rest. This too is meaningless.   *See also* **Job** 7:16; 10:1; **Ecc** 2:17; **Jnh** 4:8

---

male and female

God created humanity as male and female. Although gender differences are evident in behaviour and role, Scripture teaches the equality and complementarity of the sexes.

The creation of male and female

Ge 1:27 So God created human beings in his own image, in the image of God he created them; male and female he created them.
See also **Ge** 2:20–24; 5:2

The fall disrupted relationships between male and female

Ge 3:14–19 . . . To the woman he [the LORD God] said, "I will greatly increase your pains in childbearing; with pain you will give birth to children. Your desire will be for your husband, and he will rule over you." . . .   *See also* **2Sa** 13:1–19; **Pr** 5:3–14; **Mt** 5:28; **Ro** 1:26–27

The equality of male and female
Equality under many old covenant regulations

Nu 5:5–7 The LORD said to Moses, "Say to the Israelites: 'When a man or woman wrongs another in any way and so is unfaithful to the LORD, such people are guilty and must confess the sin they have committed . . .'"   *See also* **Lev** 20:10–12; **Nu** 5:1–4; **Dt** 15:12–15; 23:17–18

Equality in religious observance

Ex 35:22 All who were willing, men and women alike, came and brought gold jewellery of all kinds: brooches, ear-rings, rings and ornaments. They all presented their gold as a wave offering to the LORD.   *See also* **Nu** 6:1–4; **Dt** 31:12; **2Sa** 6:19

Equality of accountability

La 2:21 "Young and old lie together in the dust of the streets; my young men and young women have fallen by the sword. You have slain them in the day of your anger; you have slaughtered them without pity."   *See also* **Lev** 20:27; **2Ch** 36:15–17; **Ac** 5:1–11

Equality in Christ

Gal 3:26–28 You are all children of God through faith in Christ Jesus, for all of you who were baptised into Christ have clothed yourselves with Christ. There is neither Jew nor Greek, slave nor free, male nor female, for you are all one in Christ Jesus.   *See also* **Ac** 2:17–18; **Joel** 2:28–29; **1Co** 11:11–12

Variations in the treatment of male and female
In OT patriarchal society
Lev 27:1–7 . . . "*. . . '* . . . set the value of a male between the ages of twenty and sixty at fifty shekels of silver, according to the sanctuary shekel; and if it is a female, set her value at thirty shekels . . .'" *See also* **Ge** 17:9–14; **Ex** 13:1–2,14–15; **Nu** 3:14–15; 5:11–31; 18:8–10
In legislation protecting women under the old covenant
Nu 27:1–7 . . . "What Zelophehad's daughters are saying is right. You [Moses] must certainly give them property as an inheritance among their father's relatives and give their father's inheritance over to them." *See also* **Nu** 36:1–12; **Dt** 22:13–19,25–29
In roles within the NT church community
1Co 14:33–35 . . . As in all the congregations of the saints, women should remain silent in the churches. They are not allowed to speak, but must be in submission, as the Law says. If they want to enquire about something, they should ask their own husbands at home; for it is disgraceful for a woman to speak in the church. *See also* **1Co** 11:3–10; **Eph** 5:22–24 *The idea of "headship" is complex, but is generally regarded as including the ideas of responsibility and authority within a relationship;* **1Ti** 2:11–15; **Tit** 2:1–5
In behaviour within the NT church community
1Ti 2:8–10 I [Paul] want men everywhere to lift up holy hands in prayer, without anger or disputing. I also want women to dress modestly, with decency and propriety, not with braided hair or gold or pearls or expensive clothes, but with good deeds, appropriate for women who profess to worship God. *See also* **1Co** 11:3–16; **1Ti** 5:1–2

Male and female roles within marriage
1Co 7:1–7 . . . The husband should fulfil his marital duty to his wife, and likewise the wife to her husband. The wife's body does not belong to her alone but also to her husband. In the same way, the husband's body does not belong to him alone but also to his wife . . . *See also* **Pr** 31:10–31; **Eph** 5:22–33; **Col** 3:18–19; **1Pe** 3:1–7

Male and female imagery used of God
Female imagery
Mt 23:37 "O Jerusalem, Jerusalem, you who kill the prophets and stone those sent to you, how often I have longed to gather your children together, as a hen gathers her chicks under her wings, but you were not willing." pp Lk 13:34 *See also* **Pr** 8:1–11; **Isa** 66:12–13
Male imagery
Ps 47:2 How awesome is the LORD Most High, the great King over all the earth! *See also* **Ex** 15:3; **Ps** 23:1; **Mt** 6:6; **Lk** 11:11–13 pp Mt 7:9–11 *See also* fathers; marriage; mothers.

---

market
The market was a central feature of life in biblical times. Some of the biblical terms for redemption are drawn from the market-place.

Ancient market-places
1Ki 20:34
International trade in Tyre: **Isa** 23:3; **Eze** 27:24

The market as a place of commerce
Methods of trading
Cash: **Ge** 23:10–18; **Jn** 2:14–16
Bartering: **Ge** 47:17; **Hos** 3:2
Sealing transactions Ru 4:7; **Jer** 32:11–12

Other activities in the market-place
It was where children played Mt 11:16–17 pp Lk 7:32
It was where labourers waited for hire Mt 20:3
It was where meat was sold 1Co 10:25
It was where magistrates were present Ac 16:19

God's work in the market-place
Jesus Christ healed the sick
Mk 6:56 And wherever he went—into villages, towns or countryside—they placed the sick in the market-places. They begged him to let them touch even the edge of his cloak, and all who touched him were healed.

Paul preached
Ac 17:16–17 While Paul was waiting for them [Silas and Timothy] in Athens, he was greatly distressed to see that the city was full of idols. So he reasoned in the synagogue with the Jews and the God-fearing Greeks, as well as in the market-place day by day with those who happened to be there.

Sins in the market-place
Greed, dishonesty and materialism Hos 12:7; **Am** 8:5; **Mic** 6:11
The hypocrisy of the Pharisees Mt 23:7 pp Mk 12:38 pp Lk 20:46; **Mk** 7:4; **Lk** 11:43
Rough crowds Ac 16:22; 17:5

The temple courts become a market
Jn 2:14–16 In the temple courts he [Jesus] found people selling cattle, sheep and doves, and others sitting at tables exchanging money. So he made a whip out of cords, and drove all from the temple area, both sheep and cattle; he scattered the coins of the money changers and overturned their tables. To those who sold doves he said, "Get these out of here! How dare you turn my Father's house into a market!" pp Mt 21:12–13 pp Mk 11:15–17 pp Lk 19:45–46

Markets will be destroyed in judgment
Zep 1:11; **Rev** 18:11–13

Biblical terms for redemption are drawn from market language
In the gospel call Pr 8:3–5; **Isa** 1:18; 55:1,2; **Mt** 13:45–46
God's people have been bought
Ac 20:28 ". . . the church of God, which he bought with his own blood." *See also* **Ex** 15:16; **Ps** 74:2; **1Co** 6:20; 7:23; **2Pe** 2:1; **Rev** 5:9; 14:4
God's people have been redeemed
Gal 4:4–5 But when the time had fully come, God sent his Son, born of a woman, born under law, to redeem those under law, that we might receive adoption as God's children. *The Greek word "exagorazo" means "to buy" and was used, for example, of the buying of slaves.*

See also **Gal** 3:13–14; **Rev** 14:3   *The Greek "agorazo", translated here as "redeemed", may also be translated as "bought". Elsewhere (e.g., Tit 2:14; 1Pe 1:18), "lutro" meaning "to release" is used, conveying a similar idea.*
Redeeming the time
The Greek "exagorazo" here translated as "make the most of": **Eph** 5:16; **Col** 4:5   *See also buying and selling; trade.*

marriage
The union of a man and a woman in a permanent relationship. Though a lifelong monogamous commitment is presented as the ideal, polygamous marriages were occasionally known in OT times and carried the same legal and moral rights and responsibilities. God's relationship with his people is described in terms of the marriage bond.

marriage, customs
Marriage between two individuals united their families and involved the whole community. Parents, particularly fathers, took an active part in selecting partners for their children. There was often a long period of betrothal; wedding celebrations were usually elaborate and might last a week or more.

The choice of a marriage partner
Parents usually chose a suitable partner
Ge 38:6 Judah got a wife for Er, his firstborn, and her name was Tamar.   *See also* **Ge** 24:2–4; 21:21
The wishes of the couple
Ge 24:57–58 . . . So they called Rebekah and asked her, "Will you go with this man [Abraham's servant]?" "I will go," she said.
See also **Ge** 34:4,8–9; **Jdg** 14:2; **1Sa** 18:20

The bride-price
Daughters were "given" by their fathers Ge 29:28; **Ex** 2:21; **1Sa** 18:21
Fathers often received payment
Ge 29:18 Jacob was in love with Rachel and said, "I'll work for you [Laban] seven years in

return for your younger daughter Rachel."
Ge 34:12 "Make the price for the bride and
the gift I [Shechem] am to bring as great as you
like, and I'll pay whatever you [Dinah's father]
ask me. Only give me the girl as my wife."
See also **Ge** 29:30; **Ex** 22:16–17; **Dt** 22:28–29;
1Sa 18:17,27

Daughters were given as a reward
Jdg 1:12–13 And Caleb said, "I will give my
daughter Acsah in marriage to the man who
attacks and captures Kiriath Sepher." . . . pp Jos
15:16–17   See also **1Sa** 18:25

The exchange of wedding gifts
Gifts from the bridegroom's family Ge 24:53
Gifts from the bride's father
Servants given to the bride as a dowry: **Ge** 24:59;
29:24,29
Cities and land given as a dowry: **Jdg** 1:14–15 pp Jos
15:18–19; **1Ki** 9:16

The period of betrothal
Betrothal followed payment of the bride-price
2Sa 3:14 Then David sent messengers to Ish-
bosheth son of Saul, demanding, "Give me my
wife Michal, whom I betrothed to myself for the
price of a hundred Philistine foreskins."   See also
Ge 29:19–20
A betrothed couple were regarded as husband
and wife Ge 19:14; **Dt** 22:23–24; **Mt** 1:18–20
Sexual relationships took place only after the
wedding
Ge 29:21 Then Jacob said to Laban, "Give me
my wife. My time is completed, and I want to lie
with her."
Betrothed women were referred to as virgins: **Joel** 1:8;
Lk 1:27
Mt 1:25; **1Co** 7:36–38

Soldiers and marriage
Dt 20:7; 24:5

The wedding celebrations
The bride wore an elaborate dress and
jewellery
Eze 16:9–13 "'. . . So you [Jerusalem] were
adorned with gold and silver; your clothes were of

fine linen and costly fabric and embroidered
cloth . . .'"   *An allegorical description of God
dressing Jerusalem as a bride.   See also* **Ps**
45:13; **Isa** 61:10; **Jer** 2:32; **Rev** 21:2
Attendants on the bride and groom
Ps 45:14 In embroidered garments she [the
bride] is led to the king; her virgin companions
follow her and are brought to you.
Jn 3:29 "The bride belongs to the bridegroom.
The friend who attends the bridegroom waits and
listens for him, and is full of joy when he hears
the bridegroom's voice . . ."   See also **Jdg**
14:11,20; **Mt** 9:15 pp Mk 2:19 pp Lk 5:34; **Mt**
25:1–10
The wedding banquet Ge 29:22; **Jdg** 14:10; **Mt**
22:2; **Rev** 19:9
Wedding festivities Ps 78:63; **Isa** 62:5; **Jer**
7:34; 33:11
The invitation to a wedding Mt 22:3–4
It was an insult to the host to refuse to attend: **Mt**
22:5–7; **Lk** 14:18–21
Mt 22:11–12   See also *banquets; betrothal; bride;
bridegroom; fathers; wedding.*

---

marriage, God and his people
Marriage is used to describe the relationship
between God and Israel in the OT and between
Jesus Christ and the church in the NT.
Contemplating marriage deepens understanding of
God's love for his people; examining God's
covenant love for his people similarly enriches an
understanding of marriage.

God's marriage relationship with Israel
God's marriage covenant with Israel
Eze 16:8–14 "'Later I passed by, and when I
looked at you [Israel] and saw that you were old
enough for love, I spread the corner of my
garment over you and covered your nakedness. I
gave you my solemn oath and entered into a
covenant with you, declares the Sovereign LORD,
and you became mine . . .'"   See also **Jer**
31:32; **Eze** 16:59–60
God as Israel's husband
Isa 54:5 "For your Maker is your husband—
the LORD Almighty is his name—the Holy One of
Israel is your Redeemer; he is called the God of

all the earth.   *See also* **Hos** 2:7; **Joel** 1:8
Israel's early devotion
Jer 2:2 . . . ". . . 'I [the LORD] remember the devotion of your [Israel's] youth, how as a bride you loved me and followed me through the desert, through a land not sown.'"   *See also* **Eze** 16:43; **Hos** 2:15

The breakdown of God's marriage to Israel
Israel's adultery
Jer 3:20 "But like a woman unfaithful to her husband, so you have been unfaithful to me, O house of Israel," declares the LORD.   *See also* **Jer** 2:32; **Eze** 16:32–34; **Hos** 1:2; 9:1
Israel's alienation from God is likened to a divorce
Hos 2:2 "Rebuke your mother [Israel], rebuke her, for she is not my wife, and I [the LORD] am not her husband. Let her remove the adulterous look from her face and the unfaithfulness from between her breasts."   *See also* **Isa** 50:1; **Jer** 3:6–10

The renewal of God's marriage to Israel
God calls his bride to return
Jer 3:12–14 ". . . Return, faithless people," declares the LORD, "for I am your husband. I will choose you—one from a town and two from a clan—and bring you to Zion."
Hos 3:1–3 The LORD said to me [Hosea], "Go, show your love to your wife again, though she is loved by another and is an adulteress. Love her as the LORD loves the Israelites, though they turn to other gods and love the sacred raisin cakes." . . .   *See also* **Isa** 54:6–8; **Hos** 2:14
The renewed relationship
Isa 62:4–5 . . . As a young man marries a young woman, so will your people marry you; as a bridegroom rejoices over his bride, so will your God rejoice over you.   *See also* **Jer** 31:31–33; **Eze** 16:62; **Hos** 2:16,19–20

Jesus Christ's marriage relationship with the church
Jesus Christ's love as a model for marriage
Eph 5:25–33 Husbands, love your wives, just

as Christ loved the church and gave himself up for her . . .
Jesus Christ is described as a bridegroom
Jn 3:29 "The bride belongs to the bridegroom. The friend who attends the bridegroom waits and listens for him, and is full of joy when he hears the bridegroom's voice. That joy is mine, and it is now complete."   *See also* **Mt** 9:15 pp Mk 2:19–20 pp Lk 5:34–35; **Mt** 22:2; 25:1–13
The church as Christ's bride
2Co 11:2 I [Paul] am jealous for you [the church at Corinth] with a godly jealousy. I promised you to one husband, to Christ, so that I might present you as a pure virgin to him.
Rev 19:7–9 "Let us rejoice and be glad and give him glory! For the wedding of the Lamb has come, and his bride has made herself ready . . ." . . .   *See also* **Rev** 21:2,9–10; 22:17   *See also covenant, at Sinai.*

---

marriage, purpose
Marriage is part of God's intention for humanity from creation and forms the basis for the family which is the primary unit of society. Where marriage flourishes it blesses both the couple and the wider community.

Marriage is part of God's plan for the human race
From creation
Mt 19:4 "Haven't you read," he [Jesus] replied, "that at the beginning the Creator 'made them male and female'," pp Mk 10:6   *See also* **Ge** 1:27; **1Co** 11:11–12
It is to provide companionship
Ge 2:18 The LORD God said, "It is not good for the man to be alone. I will make a helper suitable for him."   *See also* **Ge** 2:20–22; 3:12; **Pr** 31:10–12
It is to be a committed, exclusive relationship
Ge 2:23–24 . . . For this reason a man will leave his father and mother and be united to his wife, and they will become one flesh.   *See also* **Mt** 19:5 pp Mk 10:7–8; **1Co** 7:2; **Eph** 5:31
It is a lifelong partnership
Mt 19:6 "So they [husband and wife] are no longer two, but one. Therefore what God has

joined together, let no-one separate." pp Mk 10:9   *See also* **Ro** 7:2; **1Co** 7:39

It is the intended context for raising children
Mal 2:15 Has not ₜthe Lord₎ made them [marriage partners] one? In flesh and spirit they are his. And why one? Because he was seeking godly offspring. So guard yourself in your spirit, and do not break faith with the wife of your youth.   *See also* **1Co** 7:14

It will not exist in the life to come Mt 22:30 pp Mk 12:25 pp Lk 20:34–35; **1Co** 7:29–31

Marriage as a covenant relationship
Mal 2:14 . . . the Lord is acting as the witness between you and the wife of your youth, because you have broken faith with her, though she is your partner, the wife of your marriage covenant.   *See also* **Pr** 2:17; **Eze** 16:8

Sex and marriage
Sex belongs within marriage
1Co 7:9 But if they cannot control themselves, they should marry, for it is better to marry than to burn with passion.   *See also* **Ge** 29:21
Men who violated virgins were expected to marry them: **Ex** 22:16–17; **Dt** 22:28–29
Dt 22:13–21

The sexual relationship is exclusive
SS 2:16 My lover is mine and I am his . . .
See also **Dt** 22:22–24; **Pr** 5:15–19; **1Co** 6:16; 7:3–5

Love and submission in marriage
Falling in love prior to marriage
Ge 29:20 So Jacob served seven years to get Rachel, but they seemed like only a few days to him because of his love for her.   *See also* **Ge** 34:3–4; **1Sa** 18:20

Husbands are to love their wives
Eph 5:25 Husbands, love your wives, just as Christ loved the church and gave himself up for her   *See also* **Ge** 24:67; **1Sa** 1:5; **Ecc** 9:9; **Hos** 3:1; **Eph** 5:28–29,33; **Col** 3:19

Wives are to submit to their husbands
Ge 3:16 To the woman he [the Lord God] said, ". . . Your desire will be for your husband, and he will rule over you."

Eph 5:22–24 Wives, submit to your husbands as to the Lord . . .   *See also* **Col** 3:18; **Tit** 2:4–5; **1Pe** 3:1–6

Celibacy as a calling from God
1Co 7:7–8 I [Paul] wish that all of you were as I am [unmarried]. But each of you has your own gift from God; one has this gift, another has that . . .   *See also* **Jer** 16:2; **Mt** 19:10–12; **1Co** 7:36–38; **1Ti** 5:11–14   *See also* children; husband; male and female; wife.

---

marriage, restrictions

The OT law forbade intermarriage with people who worshipped idols because it threatened the covenant relationship with God and his people. Marriage with close relations was also forbidden. Remarriage is permissible following the death of a spouse and, in certain circumstances, following divorce.

Intermarriage with foreigners
Examples of marriages to foreigners Ge 38:2; 41:45; **Ex** 2:21; **Lev** 24:10; **Ru** 1:4; **1Ch** 2:34–35; **Ezr** 10:18–44

Warnings against marrying foreigners
Ex 34:16 "And when you [Israelites] choose some of their [non-Israelite] daughters as wives for your sons and those daughters prostitute themselves to their gods, they will lead your sons to do the same."   *See also* **Dt** 7:3–4; **Jos** 23:12–13

Intermarriage with foreigners led to idolatry
Jdg 3:5–6 The Israelites lived among the Canaanites, Hittites, Amorites, Perizzites, Hivites and Jebusites. They took their daughters in marriage and gave their own daughters to their sons, and served their gods.

1Ki 11:1–8 . . . As Solomon grew old, his wives turned his heart after other gods, and his heart was not fully devoted to the Lord his God, as the heart of David his father had been . . .
See also **1Ki** 16:31; **Mal** 2:11
Intermarriage among returning exiles was a major problem facing Ezra and Nehemiah: **Ezr** 9:1–2,14; 10:1–2; **Ne** 13:23–27

Parents sought to avoid their children marrying foreigners
Ne 10:30 "We [the returning exiles] promise not to give our daughters in marriage to the peoples around us or take their daughters for our sons." *See also* **Ge** 24:3–4
Esau's foreign wives are a source of grief to his parents: **Ge** 26:34–35; 27:46
Ge 28:1–2; **Jdg** 14:3
Marriage to foreigners may be permissible Ru 4:13
Foreign wives were put aside after the exile
Ezr 10:3 "Now let us make a covenant before our God to send away all these women and their children, in accordance with the counsel of my lord and of those who fear the commands of our God. Let it be done according to the Law." *See also* **Ezr** 10:10–17

Marriages between Christians and unbelievers
Christians should not marry unbelievers 1Co 7:39; **2Co** 6:14
Christians should not leave an unbelieving spouse 1Co 7:12–16

Restrictions on marriage to close relatives
Sexual relations with close relatives is forbidden
Lev 18:6–18 " 'No-one is to approach any close relative to have sexual relations. I am the LORD . . .' " *See also* **Lev** 20:11–12,14,19–21; **Dt** 22:30; **Eze** 22:10–11; **Mt** 14:3–4 pp **Mk** 6:17–18
Examples of marriage to close relatives Ge 20:12; **2Sa** 13:13

Levirate marriage
The levirate law was instituted to preserve the dead father's name
Dt 25:5–10 If brothers are living together and one of them dies without a son, his widow must not marry outside the family. Her husband's brother shall take her and marry her and fulfil the duty of a brother-in-law to her. The first son she bears shall carry on the name of the dead brother

so that his name will not be blotted out from Israel . . .
Ru 4:10 "I [Boaz] have also acquired Ruth the Moabite, Mahlon's widow, as my wife, in order to maintain the name of the dead with his property, so that his name will not disappear from among his family or from the town records. Today you are witnesses!" *See also* **Ge** 38:8,11; **Ru** 1:11–13; 3:9; 4:5; **Mt** 22:24–26 pp **Mk** 12:19–22 pp **Lk** 20:28–31
Unwillingness to fulfil the levirate law Ge 38:9,14,26; **Ru** 4:6

Regulations governing seduction and rape
Ex 22:16; **Dt** 22:28–29

Remarriage
Widows are free to remarry
Ro 7:2–3 For example, by law a married woman is bound to her husband as long as he is alive, but if her husband dies, she is released from the law of marriage . . . *See also* **Ru** 1:9; **1Co** 7:8–9; **1Ti** 5:14
Remarriage after divorce may be adultery
Lk 16:18 "Anyone who divorces his wife and marries another woman commits adultery, and the man who marries a divorced woman commits adultery." pp **Mt** 19:9 pp **Mk** 10:11–12 *See also* **1Co** 7:10–11
Remarriage after divorce permissible in certain circumstances Dt 24:1–4; **Mt** 5:32; **1Co** 7:15,27–28 *See also divorce; widows.*

---

meals
Food eaten at set times, on special occasions or following significant events. Sacrificial meals formed part of Israelite worship in the OT, as does the Lord's Supper for worship by believers in the NT.

Regular daily meals

Breakfast
Jn 21:12 Jesus said to them [the disciples], "Come and have breakfast." . . .

Lunch

Lk 14:12–14 Then Jesus said to his host, "When you give a luncheon or dinner, do not invite your friends, brothers, sisters, relatives, or your rich neighbours; if you do, they may invite you back and so you will be repaid . . ."
See also **Ge** 43:16,31–34; **Ru** 2:14; **Ac** 10:9–10

Evening meal

Lk 17:7–8 "Suppose one of you had a servant ploughing or looking after the sheep. Would he say to the servant when he comes in from the field, 'Come along now and sit down to eat'? Would he not rather say, 'Prepare my supper, get yourself ready and wait on me while I eat and drink; after that you may eat and drink'?"
See also **Mt** 9:10–13 pp Mk 2:15–17 pp Lk 5:29–32; **Mk** 14:3 pp Lk 7:36 pp Jn 12:1–2; **Lk** 14:12–14

Royal meals

Ge 40:20 Now the third day was Pharaoh's birthday, and he gave a feast for all his officials . . . *See also* **1Sa** 20:18–34; **2Sa** 9:9–13; **1Ki** 4:22–28; 18:19; **Est** 1:1–12; 2:18; 7:1–10; **Mt** 14:6–11 pp Mk 6:21–28

Meals of the poor

Pr 15:17 Better a meal of vegetables where there is love than a fattened calf with hatred.
See also **1Ki** 17:10–16

Sacrificial meals

Ge 31:53–54 . . . Jacob took an oath in the name of the Fear of his father Isaac. He offered a sacrifice there in the hill country and invited his relatives to a meal . . . *See also* **Ex** 12:1–11; 29:31–34; **Lev** 6:14–29; 7:1–6; 8:31; 10:12–15; **Dt** 16:1–8; **1Sa** 1:3–8; 9:11–24; 20:28–29

Symbolic meals

Mt 26:20–29 . . . he [Jesus] took the cup, gave thanks and offered it to them, saying, "Drink from it, all of you. This is my blood of the covenant, which is poured out for many for the forgiveness of sins . . ." pp Mk 14:17–25 pp Lk 22:14–22 *See also* **1Co** 11:17–34

Wedding and funeral meals

Mt 22:1–14 Jesus spoke to them again in parables, saying: "The kingdom of heaven is like a king who prepared a wedding banquet for his son. He sent his servants to those who had been invited to the banquet to tell them to come, but they refused to come. "Then he sent some more servants and said, 'Tell those who have been invited that I have prepared my dinner: My oxen and fattened cattle have been slaughtered, and everything is ready. Come to the wedding banquet.' . . ." pp Lk 14:16–24 *See also* **Jer** 16:5; **Jn** 2:1–10; **Rev** 19:6–9

Meals and hospitality

2Ki 4:8 One day Elisha went to Shunem. And a well-to-do woman was there, who urged him to stay for a meal. So whenever he came by, he stopped there to eat. *See also* **Ge** 18:1–8; 19:1–3; **Jdg** 5:24–25; 13:15–16; **1Sa** 28:24–25

Meals as occasions of fellowship

Rev 3:20 "Here I am! I stand at the door and knock. If anyone hears my voice and opens the door, I will come in and eat with them, and they with me." *See also* **Pr** 15:17; **Lk** 5:29–32; 7:36 *See also banquets; covenant; eating; feast and festival; food; sacrifice, in Old Testament; wedding.*

measures, dry

These terms derive originally from the containers used, which held a fixed amount. Measures are given in ascending order, with their approximate imperial and metric equivalents.

Cab (1/18 ephah): about 2 pints (about 1 litre)

2Ki 6:25 There was a great famine in the city; the siege lasted so long that a donkey's head sold for eighty shekels of silver, and a fourth of a cab of seed pods for five shekels.

Omer (1/10 ephah): about 4 pints (about 2 litres)

Ex 16:16–22 "This is what the LORD has commanded: 'Each one is to gather as much as he needs. Take an omer for each person you have in your tent.'" . . .   *See also* **Ex** 16:32,36

Seah (1/3 ephah): about 13 pints (about 7.3 litres)
Ge 18:6 So Abraham hurried into the tent to Sarah. "Quick," he said, "get three seahs of fine flour and knead it and bake some bread." *See also* **1Sa** 25:18; **1Ki** 18:32; **2Ki** 7:1

Ephah: about 3/5 bushel (about 22 litres)
Ru 2:17 So Ruth gleaned in the field until evening. Then she threshed the barley she had gathered, and it amounted to about an ephah. *See also* **Lev** 5:11; 24:5; **Nu** 15:4–9; **Jdg** 6:19; **1Sa** 17:17; **Eze** 45:10–11; **Zec** 5:6–8   *The word for "measuring basket" in the Hebrew is "ephah".*

Lethek (5 ephahs or 1/2 homer): about 3 bushels (about 110 litres)
Hos 3:2 So I [Hosea] bought her [his wife] for fifteen shekels of silver and about a homer and a lethek of barley.

Cor or homer (10 ephahs): about 6 bushels (about 220 litres)
Cor
1Ki 4:22 Solomon's daily provisions were thirty cors of fine flour and sixty cors of meal, *See also* **1Ki** 5:11; **2Ch** 2:10; 27:5; **Ezr** 7:22; **Eze** 45:14
Homer
Lev 27:16 "'If you dedicate to the LORD part of your family land, its value is to be set according to the amount of seed required for it— fifty shekels of silver to a homer of barley seed.'"   *See also* **Nu** 11:32; **Isa** 5:10; **Eze** 45:11,13–14; **Hos** 3:2

Other dry measures found in the NT
Quart (choinix): about 1 1/2–2 pints (about 1 litre) **Rev** 6:6
Saton (equivalent to the OT seah) **Mt** 13:33 pp Lk 13:21   *The "large amount" referred to is "three sata" in the Greek.*
Bowl (modius): about 15 1/2 pints (about

8.75 litres) **Mt** 5:15 pp Mk 4:21 pp Lk 11:33
Koros (equivalent to the OT cor) **Lk** 16:7   *The measure translated as "a thousand bushels" is "one hundred korous" in the Greek.   See also sacrifice, in Old Testament; weights.*

---

measures, linear
These terms were based on natural units of measurement that could be easily applied. Measures are given in ascending order, with their approximate imperial and metric equivalents.

Finger (1/4 handbreadth): about 3/4 inch (about 1.85 centimetres)
Jer 52:21 Each of the pillars was eighteen cubits high and twelve cubits in circumference; each was four fingers thick, and hollow.

Handbreadth (4 fingers): about 3 inches (about 8 centimetres)
Ex 25:25 "Also make around it [the table] a rim a handbreadth wide and put a gold moulding on the rim." pp Ex 37:12   *The handbreadth was the width of the hand at the base of the four fingers.   See also* **1Ki** 7:26 pp 2Ch 4:5; **Ps** 39:5   *The handbreadth is here used figuratively of the shortness of human life;* **Eze** 40:5

Span (half a cubit): about 9 inches (about 23 centimetres)
Ex 28:16 "It [the breastpiece] is to be square—a span long and a span wide—and folded double." pp Ex 39:9   *The span was the width of the outstretched hand from thumb to little finger.   See also* **1Sa** 17:4; **Ps** 90:10; **Eze** 43:13

Cubit (2 spans): about 18 inches (about 0.5 metre)
Ex 25:10 "Have them [the Israelites] make a chest of acacia wood—two and a half cubits long, a cubit and a half wide, and a cubit and a half high." pp Ex 37:1   *The cubit was the distance from the fingertip to the elbow, and was used to measure height, size, depth and distance.   See also* **Ge** 7:20   *The Hebrew describes the depth of the water as "fifteen cubits";*

Ex 27:9–18 pp Ex 38:9–15; **1Ki** 6:2–3 pp 2Ch 3:3–4; **1Ch** 11:23 *The Hebrew describes the man as "five cubits tall";* **Eze** 40:5; 45:1–6; 47:3–5; **Jn** 21:8 *The Greek text describes the distance as "about two hundred cubits";* **Rev** 21:17

Reed (6 cubits): about 10 feet (about 3 metres)

Eze 41:8 I [Ezekiel] saw that the temple had a raised base all round it, forming the foundation of the side rooms. It was the length of the rod, six long cubits. *See also* **Eze** 40:3,5–7; **Rev** 11:1; 21:15–16

Mile

Mt 5:41 "If someone forces you to go one mile, go two miles." *See also* **Lk** 24:13 *The measurement in the Greek is "sixty stadia". Eight stadia were about one mile (about 1480 metres);* **Jn** 6:19 *The measurement in the Greek is "twenty-five or thirty stadia";* **Jn** 11:18 *The measurement in the Greek is "fifteen stadia".*

measures, liquid

These terms derive originally from the containers used, which held a fixed amount. There is some uncertainty about the capacity of the bath, and therefore of other liquid measures dependent upon it. Measures are given in ascending order, with their approximate imperial and metric equivalents.

Log (1/72 bath): about 1/2 pint (about 0.3 litre)

Lev 14:10 "On the eighth day they must each bring two male lambs and one ewe lamb a year old, each without defect, along with three-tenths of an ephah of fine flour mixed with oil for a grain offering, and one log of oil." *See also* **Lev** 14:12–18,21–22

Hin (1/6 bath): about 7 pints (about 4 litres)

Ex 29:38–41 ". . . With the first lamb offer a tenth of an ephah of fine flour mixed with a quarter of a hin of oil from pressed olives, and a quarter of a hin of wine as a drink offering . . ." *See also* **Lev** 23:12–13; **Nu** 15:4–10; **Eze** 4:11; 46:5–7

Bath (1 ephah): about 5 gallons (about 22 litres)

Eze 45:11 " 'The ephah and the bath are to be the same size, the bath containing a tenth of a homer and the ephah a tenth of a homer; the homer is to be the standard measure for both.' " *See also* **1Ki** 5:11; 7:38; **2Ch** 2:10; **Ezr** 7:21–22; **Isa** 5:10; **Eze** 45:14; **Lk** 16:6 *The measure translated as "eight hundred gallons" is "one hundred batous" in the original ("batos" being the Greek form of the Hebrew "bath");* **Jn** 2:6 *The measure translated as "twenty to thirty gallons" is "two to three metretas" in the original, a Greek measure roughly equivalent to the bath. See also water; wine.*

meat

The flesh of animals, consumed as food. In biblical times it was a luxury, eaten on special occasions, usually in the context of sacrificial worship.

Meat a luxury food

Ex 16:3 The Israelites said to them [Moses and Aaron], "If only we had died by the LORD's hand in Egypt! There we sat round pots of meat and ate all the food we wanted, but you have brought us out into this desert to starve this entire assembly to death." *See also* **Nu** 11:4–5; **1Sa** 25:11; **Isa** 22:12–13; **Da** 10:3

Meat served to honoured guests

1Sa 28:21–25 . . . The woman had a fattened calf at the house, which she slaughtered at once. She took some flour, kneaded it and baked bread without yeast. Then she set it before Saul and his men, and they ate. That same night they got up and left. *See also* **Ge** 18:1–8; **Jdg** 6:11–21; 13:9–16; **1Sa** 9:22–24; **2Sa** 12:1–4; **1Ki** 19:19–21; **Pr** 9:1–6; **Isa** 25:6; **Lk** 15:20–24

Meat provided by God

1Ki 17:2–6 . . . The ravens brought him [Elijah] bread and meat in the morning and bread and meat in the evening, and he drank from the brook. *See also* **Ex** 16:1–14; **Nu** 11:4–34; **Ps** 78:17–31

Restrictions on eating certain types of meat
Unclean meat
Lev 11:1–47 . . . ". . . '. . . You must distinguish between the unclean and the clean, between living creatures that may be eaten and those that may not be eaten.'" pp Dt 14:3–20   *See also* **Isa** 65:2–5
Other prohibited meat
Ge 9:4 ". . . you must not eat meat that has its lifeblood still in it."   *See also* **Ex** 21:28; 22:31; **Lev** 19:26; **Dt** 12:23; 14:21; **1Sa** 14:33–34; **Eze** 4:14; 33:25; **Ac** 15:20,29; 21:25

Eating meat in worship
The Passover lamb
Ex 12:1–11 . . . ". . . That same night they are to eat the meat roasted over the fire, along with bitter herbs, and bread made without yeast. Do not eat the meat raw or cooked in water, but roast it over the fire—head, legs and inner parts. Do not leave any of it till morning; if some is left till morning, you must burn it . . ."   *See also* **Ex** 12:43–49; **Dt** 16:1–8
Other sacrifices
Ex 29:31–34 "Take the ram for the ordination and cook the meat in a sacred place. At the entrance to the Tent of Meeting, Aaron and his sons are to eat the meat of the ram and the bread that is in the basket . . ."   *See also* **Lev** 7:11–18; **Nu** 18:14–19; **Dt** 12:27; **1Sa** 1:3–8; 2:12–16; **Jer** 7:21; **Hos** 8:13

Non-consecrated meat
Dt 12:4–25

Allegorical and metaphorical references to meat
Mic 3:1–3 Then I [the LORD] said, "Listen, you leaders of Jacob, you rulers of the house of Israel. Should you not know justice, you who hate good and love evil; who tear the skin from my people and the flesh from their bones; who eat my people's flesh, strip off their skin and break their bones in pieces; who chop them up like meat for the pan, like flesh for the pot."   *See also* **Eze** 11:1–12; 24:1–13

Varying convictions about eating meat
Ro 14:1–23   *See also clean and unclean; food; meals; Passover; sacrifice, in Old Testament; unleavened bread.*

---

medicine
The means that God has given for the cure of physical troubles. Medicine often symbolises the application of the gospel of God's grace in Jesus Christ for the healing of moral and spiritual ills.

Preventative medicine
A cheerful disposition
Pr 17:22 A cheerful heart is good medicine, but a crushed spirit dries up the bones.
Disinfection Lev 14:41; 15:5
Salt Eze 16:4
Physical exercise 1Ti 4:8

Curative medicine
Balm
Jer 51:8 ". . . Get balm for her [Babylon's] pain; perhaps she can be healed."   *See also* **Jer** 8:22; 46:11
Leaves
Eze 47:12 ". . . Their fruit will serve for food and their leaves for healing."   *See also* **Rev** 22:2
Mud Jn 9:6
Oil Mk 6:13; **Lk** 10:34; **Jas** 5:14
A poultice
2Ki 20:7 Then Isaiah said, "Prepare a poultice of figs." They did so and applied it to the boil, and he recovered.   *See also* **Isa** 38:21
Spittle Mk 7:33
Water Lev 15:5; **2Ki** 5:10; **Jn** 9:7
Wine
1Ti 5:23 Stop drinking only water, and use a little wine because of your [Timothy's] stomach and your frequent illnesses.   *See also* **Lk** 10:34
Eye salve
Rev 3:18 "I [Jesus Christ] counsel you to buy from me gold refined in the fire, so that you can become rich; and white clothes to wear, so that you can cover your shameful nakedness; and salve to put on your eyes, so that you can see."

Music

The music was intended to cure moods of depression in Saul's case, and extreme agitation in Elisha: **1Sa** 16:23; 18:10; **2Ki** 3:14–15
Spiritual surgery Mt 5:27–30; **Ro** 8:13

Soothing medicine
Myrrh
Mk 15:23 Then they [soldiers] offered him wine mixed with myrrh, but he did not take it.
Oil Isa 1:6
Wine Pr 31:6; **Mt** 27:48; **Lk** 23:36

Medicine cannot cure everything
Dt 28:27; **Jer** 17:9; 30:12–13; 46:11; **Mk** 5:25–26

Application of the gospel as medicine
Mt 11:28 "Come to me [Jesus Christ], all you who are weary and burdened, and I will give you rest."   *See also* **Lk** 5:31–32

Resurrection as the ultimate medicine for all ills
1Co 15:42–44 . . . The body that is sown is perishable, it is raised imperishable; it is sown in dishonour, it is raised in glory; it is sown in weakness, it is raised in power; it is sown a natural body, it is raised a spiritual body. If there is a natural body, there is also a spiritual body.   *See also* **Php** 3:20–21   *See also cures; disease; healing; wine.*

---

metals
Gold, silver, bronze, iron, copper, tin and lead are all mentioned in Scripture. Prized for their value, they were used in a variety of ways. Scripture uses as an image a metal refiner's fire for the purification of the lives of believers.

Gold
Job 23:10 "But he [the LORD] knows the way that I [Job] take; when he has tested me, I shall come forth as gold."   *See also* **Ex** 25:10–22; 38:21–24; **1Ki** 6:27–35; 7:48–50; 10:14–21; **Ps** 19:7–11; **Rev** 3:18; 17:4

Silver
Ps 12:6 . . . the words of the LORD are flawless, like silver refined in a furnace of clay, purified seven times.   *See also* **Ge** 37:26–28; **Ex** 38:25–28; **2Ch** 9:26–27; **Ps** 119:72; **Mt** 27:3–10

Bronze
Ge 4:22 Zillah also had a son, Tubal-cain, who forged all kinds of tools out of bronze and iron . . .   *See also* **Ex** 27:1–7; 38:29–31; **Nu** 16:31–40; **2Ch** 4:9–18

Iron
Dt 3:11 (Only Og king of Bashan was left of the remnant of the Rephaites. His bed was made of iron and was more than thirteen feet long and six feet wide. It is still in Rabbah of the Ammonites.)   *See also* **Dt** 8:7–9; **Jdg** 4:2–3; **Job** 40:15–18; **Eze** 27:19

Copper
Job 28:2 "Iron is taken from the earth, and copper is smelted from ore."   *See also* **Mk** 12:41–44 pp Lk 21:1–4

Tin
Eze 27:12 "'Tarshish did business with you [Tyre] because of your great wealth of goods; they exchanged silver, iron, tin and lead for your merchandise.'"   *See also* **Eze** 22:18

Lead
It was an exceptionally heavy metal
Ex 15:10 ". . . you [the LORD] blew with your breath, and the sea covered them [the enemy]. They sank like lead in the mighty waters."
See also **Zec** 5:5–8
It was refined before use
Jer 6:29 "The bellows blow fiercely to burn away the lead with fire . . ."   *See also* **Nu** 31:21–23; **Eze** 22:18–20
Inscriptions were sometimes made on lead
Job 19:23–24 "Oh, that my [Job's] words were recorded, that they were written on a scroll, that they were inscribed with an iron tool on lead, or engraved in rock for ever!"
It was traded between nations
Eze 27:12 "'Tarshish did business with you

[Tyre] because of your great wealth of goods; they exchanged silver, iron, tin and lead for your merchandise.'"

The value of metals
All metals were of value
Jos 22:8 . . . "Return to your homes with your great wealth—with large herds of livestock, with silver, gold, bronze and iron, and a great quantity of clothing—and divide with your people the plunder from your enemies."   *See also* **1Ch** 18:10; 22:14; 29:1–7; **Rev** 18:11–12
The relative value of metals
Isa 60:17 "Instead of bronze I [the LORD] will bring you [Israel] gold, and silver in place of iron. Instead of wood I will bring you bronze, and iron in place of stones. I will make peace your governor and righteousness your ruler."   *See also* **1Ki** 10:21 pp 2Ch 9:20; **1Ki** 14:25–28

Trade with metals
1Ki 10:22 The king had a fleet of trading ships at sea along with the ships of Hiram. Once every three years it returned carrying gold, silver and ivory, and apes and baboons. pp 2Ch 9:21 *See also* **Ge** 37:28; **1Ki** 10:11,14–15 pp 2Ch 9:13–14; **1Ki** 22:48; **Eze** 27:13,22; **Zep** 1:11

Idols were often made from various metals
Lev 19:4 " 'Do not turn to idols or make gods of cast metal for yourselves. I am the LORD your God.' "   *See also* **1Ki** 14:9; **Ps** 106:19; **Isa** 48:5; **Da** 5:22–23; 11:8

The refining of metals as an image of purification
Isa 48:10 "See, I have refined you, though not as silver; I have tested you in the furnace of affliction."

Mal 3:2 But who can endure the day of his coming? Who can stand when he appears? For he will be like a refiner's fire or a launderer's soap.   *See also* **Ps** 12:6; **Zec** 13:9   *See also idolatry; minerals; refining; trade.*

minerals
Material mined from the earth, especially metal ores and other substances of neither animal nor vegetable origin.

Bitumen
Ge 11:1–4

Chalk
Isa 27:9 By this, then, will Jacob's guilt be atoned for, and this will be the full fruitage of the removal of his sin: When he makes all the altar stones to be like chalk stones crushed to pieces, no Asherah poles or incense altars will be left standing.

Crystal
Job 28:17; **Rev** 4:6

Flint
Eze 3:9 "I [the LORD] will make your [Ezekiel's] forehead like the hardest stone, harder than flint. Do not be afraid of them or terrified by them, though they are a rebellious house." *See also* **Job** 28:9; **Zec** 7:12

Lime
Am 2:1 This is what the LORD says: "For three sins of Moab, even for four, I will not turn back ⌐my wrath⌐. Because he burned, as if to lime, the bones of Edom's king,"   *See also* **Isa** 33:10–12

Marble
Est 1:6 The garden had hangings of white and blue linen, fastened with cords of white linen and purple material to silver rings on marble pillars. There were couches of gold and silver on a mosaic pavement of porphyry, marble, mother-of-pearl and other costly stones.   *See also* **1Ch** 29:2; **SS** 5:15; **Rev** 18:11–12

Pitch
Ge 6:14 "So make yourself [Noah] an ark of cypress wood; make rooms in it and coat it with pitch inside and out."   *See also* **Ex** 2:3; **Isa** 34:9

Salt

Lev 2:13 " 'Season all your grain offerings with salt. Do not leave the salt of the covenant of your God out of your grain offerings; add salt to all your offerings.' " *See also* **Dt** 29:23; **Job** 39:5–6; **Eze** 47:6–11

Soda

Pr 25:20 Like one who takes away a garment on a cold day, or like vinegar poured on soda, is one who sings songs to a heavy heart. *See also* **Job** 9:30–31; **Jer** 2:22

Sulphur

Ge 19:24 . . . the LORD rained down burning sulphur on Sodom and Gomorrah—from the LORD out of the heavens. *See also* **Dt** 29:23; **Lk** 17:29; **Rev** 19:20

Tar

Ge 14:10 Now the Valley of Siddim was full of tar pits, and when the kings of Sodom and Gomorrah fled, some of the men fell into them and the rest fled to the hills. *See also* **Ex** 2:3

Precious stones

Eze 28:13 " 'You [the king of Tyre] were in Eden, the garden of God; every precious stone adorned you: ruby, topaz and emerald, chrysolite, onyx and jasper, sapphire, turquoise and beryl . . .' " *See also* **Ex** 28:15–21; **Job** 28:5–6; **Isa** 54:11–12; **Eze** 27:16; **Rev** 21:18

Metals

Isa 60:17 "Instead of bronze I [the LORD] will bring you gold, and silver in place of iron. Instead of wood I will bring you bronze, and iron in place of stones . . ." *See also* **Nu** 31:21–23; **Dt** 8:7–9; **Job** 28:2; **Ps** 119:72; **Eze** 27:12

Stone

Pr 27:3 Stone is heavy and sand a burden, but provocation by a fool is heavier than both. *See also* **Jos** 7:3–5; **Job** 6:12; 38:29–30; **Jer** 5:3

Sand

Mt 7:24–27 *See also* metals; stones.

money

Scripture stresses the positive and negative aspects of money, making it clear that the pursuit or love of money can easily lead to spiritual decay.

money, stewardship

The righteous handling of money is an important practical test of godliness.

Money must be obtained honestly
Not by theft
Ex 20:15 "You shall not steal." pp Dt 5:19
See also **Pr** 10:2; 19:26; **Mk** 10:19
Not by fraudulent practices
Lev 19:13 " 'Do not defraud your neighbours or rob them . . .' " *See also* **Pr** 11:1; 13:11; 20:10; **Eze** 28:18
Not by usury
Ex 22:25 "If you lend money to one of my people among you who is needy, do not be like a money-lender; charge no interest." *See also* **Ps** 15:5; **Pr** 28:8
Not at the expense of justice
Ex 23:8 "Do not accept a bribe . . ."
See also **Pr** 15:27; 16:8; **Jer** 17:11
Not by extortion
Lk 3:13 "Don't collect any more than you [tax collectors] are required to," . . . *See also* **Eze** 22:12
Not by oppression
Jas 5:4 Look! The wages you [rich people] failed to pay the workers who mowed your fields are crying out against you . . . *See also* **Pr** 22:16; **Eze** 18:7–8; **Am** 5:11; **Mal** 3:5
Not at the expense of health **Pr** 23:4
Not at the expense of witness **Ge** 14:22–23; **3Jn** 7
Not at the expense of spiritual well-being **Mt** 16:26 pp Mk 8:36 pp Lk 9:25; **Lk** 12:16–21; **1Ti** 6:9
By work, trade, investment or inheritance
2Th 3:12 Such people we command and urge in the Lord Jesus Christ to settle down and earn the bread they eat. *See also* **Ge** 15:2; 34:21; **Pr** 13:11,22; 14:23; 19:14; **Mt** 25:27 pp Lk 19:23

Money must be cared for diligently
Personal money Pr 27:23–24
Money held on trust 2Ki 22:4–7; **Mt** 25:14–27; **Lk** 16:10–12; **1Co** 4:2

Money must be used in a God-honouring way
For the support of the family
1Ti 5:8 Anyone who does not provide for relatives, and especially for immediate family members, has denied the faith and is worse than an unbeliever. *See also* **1Ti** 5:16
For benefiting the poor, especially God's people
Gal 6:10 Therefore, as we have opportunity, let us do good to all people, especially to those who belong to the family of believers. *See also* **Pr** 19:17; 28:27; **Mt** 6:3–4; **Lk** 12:33; **Jn** 13:29; **Ac** 2:45; **Ro** 15:26; **Gal** 2:10; **1Ti** 6:18
For the work of God's kingdom
Gal 6:6 Those who receive instruction in the word must share all good things with their instructor. *See also* **Pr** 3:9–10; **Mal** 3:10; **Lk** 8:3; 16:9; **Php** 4:14–19; **1Ti** 5:17–18

Examples of godly people who have used their money well
Those who were wealthy but godly Ge 13:2; 26:14; 30:43; **2Sa** 19:32; **2Ch** 9:22; **Job** 1:3; **Mt** 27:57; **Ac** 4:34–36
Those who had little but gave much Mk 12:41–44 pp **Lk** 21:1–4; **2Co** 8:1–4 *See also poverty; property; shepherd; stewardship; tithing.*

money, uses
Monetary transactions have taken place from the earliest biblical times. Originally precious metals were weighed out; coins were introduced later.

The first mention of money
Ge 17:12 ". . . every male . . . must be circumcised, including those born in your household or bought with money from a foreigner . . ."

The use of money
For the purchase and sale of land
Ge 23:14–15 Ephron answered Abraham, "Listen to me, my lord; the land [the burial place at Machpelah] is worth four hundred shekels of silver . . ." *See also* **Jer** 32:9–10; **Mt** 27:7; **Ac** 4:34; 5:1–2; 7:16
For the purchase and sale of food Ge 41:57; 42:5,35; **2Ki** 7:16; **Jn** 6:5,7; **Rev** 6:6
For other merchandise
Rev 18:11–13 ". . . cargoes of gold, silver, precious stones and pearls; fine linen, purple, silk and scarlet cloth; every sort of citron wood, and articles of every kind made of ivory, costly wood, bronze, iron and marble; cargoes of cinnamon and spice, of incense, myrrh and frankincense, of wine and olive oil, of fine flour and wheat; cattle and sheep; horses and carriages; and slaves—human beings!" *See also* **Ge** 37:25; **Jas** 4:13
For religious offerings
Ex 30:11–16 . . . ". . . Receive the atonement money from the Israelites and use it for the service of the Tent of Meeting . . ." *See also* **Nu** 3:44–48; **Dt** 12:4–6; **2Ki** 22:4–6 pp 2Ch 34:9–11; **Ezr** 7:15–17
For gifts to the poor
Mt 26:9 "This perfume could have been sold at a high price and the money given to the poor." pp Mk 14:5 pp Jn 12:5 *See also* **Ac** 3:3
For wages
Mt 20:2 "He agreed to pay them a denarius for the day and sent them into his vineyard." *See also* **Jas** 5:4
For investment and moneylending
Mt 25:27 "'. . . you should have put my money on deposit with the bankers, so that when I [the master] returned I would have received it back with interest.'" pp Lk 19:23 *See also* **Ex** 22:25; **Ne** 5:10–11; **Lk** 6:34–35
For provision for the future Ecc 7:12
For the settlement of disputes Ex 21:8–11,35; 22:15
For taxes
Mt 17:24 . . . "Doesn't your teacher pay the temple tax?" *See also* **1Ki** 10:15; **Ne** 5:4; **Mt** 22:17–19 pp Mk 12:15 pp Lk 20:22–24
For tribute money 2Ki 15:19–20
For the purchase of slaves Lev 22:11
For bribery Est 3:9; **Mt** 28:12–13; **Ac** 24:26
Fortune-telling for money Mic 3:11; **Ac** 16:16
Blood money Mt 27:6

Money changers
Mt 21:12 Jesus entered the temple area and drove out all who were buying and selling there. He overturned the tables of the money changers and the benches of those selling doves. pp Mk 11:15 pp Jn 2:14   *See also buying and selling; coinage; slavery; taxation.*

Most Holy Place

The inner sanctuary of the tabernacle set up at Sinai and of Solomon's temple, where the ark of the covenant was kept. It is a symbol of the unapproachable presence of God.

Terms used to describe the Most Holy Place
The Most Holy Place Ex 26:33
The inner sanctuary 1Ki 6:16
Literally, "the second (tabernacle)" Heb 9:7

The structure and design of the Most Holy Place
In the wilderness tabernacle
The only details concern the curtains forming the walls of the two sanctuaries, and in particular the dividing curtain which separates the Most Holy Place from the outer sanctuary: **Ex** 26:31–33; 36:35–36; 40:21
In Solomon's temple 1Ki 6:16,19–20 pp 2Ch 3:8; **1Ki** 6:23–28 pp 2Ch 3:10; **1Ki** 6:31–32; **2Ch** 3:14
In the temple in Ezekiel's vision Eze 41:4,15–21,23; 45:3

The significance and function of the Most Holy Place
To house the ark of the covenant
Ex 26:33 "Hang the curtain from the clasps and place the ark of the Testimony behind the curtain. The curtain will separate the Holy Place from the Most Holy Place."   *See also* **Ex** 40:3; **1Ki** 6:19; 8:6–9 pp 2Ch 5:7–9
To house the incense altar (in Solomon's temple)
1Ki 6:22 . . . he [Solomon] overlaid the whole interior with gold. He also overlaid with gold the altar that belonged to the inner sanctuary.
Heb 9:3–4 Behind the second curtain was a

room called the Most Holy Place, which had the golden altar of incense and the gold-covered ark of the covenant. This ark contained the gold jar of manna, Aaron's staff that had budded, and the stone tablets of the covenant.
To be a symbol of the presence of God
Ps 28:2 Hear my cry for mercy as I call to you for help, as I lift up my hands towards your Most Holy Place.   *See also* **Ex** 26:33; **Lev** 16:2

The Most Holy Place on the Day of Atonement
Heb 9:7 But only the high priest entered the inner room, and that only once a year, and never without blood, which he offered for himself and for the sins the people had committed in ignorance.   *See also* **Lev** 16:16–17

The NT understanding of the Most Holy Place as the place of God's heavenly presence
Jesus Christ enters the Most Holy Place as Mediator
Heb 9:8 The Holy Spirit was showing by this that the way into the Most Holy Place had not yet been disclosed as long as the first tabernacle was still standing.   *See also* **Heb** 6:19–20; 9:11–12,24
Entry to the Most Holy Place is open to all believers
Heb 10:19–22 Therefore, brothers and sisters, since we have confidence to enter the Most Holy Place by the blood of Jesus, by a new and living way opened for us through the curtain, that is, his body, and since we have a great priest over the house of God, let us draw near to God with a sincere heart in full assurance of faith, having our hearts sprinkled to cleanse us from a guilty conscience and having our bodies washed with pure water.   *See also* **Mt** 27:51 pp Lk 23:45
See also ark of the covenant; Atonement, Day of; curtain; tabernacle, in Old Testament; temple, Solomon's.

---

mothers

The female parent of children. The role and influence of mothers are frequently stressed in

Scripture, and their care for children is used as a picture of God's care for his people.

mothers, examples
Examples are given in Scripture of notable mothers, mothers-in-law and grandmothers.

Eve, the mother of all the living
Ge 3:20 Adam named his wife Eve, because she would become the mother of all the living. *See also* **Ge** 3:16

Hagar, the mother of Ishmael
Ge 16:1-4,15

Sarah, the mother of Isaac
Ge 21:1-3 Now the LORD was gracious to Sarah as he had said, and the LORD did for Sarah what he had promised. Sarah became pregnant and bore a son to Abraham in his old age, at the very time God had promised him. Abraham gave the name Isaac to the son Sarah bore him. *See also* **Ge** 17:15-19; 18:10-14

Rebekah, mother of Esau and Jacob
Ge 25:21,24; 27:5-17

Rachel, mother of Joseph and Benjamin
Ge 30:22-24; 35:16-18

Jochebed, mother of Moses
Ex 2:1-2; 6:20; **Heb** 11:23

Naomi, Ruth's mother-in-law
Ru 1:15; 4:13-17

Hannah, mother of Samuel
1Sa 1:2,11,20

Jezebel, who taught her sons to worship Baal rather than the LORD
1Ki 22:52; **2Ki** 9:22

The Shunammite woman
2Ki 4:16-22,32-37

Elizabeth, mother of John the Baptist
Lk 1:5-7,13,24-25,57

Mary, mother of Jesus Christ
Lk 2:6-7 While they [Joseph and Mary] were there [Bethlehem], the time came for the baby to be born, and she gave birth to her firstborn, a son. She wrapped him in cloths and placed him in a manger, because there was no room for them in the inn. *See also* **Mt** 1:18; **Lk** 1:26-31,38; 2:19; **Jn** 2:1-5; 19:25-27; **Ac** 1:14

Herodias, a treacherous mother
Mt 14:8 pp Mk 6:24-25

Rufus' mother, a mother to Paul
Ro 16:13

Lois and Eunice, a godly grandmother and a mother
2Ti 1:5   *See also firstborn.*

mothers, responsibilities
The fundamental importance of motherhood is recognised throughout Scripture.

Motherhood and childbirth
God plans happiness for women in motherhood
Ps 113:9 He settles the barren woman in her home as a happy mother of children . . .
The need for a mother's cleansing after childbirth Lev 12:1-8; **Lk** 2:22-24

A mother's relationship with her children
A mother loves and cares for her children
1Th 2:7 . . . we were gentle among you, like a mother caring for her little children. *See also* **Lk** 2:48
A mother's role as teacher
Pr 1:8 Listen, my son, to your father's instruction and do not forsake your mother's teaching. *See also* **Pr** 6:20; **2Ti** 1:5
The responsibility to discipline children
Pr 29:15 The rod of correction imparts wisdom, but children left to themselves disgrace their mothers.

The joy or sorrow of parents at their children's conduct
Pr 10:1 . . . Wise children bring joy to their fathers, but the foolish bring grief to their mothers.   *See also* **Pr** 23:25

The negative influence of some mothers upon their children
2Ch 22:3 He [Ahaziah] too walked in the ways of the house of Ahab, for his mother encouraged him in doing wrong.   *See also* **Ge** 27:5–17; **1Ki** 22:52; **Mt** 14:6–8; 20:20–22

Children's responsibility to honour their parents
Ex 20:12 "Honour your father and your mother, so that you may live long in the land the LORD your God is giving you." pp Dt 5:16   *See also* **Lev** 19:3; **Mt** 19:19 pp Mk 10:19 Lk 18:20; **Eph** 6:1–3
This honour is due especially to mothers in old age Pr 23:22

Penalties for disobeying parents
Ex 21:15,17; **Dt** 21:18–21; **Pr** 20:20; **Mt** 15:4–6 pp Mk 7:10–13

Sexual relations with one's mother or mother-in-law are forbidden
Lev 18:7; **Dt** 27:23

Upon marriage the mother-child relationship becomes secondary
Ge 2:24 For this reason a man will leave his father and mother and be united to his wife, and they will become one flesh.   *See also* **Mt** 19:5 pp Mk 10:7; **Eph** 5:31

Care for a mother-in-law
Ru 2:11 Boaz replied, "I've been told all about what you have done for your mother-in-law since the death of your husband—how you left your father and mother and your homeland and came to live with a people you did not know before."   *See also* **Mt** 8:14–15 pp Mk 1:29–31 pp Lk 4:38

The ministry of Jesus Christ may produce conflict within families
Lk 12:53 "They will be divided, father against son and son against father, mother against daughter and daughter against mother, mother-in-law against daughter-in-law and daughter-in-law against mother-in-law." pp Mt 10:35–36

Following Jesus Christ involves a commitment to him even deeper than love of one's parents
Mt 10:37 "Anyone who loves father or mother more than me is not worthy of me,"   *See also* **Lk** 14:26

Jesus Christ regards those who do God's will as his own family
Mt 12:49–50 Pointing to his disciples, he said, "Here are my mother and my brothers. For whoever does the will of my Father in heaven is my brother and sister and mother." pp Mk 3:31–35 pp Lk 8:19–21   *See also* **Mt** 19:29 pp Mk 10:29 pp Lk 18:29–30   *See also children, responsibilities to parents; fathers.*

---

mourning
The expression of grief at a time of bereavement or repentance, often accompanied by weeping, tearing of clothes and wearing sackcloth.

Regulations for the mourning of priests after bereavement
Lev 21:1–4,10–11

Mourning of God's people after bereavement
Israel for Aaron
Nu 20:29 and when the whole community learned that Aaron had died, the entire house of Israel mourned for him thirty days.
Israel for Moses
Dt 34:8 The Israelites grieved for Moses in the plains of Moab thirty days, until the time of weeping and mourning was over.
David for Saul and Jonathan
2Sa 1:11–12 Then David and all those with

him took hold of their clothes and tore them. They mourned and wept and fasted till evening for Saul and his son Jonathan . . .   *See also* **2Sa** 1:17–27

David for Absalom
2Sa 18:33 The king was shaken. He went up to the room over the gateway and wept. As he went, he said: "O my son Absalom! My son, my son Absalom! If only I had died instead of you—O Absalom, my son, my son!"

Job for his children
Job 1:20–21 At this, Job got up and tore his robe and shaved his head. Then he fell to the ground in worship and said: "Naked I came from my mother's womb, and naked I shall depart. The LORD gave and the LORD has taken away; may the name of the LORD be praised."
Other examples Ge 37:34–35; 50:11; **2Sa** 13:31; 14:2; **2Ch** 35:23–25; **Mt** 2:18; **Jn** 11:31,33; **Ac** 8:2

Examples of heathen mourning after bereavement
Isa 15:2–3; **Jer** 47:5; 48:37; **Eze** 27:30–32

Mourning as an expression of repentance
Ex 33:4; **Ezr** 9:3–6

Mourning because of misfortune
2Sa 13:9; **Job** 2:12–13

The employment of professional mourners
Jer 9:17–18; **Am** 5:16; **Mt** 9:23 pp Mk 5:39 pp Lk 8:52

Mourning spoken of metaphorically
Jer 7:29 "'Cut off your [Judah's] hair and throw it away; take up a lament on the barren heights, for the LORD has rejected and abandoned this generation that is under his wrath.'"
See also **Isa** 3:18–24; **Eze** 7:18; **Joel** 1:8; **Am** 8:10; **Mic** 1:16

As a sign of repentance for sin
Joel 2:12–13 . . . [People of Judah] Rend your heart and not your garments . . .   *See also* **Isa** 22:12   *See also burial.*

music

Music played a major role in the lives of people in biblical times. It was used in both sacred and secular activities and was most often associated with joy and celebration.

Music comes from God
God's presence inspires music
Ps 96:13 they will sing before the LORD, for he comes, he comes to judge the earth . . .
See also **Ps** 98:4
It is a gift of God
Job 35:10 ". . . 'Where is God my Maker, who gives songs in the night,'"

Music was closely associated with praise and worship
Ps 33:2 Praise the LORD with the harp; make music to him on the ten-stringed lyre.   *See also* **Jdg** 5:3; **Ne** 12:27; **Ps** 27:6; 57:7; 81:1–2; 87:7; 92:3; 95:2; 98:4; 108:1; 144:9; 147:7; 149:3; 150:1–6; **Eph** 5:19–20; **Col** 3:16

Music was employed extensively in the tabernacle and the temple
1Ch 25:6–7 All these men were under the supervision of their fathers for the music of the temple of the LORD, with cymbals, lyres and harps, for the ministry at the house of God. Asaph, Jeduthun and Heman were under the supervision of the king. Along with their relatives—all of them trained and skilled in music for the LORD—they numbered 288.   *See also* **1Ch** 6:31–32; 25:1; **2Ch** 5:12–14; 35:15; **Ezr** 2:65

Music and the psalms
Many psalms are dedicated to the "director of music"
Ps 11 Title For the director of music. Of David.   *See also* **Ps** 13 Title; 31 Title; 42 Title; 49 Title; 77 Title; 139 Title; **Hab** 3:19
The titles of some psalms probably give an indication of melody
Ps 9 Title For the director of music. To the tune of, "The Death of the Son". A psalm of David.   *See also* **Ps** 22 Title; 45 Title; 56 Title; 57

Title; 58 Title; 59 Title; 60 Title; 69 Title; 75 Title; 80 Title

The titles of some psalms indicate specific musical accompaniment

Ps 4 Title For the director of music. With stringed instruments. A psalm of David. *See also* **Ps** 5 Title; 6 Title; 54 Title; 55 Title; 61 Title; 67 Title; 76 Title; **Hab** 3:19

Uses of music
To celebrate victory
2Ch 20:27-28 Then, led by Jehoshaphat, all the men of Judah and Jerusalem returned joyfully to Jerusalem, for the LORD had given them cause to rejoice over their enemies. They entered Jerusalem and went to the temple of the LORD with harps and lutes and trumpets. *See also* **Ex** 15:1-21; **Jdg** 5:1-31; **1Sa** 18:6-7; **Isa** 30:32
At times of celebration
Ge 31:27 "Why did you [Jacob] run off secretly and deceive me [Laban]? Why didn't you tell me, so that I could send you away with joy and singing to the music of tambourines and harps?" *See also* **Job** 21:12; **Isa** 16:10; **La** 5:14; **Eze** 26:13; **Lk** 15:25; **Rev** 18:22

At banquets
Isa 5:12 They have harps and lyres at their banquets, tambourines and flutes and wine, but they have no regard for the deeds of the LORD, no respect for the work of his hands. *See also* **Am** 6:4-6
As an expression of joy
1Sa 18:6-7 When the men were returning home after David had killed the Philistine, the women came out from all the towns of Israel to meet King Saul with singing and dancing, with joyful songs and with tambourines and lutes . . . *See also* **2Sa** 6:5; **1Ki** 1:40; **Job** 21:12; **Jas** 5:13
For pleasure
Ecc 2:8 I amassed silver and gold for myself, and the treasure of kings and provinces. I acquired male and female singers, and a harem as well—the delights of the human heart. *See also* **2Sa** 19:35
For divine inspiration 2Ki 3:14-15; 1Sa 18:10

To relieve depression
1Sa 16:23 Whenever the spirit from God came upon Saul, David would take his harp and play. Then relief would come to Saul; he would feel better, and the evil spirit would leave him. *See also* **1Sa** 16:16-18
At times of mourning
2Sa 1:17-18 David took up this lament concerning Saul and his son Jonathan, and ordered that the people of Judah be taught this lament of the bow . . .
Mt 9:23 . . . Jesus entered the ruler's house and saw the flute players and the noisy crowd, *See also* **Job** 30:31; 35:10; **Jer** 48:36

Prophets sometimes prophesied to musical accompaniment
1Sa 10:5-6 ". . . As you [Saul] approach the town, you will meet a procession of prophets coming down from the high place with lyres, tambourines, flutes and harps being played before them, and they will be prophesying. The Spirit of the LORD will come upon you in power, and you will prophesy with them . . ." *See also* **2Ki** 3:14-19

Lack of music is a sign of judgment
Isa 24:8 The gaiety of the tambourines is stilled, the noise of the revellers has stopped, the joyful harp is silent. *See also* **Rev** 18:22

Music in pagan worship
Da 3:5 "As soon as you [all people] hear the sound of the horn, flute, zither, lyre, harp, pipes and all kinds of music, you must fall down and worship the image of gold that King Nebuchadnezzar has set up." *See also* **Da** 3:7,10,15

Music played by prostitutes
Isa 23:16 "Take up a harp, walk through the city, O prostitute forgotten; play the harp well, sing many a song, so that you will be remembered."

The misuse of music
Ps 69:12 Those who sit at the gate mock me,

and I am the song of the drunkards.   *See also*
Ps 137:3; **Da** 3:4–7; **Am** 5:23; 6:5   *See also*
musical instruments; musicians; singing.

musical instruments

Scripture names a large number of musical
instruments, particularly in the OT, reflecting the
importance of music in Israelite worship and
culture.

Wind instruments
Trumpets Ex 19:16; 20:18; **Lev** 25:9; **Jdg** 3:27;
1Ki 1:39; **Ps** 150:3; **Rev** 8:7–13
Flutes Ge 4:21; **Job** 21:12; **Ps** 150:4; **Da** 3:5–15;
Mt 9:23; 11:17
Horns
Ps 98:4–6 Shout for joy to the Lord, all the
earth, burst into jubilant song with music . . .
with trumpets and the blast of the ram's horn—
shout for joy before the Lord, the King.   *See also*
Ex 19:13; **2Ch** 15:14; **Ps** 81:3

Stringed instruments
Harps Ge 4:21; **1Sa** 16:18; **Job** 30:31; **Ps** 43:4;
81:2; 149:3; 150:3; **Da** 3:5–11; **Rev** 5:8
Lyres Ps 33:2; 71:22; 81:2; 108:2; 144:9; **Da**
3:5–10
**Several of the psalms were intended to be
sung to the accompaniment of stringed
instruments**
Ps 4 Title For the director of music. With
stringed instruments. A psalm of David.
See also **Ps** 6 Title; 54 Title; 55 Title; 61 Title;
67 Title; 76 Title

Percussion instruments
Tambourines
Ps 149:3 Let them praise his name with
dancing and make music to him with tambourine
and harp.
Isa 5:12 They have harps and lyres at their
banquets, tambourines and flutes and wine, but
they have no regard for the deeds of the Lord,
no respect for the work of his hands.   *See also*
Ge 31:27; **Ex** 15:20–21; **Jdg** 11:34; **1Sa** 10:5;
18:6–7; **2Sa** 6:5 pp 1Ch 13:8; **Job** 21:12;

Ps 68:24–25; 81:1–2; 150:4; **Isa** 24:8; 30:32; **Jer**
31:4
Cymbals
Ps 150:1–6 Praise the Lord. Praise God in his
sanctuary; praise him in his mighty heavens. Praise
him for his acts of power; praise him for his
surpassing greatness . . . praise him with the
clash of cymbals, praise him with resounding
cymbals . . .
1Co 13:1 If I [Paul] speak in human or angelic
tongues, but have not love, I am only a
resounding gong or a clanging cymbal.   *See also*
2Sa 6:5 pp 1Ch 13:8
David's appointment of the Levites to sound the cymbals
in the temple worship: **1Ch** 15:16,19; 16:5,42; 25:1,6
1Ch 15:28; **2Ch** 5:12–13; 29:25; **Ezr** 3:10; **Ne**
12:27
Sistrums
2Sa 6:3–5 . . . David and the whole house of
Israel were celebrating with all their might before
the Lord, with songs and with harps, lyres,
tambourines, sistrums and cymbals.

Babylonian instruments
Da 3:4–5 Then the herald loudly proclaimed,
"This is what you are commanded to do, O
nations and peoples of every language: As soon
as you hear the sound of the horn, flute, zither,
lyre, harp, pipes and all kinds of music, you must
fall down and worship the image of gold that
King Nebuchadnezzar has set up."   *See also* **Da**
3:7,10,15; **Rev** 18:21–22   *See also music;*
musicians.

musicians

Players of musical instruments. Levitical musicians
played an extensive role in Israelite worship. Other
musicians are also mentioned in Scripture, in both
sacred and secular contexts.

Levitical musicians in the tabernacle
Appointed by David
1Ch 6:31–47 These are the men David put in
charge of the music in the house of the Lord
after the ark came to rest there. They ministered
with music before the tabernacle, the Tent of

Meeting, until Solomon built the temple of the
LORD in Jerusalem . . . Here are the men who
served, together with their sons: From the
Kohathites: Heman, the musician . . . and
Heman's associate Asaph, who served at his right
hand . . . and from their associates, the
Merarites, at his left hand: Ethan son of
Kishi . . .   *See also* **1Ch** 15:16–17; 25:1–5

Responsibilities
1Ch 15:19–21 The musicians Heman, Asaph
and Ethan were to sound the bronze cymbals;
Zechariah, Aziel, Shemiramoth, Jehiel, Unni, Eliab,
Maaseiah and Benaiah were to play the lyres
according to *alamoth*, and Mattithiah, Eliphelehu,
Mikneiah, Obed-Edom, Jeiel and Azaziah were to
play the harps, directing according to *sheminith*.
See also **1Ch** 15:16; 25:6–7

Allocation of duties
1Ch 25:8–31 Young and old alike, teacher as
well as student, cast lots for their duties . . .

Levitical musicians in the temple
2Ch 5:12–13 All the Levites who were
musicians—Asaph, Heman, Jeduthun and their
sons and relatives—stood on the east side of the
altar, dressed in fine linen and playing cymbals,
harps and lyres. They were accompanied by 120
priests sounding trumpets . . .   *See also* **1Ch**
9:33; **2Ch** 35:15

Other musicians
Jubal was the first musician
Ge 4:17–21 . . . Adah gave birth to Jabal; he
was the father of those who live in tents and
raise livestock. His brother's name was Jubal; he
was the father of all who play the harp and flute.
King David was a renowned musician
1Sa 16:15–18 . . . Saul said to his
attendants, "Find someone who plays well and
bring him to me." One of the servants answered,
"I have seen a son of Jesse of Bethlehem who
knows how to play the harp. He is a brave man
and a warrior. He speaks well and is a fine-
looking man. And the LORD is with him."
See also **1Sa** 16:23; 18:10–11; 19:9–10; **2Sa** 6:5;
23:1

Unidentified musicians
Ps 68:24–25 Your procession has come into
view, O God, the procession of my God and King
into the sanctuary. In front are the singers, after
them the musicians; with them are the young
women playing tambourines.   *See also* **2Ki**
3:11–19; **Ps** 137:1–3; **Rev** 18:21–22   *See also
music; musical instruments; singing; tabernacle, in Old
Testament; temple, Solomon's.*

---

nomads

**People who moved about from place to
place, having no settled abode. They
lived in tents and frequented desert
places**

Examples of nomads
The patriarchs
Ps 105:12–13 When they were but few in
number, few indeed, and strangers in it [the land
of Canaan], they wandered from nation to nation,
from one kingdom to another.
Heb 11:8–9 By faith Abraham, when called to
go to a place he would later receive as his
inheritance, obeyed and went, even though he did
not know where he was going. By faith he made
his home in the promised land like a stranger in
a foreign country; he lived in tents, as did Isaac
and Jacob, who were heirs with him of the same
promise.   *See also* **Ge** 12:8; 13:3,15,18; 26:25;
31:25; 35:21; **Dt** 26:5; **1Ch** 16:18–20
Israel during her desert wanderings
Nu 32:13 "The LORD's anger burned against
Israel and he made them wander in the desert for
forty years, until the whole generation of those
who had done evil in his sight was gone."
See also **1Ch** 17:5–6
Other nomadic peoples Ge 4:20; **Jdg** 4:17
The Midianites: **Jdg** 6:3; **Hab** 3:7
Kedar: **Ps** 120:5; **Jer** 49:28–29; **Eze** 25:4
Isa 13:20; **Jer** 35:1–11
Desert tracks followed by nomads Jdg 8:11;
Jer 3:2

The nomadic life as a spiritual symbol
1Pe 2:11 Dear friends, I urge you, as aliens and strangers in the world, to abstain from sinful desires, which war against your soul.   *See also* **Heb** 11:13–16; **1Pe** 1:17

Jesus Christ as a nomad
Mt 8:20   *See also tabernacle, in Old Testament; tents.*

oaths, human
Solemn, binding statements made in God's name. The OT forbids the making of oaths in the name of other gods and the NT suggests that it is best to refrain from making oaths.

Oaths are considered binding
Nu 30:2 "When a man . . . takes an oath to bind himself by a pledge, he must not break his word but must do everything he said."   *See also* **Dt** 23:21; **Mt** 23:16–22

Oaths to be taken only in God's name
Dt 6:13 Fear the LORD your God, serve him only and take your oaths in his name.   *See also* **Ps** 24:3–4; **Jer** 12:16

False oaths forbidden
Lev 19:12 " 'Do not swear falsely by my name and so profane the name of your God. I am the LORD.' "   *See also* **Ex** 20:7 pp Dt 5:11; **Lev** 6:3–5; **Zec** 5:3–4

Examples of oaths
In bearing witness Ex 22:11; **Nu** 5:19; **1Ki** 8:31
In showing allegiance 2Ki 11:4; **Ecc** 8:2; **Jer** 38:16; **Eze** 17:13
In covenants Ge 21:22–31; 26:26–31; 31:44–53; **Jos** 9:3–21
As a curse Jos 6:26; **Mt** 26:71–74 pp Mk 14:70–71
As assurance that a promise will be kept
Ge 14:22–23 But Abram said to the king of Sodom, "I have raised my hand to the LORD, God Most High, Creator of heaven and earth, and have taken an oath that I will accept nothing belonging

to you, not even a thread or the thong of a sandal, so that you will never be able to say, 'I made Abram rich.' "   *See also* **Ge** 24:3–9,37–41; 47:28–31; 50:24–25; **Ps** 132:1–5

Unwise or thoughtless oaths
Ge 25:33 But Jacob said, "Swear to me first." So he [Esau] swore an oath to him, selling his birthright to Jacob.   *See also* **Lev** 5:4; **Mt** 14:6–7 pp Mk 6:22–23

Advice against taking oaths
Jas 5:12 Above all, my brothers and sisters, do not swear—not by heaven or by earth or by anything else. Let your "Yes" be yes, and your "No", no, or you will be condemned.   *See also* **Mt** 5:33–37   *See also covenant; pledges; vows.*

occupations
Professions, trades and means of employment. A great variety of occupations, both secular and religious, are mentioned in Scripture.

Builders
Ps 127:1 Unless the LORD builds the house, its builders labour in vain . . .   *See also* **Ps** 118:22; **Mt** 21:42 pp Mk 12:10 pp Lk 20:17; **Ac** 4:11; **1Co** 3:10–15; **Heb** 3:3; **1Pe** 2:7

Embroiderers
Ex 38:23

Weavers and spinners
Ex 39:22; **Pr** 31:19

Stonemasons
2Ki 12:12; 22:5–6

Carpenters and woodworkers
2Ki 22:5–6; **Mt** 13:55

Musicians
1Ch 15:19–22; 16:42; **Hab** 3:19

Tanners
Ac 9:43 Peter stayed in Joppa for some time

with a tanner named Simon.   *See also* **Ac** 10:6,32

Linen workers
1Ch 4:21 The sons of Shelah son of Judah: Er the father of Lecah, Laadah the father of Mareshah and the clans of the linen workers at Beth Ashbea,

Launderers
Isa 7:3 . . . the LORD said to Isaiah, "Go out, you and your son Shear-Jashub, to meet Ahaz at the end of the aqueduct of the Upper Pool, on the road to the Laundry Field."   *See also* **2Ki** 18:17 pp Isa 36:2

Blacksmiths
Isa 44:12 The blacksmith takes a tool and works with it in the coals; he shapes an idol with hammers, he forges it with the might of his arm . . .   *See also* **1Sa** 13:19–21; **Isa** 54:16

Merchants
Ne 3:31-32 . . . Malkijah, one of the goldsmiths, made repairs as far as the house of the temple servants and the merchants, opposite the Inspection Gate, and as far as the room above the corner; and between the room above the corner and the Sheep Gate the goldsmiths and merchants made repairs.   *See also* **1Ki** 10:14–15,28–29 pp 2Ch 1:16–17; **Ne** 13:19–21; **Hos** 12:7; **Mt** 13:45–46

Tentmakers
Ac 18:1-3 After this, Paul left Athens and went to Corinth. There he met a Jew named Aquila, a native of Pontus, who had recently come from Italy with his wife Priscilla, because Claudius had ordered all the Jews to leave Rome. Paul went to see them, and because he was a tentmaker as they were, he stayed and worked with them.

Soldiers
2Ki 5:1 Now Naaman was commander of the army of the king of Aram. He was a great man in the sight of his master and highly regarded, because through him the LORD had given victory

to Aram. He was a valiant soldier, but he had leprosy.   *See also* **Mt** 8:5–13 pp Lk 7:1–10; **Lk** 3:14; **Ac** 10:1–8; **2Ti** 2:3–4

Priests
Ge 46:20 In Egypt, Manasseh and Ephraim were born to Joseph by Asenath daughter of Potiphera, priest of On.   *See also* **Ge** 14:18; **Ex** 18:1; 28:3; 40:13; **Jdg** 17:12–13; **1Sa** 2:27–29; **1Ki** 4:2–5; **Mal** 2:7; **Mt** 8:4

Levites and temple servants
Nu 1:50-51 ". . . appoint the Levites to be in charge of the tabernacle of the Testimony—over all its furnishings and everything belonging to it. They are to carry the tabernacle and all its furnishings; they are to take care of it and encamp round it. Whenever the tabernacle is to move, the Levites are to take it down, and whenever the tabernacle is to be set up, the Levites shall do it . . ."   *See also* **1Ch** 15:16,22; 16:4; **Ezr** 2:70; **Ne** 12:44–47; **Lk** 10:32

Guards
Ps 127:1 . . . Unless the LORD watches over the city, the guards stand watch in vain. *See also* **2Sa** 18:24–27; **SS** 3:1–4; 5:7; **Isa** 21:11–12; 56:10; **Eze** 33:2–6; **Jn** 10:1–3

Shepherds
Ge 47:3 Pharaoh asked the brothers, "What is your occupation?" "Your servants are shepherds," they replied to Pharaoh, "just as our fathers were."   *See also* **Ge** 29:1–10; 46:31–34; **Ex** 2:16–17; **1Sa** 17:20; 21:7; **Am** 1:1; **Lk** 2:8–18; **Jn** 10:2–4

Farmers
Zec 13:4-5 "On that day the prophets will all be ashamed of their prophetic visions. They will not put on a prophet's garment of hair in order to deceive. Every one of them will say, 'I am not a prophet. I am a farmer; the land has been my livelihood since my youth.'"   *See also* **Isa** 28:24–25; **Jer** 31:5; **Joel** 1:11; **Mt** 13:3–9 pp Mk 4:3–8 pp Lk 8:5–8; **Mt** 21:33 pp Mk 12:1 pp Lk 20:9; **2Ti** 2:6; **Jas** 5:7

Fishermen
Mt 13:48 "When it was full, the fishermen pulled it up on the shore. Then they sat down and collected the good fish in baskets, but threw the bad away." *See also* **Isa** 19:8; **Jer** 16:16; **Eze** 47:10; **Mt** 4:18–19 pp Mk 1:16–17; **Lk** 5:2

Doctors
Mk 5:25–26 And a woman was there who had been subject to bleeding for twelve years. She had suffered a great deal under the care of many doctors and had spent all she had, yet instead of getting better she grew worse. pp Lk 8:43
See also **Mt** 9:12 pp Mk 2:17 pp Lk 5:31; **Col** 4:14

Lawyers
Ac 24:1 Five days later the high priest Ananias went down to Caesarea with some of the elders and a lawyer named Tertullus, and they brought their charges against Paul before the governor.
See also **Tit** 3:13 *See also agriculture; building; shepherd, occupation; tax collectors.*

offerings
Anything offered up to God by human beings, including sacrificial offerings. A distinction can be made between offerings which involve the taking of life and other gifts made to God.

Sacrificial offerings as a sign of gratitude or repentance
Ge 4:4 But Abel brought fat portions from some of the firstborn of his flock. The LORD looked with favour on Abel and his offering,
Ps 107:22 Let them sacrifice thank-offerings and tell of his works with songs of joy.

Tithes were a regular form of offering
Ge 28:20–22 Then Jacob made a vow, saying, "If God will be with me and will watch over me on this journey I am taking . . . of all that you give me I will give you a tenth."
Lev 27:30 " 'A tithe of everything from the land, whether grain from the soil or fruit from the trees, belongs to the LORD; it is holy to the LORD.' " *See also* **Ge** 14:20

Part of every harvest was given as a freewill offering to God
As firstfruits: **Ex** 22:29; **Nu** 18:12; **Dt** 18:4; **Ne** 10:35
Lev 19:23–25; **Lev** 23:38

Offerings and the tabernacle
For its construction
Ex 25:1–2 The LORD said to Moses, "Tell the Israelites to bring me an offering. You are to receive the offering for me from each man whose heart prompts him to give." pp Ex 35:5
At its dedication Nu 7:2–3

Offerings and Solomon's temple
David's personal gift 1Ch 29:2–5
Offerings for upkeep and restoration
In the reign of Joash: **2Ki** 12:4–5; **2Ch** 24:8–12
In the reign of Josiah: **2Ki** 22:4–6 pp 2Ch 34:9–11

Offerings and the second temple
Ezr 3:5; 7:16; 8:24–30

Offerings and Herod's temple
Mk 12:41–43 pp Lk 21:1–3; **Lk** 21:5

Some offerings are not acceptable
Mt 5:23–24 "Therefore, if you are offering your gift at the altar and there remember that your brother or sister has something against you, leave your gift there in front of the altar. First go and be reconciled to them; then come and offer your gift." *See also* **Ge** 4:3–5
Boasting about offerings makes them unacceptable: **Am** 4:4–5; **Lk** 18:12
Mt 23:23 pp Lk 11:42

Offerings in the future kingdom
From the Gentile nations Ps 76:11; **Isa** 18:7; **Mal** 1:11
From God's people Eze 20:40; 44:30

Gifts and offerings in the NT
To help the needy Ac 4:34–35; 11:29–30; **1Co** 16:1–4; **Heb** 13:16
To support God's servants Php 4:10–18

Offerings of praise
Heb 13:15

God's people are themselves an offering to God
Jer 2:3; **Jas** 1:18; **Rev** 14:4

Offerings as "Corban"
Mk 7:9–13 And he [Jesus] said to them [the Pharisees and teachers of the law]: "You have a fine way of setting aside the commands of God in order to observe your own traditions! For Moses said, 'Honour your father and your mother,' and, 'Anyone who curses father or mother must be put to death.' But you say that if anyone says to father or mother: 'Whatever help you might otherwise have received from me is Corban' (that is, a gift devoted to God), then you no longer let them do anything for their father or mother. Thus you nullify the word of God by your tradition that you have handed down. And you do many things like that." *"Corban" is a technical Jewish religious term, meaning "something dedicated, especially on oath". What Jesus Christ says implies that once the children had donated the amount they would have spent on their ageing parents for religious purposes, they were no longer responsible for their upkeep.*   See also burnt offering; drink offering; fellowship offering; firstfruits; freewill offering; grain offering; guilt offering; sacrifice; sin offering; thank-offering; tithing; wave offering.

---

ornaments

The use of jewellery and other adornments is not forbidden in Scripture, but excessive use can indicate worldliness. Inner spiritual adornment is of greater value.

Possession and use of various ornaments show wealth
Ornaments used to beautify
SS 1:10–11 Your cheeks are beautiful with earrings, your neck with strings of jewels. We will make you ear-rings of gold, studded with silver. *See also* **Ge** 37:3,23,32; **2Sa** 1:24; **Jer** 2:32
Rings, ear-rings and nose rings Ge 35:4;

Ex 32:2–3; **Jdg** 8:24; **Est** 8:8; **Pr** 25:12; **Isa** 3:19,21; **Eze** 16:12; **Lk** 15:22; **Jas** 2:2
Bracelets and gold chains Ge 24:22; 41:42; **Pr** 1:9; **Eze** 16:11; **Da** 5:29
Bells Ex 28:33–35

Ornaments plundered from Egypt
Ex 3:22 "Every woman is to ask her neighbour and any woman living in her house for articles of silver and gold and for clothing, which you will put on your sons and daughters. And so you will plunder the Egyptians."

The misuse of ornaments for pride and seduction
Isa 3:16 The LORD says, "The women of Zion are haughty, walking along with outstretched necks, flirting with their eyes, tripping along with mincing steps, with ornaments jingling on their ankles."   *See also* **Eze** 23:40,42; **Hos** 2:13

Ornaments as gifts
Ge 24:53 Then the servant brought out gold and silver jewellery and articles of clothing and gave them to Rebekah; he also gave costly gifts to her brother and to her mother.   *See also* **Ge** 24:22; **Job** 42:11

Adornment as a picture of God's love
Eze 16:11–13 "'I [the LORD] adorned you [Jerusalem] with jewellery: I put bracelets on your arms and a necklace around your neck . . .'" *See also* **Isa** 61:10; **Lk** 15:22

Ornaments as symbols of authority
Ge 41:42 Then Pharaoh took his signet ring from his finger and put it on Joseph's finger. He dressed him in robes of fine linen and put a gold chain around his neck.   *See also* **2Sa** 1:10; **Est** 3:10; **Da** 5:29

Ornaments discarded
In mourning
Ex 33:4–6 When the people heard these distressing words, they began to mourn and no-one put on any ornaments . . .   *See also* **Eze** 26:16

To make idols

Ex 32:2–4 Aaron answered them, "Take off the gold ear-rings that your wives, your sons and your daughters are wearing, and bring them to me." So all the people took off their ear-rings and brought them to Aaron. He took what they handed him and made it into an idol cast in the shape of a calf, fashioning it with a tool . . . *See also* **Jdg** 8:24–27

As offerings to God

Ex 35:22 All who were willing, men and women alike, came and brought gold jewellery of all kinds: brooches, ear-rings, rings and ornaments. They all presented their gold as a wave offering to the Lord. *See also* **Nu** 31:50

Inner, not outer, adornment encouraged

1Pe 3:3–4 Your beauty should not come from outward adornment, such as braided hair and the wearing of gold jewellery and fine clothes. Instead, it should be that of your inner self, the unfading beauty of a gentle and quiet spirit, which is of great worth in God's sight. *See also* **bride; clothing.**

---

palaces

Fortified, luxurious residences for kings. They normally served as the seat and symbol of royal authority.

David's palace on Mount Zion

1Ch 14:1 Now Hiram king of Tyre sent messengers to David, along with cedar logs, stonemasons and carpenters to build a palace for him. *See also* **2Sa** 5:6–11 pp 1Ch 11:4–8; **2Sa** 7:1–2 pp 1Ch 17:1

Solomon's palace in Jerusalem

1Ki 10:4–5 When the queen of Sheba saw all the wisdom of Solomon and the palace he had built . . . she was overwhelmed. pp 2Ch 9:3–4 *See also* **1Ki** 7:1–12; 10:16–21 pp 2Ch 9:15–20; **2Ch** 8:11

Gold and valuable items were stored in the palace in Jerusalem

1Ki 15:18–19 Asa then took all the silver and gold that was left in the treasuries of the Lord's temple and of his own palace. He entrusted it to his officials and sent them to Ben-hadad son of Tabrimmon, the son of Hezion, the king of Aram, who was ruling in Damascus. "Let there be a treaty between me and you," he said, "as there was between my father and your father. See, I am sending you a gift of silver and gold. Now break your treaty with Baasha king of Israel so that he will withdraw from me." pp 2Ch 16:2–3 *See also* **1Ki** 14:25–26 pp 2Ch 12:9; **2Ki** 12:17–18; 14:13–14 pp 2Ch 25:23–24; **2Ki** 16:7–8 pp 2Ch 28:20–21; **2Ki** 18:14–15; 24:13; **2Ch** 21:16–17; **Jer** 27:18–22

The royal palace in Jerusalem was destroyed by the Babylonians

2Ki 25:9 He [Nebuzaradan] set fire to the temple of the Lord, the royal palace and all the houses of Jerusalem. Every important building he burned down. pp 2Ch 36:19 pp Jer 52:13 *See also* **Jer** 22:1–6; 39:8

Other palaces

The kings of Israel had palaces in Samaria

1Ki 21:1 . . . The vineyard [Naboth's] was in Jezreel, close to the palace of Ahab king of Samaria. *See also* **1Ki** 16:18; 20:5–6,43; **2Ki** 15:25

Foreign palaces

Pharaoh's palace in Egypt: **Ge** 12:15; 41:40; 47:14; **Ex** 8:3

The royal palace in Babylon: **Da** 4:29–30; 5:5 **Est** 1:9

Summer palaces Jdg 3:20–21

Palaces in NT times

Mt 26:3–4; **Jn** 18:28; **Ac** 23:35; **Php** 1:12–13

Features of palaces

Palace gardens

2Ki 21:18 Manasseh rested with his ancestors and was buried in his palace garden, the garden of Uzza . . .   *See also* **2Ki** 21:25–26; **Est** 1:5–6

The luxury of palaces

1Ki 22:39 As for the other events of Ahab's reign, including all he did, the palace he built and inlaid with ivory, and the cities he fortified, are they not written in the book of the annals of the kings of Israel?   *See also* **Nu** 22:18; **Ps** 45:8–9; **Isa** 13:22; **Jer** 22:13–17; **Mt** 11:8 pp Lk 7:25

Palaces were administered by royal officials

2Ki 10:5 So the palace administrator, the city governor, the elders and the guardians sent this message to Jehu: "We are your servants and we will do anything you say. We will not appoint anyone as king; you do whatever you think best."   *See also* **1Ki** 4:6; 18:3; **2Ki** 15:5; **2Ch** 28:7; **Isa** 22:15   *See also banquets; king; queen.*

Passover

One of the major OT feasts. It specifically commemorates the exodus from Egypt as an act of God's deliverance. In Israel's calendar of feasts it was always celebrated with the Feast of Unleavened Bread.

The institution of the Passover

Ex 12:25–27 "When you enter the land that the Lᴏʀᴅ will give you as he promised, observe this ceremony. And when your children ask you, 'What does this ceremony mean to you?' then tell them, 'It is the Passover sacrifice to the Lᴏʀᴅ, who passed over the houses of the Israelites in Egypt and spared our homes when he struck down the Egyptians.'" . . .   *The Hebrew term "Passover" comes from a verb meaning "to pass over" with the sense of "to spare".*

Celebrating the Passover

Instructions concerning its observance Ex 12:2–11,46–47; **Nu** 9:1–5; **Dt** 16:1–8
Combined with the Feast of Unleavened Bread Ex 34:25
The need for ritual cleansing Jn 11:55

Provision for ritual uncleanness Nu 9:6–13
Provision for non-Jews Ex 12:43–45,48–49; **Nu** 9:14
Its observance in the OT
These occasions are times of spiritual renewal, when the nation remembered how the Lᴏʀᴅ had saved them: **Jos** 5:10; **2Ki** 23:21–23; **2Ch** 30:1–5,13–20; **Ezr** 6:19–21
Ezekiel's vision of the future observance of the Passover Eze 45:21–24

The Passover in the NT
Its observance Lk 2:41–42; **Jn** 6:4; **Ac** 12:4
It was celebrated by Jesus Christ
Lk 22:15 . . . "I have eagerly desired to eat this Passover with you [the disciples] before I suffer."   *See also* **Mt** 26:17–19 pp Mk 14:12–16 pp Lk 22:7–13; **Jn** 2:23
Jesus Christ identified with the Passover lamb
1Co 5:7 . . . For Christ, our Passover lamb, has been sacrificed.   *See also* **Jn** 1:29,36; 19:36; **Ex** 12:46; **Rev** 5:5–6   *See also circumcision, physical; feast and festival; sacraments.*

Pentecost

One of Israel's three major agricultural festivals, the second great feast of the Jewish year. It is a harvest festival, also known as the Feast of Weeks. The original Jewish significance of this festival has been overshadowed by the Christian celebration of the coming of the Holy Spirit at Pentecost.

Pentecost was one of Israel's three major agricultural festivals

It was also known as the Feast of Weeks
Dt 16:9–10 Count off seven weeks from the time you begin to put the sickle to the standing corn. Then celebrate the Feast of Weeks to the Lᴏʀᴅ your God by giving a freewill offering in proportion to the blessings the Lᴏʀᴅ your God has given you.   *See also* **Ex** 34:22; **Dt** 16:16–17; **2Ch** 8:13
It is also referred to as the Feast of Harvest Ex 23:16

Instructions for the celebration of Pentecost
Its timing and sacrifices Lev 23:15–21   *The "fifty days" (verse 16) gives rise to the term "Pentecost" which is derived from the Greek word for "fiftieth";* **Nu** 28:26–31; **Jer** 5:24
Its link with the deliverance from Egypt Dt 16:12 Remember that you were slaves in Egypt, and follow carefully these decrees. *Pentecost later became associated with covenant renewal and the giving of the Law.*

Pentecost in the NT
It was observed by Paul Ac 20:16; **1Co** 16:8
Its association with the coming of the Holy Spirit
Ac 2:1–4 When the day of Pentecost came, they were all together in one place . . . All of them [the apostles] were filled with the Holy Spirit and began to speak in other tongues as the Spirit enabled them.
Ac 2:16–21 ". . . this is what was spoken by the prophet Joel: 'In the last days, God says, I will pour out my Spirit on all people . . .'"
Ac 11:15 "As I [Peter] began to speak, the Holy Spirit came on them [those in the house of Cornelius] as he had come on us at the beginning." *See also* **Joel** 2:28–32   *See also covenant; Feast of Weeks; harvest.*

---

plague
Affliction with disease, destruction or environmental disaster as an expression of divine judgment, usually resulting in death. The purpose may be as a punishment or to encourage repentance.

The nature of plague
Eze 6:11–12 " 'This is what the Sovereign LORD says: Strike your hands together and stamp your feet and cry out "Alas!" because of all the wicked and detestable practices of the house of Israel, for they will fall by the sword, famine and plague. Those who are far away will die of the plague, and those who are near will fall by the sword, and those who survive and are spared will die of famine. So will I spend my wrath upon

them.' "   *See also* **2Ch** 20:9; **Jer** 14:12; 27:8; **Eze** 14:21; **Rev** 6:8

Plagues sent upon Egypt
Plagues described Ex 7:17–18; 8:5–6,16–17,21,24; 9:6,9–10,22–25; 10:4–6,13–15,21–23; 11:4–6; 12:29–30
Plagues withdrawn in answer to prayer Ex 8:12–13,29; 9:29,33; 10:18–19
Plagues recalled and celebrated Ps 78:41–51; 105:26–36; 135:8–9; **Am** 4:10; **Ac** 7:36

Plagues sent upon Israel
Plagues threatened for breaking God's covenant
Lev 26:23–26 " '. . . And I [the LORD] will bring the sword upon you to avenge the breaking of the covenant. When you withdraw into your cities, I will send a plague among you, and you will be given into enemy hands . . .'"   *See also* **Lev** 26:14–16; **Dt** 28:20–24
Plagues experienced in fulfilment of God's covenant Ex 32:33–35; **Nu** 11:31–34; 14:36–38; 16:41–50; 25:3–9; **2Sa** 24:11–17 pp 1Ch 21:9–17; **Joel** 1:2–12; **Am** 4:6–11
Plagues withdrawn after intercession or obedience Nu 14:10–20; 16:46–48; 21:6–9; 25:6–11; **2Sa** 24:18–25 pp 1Ch 21:18–26; **1Ki** 8:37–40 pp 2Ch 6:28–31; **Ps** 106:23,28–31
Plagues announced by prophets as God's judgment
Jer 21:5–10 "I [the LORD] myself will fight against you with an outstretched hand and a mighty arm in anger and fury and great wrath. I will strike down those who live in this city—both people and animals—and they will die of a terrible plague . . .' . . ."   *See also* **Jer** 24:10; 29:17–19; 34:17; 44:13; **Eze** 5:12,17; 33:27

Plagues sent upon other nations
1Sa 5:6–12; **Isa** 19:22; **Jer** 28:8; **Eze** 28:22–23; **Hab** 3:5–6; **Zec** 14:12–15

Apocalyptic visions of plague as God's judgment
Lk 21:11 "There will be great earthquakes, famines and pestilences in various places, and

fearful events and great signs from heaven." pp
Mt 24:7 pp Mk 13:8   See also **Rev** 6:8; 11:6;
15:1,6–8; 16:1–21; 18:4–8; 22:18

Divine protection from plague

Ps 91:3–8 Surely he will save you from the
fowler's snare and from the deadly pestilence. He
will cover you with his feathers, and under his
wings you will find refuge; his faithfulness will be
your shield and rampart. You will not fear the
terror of night, nor the arrow that flies by day,
nor the pestilence that stalks in the darkness, nor
the plague that destroys at midday. A thousand
may fall at your side, ten thousand at your right
hand, but it will not come near you. You will
only observe with your eyes and see the
punishment of the wicked.   See also **Ex**
8:22–23; 9:4,6,26; 10:23; 11:7; 12:13,23,27; **2Ch**
20:9   See also *disease; famine.*

---

plants

Plants are an important aspect of God's creation,
and a major source of food and materials.
Scripture refers to many plants, with their various
uses.

Plants as a source of food

Ge 1:29–30 Then God said, "I give you every
seed-bearing plant on the face of the whole earth
and every tree that has fruit with seed in it. They
will be yours for food. And to all the beasts of
the earth and all the birds of the air and all the
creatures that move on the ground—everything
that has the breath of life in it—I give every
green plant for food." And it was so.   See also
Ge 1:11–12; 3:17–19; 9:3; **Ps** 104:14

Growth of plants dependent upon soil, sun and irrigation

Dt 32:2 Let my [Moses'] teaching fall like rain
and my words descend like dew, like showers on
new grass, like abundant rain on tender plants.
See also **Ge** 2:4–5; **2Ki** 19:26 pp Isa 37:27; **Job**
8:16–19; **Isa** 61:11; **Zec** 10:1; **Mt** 13:3–8 pp Mk
4:3–8 pp Lk 8:5–8; **Jas** 1:11

Individual plants
Aloes
Nu 24:5–6 "How beautiful are your tents, O
Jacob, your dwelling-places, O Israel! Like valleys
they spread out, like gardens beside a river, like
aloes planted by the LORD, like cedars beside the
waters."   See also **Ps** 45:8; **Pr** 7:17; **SS**
4:13–14

Calamus
Jer 6:20 "What do I care about incense from
Sheba or sweet calamus from a distant land?
Your burnt offerings are not acceptable; your
sacrifices do not please me."   See also **SS**
4:12–14; **Isa** 43:24; **Eze** 27:19

Crocus
Isa 35:1–2 The desert and the parched land
will be glad; the wilderness will rejoice and
blossom. Like the crocus, it will burst into bloom;
it will rejoice greatly and shout for joy. The glory
of Lebanon will be given to it, the splendour of
Carmel and Sharon; they will see the glory of the
LORD, the splendour of our God.

Hyssop
1Ki 4:33 He [Solomon] described plant life,
from the cedar of Lebanon to the hyssop that
grows out of walls. He also taught about animals
and birds, reptiles and fish.   See also **Ex** 12:22;
Ps 51:7; **Jn** 19:29

Lily
Lk 12:27 "Consider how the lilies grow. They
do not labour or spin. Yet I [Jesus] tell you, not
even Solomon in all his splendour was dressed
like one of these." pp Mt 6:28–29   See also
SS 2:1–2; **Hos** 14:5

Lotus
Job 40:21–22 Under the lotus plant it [the
behemoth] lies, hidden among the reeds in the
marsh. The lotuses conceal it in their shadow; the
poplars by the stream surround it.

Mandrake
SS 7:13 The mandrakes send out their fragrance,
and at our door is every delicacy, both new and
old, that I have stored up for you, my lover.
See also **Ge** 30:14–16

Mustard
Mt 13:31–32 . . . "The kingdom of heaven is
like a mustard seed, which a man took and

planted in his field. Though it is the smallest of
all your seeds, yet when it grows, it is the largest
of garden plants and becomes a tree, so that the
birds of the air come and perch in its branches."
pp Mk 4:30–32 pp Lk 13:18–19

Myrtle
Isa 55:13 "Instead of the thornbush will grow
the pine tree, and instead of briers the myrtle will
grow. This will be for the LORD's renown, for an
everlasting sign, which will not be destroyed."
See also **Isa** 41:18–20; **Zec** 1:8–10

Reed
Ex 2:3 . . . when she [Moses' mother] could
hide him no longer, she got a papyrus basket for
him and coated it with tar and pitch. Then she
placed the child in it and put it among the reeds
along the bank of the Nile.   *See also* **Job** 8:11;
Isa 19:6–7

Rose
SS 2:1 I [the beloved] am a rose of Sharon, a
lily of the valleys.

Rush
Isa 19:6–7 The canals will stink; the streams of
Egypt will dwindle and dry up. The reeds and
rushes will wither, also the plants along the Nile,
at the mouth of the river. Every sown field along
the Nile will become parched, will blow away and
be no more.   *See also herbs and spices; life, animal
and plant; vine.*

---

pledges
A solemn, binding promise, often involving the
deposit of valuable items or property as a
guarantee that the promise will be kept. To break
a pledge is to sin against God.

Pledges were binding
Nu 30:2 "When a man makes a vow to the
LORD or takes an oath to bind himself by a
pledge, he must not break his word but must do
everything he said."   *See also* **Nu** 30:3–15   *In
certain cases pledges made by daughters or wives could
be nullified by fathers or husbands respectively.*

Pledges were solemn promises
2Ki 23:3 The king [Josiah] stood by the pillar

and renewed the covenant in the presence of the
LORD—to follow the LORD and keep his
commands, regulations and decrees with all his
heart and all his soul, thus confirming the words
of the covenant written in this book. Then all the
people pledged themselves to the covenant. pp
2Ch 34:31–32   *See also* **1Ch** 29:24; **Ezr** 10:19;
Eze 17:16–18; **Mic** 7:20; **1Pe** 3:21

Pledges were guarantees that a
promise would be kept
Items deposited to secure a pledge
Ge 38:17–18 "I'll send you [Tamar] a young
goat from my flock," he [Judah] said. "Will you
give me something as a pledge until you send
it?" she asked. He said, "What pledge should I
give you?" "Your seal and its cord, and the staff
in your hand," she answered. So he gave them
to her . . .   *See also* **Ex** 22:26–27; **Dt**
24:10–13; **Pr** 20:16; 27:13
Unjust exaction of pledges condemned
Dt 24:17 Do not . . . take the cloak of the
widow as a pledge.   *See also* **Job** 22:4–6;
24:2–3; **Am** 2:6–8

Warning against making pledges on
behalf of others
Pr 11:15 The one who puts up security for
another will surely suffer, but whoever refuses to
strike hands in pledge is safe.   *See also* **Pr**
6:1–5; 17:18; 22:26–27

Pledges and betrothal
Mt 1:18–19 . . . His [Jesus'] mother Mary
was pledged to be married to Joseph, but before
they came together, she was found to be with
child through the Holy Spirit. Because Joseph her
husband was a righteous man and did not want
to expose her to public disgrace, he had in mind
to divorce her quietly.   *See also* **Ex** 22:16; **Dt**
22:23–25; **Lk** 1:27   *See also betrothal; covenant,
nature of; marriage; seal; vows.*

---

ploughing
Cutting up the furrows in soil and turning it up
before work can be done on the land.

Ploughing as a way of life

1Ki 19:19-21 So Elijah went from there and found Elisha son of Shaphat. He was ploughing with twelve yoke of oxen, and he himself was driving the twelfth pair. Elijah went up to him and threw his cloak around him . . . So Elisha . . . took his yoke of oxen and slaughtered them. He burned the ploughing equipment to cook the meat and gave it to the people, and they ate . . .
Lk 17:7 "Suppose one of you had a servant ploughing or looking after the sheep. Would he say to the servant when he comes in from the field, 'Come along now and sit down to eat'?" *See also* **1Sa** 8:12; 13:19–21; **Job** 1:14; **Pr** 20:4; **Isa** 28:24; **Eze** 36:9; **Am** 9:13

Rules concerning ploughing
Ex 23:10–11; 34:21; **Dt** 22:10

Ploughing used figuratively

Job 4:8 "As I have observed, those who plough evil and those who sow trouble reap it."
Lk 9:62 Jesus replied, "No-one who takes hold of the plough and looks back is fit for service in the kingdom of God." *See also* **Jdg** 14:18; **Ps** 129:3; 141:7; **Isa** 2:4; **Jer** 4:3; **Hos** 10:11–12; **Am** 6:12; **1Co** 9:10 *See also agriculture; harvest; land; divine responsibility; sowing and reaping.*

potters and pottery

Pottery was in common use for both household and ceremonial utensils, though for sacred use precious metals were often preferred. Broken pottery symbolises worthlessness and judgment. The potter formed clay with his hands on a wheel which he turned with his feet. The descriptions of God as a potter and of his people as clay emphasise God's sovereignty and also his concern for what he has made.

Potters in Scripture
Examples of potters
Jer 18:2 "Go down to the potter's house, and there I [the Lord] will give you [Jeremiah] my message." *See also* **1Ch** 4:23; **Jer** 19:1; **Zec** 11:13; **Mt** 27:7

Description of the potter's work Pr 26:23; **Jer** 18:3–4

God depicted as a potter
God's authority over what he has made
Jer 18:6 "O house of Israel, can I not do with you as this potter does?" declares the Lord. "Like clay in the hand of the potter, so are you in my hand, O house of Israel." *See also* **Isa** 29:16; 45:9–10; **Ro** 9:20–21
God's concern for what he has made
Isa 64:8-9 Yet, O Lord, you are our Father. We are the clay, you are the potter; we are all the work of your hand. Do not be angry beyond measure, O Lord; do not remember our sins for ever. Oh, look upon us we pray, for we are all your people. *See also* **Ge** 2:7–8; **Job** 10:8–9; **Ps** 103:14; 119:73; **Isa** 43:1

Broken pottery
Contaminated pottery to be broken Lev
11:33–35; 15:12
Broken pottery as a symbol of judgment
Jer 19:10-11 ". . . 'This is what the Lord Almighty says: I will smash this nation [Judah] and this city [Jerusalem] just as this potter's jar is smashed and cannot be repaired . . .'"
See also **Ps** 2:9; **Rev** 2:27; **Isa** 30:14; **Jer** 25:34; 48:12
Broken pottery as a symbol of worthlessness
Ps 31:12 I am forgotten by them [my friends] as though I were dead; I have become like broken pottery. *See also* **Jer** 22:28; 19:2 *The Potsherd Gate was so called because it overlooked the dump for broken pottery.*

Pottery of little value
La 4:2 How the precious children of Zion, once worth their weight in gold, are now considered as pots of clay, the work of a potter's hands!
See also **Ps** 60:8 pp Ps 108:9
2Co 4:7 But we [believers] have this treasure in jars of clay to show that this all-surpassing power is from God and not from us.

Examples of items of pottery
2Sa 17:28; **2Ti** 2:20

Cooking pots Jdg 6:19; **1Sa** 2:14; **2Ki** 4:38–41; **Job** 41:20; **Mic** 3:3

Pitchers to carry water Ge 24:17–20; **Jdg** 7:16; **Mk** 14:13 pp Lk 22:10; **Jn** 4:28

Water jugs 1Sa 26:11–12; **1Ki** 17:10; 19:6

Drinking vessels Jdg 5:25; **Jer** 35:5; **Mt** 26:27–28 pp Mk 14:23–24 pp Lk 22:20 pp 1Co 11:25

Other pottery containers 1Ki 14:3; **2Ki** 4:3–4; 21:13; **Jer** 32:14; **Mt** 26:23; **Jn** 13:5

Household lamps 2Ki 4:10; **Mt** 5:15

Pottery used in religious rituals
Basins to hold the blood of sacrifices
Ex 12:21–22 . . . ". . . Take a bunch of hyssop, dip it into the blood in the basin and put some of the blood on the top and on both sides of the door-frame . . ."   *See also* **Ex** 24:6; **Lev** 14:5,50

Utensils to cook or bake offerings
Lev 6:28 " 'The clay pot that the meat is cooked in must be broken . . .' "   *See also* **Lev** 2:5; 6:21; 7:9

Clay water jars Nu 5:17; 19:17

Lamps
Ex 25:37 "Then make its [the lampstand's] seven lamps and set them up on it so that they light the space in front of it."   *See also* **Ex** 27:21; 30:8; **Lev** 24:3–4; **1Sa** 3:3; **1Ki** 7:49
See also cooking; washing.

poverty
The state of being without material possessions or wealth. Scripture indicates that poverty is contrary to God's intention for his people, and that those who are poor and destitute are to be treated with special consideration and compassion.

poverty, attitudes to
The plight of those in need calls for compassionate action of which Jesus Christ is the great example and in which the early church was faithful. Such compassion will be rewarded.

The treatment of the poor
They are not to be neglected
Dt 15:7–8 If there are poor among your people

in any of the towns of the land that the LORD your God is giving you, do not be hard-hearted or tight-fisted towards them. Rather be open-handed and freely lend them whatever they need.
See also **Pr** 17:5; **Ro** 12:13; **Gal** 6:10; **Jas** 2:15–16; **1Jn** 3:17

They are not to be unjustly treated Lev 25:35–37

Ex 23:6 "Do not deny justice to your poor people in their lawsuits."   *See also* **Dt** 24:14–15; **2Sa** 12:1–4; **Job** 24:1–4; **Pr** 22:22; 29:7; **Jer** 22:2–3,16; **Eze** 18:10–13; **Am** 2:6–7; **Zec** 7:10; **Jas** 2:2–4

They are to have special rights and privileges Dt 14:28–29 At the end of every three years, bring all the tithes of that year's produce and store it in your towns, so that the Levites (who have no allotment or inheritance of their own) and the aliens, the fatherless and the widows who live in your towns may come and eat and be satisfied, and so that the LORD your God may bless you in all the work of your hands.
See also **Ex** 23:11; **Lev** 19:9–10; 25:5–6; **Pr** 19:17

They are to be cared for
Ps 82:3–4 "Defend the cause of the weak and fatherless; maintain the rights of the poor and oppressed. Rescue the weak and needy; deliver them from the hand of the wicked."   *See also* **Job** 29:11–17; **Lk** 3:11; **Ac** 9:36

They are to be helped generously
Dt 15:9–11 Be careful not to harbour this wicked thought: "The seventh year, the year for cancelling debts, is near," so that you do not show ill will towards the needy among your people and give them nothing. They may then appeal to the LORD against you, and you will be found guilty of sin. Give generously to them and do so without a grudging heart; then because of this the LORD your God will bless you in all your work and in everything you put your hand to. There will always be poor people in the land. Therefore I command you to be open-handed towards those of your people who are poor and needy in your land.   *See also* **Dt** 14:29; **Ru** 2:14; **Ps** 112:9; **Jer** 39:10; **Lk** 19:8; **Ac** 10:2; **2Co** 9:7

They are to be helped without ostentation
Mt 6:2 "So when you give to the needy, do

not announce it with trumpets, as the hypocrites do in the synagogues and on the streets, to be honoured by others. I tell you the truth, they have received their reward in full."

Jesus Christ's compassion for the poor
Mt 15:32 Jesus called his disciples to him and said, "I have compassion for these people; they have already been with me three days and have nothing to eat. I do not want to send them away hungry, or they may collapse on the way." pp Mk 8:1–3   *See also* **Lk** 4:18–19; **Jn** 13:29; **Ac** 10:38

The attitude of the first Christians towards poverty
Ac 2:44–45 All the believers were together and had everything in common. Selling their possessions and goods, they gave to anyone who had need.   *See also* **Ac** 4:32–35; 11:29–30; 20:35; 24:17; **Ro** 15:25–27; **2Co** 8:13–15; **Gal** 2:10

Compassion for the poor will be rewarded
Ps 41:1 Blessed are those who have regard for the weak; the LORD delivers them in times of trouble.   *See also* **Pr** 19:17; 28:27; **Mt** 19:21; 25:34–36; **Mk** 9:41; **Heb** 13:16

Examples of the poor who need help
Orphans Dt 10:18; 14:28–29; **Ps** 10:14; 146:9; **Pr** 23:10; **Isa** 10:2
Widows Dt 14:29; 16:11; **Ru** 4:5; **2Ki** 4:1; **Job** 22:9; **Mal** 3:5; **Ac** 6:1; **1Ti** 5:3,9,16; **Jas** 1:27
See also justice; widows.

---

poverty, causes
To want for the necessities of life is ultimately the result of human sin.

Poverty arises from human sin
Ge 3:17–19 To Adam he said, "Because you listened to your wife and ate from the tree about which I commanded you, 'You must not eat of it,' Cursed is the ground because of you; through painful toil you will eat of it all the days of your life. It will produce thorns and thistles for you, and you will eat the plants of the field. By the sweat of your brow you will eat your food until you return to the ground, since from it you were taken; for dust you are and to dust you will return."   *Compare this with the description of Eden in Ge 2:9–14.*

Causes of poverty
Divine retribution brings poverty
Dt 28:47–48 Because you [disobedient Israel] did not serve the LORD your God joyfully and gladly in the time of prosperity, therefore in hunger and thirst, in nakedness and dire poverty, you will serve the enemies the LORD sends against you . . .   *See also* **Pr** 22:16; **Isa** 3:1; **Am** 4:6; 5:11

Idleness brings poverty
Pr 6:10–11 A little sleep, a little slumber, a little folding of the hands to rest—and poverty will come on you like a bandit and scarcity like an armed man.   *See also* **Pr** 10:4; 14:23; 20:13; 24:33–34

Dissolute living brings poverty
Pr 21:17 Whoever loves pleasure will become poor; whoever loves wine and oil will never be rich.   *See also* **Pr** 6:26; 28:19; **Lk** 15:14

Lack of discipline brings poverty Pr 13:18; 21:5
Rash promises bring poverty Pr 22:26–27
Debt brings poverty Mt 18:23–25
Neglect of God's law of giving brings poverty Pr 11:24; 28:22; **Ac** 20:35
Neglect of God's work brings poverty Hag 1:9
Oppression brings poverty Jdg 6:6; **Job** 20:19; **Pr** 13:23; **Isa** 1:7; **Jas** 5:4
Famine brings poverty Ge 45:11; 47:20–21
Misfortune brings poverty Job 1:13–21

Poverty affects good as well as evil people
The righteous often escape poverty Dt 8:7–9; **Ps** 34:9–10; 37:25
Many of the godly have been poor 2Ki 4:1; **Lk** 16:20; **Ro** 15:26
Jesus Christ was poor Mt 8:20

Results of poverty
Poverty results in ruin
Pr 10:15 . . . poverty is the ruin of the poor.
Poverty results in shame Pr 13:18; **Lk** 16:3
Poverty results in misery Pr 31:7
Poverty results in crime Pr 6:30; 30:8–9
Poverty need not lead to ungodliness Ps 119:71; **Mk** 12:44 pp Lk 21:4; **2Co** 8:2; **Jas** 2:5; **Rev** 2:9

Voluntary poverty
Jesus Christ's example of voluntary poverty
2Co 8:9 For you [Corinthians] know the grace of our Lord Jesus Christ, that though he was rich, yet for your sakes he became poor, so that you through his poverty might become rich.
Voluntary poverty commanded of some
Mt 19:21–22 Jesus answered, "If you [rich young man] want to be perfect, go, sell your possessions and give to the poor, and you will have treasure in heaven. Then come, follow me." . . .
Voluntary poverty experienced by others Heb 10:34
Love essential in voluntary poverty 1Co 13:3; **2Co** 6:10   *See also beggars; famine; warfare.*

---

poverty, remedies
Although poverty can never be totally eliminated from this sinful world, it can be alleviated. Scripture provides guidance concerning how this may be done.

Poverty will always exist in this world
Mt 26:11 "The poor you will always have with you [Jesus' disciples] . . ." pp Jn 12:8
See also **Dt** 15:11

God's concern over poverty
God cares for the poor
Ps 35:10 My whole being will exclaim, "Who is like you, O LORD? You rescue the poor from those too strong for them, the poor and needy from those who rob them."
Ps 68:10 . . . from your bounty, O God, you provided for the poor.   *See also* **Dt** 15:4–5; **Job** 5:16; **Ps** 14:6; 113:7; 140:12; **Isa** 25:4

The law made concessions for poverty Lev 5:7,11; 12:8; 14:21–22; 27:8
God judges those who oppress the poor Eze 18:12–13; **Am** 4:1–2

The poor should be encouraged to help themselves
Mosaic law enabled the poor to help themselves Ex 23:11; **Lev** 19:10; 23:22; 25:25,28,39,41; **Dt** 23:25
Paul exhorts the poor to work 1Th 4:11; **2Th** 3:10
Paul sets the poor an example Ac 20:34; **1Th** 2:9; **2Th** 3:8

The relatives of the poor should help
1Ti 5:4 But if a widow has children or grandchildren, these should learn first of all to put their religion into practice by caring for their own family and so repaying their parents and grandparents, for this is pleasing to God.
See also **Ge** 45:9–11; **Lev** 25:25; **1Ti** 5:8,16

Those better off should help the poor
The poor can be helped by means of gifts
Ac 10:4 . . . "Your prayers [Cornelius'] and gifts to the poor have come up as a memorial offering before God.   *See also* **Dt** 15:7–8; **Ps** 112:9; **Pr** 31:20; **Mt** 19:21 pp Mk 10:21 pp Lk 18:22; **Lk** 19:8; **Ac** 9:36; **Eph** 4:28; **1Ti** 6:17–18
The poor can be helped in practical ways Mt 25:34–40; **Lk** 11:41; 14:13; **Ac** 9:36,39; **1Ti** 5:9–10; **Jas** 2:15–16; **1Jn** 3:17
The poor can be helped by others upholding justice
Ps 82:3 "Defend the cause of the weak and fatherless; maintain the rights of the poor and oppressed."   *See also* **Dt** 24:12–15; **Pr** 22:22; 29:7,14; 31:9; **Isa** 10:1–2; **Jer** 22:16

The church should help the poor
Gal 2:10 All they [James, Peter and John] asked was that we [Paul and Barnabas] should continue to remember the poor, the very thing I was eager to do.   *See also* **Ac** 24:17; **Ro** 15:26; **1Ti** 5:16

God's greatest gift to the poor is the good news of Jesus Christ

Lk 4:18 "The Spirit of the Lord is on me [Jesus], because he has anointed me to preach good news to the poor . . ."   *See also* **Isa** 61:1; **Mt** 11:5 pp Lk 7:22; **Lk** 14:21

priesthood

The body of people responsible for priestly duties, especially in relation to worship and sacrifice. The OT identifies Aaron and his heirs as having special priestly duties. In the NT, all believers are understood to share in this priesthood. Jesus Christ fulfils the OT concept of priesthood by being both the high priest and sacrifice, through which forgiveness of sins is completely achieved.

priesthood, New Testament

Jesus Christ recognised the function of the OT priesthood, but the gospel belief in Christ as high priest and the priesthood of all believers superseded the earlier concept.

Jesus Christ acknowledged the role of the Jerusalem priesthood

Mt 8:4 pp Mk 1:44 pp Lk 5:14

Characteristics of the Levitical priesthood

It was equivalent to the order of Aaron

Heb 7:11 If perfection could have been attained through the Levitical priesthood (for on the basis of it the law was given to the people), why was there still need for another priest to come—one in the order of Melchizedek, not in the order of Aaron?

It was incompatible with membership of the tribe of Judah

Heb 7:14 For it is clear that our Lord descended from Judah, and in regard to that tribe Moses said nothing about priests.

It was not established by divine oath

Heb 7:20 . . . Others [those with Levitical qualifications] became priests without any oath,

Characteristics of the Melchizedek priesthood

Heb 7:15–16 And what we have said is even more clear if another priest like Melchizedek appears, one who has become a priest not on the basis of a regulation as to his ancestry but on the basis of the power of an indestructible life.

How Jesus Christ's priesthood resembled the OT priesthood

He fulfilled the requirement of humanity

Heb 2:17 For this reason he had to be made like his brothers and sisters in every way, in order that he might become a merciful and faithful high priest in service to God, and that he might make atonement for the sins of the people.   *See also* **Heb** 5:1

He was not self-appointed

Heb 5:4–5 No-one takes this honour upon himself; he must be called by God, just as Aaron was. So Christ also did not take upon himself the glory of becoming a high priest . . .

He resembled Melchizedek

Heb 5:10 . . . [Jesus] was designated by God to be high priest in the order of Melchizedek.

How Jesus Christ's priesthood contrasts with the Levitical priesthood

It involves a change in the applicability of the law

Heb 7:12–13 . . . He of whom these things are said belonged to a different tribe, and no-one from that tribe has ever served at the altar.

It lasts for ever

Heb 7:23–24 Now there have been many of those priests, since death prevented them from continuing in office; but because Jesus lives for ever, he has a permanent priesthood.   *See also* **Heb** 10:11–12

It was based on a once-for-all sacrifice, not of animals but of himself

Heb 9:26 Then Christ would have had to suffer many times since the creation of the world. But now he has appeared once for all at the end of the ages to do away with sin by the sacrifice of himself.   *See also* **Heb** 9:12

It is effective, not simply illustrative
Heb 10:14 . . . by one sacrifice he has made perfect for ever those who are being made holy.   *See also* **Heb** 8:5; 10:1,4

It is not that of a mere man, but of the Son of God
Heb 7:28 For the law appoints as high priests men who are weak; but the oath, which came after the law, appointed the Son, who has been made perfect for ever.   *See also* **Heb** 4:14; 7:26

Characteristics of the priesthood of all believers
1Pe 2:9 But you are a chosen people, a royal priesthood, a holy nation, a people belonging to God, that you may declare the praises of him who called you out of darkness into his wonderful light.

They are to reflect the holiness of their great high priest
1Pe 1:15 But just as he who called you is holy, so be holy in all you do;   *See also* **Heb** 10:10

They are to offer spiritual sacrifices
1Pe 2:5 you also, like living stones, are being built into a spiritual house to be a holy priesthood, offering spiritual sacrifices acceptable to God through Jesus Christ.   *See also* **Ro** 12:1; **Php** 4:18; **Heb** 13:15

They are to intercede for others before God
1Ti 2:1 I urge, then, first of all, that requests, prayers, intercession and thanksgiving be made for everyone—   *See also* **Rev** 5:8,10

They are to represent God before other human beings
2Co 5:20 We are therefore Christ's ambassadors, as though God were making his appeal through us . . .   *See also* **Eph** 3:7–11
See also atonement.

priesthood, Old Testament
The institution of the priesthood or the particular body of people responsible for priestly duties.

The priesthood as an institution
It was a perpetual institution
Ex 40:15 "Anoint them [Aaron and his sons] just as you anointed their father, so that they may serve me as priests. Their anointing will be to a priesthood that will continue for all generations to come."   *See also* **Nu** 18:1; 25:13

It was distinct from the laity
Nu 3:10 "Appoint Aaron and his sons to serve as priests; anyone else who approaches the sanctuary must be put to death."

It was subject to the king's authority
1Ki 2:27 So Solomon removed Abiathar from the priesthood of the LORD, fulfilling the word the LORD had spoken at Shiloh about the house of Eli.

It was a privilege
Nu 18:7 ". . . I [the LORD] am giving you the service of the priesthood as a gift . . ."
See also **Ex** 29:9; **Nu** 16:10; **Jos** 18:7

The priesthood as the body of people responsible for priestly duties
The Aaronic priesthood
Ex 28:41 "After you [Moses] put these clothes on your brother Aaron and his sons, anoint and ordain them. Consecrate them so they may serve me as priests."   *See also* **1Ch** 6:49; **Ne** 10:38

The Shiloh priesthood
Jos 18:1 The whole assembly of the Israelites gathered at Shiloh and set up the Tent of Meeting there . . .   *See also* **1Sa** 3:14; **1Ki** 2:27; **Ps** 78:60; **Jer** 7:12

The Melchizedek priesthood
Ps 110:4 The LORD has sworn and will not change his mind: "You are a priest for ever, in the order of Melchizedek."   *See also* **Ge** 14:18; **Heb** 5:10; 7:11–17

The Anathoth priesthood
Jer 1:1 The words of Jeremiah son of Hilkiah, one of the priests at Anathoth in the territory of Benjamin.   *See also* **Jos** 21:18; **1Ki** 2:27

The Zadokite priesthood
Eze 40:46 ". . . These are the sons of Zadok, who are the only Levites who may draw near to the LORD to minister before him."

The Levitical priesthood
Dt 17:9 Go to the priests, who are Levites, and to the judge who is in office at that time. Enquire of them and they will give you the verdict.

prison

A place of confinement, such as a jail or dungeon, used to imprison individuals.

Irregular prisons

Ge 37:22 [Reuben said] ". . . Throw him [Joseph] into this cistern here in the desert, but don't lay a hand on him." . . .   *See also* **Nu** 12:14–15; **Jer** 38:6,13

Houses used as prisons

Jer 37:15 They [the officials] were angry with Jeremiah and had him beaten and imprisoned in the house of Jonathan the secretary, which they had made into a prison.   *See also* **2Sa** 20:3; **Lk** 22:54; **Ac** 28:16

Legally established prisons

Ge 39:20 Joseph's master took him and put him in prison, the place where the king's prisoners were confined . . .

Ac 5:18 They [the Jewish authorities] arrested the apostles and put them in the public jail.
See also **Ge** 42:16–19; **Jdg** 16:21; **1Ki** 22:27; **2Ki** 17:4; 25:27; **2Ch** 16:10; **Mt** 14:3; **Lk** 21:12; **Ac** 4:3; 12:4–7; 16:37

Barracks or guardhouses as prisons

Jer 32:2; **Ac** 22:24; **Php** 1:12–13

Figurative and poetic use of prisons

Isa 42:7 "to open eyes that are blind, to free captives from prison and to release from the dungeon those who sit in darkness."   *See also* **Job** 11:10; **Ps** 88:8; 142:7; **Isa** 24:22; **Lk** 12:58; **1Pe** 3:19; **2Pe** 2:4; **Rev** 1:18

The restriction of Satan's activity is pictured as his binding and imprisonment: **Rev** 20:1,7

property

The ultimate source of all property is God. While property is entrusted to human beings, they have responsibilities towards God as a result of their stewardship.

property

Possessions are a gift from God to be used for his glory, for human pleasure and in benefiting others.

Possessions are a cause for thanksgiving

Ecc 5:19 . . . when God gives people wealth and possession and the ability to enjoy them, to accept their lot and be happy in their work—this is a gift of God.   *See also* **Ge** 39:2–4; **Dt** 8:18; **1Ch** 29:12; **2Ch** 31:21; **Hos** 2:8

Owning possessions is open to abuse
They can be coveted

Ex 20:17 "You shall not covet your neighbour's house. You shall not covet your neighbour's wife, or his male or female servant, his ox or donkey, or anything that belongs to your neighbour."
See also **1Ki** 21:1–4; **Jer** 6:13; **Mic** 2:2; **Lk** 12:15; **1Co** 7:29–31
They can cause deceit **Ac** 5:1–9
They can cause pride and forgetfulness
Pr 30:9 "Otherwise, I may have too much and disown you and say, 'Who is the Lord?' Or I may become poor and steal, and so dishonour the name of my God."   *See also* **2Ki** 20:13–17; **Da** 4:30; 5:20; **Hos** 13:6; **Mt** 19:24; **Lk** 12:13–21
Abuse of ownership leads to judgment **Isa** 3:16–24; 5:8; **Hab** 2:6–9

Property is for benefiting others
It is to be used to help others **Ac** 2:44–45; 4:32–35; **Gal** 6:6,10; **Eph** 4:28; **1Ti** 6:17–18; **Jas** 2:15–16; **1Jn** 3:17–18
It is to be used to assist strangers **Lev** 25:35; **Nu** 35:15; **Dt** 10:19; **Mt** 5:42

Property provides no lasting satisfaction

Ecc 2:26 To the one who pleases him, God gives wisdom, knowledge and happiness, but to the sinner he gives the task of gathering and storing up wealth to hand it over to the one who pleases God. This too is meaningless, a chasing after the wind.   *See also* **Job** 27:16–17; **Ps** 39:6; **Ecc** 2:21; **Eze** 28:4–7; **Hag** 1:6; **Mt** 6:19–21;

Lk 12:20–21; **Jas** 5:3

Laws governing the inheritance of property
Nu 27:3–11; **Dt** 21:15–17; **Eze** 46:16–18

Godly men of property
Abraham Ge 13:2
Isaac Ge 26:14
Jacob Ge 30:43; 32:5; 36:7
Barzillai 2Sa 19:32
David 1Ch 29:28
Solomon 2Ch 1:15; 9:22
Hezekiah 2Ch 32:27–29
Job Job 1:3
Joseph of Arimathea Mt 27:57
Barnabas Ac 4:36–37 *See also stewardship.*

property, houses

From at least the time of the flood people have built houses to live in and these have been a major part of their property; the temple was seen as God's house.

Houses are a major part of people's property
Ex 12:22; **Hag** 1:4; **Mt** 7:24–27; **Heb** 3:3

The homeless have no property
1Co 4:11 To this very hour we go hungry and thirsty, we are in rags, we are brutally treated, we are homeless. *See also* **Job** 24:8; **La** 4:5; **Lk** 9:58

Property has no lasting value
Heb 10:34 You sympathised with those in prison and joyfully accepted the confiscation of your property, because you knew that you yourselves had better and lasting possessions. *See also* **Dt** 6:11–12; **Mt** 19:29

Materials used in house building
Clay Job 4:19
Brick Ex 1:11–14; **Isa** 9:10
Stone and wood Lev 14:40,42; **Hab** 2:11
Luxurious building materials 1Ki 22:39; **Est** 1:6; **Am** 3:15

Houses are protected by God
Ps 127:1 Unless the LORD builds the house, its builders labour in vain . . . *See also* **Ex** 12:27

Houses as dwellings
For sinners Jos 2:1; **Pr** 7:27; 21:9
For friends Zec 13:6; **Lk** 10:38; **Jn** 12:1–2

Other uses for houses
For work Jer 18:2
For hospitality
Lk 10:5–7 "When you enter a house, first say, 'Peace to this house.' If anyone there loves peace, your peace will rest on that person; if not, it will return to you. Stay in that house, eating and drinking whatever they give you, for workers deserve their wages. Do not move around from house to house." pp Mt 10:11 pp Mk 6:10
See also **Ge** 19:3; **Mt** 25:35; **Ac** 16:15; **1Ti** 5:10; **Heb** 13:2
For church gatherings
Ac 20:20 You know that I have not hesitated to preach anything that would be helpful to you but have taught you publicly and from house to house. *See also* **Ro** 16:5; **1Co** 16:19; **Col** 4:15; **Phm** 2
As palaces 2Sa 7:2; **1Ki** 7:1–2; 22:39; **Da** 4:29–30; **Mt** 11:8

Legislation concerning houses
Respecting the houses of others Ex 20:17; **Mic** 2:2
Redemption of property Lev 25:29–33

The LORD's house
God's promise to David 2Sa 7:11; **1Ki** 5:5
Solomon's building 1Ki 6:1,2,7,12,14
Ezra's rebuilding Ezr 3:9–10
It was a place to meet God Ps 23:6; 27:4; 84:10; 122:1; **Isa** 56:7; **Joel** 3:18; **Jn** 2:16–17; **Ps** 69:9
It is a picture of the church
Eph 2:19–20 Consequently, you are no longer foreigners and aliens, but fellow-citizens with God's people and members of God's household, built on the foundation of the apostles and prophets, with Christ Jesus himself as the chief cornerstone."

See also **1Co** 3:9–11   See also *building; house; palaces; temple, Solomon's.*

property, land

All land belongs to God, and he allows people to care for it and use it for their own needs and the needs of others. The land promised to Israel is a special case illustrating the spiritual inheritance of all believers and God's ultimate purpose for the world.

All land belongs to God
It is in his possession and care
Ps 24:1 The earth is the Lord's, and everything in it, the world, and all who live in it;   *See also* **Ex** 9:29; **Ps** 33:5; **1Co** 10:26
It is given to human beings to manage
Ge 2:15 The Lord God took the man and put him in the Garden of Eden to work it and take care of it.   *See also* **Ps** 8:6; 115:16

The land promised to Israel
It was promised on oath
Ge 12:6–7 Abram travelled through the land as far as the site of the great tree of Moreh at Shechem. At that time the Canaanites were in the land. The Lord appeared to Abram and said, "To your offspring I will give this land." . . .
See also **Ge** 13:14–17; 15:7,18; 17:8; 50:24; **Ex** 6:8; **Dt** 6:10–11; 31:20–21; **Jdg** 2:1
It was a fruitful land
Ex 3:8 "So I [the Lord] have come down to rescue them from the hand of the Egyptians and to bring them up out of that land into a good and spacious land, a land flowing with milk and honey . . ."   *See also* **Lev** 20:24; **Nu** 14:7–8; **Jos** 5:6
The distribution of the land Lev 25:34; **Nu** 33:53–54; 35:2–5

Individual land rights
Legitimate purchase or sale Ge 23:15–16; 33:19; 47:20; **2Sa** 24:24; **Pr** 31:16; **Jer** 32:6–15
Judas bought land with blood money: **Mt** 27:7–10; **Ac** 1:18
Examples of renting SS 8:11; **Mt** 21:33–41 pp Mk 12:1–9 pp Lk 20:9–16

Laws of inheritance Nu 36:6–9; **Mic** 2:2
Encroachment was forbidden Dt 19:14; 27:17; **Job** 24:2; **Pr** 22:28; 23:10; **Hos** 5:10
Redemption of land Lev 25:23–28; **Ru** 4:2–9

God's ultimate purpose for the world
The heavenly land
Heb 11:13–16 . . . If they [the Israelites] had been thinking of the country they had left, they would have had opportunity to return. Instead, they were longing for a better country—a heavenly one. Therefore God is not ashamed to be called their God, for he has prepared a city for them.   *See also* **Heb** 11:8–10
A new heaven and earth
Isa 65:17 "Behold, I [the Lord] will create new heavens and a new earth. The former things will not be remembered, nor will they come to mind."   *See also* **Isa** 66:22; **Rev** 21:1–2
The inheritance of the righteous
Mt 5:5 "Blessed are the meek, for they will inherit the earth."   *See also* **Ps** 37:11,29; **2Pe** 3:13   *See also land.*

queen

In OT times the chief wife of a king's harem or a female monarch. A queen mother, as a king's widow and the mother of the reigning king, would have held a position of some authority and influence.

A queen as the wife of a king
A chief wife among several
Est 2:17 Now the king [Xerxes] was attracted to Esther more than to any of the other women, and she won his favour and approval more than any of the other virgins. So he set a royal crown on her head and made her queen instead of Vashti.   *See also* **Est** 1:9–12; 2:4
Enjoying a position of some influence Est 1:15–18; 2:22; 5:12; 7:5–8
Enjoying the king's special favour
Est 5:2–3 When he [King Xerxes] saw Queen Esther standing in the court, he was pleased with her and held out to her the gold sceptre that was in his hand. So Esther approached and touched

the tip of the sceptre. Then the king asked, "What is it, Queen Esther? What is your request? Even up to half the kingdom, it will be given you." *See also* **Est** 7:1–3; 8:1,7; 9:12; **SS** 6:8–9; **Ne** 2:6; **Ps** 45:9

Sometimes granted considerable authority
Est 9:29 So Queen Esther, daughter of Abihail, along with Mordecai the Jew, wrote with full authority to confirm this second letter concerning Purim. *See also* **Est** 9:31

A queen as a female monarch
The queen of Sheba
1Ki 10:1 When the queen of Sheba heard about the fame of Solomon and his relation to the name of the LORD, she came to test him with hard questions. pp 2Ch 9:1 *See also* **1Ki** 10:2–10 pp 2Ch 9:1–9; **1Ki** 10:13 pp 2Ch 9:12; **Mt** 12:42 pp Lk 11:31
Queen Athaliah of Judah 2Ki 11:1–21 pp 2Ch 22:10—23:21

Queen used figuratively
Of Jerusalem La 1:1; **Eze** 16:13
Of Babylon Isa 47:5,7; **Rev** 18:7

Queen of Heaven: a title for the Babylonian goddess Ishtar
Jer 7:18; 44:17–19,25

A queen mother as a king's widow and mother of the reigning king
1Ki 2:19 When Bathsheba went to King Solomon to speak to him for Adonijah, the king stood up to meet her, bowed down to her and sat down on his throne. He had a throne brought for the king's mother, and she sat down at his right hand. *See also* **1Ki** 15:13 pp 2Ch 15:16; **2Ki** 10:13; 24:8,12,15; **Jer** 13:18; 22:26; 29:2; **Da** 5:10; **Ac** 8:27 *See also* **king.**

---

rain

Rain as a natural phenomenon
2Sa 21:10; **1Ki** 18:41,44; **Ezr** 10:9; **Ecc** 11:3; **Isa** 4:6; **Lk** 12:54; **Heb** 6:7

Associated with cold weather
Ac 28:2 The islanders [of Malta] showed us unusual kindness. They built a fire and welcomed us all [Paul and all who had been shipwrecked] because it was raining and cold.

God controls the rain
Ge 2:5 and no shrub of the field had yet appeared on the earth and no plant of the field had yet sprung up, for the LORD God had not sent rain on the earth and there was no-one to work the ground,
Jer 51:16 "When he [the LORD] thunders, the waters in the heavens roar; he makes clouds rise from the ends of the earth. He sends lightning with the rain and brings out the wind from his storehouses." *See also* **1Ki** 18:1; **Job** 5:10; 28:26; 37:6; 38:25; **Ps** 68:8; 135:7; 147:8; **Jer** 10:13; 14:22

God's bounty in giving rain to Israel
Dt 28:12 The LORD will open the heavens, the storehouse of his bounty, to send rain on your land in season and to bless all the work of your hands. You will lend to many nations but will borrow from none. *See also* **Lev** 26:4; **Dt** 11:14

God's bounty in giving rain to all humanity
Mt 5:45 ". . . your Father in heaven. He causes his sun to rise on the evil and the good, and sends rain on the righteous and the unrighteous."
Ac 14:17 "Yet he [God] has not left himself without testimony: He has shown kindness by giving you rain from heaven and crops in their seasons; he provides you with plenty of food and fills your hearts with joy." *See also* **Zec** 10:1

God's punishment through rain and flood
Ge 7:4 "Seven days from now I will send rain on the earth for forty days and forty nights, and I will wipe from the face of the earth every living creature I have made." *See also* **Ex** 9:33–34; **1Sa** 12:17–18; **Eze** 38:22

God's punishment through drought
Dt 11:17 Then the LORD's anger will burn against you, and he will shut the heavens so that it will not rain and the ground will yield no produce, and you will soon perish from the good land the LORD is giving you. *See also*

1Ki 8:35–36 pp 2Ch 6:26–27; 1Ki 17:1; Isa 5:6; Am 4:7; Zec 14:17–18; Jas 5:17; Rev 11:6

Rain as a symbol of spiritual truth
God's power to save
Isa 55:10–11 "As the rain and the snow come down from heaven, and do not return to it without watering the earth and making it bud and flourish, so that it yields seed for the sower and bread for the eater, so is my word that goes out from my mouth: It will not return to me empty, but will accomplish what I desire and achieve the purpose for which I sent it." *See also* **2Sa** 23:4; **Isa** 45:8

God's powerful anger
Eze 13:11–13 "'. . . In my wrath I will unleash a violent wind, and in my anger hailstones and torrents of rain will fall with destructive fury.'" *See also* **2Sa** 22:12; **Job** 20:23; **Isa** 28:2

Power of circumstances
Mt 7:27 "The rain came down, the streams rose, and the winds blew and beat against that house, and it fell with a great crash." *See also* **Mt** 7:25

Rain in other imagery
Ability to satisfy: **Dt** 32:2; **Job** 29:23; **Ps** 72:6; **Pr** 16:15

Clouds without rain: uselessness: **Pr** 25:14; **Jude** 12 **Pr** 25:23; 26:1

The rainbow
Ge 9:14–16; **Eze** 1:28; **Rev** 4:3; 10:1
See also water; weather; God's sovereignty.

---

reading
The gaining of information through written documents. The Law was read regularly in the synagogue. Jesus Christ expected the Scriptures to be read. NT letters were read in the churches to which they were sent.

Reading of the Law to Israel
By Moses
Ex 24:7 Then he [Moses] took the Book of the Covenant and read it to the people . . .
See also **Dt** 31:10–11
By Joshua Jos 8:34–35
By Josiah 2Ki 23:2 pp 2Ch 34:30
In Ezra's time Ne 8:2–3,18; 9:3; 13:1

Reading of the Law in the synagogue
Ac 15:21 "For Moses . . . is read in the synagogues on every Sabbath." *See also* **Lk** 4:16; **Ac** 13:15,27; **2Co** 3:14–15

Other examples of reading
Dt 17:18–20
Jeremiah's words were to be read in public: **Jer** 36:6–8; 51:61
Da 9:2

Jesus Christ expected the Scriptures to be read
Mt 12:3–5 He [Jesus] answered, "Haven't you read what David did when he and his companions were hungry? He entered the house of God, and he and his companions ate the consecrated bread—which was not lawful for them to do, but only for the priests. Or haven't you read in the Law that on the Sabbath the priests in the temple desecrate the day and yet are innocent?" pp Mk 2:25–26 pp Lk 6:3–4 *See also* **Mt** 19:4; 21:16,42 pp Mk 12:10–11 pp Lk 20:17; **Mt** 22:31; 24:15 pp Mk 13:14

Reading of NT letters
Col 4:16 After this letter has been read to you, see that it is also read in the church of the Laodiceans and that you in turn read the letter from Laodicea. *See also* **Ac** 15:31; **1Th** 5:27

Reasons for reading the Scriptures
They are God-breathed 2Ti 3:16
God's word is true Jn 17:7
To understand the truth about Jesus Christ Lk 24:26–27; **Eph** 3:4
To believe and be saved from God's wrath Jn 20:31; **2Ti** 3:15
To learn how to serve and please God Ps 119:105,130; **2Ti** 3:16; **Rev** 1:3

They teach Christians and give them hope Ro 15:4; **1Jn** 2:1,12–14,21

They enable Christians to discern truth from error

Ac 18:28 For he [Apollos] vigorously refuted the Jews in public debate, proving from the Scriptures that Jesus was the Christ.   *See also* **Ac** 17:11; **Gal** 1:6–9; **2Pe** 3:14–16; **1Jn** 2:26; 4:1   *See also book; law; writing.*

redemption, in life

The purchase of a person's freedom or the buying back of an object from the possession of another. Scripture provides illustrations of these everyday meanings of the word.

The OT redemption of property, animals and individuals
Redemption of property
Lev 25:24–28 " . . . 'If any of your own people become poor and sell some of their property, their nearest relative is to come and redeem what they have sold . . .'"   *See also* **Lev** 27:15–20; **Ru** 4:1–6; **Jer** 32:8

Redemption of animals
Ex 13:13 "Redeem with a lamb every firstborn donkey, but if you do not redeem it, break its [the donkey's] neck . . ."   *See also* **Ex** 34:20; **Lev** 27:13,27; **Nu** 18:14–17

Redemption of individuals
Ex 30:12–16 "When you take a census of the Israelites to count them, each one must pay the LORD a ransom for his life at the time he is counted. Then no plague will come on them when you number them . . ."   *See also* **Ex** 13:12–13; 21:8,28–32; 34:19–20; **Lev** 25:47–55; **Nu** 3:44–51

The redemption of the nation of Israel
Ex 6:6 "Therefore, say to the Israelites: 'I am the LORD, and I will bring you out from under the yoke of the Egyptians. I will free you from being slaves to them, and I will redeem you with an outstretched arm and with mighty acts of judgment."   *See also* **Dt** 9:26; **2Sa** 7:23–24 pp 1Ch 17:21–22; **Ne** 1:10; **Ps** 77:15; 78:35; 106:10; **Isa** 43:1–3; **Mic** 6:4

Redemption as release from sin
Ps 130:8 He [the LORD] himself will redeem Israel from all their sins.   *See also* **Isa** 40:2

The role of the redeemer
In helping close relatives regain property or freedom
Lev 25:25 " 'If any of your own people become poor and sell some of their property, their nearest relative is to come and redeem what they have sold.' "   *See also* **Lev** 25:47–49; 27:15–20; **Ru** 2:20; 3:9; 4:1–8

In avenging death Nu 35:12,19–21

refining

The process of heating metals to high temperatures in order to burn away impurities. It is often used in a metaphorical sense to depict God refining his people to get rid of impurities in their faith.

Precious metals produced by refining
Ps 12:6 . . . the words of the LORD are flawless, like silver refined in a furnace of clay, purified seven times.   *See also* **1Ch** 28:14–18; 29:3–5; **Job** 28:1–2; **1Pe** 1:7; **Rev** 3:18

God refines his people
Refining involves suffering
Ps 66:10–12 For you, O God, tested us [your people]; you refined us like silver. You brought us into prison and laid burdens on our backs. You let people ride over our heads; we went through fire and water, but you brought us to a place of abundance.   *See also* **Isa** 48:9–11; **Jer** 9:7–9

Refining for purging and purification
Zec 13:8–9 "In the whole land," declares the LORD, "two-thirds will be struck down and perish; yet one-third will be left in it. This third I will bring into the fire; I will refine them like silver and test them like gold. They will call on my name and I will answer them; I will say, 'They are my people,' and they will say, 'The LORD is our God.' "   *See also* **Jer** 6:27–30; **Da** 11:35; 12:10; **Mal** 3:2–4   *See also metals.*

refugees

Fugitives driven from home because of personal, political or religious persecution, or because of physical danger.

Examples of refugees
Ge 16:6-8; 46:1; **Ex** 12:37-39; **Ru** 1:1; **Mt** 2:13-15; **Ac** 18:2

Refugees are to be treated kindly
Dt 23:15-16; **Mt** 25:35; **Phm** 10:16

Refugees from legal accusation are to be provided for
Nu 35:6; **Jos** 20:1-6

The LORD is a place of spiritual refuge
Dt 33:27; **2Sa** 22:3; **Ps** 9:9; 59:16; **Isa** 25:4; **Jer** 16:19; **Na** 1:7   *See also poverty.*

restitution

The return of something lost or stolen so that the original situation is restored. This central theme of the OT law is supremely fulfilled through Jesus Christ making restitution for Adam's sin, thus restoring fellowship with God and hope of eternal life.

Reasons for restitution
For crimes committed
Ex 22:2-3 ". . . Thieves must certainly make restitution, but if they have nothing, they must be sold to pay for their theft." *See also* **Ex** 22:7,16-17; **Lev** 6:1-6; 24:17-21; **Nu** 5:6-7; **Eze** 33:14-15
For accidental loss
Ex 22:5-6 ". . . If a fire breaks out and spreads into thornbushes so that it burns shocks of grain or standing corn or the whole field, the one who started the fire must make restitution." *See also* **Ex** 21:33-34; 22:10-15
For unintentional sin Lev 5:14-16
As part of confession Nu 5:5-7
In cases of misplaced accusation Ps 69:4

The basis of decisions regarding restitution
Arbitration Ex 22:8-9
The amount of restitution is to exceed the amount stolen
Ex 22:1 "Whoever steals an ox or a sheep and slaughters it or sells it must pay back five head of cattle for the ox and four sheep for the sheep." *See also* **Ex** 22:4; **Lev** 6:5; **2Sa** 12:5-6; **Pr** 6:31
Land should belong to its rightful owners 2Sa 9:7

Examples of restitution
1Sa 6:17; **1Ki** 20:34; **2Ki** 8:1-6; **Ne** 5:10-12; **Lk** 19:8-9

The act of restitution is to be motivated by love
Ro 13:8-10 Let no debt remain outstanding, except the continuing debt to love one another, for whoever loves others has fulfilled the law . . . *See also* **Mt** 5:23-24,44; **Col** 3:13-14

God promises physical restitution
Isa 57:18; 61:3-4; **Jer** 30:17-18

Jesus Christ makes restitution for sin
He restores fellowship with God
Ro 5:19 For just as through the disobedience of the one man the many were made sinners, so also through the obedience of the one man the many will be made righteous. *See also* **2Co** 5:21; **Heb** 9:28
He restores the hope of eternal life
1Co 15:21-22 . . . For as in Adam all die, so in Christ all will be made alive. *See also* **1Co** 15:45-49

Restitution is made to Jesus Christ
Php 2:8-9 . . . he [Jesus] humbled himself and became obedient to death—even death on a cross! Therefore God exalted him to the highest place and gave him the name that is above every name, *Here God's exaltation of Jesus Christ is seen as restitution to his position of glory.*
See also **Isa** 53:10-12

Restitution is made to those who make sacrifices for the gospel
Mt 19:21 Jesus answered, "If you want to be perfect, go, sell your possessions and give to the poor, and you will have treasure in heaven . . ." pp Mk 10:21 pp Lk 18:22   *See also* **Mt** 19:29 pp Mk 10:29–30 pp Lk 18:29–30; **Mk** 8:35 pp Mt 16:25 pp Lk 9:24; **Jn** 12:24–25; **Php** 3:8–10 *See also guilt offering.*

---

rich, the
It is hard but not impossible for rich people to enter God's kingdom. They must put their hope in God, not in their riches. Rich people who live selfishly, abuse their position and fail to repent and live for Jesus Christ, are in peril.

Parables concerning rich people
2Sa 12:1–10; **Mt** 13:44–46; 18:23; 22:2 pp Lk 14:16; **Mt** 25:14 pp Lk 19:12; **Lk** 12:16; 15:11–13; 16:1; 18:10

Rich people have received blessing
1Ti 6:17 Command those who are rich in this present world not to be arrogant nor to put their hope in wealth, which is so uncertain, but to put their hope in God, who richly provides us with everything for our enjoyment.   *See also* **Ps** 1:3; 112:1–3
They have friends Pr 14:20; 19:4
They have power Pr 22:7
They have security Pr 10:15; 18:11

Warnings to rich people
They should recognise that God is the giver of riches
Dt 8:17–18 . . . remember the LORD your God, for it is he who gives you the ability to produce wealth, and so confirms his covenant . . .
See also **Dt** 32:13–15; **Hos** 2:8
They should not be arrogant or complacent on account of their riches
Jer 9:23–24 This is what the LORD says: "Let not the wise boast of their wisdom or the strong boast of their strength or the rich boast of their riches . . ." . . .   *See also* **Ps** 49:5–6; **Jer** 49:4;

Hos 12:8; **1Ti** 6:17; **Rev** 3:17
They should not trust in their riches
Pr 11:28 Those who trust in their riches will fall . . .   *See also* **Ps** 49:6; 52:7; 62:10; **Jer** 48:7
They face disaster if they lack wisdom
Ps 49:20 Human beings who have riches without understanding are like the beasts that perish.   *See also* **Pr** 28:11; **Jer** 9:23–24
They must live moral lives
Pr 28:6 Better the poor whose walk is blameless than the rich whose ways are perverse.   *See also* **Pr** 22:16; **Jer** 5:27–28; 17:11; **Mic** 6:12
Wealth can bring anxiety
Ecc 5:12 . . . the abundance of the rich permits them no sleep.   *See also* **Mt** 6:25–34 pp Lk 12:22–31
Riches are of fleeting value
Lk 12:16–21 . . . "". . . But God said to him [a rich man], 'You fool! This very night your life will be demanded from you. Then who will get what you have prepared for yourself ?' . . ."
See also **Ps** 49:5–12; **Pr** 27:24; **Ecc** 5:15; **Isa** 10:3; **Mt** 6:19; **1Ti** 6:7; **Job** 1:21; **Jas** 1:10–11
Ultimate security is found in God alone Ex 15:2; **2Sa** 22:33; **1Ch** 16:11; **Ps** 28:7; 29:11; 46:1; 52:6–7; **Isa** 12:2; **Hab** 3:19
It is hard for rich people to enter God's kingdom
Mt 19:23–26 Then Jesus said to his disciples, "I tell you the truth, it is hard for the rich to enter the kingdom of heaven. Again I tell you, it is easier for a camel to go through the eye of a needle than for the rich to enter the kingdom of God." When the disciples heard this, they were greatly astonished and asked, "Who then can be saved?" Jesus looked at them and said, "Humanly, this is impossible, but with God all things are possible." pp Mk 10:23–27 pp Lk 18:24–27   *See also* **Mt** 13:22 pp Mk 4:18–19 pp Lk 8:14; **Mt** 19:16–22 pp Mk 10:17–22 pp Lk 18:18–23

Rich people will be judged for their behaviour
Zec 11:5–6; **Lk** 1:53

If they exploit, oppress or kill the poor
Jas 5:1–4 . . . you rich people, weep and wail
because of the misery that is coming upon
you . . . The wages you failed to pay the
workers who mowed your fields are crying out
against you. The cries of the harvesters have
reached the ears of the Lord Almighty.   *See also*
Pr 14:31; 22:16; 28:3; **Eze** 18:12–13; 22:29–31;
Jas 2:6; 5:6
If they hoard wealth and live selfishly
Jas 5:5 You have lived on earth in luxury and
self-indulgence . . .   *See also* **Lk** 12:16–21;
16:19–31
If they slander the name of Jesus Christ Jas 2:7

Commands to rich people
To seek God's kingdom as first priority Mt
6:19–21,31–33 pp Lk 12:29–31; **1Ti** 6:19
To repent from sin Rev 3:17,19
To be generous towards the needy
1Ti 6:18 Command them [the rich] to do good,
to be rich in good deeds, and to be generous and
willing to share.   *See also* **Mt** 19:21 pp Mk
10:21 pp Lk 18:22; **Lk** 3:11; 11:41; 12:33–34;
14:12–14; 16:9; 19:8; **2Co** 8:1–5,9,13–15; 9:6–15

Incorrect attitudes to the rich
Ecc 10:20; **Ps** 49:5–6,16–17
Showing favouritism to them: **Job** 34:18–19; **Pr** 22:2;
Jas 2:1–4

God brings good news for rich people
Ps 22:29–31; **Mt** 9:9–10 pp Mk 2:14–15 pp
Lk 5:27–29; **Mt** 27:57 pp Mk 15:43 pp Lk
23:50–51; **Lk** 19:1–10

Examples of rich people
Abraham: **Ge** 12:10–16; 13:2
Ge 26:1–14
Jacob: **Ge** 27:19,28; 30:29–43; 35:11–12
The Israelites, who entered a fertile promised land with
an abundance of wealth plundered from the Egyptians:
Ge 15:14; **Ex** 3:22; 12:36; **Ps** 105:37
1Ki 10:23 pp 2Ch 9:22
Hezekiah: **2Ki** 20:13; **2Ch** 32:27–29; **Mt** 27:57–60
pp Mk 15:43–46 pp Lk 23:50–53; **Jn** 19:38–42
See also money; poverty.

ritual

The regulations governing Jewish religious life and
worship, especially sacrifices, ritual cleanliness and
food laws. By the sacrificial death of Jesus Christ
these rituals have been fulfilled and play no part
in the new covenant.

The purpose of ritual sacrifices
To atone for sin
Lev 5:12–13 "'. . . It is a sin offering. In
this way the priest will make atonement for them
for any of these sins they have committed, and
they will be forgiven . . .'"   *See also* **Ex**
29:38–43; **Lev** 1:3–13;
4:1–3,13–14,20–23,26–28,31–35; 5:13; 6:1–7;
7:1–7; 16:1–34
To maintain fellowship between God and his
people Lev 3:1–5; 7:11–15
To express worship and gratitude to God
The grain offering was the only bloodless offering but it
accompanied the other offerings and was burnt whole to
express gratitude to God for the harvest and for
particular blessings: **Lev** 2:1–3,8–16; 6:14–23;
7:9–10; 9:4; **Nu** 6:14–17; 28:3–13

Rituals for purification from ritual
uncleanness
Childbirth
Lk 2:22–24 When the time of their purification
according to the Law of Moses had been
completed, Joseph and Mary took him [Jesus] to
Jerusalem to present him to the Lord (as it is
written in the Law of the Lord, "Every firstborn
male is to be consecrated to the Lord"), and to
offer a sacrifice in keeping with what is said in
the Law of the Lord . . .   *See also* **Lev** 12:1–8
Unclean diseases
Mk 1:40–44 A man with leprosy came to him
[Jesus] and begged him on his knees, "If you
are willing, you can make me clean." . . . Jesus
reached out his hand and touched the man. "I
am willing," he said. "Be clean!" . . .
". . . show yourself to the priest and offer the
sacrifices that Moses commanded for your
cleansing, as a testimony to them." pp Mt 8:2–4
pp Lk 5:12–14   *See also* **Lev** 14:2–7

Unclean discharges Lev 15:32–33
Touching dead bodies Nu 19:11–13

Rituals relating to food
Clean and unclean foods
Lev 11:1–2 The Lord said to Moses and Aaron, "Say to the Israelites: 'Of all the animals that live on land, these are the ones you may eat:'"
See also **Lev** 11:44–47
The eating of blood is forbidden Ge 9:4–5; **Lev** 17:11–12; **Ac** 15:20

Rituals relating to the priesthood
Lev 8:30 Then Moses took some of the anointing oil and some of the blood from the altar and sprinkled them on Aaron and his garments and on his sons and their garments. So he consecrated Aaron and his garments and his sons and their garments. *See also* **Ex** 29:1–9

Rituals relating to the place of worship
2Ch 29:4–5 . . . "'. . . consecrate the temple of the Lord, the God of your ancestors. Remove all defilement from the sanctuary." *See also* **Lev** 16:15–20; **1Ki** 8:62–63 pp 2Ch 7:4–5; **Ezr** 6:16–17

Rituals relating to special days
Festivals Lev 23:37
The Sabbath Ex 31:12–17; **Mt** 12:2 pp Mk 2:24 pp Lk 6:2

The initiation ritual of circumcision
Ge 17:10–14

Ritual only has meaning when accompanied by obedience
Ro 2:25 Circumcision has value if you observe the law, but if you break the law, you have become as though you had not been circumcised. *See also* **Isa** 1:11–17; **Mt** 15:16–20 pp Mk 7:18–23; **Mt** 23:25; **Ro** 2:28–29; **1Co** 7:19; 8:8

Rituals of the old covenant are fulfilled by Jesus Christ
Col 2:17 These [rituals] are a shadow of the things that were to come; the reality, however, is found in Christ. *See also* **Mk** 2:27–28; **Col** 2:11; **Heb** 10:1–3,8–10

Old covenant rituals are abolished under the new covenant
Heb 9:10 They [rituals] are only a matter of food and drink and various ceremonial washings—external regulations applying until the time of the new order. *See also* **Mk** 7:19; **Ac** 10:9–15; **Ro** 7:6; 14:14,20; **Gal** 5:6; 6:15; **Eph** 2:15; **Col** 2:13–16 *See also blood; ceremonies; circumcision; clean and unclean; offerings; priesthood; ritual law; ritual washing; sacrifice, in Old Testament.*

ritual law
The rules and regulations regarding the conduct of the priests and people of Israel in approaching God, especially in worship. They were to be holy as God is holy. The perfect sacrifice of Jesus Christ on the cross is seen by NT writers as fulfilling this demand for holiness and obedience.

The ritual law and the priesthood
The priests were to be careful to obey God's commandments
Lev 22:9 "'The priests are to keep my requirements so that they do not become guilty and die for treating them with contempt. I am the Lord, who makes them holy.'" *See also* **Lev** 10:10; 22:3
The priests had to avoid ceremonial uncleanness
Contact with the dead caused uncleanness and was forbidden to the high priest: **Lev** 21:1–3,11; **Nu** 19:11,14
Lev 21:16–23; 22:20–25

The ritual law and the people of Israel
The people were called to holiness
Lev 19:2 "Speak to the entire assembly of Israel and say to them: 'Be holy because I, the Lord your God, am holy.'"
Lev 20:26 "'You are to be holy to me because I, the Lord, am holy, and I have set you apart from the nations to be my own.'"

See also **Lev** 11:44–45; 20:7; 21:8; 22:32

The ritual law stipulated what they could eat

Lev 11:46–47 " 'These are the regulations concerning animals, birds, every living thing that moves in the water and every creature that moves about on the ground. You must distinguish between the unclean and the clean, between living creatures that may be eaten and those that may not be eaten.' "   *See also* **Ge** 7:2; 8:20; **Lev** 11:1–23 pp Dt 14:3–20; **Dt** 14:21

The ritual law regarding childbirth Lev 12:1–5; **Lk** 2:22–24

Jesus Christ's obedience and perfect sacrifice on the cross fulfilled the demands of the ritual law

Heb 10:8–10 First he [Jesus] said, "Sacrifices and offerings, burnt offerings and sin offerings you did not desire, nor were you pleased with them" (although the law required them to be made). Then he said, "Here I am, I have come to do your will." He sets aside the first to establish the second. And by that will, we have been made holy through the sacrifice of the body of Jesus Christ once for all.   *See also* **Eph** 2:15; **Col** 2:14; **Heb** 7:11,18,27; 10:1–3,11–14   *See also clean and unclean; law; offerings; ritual; ritual washing; sacrifice.*

---

ritual washing

The act of washing for consecration or for purification from uncleanness. It involved washing all or part of the body or one's clothing. Jesus Christ's attitude to the Pharisees reflected, not a disavowal of ritual washing, but disapproval of their emphasis on the outward, rather than inward, forms of religion.

Ritual washing for consecration

Ex 19:10–11 And the LORD said to Moses, "Go to the people and consecrate them today and tomorrow. Make them wash their clothes and be ready by the third day . . ."   *See also* **Ex** 19:14; 40:12–15; **Nu** 8:5–7,21–22

Ritual washing for cleansing

Lev 17:15 " 'Anyone, whether native-born or alien, who eats anything found dead or torn by wild animals must wash their clothes and bathe with water, and they will be ceremonially unclean till evening; then they will be clean.' "   *See also* **Lev** 13:6,34; 15:16–18,21–23; **Nu** 19:10,19

Methods of ritual washing
Washing clothes

Nu 31:24 "On the seventh day wash your [soldiers'] clothes and you will be clean . . ." *See also* **Lev** 6:27; 11:24–28,39–40; 13:58; 14:43–47; **Nu** 19:21; **Rev** 7:14; 22:14

Bathing

Lev 14:8–9 "The person to be cleansed must wash their clothes, shave off all their hair and bathe with water; then they will be ceremonially clean. After this they may come into the camp, but they must stay outside their tent for seven days. On the seventh day they must shave off all their hair; they must shave their head, their beard, their eyebrows and the rest of their hair. They must wash their clothes and bathe themselves with water, and they will be clean."   *See also* **Lev** 15:4–13,27; 16:26–28; 17:15; **Nu** 19:7–8; **Dt** 23:9–11; **2Ki** 5:9–14; **Ps** 51:7; **Heb** 10:19–22

Sprinkling with the water of purification

Nu 19:17–19 ". . . someone who is ceremonially clean is to take some hyssop, dip it in the water and sprinkle the tent and all the furnishings and the people who were there. That person must also sprinkle anyone who has touched a human bone or a grave or anyone who has been killed or anyone who has died a natural death. The one who is clean is to sprinkle those who are unclean on the third and seventh days, and on the seventh day he is to purify them. Those who are being cleansed must wash their clothes and bathe with water, and that evening they will be clean."   *See also* **Nu** 8:5–7; 19:13; **Eze** 36:24–25

Washing hands and feet

Ex 30:17–21 . . . ". . . Aaron and his sons are to wash their hands and feet with water from it [the bronze basin]. Whenever they enter the Tent of Meeting, they shall wash with water so

that they will not die. Also, when they approach the altar to minister by presenting an offering made to the LORD by fire, they shall wash their hands and feet so that they will not die. This is to be a lasting ordinance for Aaron and his descendants for the generations to come."
See also **Ex** 40:30–32; **Dt** 21:6–9; **Jn** 13:5–10; **Jas** 4:8

Consequences of the failure to perform ritual washing
Nu 19:20 ". . . if those who are unclean do not purify themselves, they must be cut off from the community, because they have defiled the sanctuary of the LORD. The water of cleansing has not been sprinkled on them, and they are unclean."   See also **Lev** 17:15–16; **Nu** 19:13

The NT perception of ritual washing
It was practised in NT times
Jn 2:6 Nearby stood six stone water jars, the kind used by the Jews for ceremonial washing, each holding from twenty to thirty gallons.
See also **Jn** 3:25

The Pharisees over-emphasised its importance
Mt 15:1–11 Then some Pharisees and teachers of the law came to Jesus from Jerusalem and asked, "Why do your disciples break the tradition of the elders? They don't wash their hands before they eat!" . . . Jesus called the crowd to him and said, "Listen and understand. What goes into your mouth does not make you 'unclean', but what comes out of your mouth, that is what makes you 'unclean'." pp **Mk** 7:1–23   See also **Lk** 11:37–41

Jesus Christ's atoning work rendered it unnecessary
Heb 9:6–14 . . . The blood of goats and bulls and the ashes of a heifer sprinkled on those who are ceremonially unclean sanctify them so that they are outwardly clean. How much more, then, will the blood of Christ, who through the eternal Spirit offered himself unblemished to God, cleanse our consciences from acts that lead to death, so that we may serve the living God!   See also *clean and unclean; ritual; ritual law; washing.*

Sabbath
The day of rest laid down for the people of God. The OT treated the seventh day of the week (Saturday) as the Sabbath, a custom continued in modern Judaism. The Christian church, in recognition of the importance of the resurrection of Jesus Christ, observed a day of rest on the first day of the week (Sunday).

Sabbath, in New Testament
The NT develops the OT teaching on the Sabbath in three important directions. It declares that the Sabbath should not be observed in a legalistic manner; the Sabbath-rest is treated as an important symbol of the Christian doctrine of salvation; and finally, the NT itself indicates how Sunday, rather than Saturday, came to be seen as the Christian Sabbath.

Gospel incidents connected with the Sabbath
Exorcism Mk 1:21–25 pp **Lk** 4:31–35
Healing Mt 12:9–14 pp **Mk** 3:1–6 pp **Lk** 6:6–11; **Mk** 1:30–31 pp **Lk** 4:38–40; **Lk** 13:10–17; 14:1–6; **Jn** 5:5–18; 9:1–16
Teaching Mk 6:2 pp **Mt** 13:54; **Lk** 4:16
Other references Mt 28:1 pp **Mk** 16:1; **Lk** 23:55–56; **Jn** 12:2

Jesus Christ's teaching regarding the Sabbath
Jesus Christ observes the Sabbath regulation
Lk 4:16 He went to Nazareth, where he had been brought up, and on the Sabbath day he went into the synagogue, as was his custom . . .   See also **Mt** 24:20; **Ac** 1:12
Human well-being is more important than rigid observance of the Law
Mk 2:27–28 Then he [Jesus] said to them [the Pharisees], "The Sabbath was made for people, not people for the Sabbath. So the Son of Man is Lord even of the Sabbath."   See also **Mt** 12:3
Ceremonial observance must give way before any higher, or more spiritual, motive
Mt 12:5–6 "Or haven't you read in the Law

that on the Sabbath the priests in the temple desecrate the day and yet are innocent? I tell you that one greater than the temple is here." *See also* **Lk** 6:5

Sabbath reading of Scripture provided an opportunity for reaching the Jews

Ac 17:2 As his custom was, Paul went into the synagogue, and on three Sabbath days he reasoned with them from the Scriptures, *See also* **Ac** 13:14,27,42,44; 15:21; 16:13; 18:4

Sabbath observance was optional for Gentile Christians

Col 2:16 Therefore do not let anyone judge you by what you eat or drink, or with regard to a religious festival, a New Moon celebration or a Sabbath day.

The Lord's Day

Rev 1:10 On the Lord's Day I was in the Spirit, and I heard behind me a loud voice like a trumpet, *At an early stage the Sabbath was replaced by Sunday (the first day of the week) as the day for rest and worship. See also* **Jn** 20:19,26; **Ac** 20:7; **1Co** 16:2

The Sabbath-rest is seen as a symbol of the salvation of the people of God

Heb 4:1 Therefore, since the promise of entering his rest still stands, let us be careful that none of you be found to have fallen short of it.
Heb 3:18–19 And to whom did God swear that they would never enter his rest if not to those who disobeyed? So we see that they were not able to enter, because of their unbelief.
Heb 4:9 There remains, then, a Sabbath-rest for the people of God;

Sabbath, in Old Testament

The Sabbath of rest is grounded in God's work of creation. Observance of a Sabbath day is distinctive of the people of God.

The Sabbath grounded in creation itself

Ge 2:3 And God blessed the seventh day and made it holy, because on it he rested from all the work of creating that he had done. *See also* **Ps** 118:24

The purpose of the Sabbath

To remember God's work in creation

Ex 20:8–11 "Remember the Sabbath day by keeping it holy. Six days you shall labour and do all your work, but the seventh day is a Sabbath to the LORD your God. On it you shall not do any work, neither you, nor your son or daughter, nor your male or female servant, nor your animals, nor the alien within your gates. For in six days the LORD made the heavens and the earth, the sea, and all that is in them, but he rested on the seventh day. Therefore the LORD blessed the Sabbath day and made it holy." *See also* **Ge** 2:2; **Ex** 35:2

To remember the exodus

Dt 5:12–15 "Observe the Sabbath day by keeping it holy, as the LORD your God has commanded you. Six days you shall labour and do all your work, but the seventh day is a Sabbath to the LORD your God. On it you shall not do any work, neither you, nor your son or daughter, nor male or female servant, nor your ox, your donkey or any of your animals, nor the alien within your gates, so that your male and female servants may rest, as you do. Remember that you were slaves in Egypt and that the LORD your God brought you out of there with a mighty hand and an outstretched arm. Therefore the LORD your God has commanded you to observe the Sabbath day." *The idea of rest relates the concept of the Sabbath to the ultimate conquest of Canaan under David and to the return from exile. See also* **Ge** 8:4; **2Sa** 7:1,11; **Ps** 95:10–11; **Heb** 4:9; **Rev** 14:13

To be a sign of the relationship between Israel and God and to give refreshment

Ex 31:17 " 'It will be a sign between me and the Israelites for ever, for in six days the LORD made the heavens and the earth, and on the seventh day he abstained from work and rested.' " *See also* **Dt** 5:12–14

The Law required the Sabbath to be a holy day free from work

Lev 23:3 "'There are six days when you may work, but the seventh day is a Sabbath of rest, a day of sacred assembly. You are not to do any work; wherever you live, it is a Sabbath to the LORD.'" *See also* **Ex** 34:21; 35:3; **Lev** 23:38; **Isa** 56:2; 58:13

The Sabbath was linked with celebration of the New Moon

2Ki 4:23 "Why go to him [Elisha] today?" he asked. "It's not the New Moon or the Sabbath." . . . *See also* **Isa** 1:13; **Eze** 46:3; **Hos** 2:11; **Am** 8:5

Abuses of the Sabbath

Ex 16:27–28; **Nu** 15:32; **Ne** 13:15–18
Engaging in commerce: **Ne** 10:31; **Am** 8:5
Jer 17:21

Punishments for infringing the Sabbath law

The death penalty Ex 31:14; **Nu** 15:35
Disaster for Jerusalem Jer 17:27; **Eze** 20:13; 22:8,15

Sacrifices to be offered on the Sabbath

Bread Lev 24:8; **1Ch** 9:32
Burnt offerings Nu 28:9–10; **1Ch** 23:31; **2Ch** 2:4
Other offerings Eze 46:4 *See also law, Old Testament.*

---

sacraments

The sacraments of baptism and the Lord's Supper were instituted by Jesus Christ as signs and seals of the covenant. They explain the basis of this covenant and apply its benefits to believers. They replace circumcision and the Passover which were the sacraments of the old covenant.

The sacraments as signs of the new covenant

Baptism

Mt 28:19 ". . . make disciples of all nations, baptising them in the name of the Father and of the Son and of the Holy Spirit," *See also* **Ac** 2:38,41

The Lord's Supper

1Co 11:23–25 For I [Paul] received from the Lord what I also passed on to you: The Lord Jesus, on the night he was betrayed, took bread, and when he had given thanks, he broke it and said, "This is my body, which is for you; do this in remembrance of me." In the same way, after supper he took the cup, saying, "This cup is the new covenant in my blood; do this, whenever you drink it, in remembrance of me." pp Mt 26:26–28 pp Mk 14:22–24 pp Lk 22:17–20

The sacraments as a participation in the body of Christ

Baptism

Gal 3:27 for all of you who were baptised into Christ have clothed yourselves with Christ. *See also* **Ro** 6:3

The Lord's Supper

1Co 10:16–17 Is not the cup of thanksgiving for which we give thanks a participation in the blood of Christ? And is not the bread that we break a participation in the body of Christ? Because there is one loaf, we, who are many, are one body, for we all partake of the one loaf. *See also* **Mt** 26:26 pp Mk 14:22 pp Lk 22:19 pp 1Co 11:24; **Jn** 6:32–35,48,50–58

The sacraments as a participation in the death of Christ

Baptism

Ro 6:3–4 . . . We were therefore buried with him [Christ] through baptism into death in order that, just as Christ was raised from the dead through the glory of the Father, we too may live a new life. *See also* **Ac** 2:38; 22:16; **Ro** 6:5–7; **Col** 2:12; **Tit** 3:5; **1Pe** 3:21

The Lord's Supper

1Co 11:26 . . . whenever you eat this bread and drink this cup, you proclaim the Lord's death until he comes. *See also* **Mt** 26:27–28 pp Mk 14:23–24 pp Lk 22:20 pp 1Co 11:25; **Jn** 6:53–56; **1Co** 10:16

The sacraments of the old covenant
Circumcision
Ac 7:8 ". . . he [God] gave Abraham the covenant of circumcision. And Abraham became the father of Isaac and circumcised him eight days after his birth . . ." *See also* **Ge** 17:10–14; **Ro** 2:28–29; 4:10–11; **Col** 2:11–12

The Passover
Ex 12:25–27 "When you [the Israelites] enter the land that the LORD will give you as he promised, observe this ceremony . . . 'It is the Passover sacrifice to the LORD, who passed over the houses of the Israelites in Egypt and spared our homes when he struck down the Egyptians.'" . . . *See also* **Lk** 22:15–16; **1Co** 5:7 *See also circumcision; covenant; Passover.*

---

sacrifice
An important aspect of the relationship between God and humanity but whereas the OT describes many sacrifices, the NT announces the fulfilment of sacrifice in Jesus Christ.

---

sacrifice, in Old Testament
An act that involved offering to God the life of an animal. It expressed gratitude for God's goodness or acknowledgment of sin. It was also associated with establishing a covenant.

Sacrifice was an integral part of worship
Ge 46:1; **Ex** 10:24–26; **Jdg** 13:19; **1Sa** 1:3; **1Ki** 3:4

Sacrifices were a means of offering thanks to God
Ge 4:4; 8:20; **Ex** 18:12; **Jdg** 11:31; **1Sa** 6:15
The returning exiles: **Ezr** 3:3; 8:35
In response to God's deliverance from danger and sickness: **Ps** 27:6; 54:6; 107:17–22

Sacrifices were offered at regular religious festivals
Lev 23:5–8,18–20,23–25
The Day of Atonement: **Lev** 16:6–10; 23:26–32
Lev 23:33–36

Special occasions were marked by sacrifices
1Ki 8:63; **2Ch** 29:31–33; **Ezr** 3:2–3; 6:17

Sacrifices as signs of individual and national penitence
Lev 4:1–3,13–14; **Jdg** 2:1–5; 20:26; **1Sa** 7:8–9; **2Sa** 24:10–25

The place of sacrifice
It was divinely chosen
Dt 12:13–14 Be careful not to sacrifice your burnt offerings anywhere you please. Offer them only at the place the LORD will choose . . .
See also **Lev** 17:3–5; **Dt** 12:2–6

Rival places of sacrifice caused the Israelites to sin **1Ki** 12:28–29,32; **2Ch** 15:17; 31:1

God condemned certain sacrifices
Sacrifices to other gods
1Ki 11:7–8 On a hill east of Jerusalem, Solomon built a high place for Chemosh the detestable god of Moab, and for Molech the detestable god of the Ammonites. He did the same for all his foreign wives, who burned incense and offered sacrifices to their gods. *See also* **Nu** 25:1–3; **2Ki** 16:4,15; **Ps** 106:28; **Isa** 57:7; 65:3,7; **Jer** 19:4

Human sacrifices **Lev** 18:21; **Dt** 12:31; **1Ki** 16:34; **2Ki** 3:26–27; 16:3; 17:31; 21:6; **Eze** 20:31

Sacrifice to the LORD may be rejected
If it is a substitute for obedience **1Sa** 15:20–22; **Jer** 7:21–22; **Hos** 8:11–13; **Am** 4:4; **Mk** 12:33
If it is a substitute for justice and mercy **Isa** 66:2–3; **Mic** 6:7–8; **Mt** 9:13
If it is imperfect **Mal** 1:13–14

Blessing is promised when right sacrifices are offered
Ge 22:15–18; **Ps** 4:5; 50:14–15,23; 51:17
See also altar; blood; feast and festival; offerings; ritual; temple, Solomon's.

sacrifice, New Testament fulfilment

For the people of the new covenant, sacrifice is fulfilled in Jesus Christ. Christians should have nothing to do with other sacrifices but are to bring their own "spiritual" offerings.

The OT points ahead to the fulfilment of sacrifice in Jesus Christ
A new sacrificial system
Isa 56:6-7 "And foreigners who bind themselves to the LORD to serve him, to love the name of the LORD, and to worship him, all who keep the Sabbath without desecrating it and who hold fast to my covenant—these I will bring to my holy mountain and give them joy in my house of prayer. Their burnt offerings and sacrifices will be accepted on my altar; for my house will be called a house of prayer for all nations." *See also* **Isa** 19:21
The new people of God Jer 33:18; **Eze** 20:40
The vision of the new temple Eze 40:46

The perfect sacrifice of Jesus Christ
Jesus Christ perceived his death as a sacrifice
Mt 26:28 "This is my blood of the covenant, which is poured out for many for the forgiveness of sins." pp Mk 14:24 pp Lk 22:20 pp 1Co 11:25 *See also* **Heb** 5:1
The contrast with the OT sacrificial system
Heb 7:27 Unlike the other high priests, he does not need to offer sacrifices day after day, first for his own sins, and then for the sins of the people. He sacrificed for their sins once for all when he offered himself. *See also* **Heb** 9:23–26; 10:1–3,12
Jesus Christ's sacrifice of a life dedicated to God makes believers holy Tit 2:14; **Heb** 10:8–10

The sacrifices of Christians
Christians offer themselves as living sacrifices
Ro 12:1 Therefore, I urge you, brothers and sisters, in view of God's mercy, to offer your bodies as living sacrifices, holy and pleasing to God—this is your spiritual act of worship.

Paul saw his own death as part of a sacrificial offering:
Php 2:17; **2Ti** 4:6
The sacrifice of praise and good works
Heb 13:15–16 Through Jesus, therefore, let us continually offer to God a sacrifice of praise—the fruit of lips that confess his name. And do not forget to do good and to share with others, for with such sacrifices God is pleased.

Christian attitudes to pagan sacrifice
1Co 10:18–22,25–26,27–29 *See also* atonement; covenant, new.

sanctuary

A place or structure set aside for the worship of God. In Scripture the word generally refers to the tabernacle or the Jerusalem temple. By extension the word signifies a location or spiritual state providing refuge from hostile forces, human, spiritual or natural.

The tabernacle
Ex 25:8–9 "Then have them make a sanctuary for me, and I will dwell among them. Make this tabernacle and all its furnishings exactly like the pattern I will show you." *See also* **Ex** 36:1; **Heb** 8:2,5
Worship in the tabernacle was divinely ordained in great detail Ex 30:7–10; **Lev** 7:37–38; 23:44; **Ex** 39:1; **Nu** 3:30–31; **Heb** 9:1
The people gave generously for the tabernacle
Ex 36:4–5 So all the skilled workers who were doing all the work on the sanctuary left what they were doing and said to Moses, "The people are bringing more than enough for doing the work the LORD commanded to be done."
Approach to God's sanctuary was strictly regulated
Lev 12:4 "'Then the woman must wait thirty-three days to be purified from her bleeding. She must not touch anything sacred or go to the sanctuary until the days of her purification are over.'" *See also* **Lev** 21:21–23; **Nu** 3:10,38; 8:19; 18:5; 19:20; **2Ch** 26:18
A reverent attitude was commanded
Lev 19:30 "'Observe my Sabbaths and have

reverence for my sanctuary. I am the LORD.' " pp
Lev 26:2

The Jerusalem temple
**David made extensive preparations for
Solomon to build the temple**
1Ch 22:17-19 Then David ordered all the
leaders of Israel to help his son Solomon . . .
"Now devote your heart and soul to seeking the
LORD your God. Begin to build the sanctuary of
the LORD God, so that you may bring the ark of
the covenant of the LORD and the sacred articles
belonging to God into the temple that will be built
for the Name of the LORD."   *See also* **1Ch**
28:2–3,6
**The inner sanctuary of the temple
corresponded to the Most Holy Place in the
tabernacle**
1Ki 6:19 He [Solomon] prepared the inner
sanctuary within the temple to set the ark of the
covenant of the LORD there.   *See also* **1Ki** 8:6
pp 2Ch 5:7; **1Ch** 6:49; **Heb** 9:1–4

Some places were considered sacred because of God's presence and activity
Ex 15:17 "You will bring them in and plant
them on the mountain of your inheritance—the
place, O LORD, you made for your dwelling, the
sanctuary, O Lord, your hands established."
See also **Ge** 28:16–17; **Ex** 3:1–5; **Ps** 15:1; 63:2;
73:16–17; **Jer** 17:12

Conduct that displeases God will lead to a nation's sanctuaries being destroyed
Disobedience to God
Lev 26:31 " 'I will turn your cities into ruins
and lay waste your sanctuaries, and I will take no
delight in the pleasing aroma of your
offerings.' "   *See also* **2Ch** 30:8; **Eze** 7:24; **La**
2:7; **Am** 7:9; **Mal** 2:11
Dishonesty in dealings
Eze 28:18 " 'By your many sins and dishonest
trade you have desecrated your sanctuaries. So I
made a fire come out from you, and it consumed
you, and I reduced you to ashes on the ground in
the sight of all who were watching.' "

Idolatry Lev 20:3; **Eze** 8:6; 23:38–39
Profaning the sanctuary Eze 44:7–8; **Zep** 3:4

Sanctuary from vengeance: the cities of refuge
Jos 20:2-3 "Tell the Israelites to designate the
cities of refuge, as I instructed you through Moses,
so that anyone who kills a person accidentally and
unintentionally may flee there and find protection
from the avenger of blood."   *See also* **Nu**
35:6,9–12

God himself is his people's sanctuary
Ps 31:20 In the shelter of your presence you
hide them from human intrigues; in your dwelling
you keep them safe from accusing tongues.
See also **Dt** 33:27; **Ps** 17:7–9; 27:1; 32:7; 46:1;
64:1–2; 91:4; **Isa** 25:4; **Eze** 11:16; **Ro** 8:38–39;
Php 4:7; **Heb** 6:19

Non-material "sanctuaries" of God
Heaven, where God is perfectly worshipped
Ps 102:19 "The LORD looked down from his
sanctuary on high, from heaven he viewed the
earth . . ."   *See also* **Heb** 9:24
**God's worshipping people, in whom God
dwells**
Ps 114:2 Judah became God's sanctuary, Israel
his dominion.   *See also* **1Co** 6:19; **Eph** 2:21;
1Pe 2:5
**Jesus Christ himself as the "place" where
God dwelt on earth Jn** 2:19–21   *See also* Most
Holy Place; tabernacle, in Old Testament; temple,
Solomon's.

---

scales and balances
Weighing devices designed to ensure fair dealing.
The terms are also used metaphorically in
Scripture.

Scales and balances were used in business transactions
Jer 32:10

Scales and balances should not be used dishonestly

Exhortations to honest dealing

Lev 19:35-36 " 'Do not use dishonest standards when measuring length, weight or quantity. Use honest scales and honest weights, an honest ephah and an honest hin. I am the LORD your God, who brought you out of Egypt.' "   *See also* **Eze** 45:10

The LORD hates dishonest dealing

Pr 20:10 Differing weights and differing measures—the LORD detests them both.
See also **Pr** 11:1; 16:11; 20:23

Dishonest dealing was one of the reasons for God's judgment on his people

Jer 5:1 "Go up and down the streets of Jerusalem, look around and consider, search through her squares. If you can find but one person who deals honestly and seeks the truth, I will forgive this city."   *See also* **Hos** 12:6-7; **Am** 8:4-8; **Mic** 6:10-13

Scales and balances used metaphorically

To emphasise Job's distress

Job 6:2 "If only my anguish could be weighed and all my misery be placed on the scales!"

To highlight God's greatness

Isa 40:15 Surely the nations are like a drop in a bucket; they are regarded as dust on the scales; he weighs the islands as though they were fine dust.   *See also* **Isa** 40:12

Of God's judgment

Da 5:25-30 ". . . You have been weighed on the scales and found wanting . . ."   *See also* **Eze** 5:1-2; **Rev** 6:5-6   *See also weights and measures, laws.*

seafaring

Ideas and images drawn from seafaring are used in Scripture to illustrate important aspects of the Christian life. Although Israel was not a seafaring nation, ships and sailing played a part in her history, as they did in the spreading of the gospel in the NT.

Israel's harbours

Ge 49:13 "Zebulun will live by the seashore and become a haven for ships; his border will extend towards Sidon."   *See also* **Jdg** 5:17

The art of shipbuilding

Eze 27:3-9

Ships used for various purposes

Deliverance from danger: Noah's ark Ge

6:1—9:17

Trade

1Ki 9:27-28 And Hiram sent his servants—sailors who knew the sea—to serve in the fleet with Solomon's servants. They sailed to Ophir and brought back 420 talents of gold, which they delivered to King Solomon. pp 2Ch 8:18

Eze 27:25 " 'The ships of Tarshish serve as carriers for your wares. You are filled with heavy cargo in the heart of the sea.' "   *See also* **1Ki** 10:11,22 pp 2Ch 9:21; **1Ki** 22:48-49 pp 2Ch 20:35-37

Slavery Dt 28:68; **Rev** 18:11-13

Invasion

Nu 24:24 "Ships will come from the shores of Kittim; they will subdue Asshur and Eber, but they too will come to ruin."   *See also* **Eze** 30:9; **Da** 11:30,40

To carry refugees

Isa 60:9 "Surely the islands look to me [the LORD]; in the lead are the ships of Tarshish, bringing your children from afar, with their silver and gold, to the honour of the LORD your God, the Holy One of Israel, for he has endowed you with splendour."

To carry passengers

Jnh 1:3 But Jonah ran away from the LORD and headed for Tarshish. He went down to Joppa, where he found a ship bound for that port. After paying the fare, he went aboard and sailed for Tarshish to flee from the LORD.

Mt 9:1 Jesus stepped into a boat, crossed over and came to his own town.

Ac 13:4 The two of them [Paul and Barnabas], sent on their way by the Holy Spirit, went down to Seleucia and sailed from there to Cyprus.
See also **Mt** 14:13; 15:39; **Mk** 3:9; **Ac** 13:13;

14:26; 15:39; 16:11; 18:18,21; 20:3,6,13–16;
21:1–3,6–7; 27:1–8; 28:11–13

Seafarers
Ps 107:23–30 Others went out on the sea in ships; they were merchants on the mighty waters. They saw the works of the Lord, his wonderful deeds in the deep. For he spoke and stirred up a tempest that lifted high the waves. They mounted up to the heavens and went down to the depths; in their peril their courage melted away. They reeled and staggered like drunkards; they were at their wits' end. Then they cried out to the Lord in their trouble, and he brought them out of their distress. He stilled the storm to a whisper; the waves of the sea were hushed. They were glad when it grew calm, and he guided them to their desired haven.
2Co 11:25 Three times I [Paul] was beaten with rods, once I was stoned, three times I was shipwrecked, I spent a night and a day in the open sea,   *See also* **1Ki** 22:48 pp 2Ch 20:37; **Jnh** 1:3–15; **Mt** 8:23–27 pp Mk 4:35–41 pp Lk 8:22–26; **Mt** 14:22–33 pp Mk 6:45–53 pp Jn 6:16–21; **Ac** 27:9–44

Judgment on seafarers
Isa 23:1 An oracle concerning Tyre: Wail, O ships of Tarshish! For Tyre is destroyed and left without house or harbour. From the land of Cyprus word has come to them.   *See also* **Isa** 2:16; 23:14; 33:21–23; 43:14; **Eze** 27:26–36; **Rev** 18:17–19

Metaphorical references to ships and seafaring
Spiritual immaturity as a ship tossed at sea
Eph 4:14 Then we will no longer be infants, tossed back and forth by the waves, and blown here and there by every wind of teaching and by the cunning and craftiness of people in their deceitful scheming.
Abandoning sound teaching as shipwreck
1Ti 1:19 . . . holding on to faith and a good conscience. Some have rejected these and so have shipwrecked their faith.
Faith as an anchor

Heb 6:19 We have this hope as an anchor for the soul, firm and secure. It enters the inner sanctuary behind the curtain,
Other seafaring analogies
Jas 3:4–5 Or take ships as an example. Although they are so large and are driven by strong winds, they are steered by a very small rudder wherever the pilot wants to go. Likewise the tongue is a small part of the body, but it makes great boasts . . .   *See also* **Ps** 48:7; **Pr** 31:14; **Jas** 1:6
Noah's ark as a symbol of Jesus Christ 1Pe 3:20   *See also fish; trade.*

seal
A personalised design used to produce an imprint in clay or wax which was then attached, usually to documents and letters as a mark of ownership, authenticity and authority. A seal might also refer to what is given as a pledge or guarantee or be used to keep something secure.

The nature and use of a seal
Seals engraved on precious stone
Ex 28:11 "Engrave the names of the sons of Israel on the two stones the way a gem cutter engraves a seal . . ." pp Ex 39:6   *See also* **Ex** 28:21 pp Ex 39:14; **Ex** 28:36 pp Ex 39:30
Seals used to imprint soft clay Job 38:14

Ways of carrying a personal seal
Figuratively used SS 8:6
Worn round the neck
Ge 38:18 He [Judah] said, "What pledge should I give you?" "Your seal and its cord, and the staff in your hand," she [Tamar] answered . . .   *See also* **Ge** 38:25
Worn as a signet ring
Jer 22:24 "As surely as I live," declares the Lord, "even if you, Jehoiachin son of Jehoiakim king of Judah, were a signet ring on my right hand, I would still pull you off."   *See also* **Nu** 31:50; **Isa** 3:21

A seal as a mark of authority
Given to signify delegation of authority Ge 41:42; **Est** 3:10; 8:2; **Rev** 7:2

God's seal validates his servants' ministry Jn 6:27; **1Co** 9:2

A seal authenticates documents
Est 8:8–10 "Now write another decree in the king's name on behalf of the Jews as seems best to you, and seal it with the king's signet ring— for no document written in the king's name and sealed with his ring can be revoked." . . .
See also **1Ki** 21:8; **Est** 3:12

A seal used to keep something secure
Da 6:17 A stone was brought and placed over the mouth of the den, and the king sealed it with his own signet ring and with the rings of his nobles, so that Daniel's situation might not be changed. *See also* **Dt** 32:34; **Job** 14:17; **Ps** 40:9; **SS** 4:12; **Mt** 27:65–66; **Rev** 20:3

Documents sealed to prevent alteration
Binding agreements
Ne 9:38—10:1 "In view of all this, we are making a binding agreement, putting it in writing, and our leaders, our Levites and our priests are affixing their seals to it." . . . *See also* **Jer** 32:10–11,14,44

The words of prophecy
Da 12:4 "But you, Daniel, close up and seal the words of the scroll until the time of the end . . ." *See also* **Isa** 8:16–17; 29:10–11; **Da** 8:26; 9:24; 12:9; **Rev** 10:4; 22:10

The scroll and its seals
Rev 5:1–4 Then I [John] saw in the right hand of him who sat on the throne a scroll with writing on both sides and sealed with seven seals. And I saw a mighty angel proclaiming in a loud voice, "Who is worthy to break the seals and open the scroll?" . . .
Rev 5:9 And they [the living creatures and elders] sang a new song: "You [the Lamb] are worthy to take the scroll and to open its seals, because you were slain, and with your blood you purchased for God members of every tribe and language and people and nation." *See also* **Rev** 5:5; 6:1–12; 8:1

A seal as a pledge or guarantee
Dt 29:12; **Hag** 2:23; **Ro** 4:11

A seal as a mark of belonging
The mark of the beast Rev 13:16–17; 14:9–11
God's seal of ownership
2Ti 2:19 Nevertheless, God's solid foundation stands firm, sealed with this inscription: "The Lord knows those who are his," and, "Everyone who confesses the name of the Lord must turn away from wickedness."
Rev 7:3–8 "Do not harm the land or the sea or the trees until we put a seal on the foreheads of the servants of our God." . . . *See also* **Eze** 9:4; **Gal** 6:17; **Rev** 9:4
The Spirit as a pledge of final redemption
2Co 1:21–22 Now it is God who makes both us and you stand firm in Christ. He anointed us, set his seal of ownership on us, and put his Spirit in our hearts as a deposit, guaranteeing what is to come. *See also* **Eph** 1:13–14; 4:30 *See also covenant, nature of; pledges; writing.*

---

seed
The means of propagating life from one generation to another. Figuratively, the term illustrates principles of spiritual life and growth, especially in later parts of the OT and throughout the NT.

How seed was used
Seed for eating Ge 1:29; 42:1–2; **Ne** 5:1–2; **Isa** 28:28; **Ecc** 11:6
Seed as an offering Lev 23:15–21 pp Nu 28:26–31; **2Ch** 31:5
Seed to measure value Lev 27:16

How seed was appreciated
The presence of seed was a blessing
Zec 8:12 "The seed will grow well, the vine will yield its fruit, the ground will produce its crops, and the heavens will drop their dew. I will give all these things as an inheritance to the remnant of this people." *See also* **Ge** 8:22; **Ps** 67:6; 85:12
The absence of seed was a curse
Joel 1:16–17 Has not the food been cut off before our very eyes—joy and gladness from the house of our God? The seeds are shrivelled beneath the clods. The storehouses are in ruins,

the granaries have been broken down, for the grain has dried up.   *See also* **Dt** 28:38–42

Regulations in the law concerning seed
Dt 22:9 Do not plant two kinds of seed in your vineyard; if you do, not only the crops you plant but also the fruit of the vineyard will be defiled. pp Lev 19:19   *See also* **Lev** 11:37–38; 27:30

Seed used figuratively to illustrate kingdom life
To illustrate those ready to enter the kingdom of God
Jn 4:35–38 "Do you not say, 'Four months more and then the harvest'? I tell you, open your eyes and look at the fields! They are ripe for harvest. Even now those who reap draw their wages, even now they harvest the crop for eternal life, so that the sower and the reaper may be glad together . . ."
To illustrate birth into eternal life
1Pe 1:23 For you have been born again, not of perishable seed, but of imperishable, through the living and enduring word of God.   *See also* **1Jn** 3:9
To illustrate the growth of the kingdom of God
Mt 13:31–32 He told them another parable: "The kingdom of heaven is like a mustard seed, which a man took and planted in his field. Though it is the smallest of all your seeds, yet when it grows, it is the largest of garden plants and becomes a tree, so that the birds of the air come and perch in its branches." pp Mk 4:30–32 pp Lk 13:18–19
Mk 4:26–29 He also said, "This is what the kingdom of God is like. A man scatters seed on the ground. Night and day, whether he sleeps or gets up, the seed sprouts and grows, though he does not know how. All by itself the soil produces corn—first the stalk, then the ear, then the full grain in the ear. As soon as the grain is ripe, he puts the sickle to it, because the harvest has come."   *See also* **Mt** 13:24–30,36–43
To illustrate the growth of the church
1Co 3:6–7 I planted the seed, Apollos watered it, but God made it grow. So neither the one

who plants nor the one who waters is anything, but only God, who makes things grow.
To illustrate God's word and people's response to it Mt 13:1–23 pp Mk 4:1–20 pp Lk 8:4–15
To illustrate faith
Mt 17:20 He [Jesus] replied, "Because you have so little faith. I tell you the truth, if you have faith as small as a mustard seed, you can say to this mountain, 'Move from here to there' and it will move. Nothing will be impossible for you."
To illustrate the principle that death comes before life
Jn 12:23–25 . . . ". . . I tell you the truth, unless a grain of wheat falls to the ground and dies, it remains only a single seed. But if it dies, it produces many seeds . . ."   *See also* **1Co** 15:36
To illustrate the resurrection body
1Co 15:35–38 But someone may ask, "How are the dead raised? With what kind of body will they come?" How foolish! What you sow does not come to life unless it dies. When you sow, you do not plant the body that will be, but just a seed, perhaps of wheat or of something else. But God gives it a body as he has determined, and to each kind of seed he gives its own body.

God calls his people to sow seeds of righteousness
Jas 3:18 Peacemakers who sow in peace raise a harvest of righteousness.   *See also* **Ps** 126:5–6; **Pr** 22:8; **Jer** 4:3–4; **Hos** 10:12; **2Co** 9:6,10; **Gal** 6:7–9   *See also flowers; harvest; life.*

---

servants
Someone who serves another. Scripture provides guidance concerning the roles of servants, noting in particular that Jesus Christ chose to be a servant and commands believers to serve one another.

---

servants, bad
Bad servants are characterised by disobedience, idleness and dishonesty.

Characteristics of bad servants
Idleness
2Th 3:11 We hear that some among you are idle. They are not busy; they are busybodies. *See also* **Pr** 18:9; **Mt** 25:24–30 pp Lk 19:20–26

Dishonesty
Lk 16:12 "And if you have not been trustworthy with someone else's property, who will give you property of your own?" *See also* **Ge** 21:25; **Lev** 6:2; **2Ki** 5:20–25; **Eph** 6:6; **Col** 3:22

Disloyalty
Lk 16:13 "No one can be a slave to two masters. Either you will hate the one and love the other, or you will be devoted to the one and despise the other . . ." *See also* **2Sa** 19:24–27; **Jn** 10:13; **Ac** 27:30

Quarrelsomeness
Mt 24:48–49 "But suppose that servant is wicked and says to himself, 'My master is staying away a long time,' and he then begins to beat his fellow-servants and to eat and drink with drunkards." *See also* **Ge** 13:7; 26:20; **Mt** 18:23–30

Discontentment
Lk 3:14 Then some soldiers asked him [John the Baptist], "And what should we do?" He replied, "Don't extort money and don't accuse people falsely—be content with your pay." *See also* **Mt** 20:9–15

Refusing correction Pr 29:19

Examples of bad servants
Ziba: **2Sa** 16:1–4; 19:26–29
1Ki 2:39;16:9–10; **2Ki** 5:19–27; **Job** 19:16; **Phm** 8–16

---

servants, good
Scripture identifies certain qualities which are found in good servants and requires that these qualities should be found in believers' service of God.

Qualities found in good servants
Diligence
Ecc 9:10 Whatever your hand finds to do, do it with all your might . . . *See also* **1Ki** 11:28; **Pr** 10:4; 22:29; **Mt** 25:14–23 pp Lk 19:12–19

Faithfulness
1Co 4:2 Now it is required that those who have been given a trust must prove faithful. *See also* **Ex** 21:5–6; **2Sa** 15:21; **2Ch** 34:11–12; **Ne** 13:13; **Pr** 25:13; **Da** 6:4

Honesty
2Ki 22:7 "But they [supervisors of the temple building work] need not account for the money entrusted to them, because they are acting faithfully." *See also* **Ge** 39:6; **2Ki** 12:15; **Tit** 2:9–10

Obedience
Eph 6:5 Slaves, obey your earthly masters with respect and fear, and with sincerity of heart, just as you would obey Christ. *See also* **Lk** 17:10; **Col** 3:22

Perseverance
Ge 31:40–41 "This was my [Jacob's] situation: The heat consumed me in the daytime and the cold at night, and sleep fled from my eyes. It was like this for the twenty years I was in your [Laban's] household. I worked for you fourteen years for your two daughters and six years for your flocks, and you changed my wages ten times." *See also* **2Th** 3:12–13

Respect
1Ti 6:1–2 All who are under the yoke of slavery should consider their masters worthy of full respect, so that God's name and our teaching may not be slandered. Those who have believing masters are not to show less respect for them because they are believers. Instead, they are to serve them even better, because those who benefit from their service are believers, and dear to them . . . *See also* **Mal** 1:6; **1Pe** 2:18

Willingness
Eph 6:6–7 Obey them [masters] not only to win their favour when their eye is on you, but like slaves of Christ, doing the will of God from your heart. Serve wholeheartedly, as if you were serving the Lord, not people. *See also* **1Ch** 28:21; **Tit** 2:9

Examples of good servants
Abraham's servant: **Ge** 24:9,49
David's servants: **2Sa** 12:18; 23:13–17
2Ki 5:13; **Mt** 8:9

Good servants are often rewarded by their employers
They are advanced by them Ge 39:4–5; **Pr** 27:18; **Mt** 25:21,23
They have their confidence Ge 24:2–4,10

Good servants often bring blessings on their employers
Ge 30:27–30; 39:2–4

Good servants have God with them
Ge 24:7,27; 31:7,42; 39:3,21; **Mt** 24:46; **Ac** 7:9–10

servants, work conditions
Those who serve are to be treated fairly and with respect. Jesus Christ himself chose to be a servant and lays responsibility of service on those who follow.

Servants are to be treated fairly
They are not to be exploited
Eph 6:9 And masters, treat your slaves in the same way. Do not threaten them, since you know that he who is both their Master and yours is in heaven, and there is no favouritism with him. *See also* **Lev** 25:39–40,53
They are to be paid fairly and promptly
Dt 24:14–15 Do not take advantage of a hired worker who is poor and needy, whether that worker is an Israelite or an alien living in one of your towns. Pay such workers their wages each day before sunset, because they are poor and are counting on it. Otherwise they may cry to the Lᴏʀᴅ against you, and you will be guilty of sin. *See also* **Ge** 29:15; **Lev** 19:13; **Nu** 18:29–31; **1Ki** 5:6; **Job** 7:1–2; **Jer** 22:13; **Mt** 20:4,8; **Ro** 4:4; **Col** 4:1; **2Th** 3:10
Examples of servants treated unfairly
Jas 5:4 Look! The wages you failed to pay the workers who mowed your fields are crying out against you. The cries of the harvesters have reached the ears of the Lord Almighty. *See also* **Ge** 31:7,41; **Ex** 2:23–24; **Job** 24:10–11; **Mal** 3:5

Jesus Christ as a servant
Mt 20:28 "just as the Son of Man did not come to be served, but to serve, and to give his life as a ransom for many." *See also* **Php** 2:7

Believers follow Jesus Christ's example as servants
They are servants of Jesus Christ and his church
Ro 1:1 Paul, a servant of Christ Jesus, called to be an apostle and set apart for the gospel of God— *See also* **Lk** 1:38; **1Co** 12:5; 16:15; **Eph** 4:12; **Col** 1:23; 3:24
They work to please God
Eph 6:5–6 Slaves, obey your earthly masters with respect and fear, and with sincerity of heart, just as you would obey Christ. Obey them not only to win their favour when their eye is on you, but like slaves of Christ, doing the will of God from your heart. *See also* **Col** 3:22–24; **Tit** 2:9–10

Christian workers should be paid honourably
1Ti 5:17–18 The elders who direct the affairs of the church well are worthy of double honour, especially those whose work is preaching and teaching. For the Scripture says, "Do not muzzle the ox while it is treading out the grain," and "Workers deserve their wages." *See also* **Lk** 10:7; **1Co** 9:7–11; **Gal** 6:6

God rewards his servants
Eph 6:8 . . . you know that the Lord will reward each one of you whatever good you do, whether you are slave or free. *See also* **Job** 34:10–11; **Pr** 10:16; **Mt** 6:3–4; 25:23; **Jn** 4:36; **2Ti** 4:8

Service of sin has its reward
Ro 6:23 . . . the wages of sin is death . . . *See also* **Pr** 11:18; **Hos** 9:1; **2Pe** 2:15 *See also slavery; wages.*

shepherd
The work of a shepherd was important and responsible in the rural world of ancient Palestine. Since it involved leading, protecting and feeding a

flock, it is seen as a metaphor for the task of leadership. Scripture declares that God is the Shepherd of his people.

shepherd, occupation

The occupation of a shepherd was both humble and honourable. In the marginal hill country of Palestine it was particularly demanding.

A shepherd as a keeper of flocks of animals
Ge 46:32

The tasks of a shepherd
Tending, feeding and watering
Ps 23:2 He makes me lie down in green pastures, he leads me beside quiet waters, *See also* **Ge** 29:3; 26:19–22; **Ex** 22:5; **Lk** 13:15; **Jn** 21:15–17
Keeping and protecting
Jer 31:10 ". . . 'He [the LORD] who scattered Israel will gather them and will watch over his flock like a shepherd.' " *See also* **Ge** 4:2; **Ps** 23:4; **1Sa** 17:34–37
Leading, not driving, sheep
Jn 10:3–4 ". . . He calls his own sheep by name and leads them out . . . he goes on ahead of them, and his sheep follow him because they know his voice." *See also* **Ex** 3:1; **Ps** 23:2; 77:20; **Isa** 40:11; **Jer** 50:6
Gathering animals together
Jn 10:3 "The gatekeeper opens the gate for him . . . He calls his own sheep by name and leads them out." *See also* **Ps** 147:4; **Isa** 40:26; **Mt** 25:32

The shepherd's routine
The search for pasture Ge 37:17
The midday rest SS 1:7
The night-watch Lk 2:8; **Jer** 43:12
Shearing, an annual festival 1Sa 25:7–8
The use of pens and folds Ps 50:9; **Hab** 3:17; **Jn** 10:1,16
Breeding Ge 30:40
Rearing
Rebekah's ruse depended on a method used to get a ewe to accept an alien lamb: **Ge** 27:16,27

The problems faced by shepherds
Drought and dry winds Jer 12:4; **Hos** 4:3; 13:15; **Joel** 1:17–20; **Am** 1:2
With animals and thieves 1Sa 17:34–37; 25:15; **Jn** 10:1,12

Shepherds as employers
Job 1:3 . . . he [Job] owned seven thousand sheep . . . *See also* **1Sa** 25:2; **2Ki** 3:4; **Am** 1:1

Shepherds as employees
The status of a shepherd 1Sa 16:11; 17:28; **Lk** 2:8
The responsibilities of a shepherd Ge 31:39; **Am** 3:12; **Mt** 18:12 pp Lk 15:4 *See also animals; occupations.*

sin offering

Offerings to make atonement for both moral and ritual offences. The NT sees them as foreshadowing the death of Jesus Christ as an offering for human sin.

Occasions when a sin offering was required
Unintentional sins against God's laws: **Lev** 4:2; **Heb** 9:7
Lev 5:1–4; 4:20
Purification after childbirth: **Lev** 12:6–8; **Lk** 2:24
Cleansing from infectious diseases: **Lev** 14:13–31; **Mk** 1:44
Cleansing from a bodily discharge: **Lev** 15:15,30

The form the sin offering took depended on who committed the sin
Lev 4:3,14,22–23
An individual who sins: **Lev** 4:27–35; 5:5–6

The ceremony when presenting an animal as a sin offering
The guilty identify themselves with the offering before killing it Lev 4:4,15,24
Confession Lev 5:5
Blood, representing the victim's lifeblood, is put on the altar Lev 4:25,30,34

The best parts, being burned on the altar, are offered to God Lev 4:8–10,26,35
Male members of priestly families may eat what remains Lev 6:26,29; 10:16–20
Special procedures for the offerings of the poor Lev 5:7–13

The special ceremony for priests and the community presenting a sin offering
Blood is taken into the sanctuary and placed on the altar Lev 4:5–7,16–18
The rest of the animal is incinerated, not eaten Lev 4:11–12,21

Significant occasions when sin offerings were made
Lev 8:14–17; 16:1–34; **2Ki** 12:16; **2Ch** 29:21–24; **Ezr** 6:17; 8:35
As part of Ezekiel's vision of restored worship: **Eze** 40:39; 42:13; 43:19,21

The NT perspective on the sin offering
Jesus Christ was the supreme sin offering
Ro 8:3 For what the law was powerless to do in that it was weakened by the sinful nature, God did by sending his own Son in the likeness of sinful humanity to be a sin offering . . .
2Co 5:21 God made him [Christ] who had no sin to be sin for us, so that in him we might become the righteousness of God. *NIV footnote.*
Animal sacrifices had limited value Heb 9:7–10
The death of Jesus Christ brings full cleansing and forgiveness
Heb 9:11–14 . . . but he [Jesus] entered the Most Holy Place once for all by his own blood, having obtained eternal redemption . . . *See also* **1Pe** 1:18–19
Unlike earthly priests, Jesus Christ needed no sin offering
Heb 7:27 . . . he [Jesus] does not need to offer sacrifices day after day, first for his own sins, and then for the sins of the people. He sacrificed for their sins once for all when he offered himself. *See also* **Heb** 5:1–3 *See also atonement; blood; offerings; sacrifice, in Old Testament.*

singing

The musical voicing of praise to God. On account of God's majesty and great acts of salvation singing was a regular part of the life of Israel and of the early church. In Israel musicians and singers were set aside solely for this purpose.

The call to sing praise to God
Ps 33:1–3 Sing joyfully to the LORD, you righteous; it is fitting for the upright to praise him . . . Sing to him a new song; play skilfully, and shout for joy.
Ps 96:1–2 Sing to the LORD a new song; sing to the LORD, all the earth. Sing to the LORD, praise his name; proclaim his salvation day after day. *See also* **Ps** 5:11; 9:11; 30:4; 47:6; 68:4,32; 81:1–2; 95:1; 98:1,4–5,8–9; 117:1; 147:7; 149:1; **Isa** 44:23; 49:13; 52:9; **Ro** 15:11

The resolve to sing praise to God
Ps 104:33 I will sing to the LORD all my life; I will sing praise to my God as long as I live. *See also* **Ps** 7:17; 9:2; 13:6; 57:8–9; 59:16–17; 89:1; 101:1; 147:1

Singing in response to God's deliverance from enemies and sin
Isa 35:10 . . . the ransomed of the LORD will return. They will enter Zion with singing; everlasting joy will crown their heads . . . *See also* **Ps** 18:47–49; 71:22–24; **Isa** 54:1; 55:12; **Rev** 5:11–14; 15:3–4

God sings of his delight and love for his people
Zep 3:17 ". . . He [the LORD your God] will take great delight in you, he will quiet you with his love, he will rejoice over you with singing."

Singing in Israel
Singing accompanied major events 1Ch 15:27–28; **2Ch** 5:12–13; 20:21–22; 23:11–13; 29:27–28
The celebration of the Passover and Feast of Unleavened Bread: **2Ch** 30:21; 35:15
Ne 12:27–29

Part of day-to-day worship 2Ch 23:18; **Ne** 11:23

Accompanied by instruments
1Ch 15:16 David told the leaders of the Levites to appoint some of their members as singers to sing joyful songs, accompanied by musical instruments.   *See also* **1Ki** 10:12 pp 2Ch 9:11; **Ps** 137:1–4

Musicians and singers appointed to lead Israel's singing
1Ch 9:33 Those who were musicians, heads of Levite families, stayed in the rooms of the temple and were exempt from other duties because they were responsible for the work day and night.
1Ch 15:22 Kenaniah the head Levite was in charge of the singing; that was his responsibility because he was skilful at it.   *See also* **1Ch** 6:31–32; 25:6–7; **Ezr** 2:41 pp Ne 7:44; **Ezr** 2:65; **Ne** 11:22; 12:46

Singing in the NT
Eph 5:19–20 Speak to one another with psalms, hymns and spiritual songs. Sing and make music in your heart to the Lord, always giving thanks to God the Father for everything, in the name of our Lord Jesus Christ.
Jas 5:13 . . . Is anyone happy? Sing songs of praise.   *See also* **Mt** 26:30 pp Mk 14:26; **Ac** 16:25; **1Co** 14:15; **Col** 3:16

Singing is not always appropriate
Pr 25:20 Like one who takes away a garment on a cold day, or like vinegar poured on soda, is one who sings songs to a heavy heart.   *See also* **Ecc** 7:5
Am 5:23 "Away with the noise of your songs! I [the Sovereign LORD] will not listen to the music of your harps."   *See also* **Isa** 24:14–17; 25:5; **Eze** 26:13; **Am** 6:5–7; 8:3,10   *See also* music; musical instruments; musicians; wedding.

slavery

The state of being an unpaid servant, whether through forcible subjection or voluntary submission. Slavery was common in biblical times, and Scripture lays down strict guidelines as to how slaves are to be treated by their masters, stressing the new status that slaves have as a result of being believers in Jesus Christ. The image of slavery is also used to describe the state of sinful human beings.

slavery, in New Testament

The NT does not condone slavery but recognises that slavery exists, and that many slaves have become believers. The status of slaves in the church is transformed by the work of Jesus Christ. Slaves were accorded greater respect because they were seen to be spiritually equal with others.

Examples of slavery in the NT
Ac 16:16–21; **Phm** 8–21

The gospel transforms the status of slaves
1Co 12:13 For we [believers] were all baptised by one Spirit into one body—whether Jews or Greeks, slave or free—and we were all given the one Spirit to drink.
Gal 3:26–28 . . . There is neither Jew nor Greek, slave nor free, male nor female, for you are all one in Christ Jesus.

Instructions concerning slavery
Instructions to Christian slaves
Eph 6:5–8 Slaves, obey your earthly masters with respect and fear, and with sincerity of heart, just as you would obey Christ. Obey them not only to win their favour when their eye is on you, but like slaves of Christ, doing the will of God from your heart. Serve wholeheartedly, as if you were serving the Lord, not people, because you know that the Lord will reward each one of you for whatever good you do, whether you are slave or free.   *See also* **1Co** 7:20–24; **Col** 3:22–24; **1Ti** 6:1–2; **Tit** 2:9–10; **1Pe** 2:18–21
Instructions to Christian masters
Eph 6:9 And masters, treat your slaves in the same way. Do not threaten them, since you know that he who is both their Master and yours is in heaven, and there is no favouritism with him.
See also **Col** 4:1; **Phm** 8–17

The immorality of trading in slaves
1Ti 1:9–10 We also know that law is made not for the righteous but for lawbreakers and rebels, the ungodly and sinful, the unholy and irreligious; for those who kill their fathers or mothers, for murderers, for adulterers and perverts, for slave traders . . . *See also servants.*

slavery, in Old Testament
Slavery in the OT occurs when someone either voluntarily or forcibly becomes completely subject to another person's control.

Reasons for slavery
War
Dt 20:10–11 When you [Israelites] march up to attack a city, make its people an offer of peace. If they accept and open their gates, all the people in it shall be subject to forced labour and shall work for you. *See also* **Ge** 14:21; **Nu** 31:9; **2Ki** 5:2; **2Ch** 28:8
Purchase
Lev 25:44–45 " 'Your male and female slaves are to come from the nations around you; from them you may buy slaves. You may also buy some of the temporary residents living among you and members of their clans born in your country, and they will become your property.' " *See also* **Ge** 37:23–28
Debt
2Ki 4:1 The wife of a man from the company of the prophets cried out to Elisha, "Your servant my husband is dead, and you know that he revered the LORD. But now his creditor is coming to take my two boys as his slaves." *See also* **Ex** 22:2–3; **Lev** 25:39,47–48; **Dt** 15:12; **Ne** 5:1–5
Birth
Ex 21:4 "If his [the slave's] master gives him a wife and she bears him sons or daughters, the woman and her children shall belong to her master, and only the man shall go free."
See also **Ge** 17:12–13; **Ecc** 2:7; **Jer** 2:14
Conscription of foreigners as forced labour
2Sa 12:29–31 . . . He [David] took a great quantity of plunder from the city and brought out the people who were there, consigning them to labour with saws and with iron picks and axes, and he made them work at brickmaking . . .

See also **Ex** 1:11–14; **Jos** 9:22–23; 16:10; **Jdg** 1:28; **1Ki** 9:20–21

Rights of slaves
Rights of protection against physical and sexual abuse
Lev 25:43 " 'Do not rule over them [slaves] ruthlessly, but fear your God.' " *See also* **Ex** 21:7–11,20–21,26–27
Rights to participate in religious feasts and festivals
Ex 23:12 "Six days do your work, but on the seventh day do not work, so that your ox and your donkey may rest and the slave born in your household, and the alien as well, may be refreshed." *See also* **Ex** 20:9–10; **Dt** 12:11–12
Rights to inherit property
Ge 15:3 And Abram said, "You have given me no children; so a servant in my household will be my heir."
Rights of asylum
Dt 23:15 If any slaves have taken refuge with you, do not hand them over to their masters.

The release of slaves
Release in the Year of Jubilee
Lev 25:54–55 " 'Even if they [the slaves] are not redeemed in any of these ways, they and their children are to be released in the Year of Jubilee, for the Israelites belong to me as servants . . .' " *See also* **Lev** 25:39–41
Release after six years of service
Ex 21:2 "If you buy a Hebrew servant, he is to serve you for six years. But in the seventh year, he shall go free, without paying anything."
See also **Ex** 21:3–6; **Dt** 15:12–18; **Jer** 34:8–20
Release through redemption by a near relative
Lev 25:47–53

The status of slaves
Slaves as property
Lev 25:46 " 'You can will them [non-Israelite slaves] to your children as inherited property and can make them slaves for life . . .' " *See also* **Ex** 21:32; **Lev** 25:39–42
Slaves as trusted advisors 1Sa 9:5–10
See also property; warfare.

sowing and reaping

OT references are mainly agricultural with regulatory laws covering crop production and festivals of thanksgiving. God's blessing was reflected in the harvest. The NT refers more to the spiritual sowing and reaping that takes place in the kingdom of God.

Regulations concerning the sowing and reaping of crops

Laws of purity related to planting Lev 19:23–25; **Dt** 22:9

Reapers are to leave gleanings for the poor Lev 19:9–10; 23:22; **Dt** 24:19; **Ru** 2:2–3,15–16

Harvest celebrations

Ex 23:16 "Celebrate the Feast of Harvest with the firstfruits of the crops you sow in your field. Celebrate the Feast of Ingathering at the end of the year, when you gather in your crops from the field." *See also* **Lev** 23:9–11,39–41; **Dt** 16:9–10,13–15

The Sabbath-rest for the land and its cultivators Ex 23:10–11; 34:21; **Lev** 25:3–5,11

Reaping a good harvest is a blessing from God

It is a consequence of obedience Ge 26:12; **Lev** 25:18–22; 26:3–5,10

It is a promise to the remnant of God's people

Am 9:13–14 "The days are coming," declares the LORD, "when the reaper will be overtaken by the one who ploughs and the planter by the one treading grapes. New wine will drip from the mountains and flow from all the hills. I will bring back my exiled people Israel; they will rebuild the ruined cities and live in them. They will plant vineyards and drink their wine; they will make gardens and eat their fruit." *See also* **Isa** 30:23; 62:8–9; 65:21–22; **Jer** 31:5; **Zec** 8:11–12

God's judgment on Israel is reflected in reaping a poor harvest

A poor yield of crops Lev 26:18–20; **Dt** 28:15,38–40; **Isa** 5:10; 17:10–11; **Jer** 8:13; 12:13; **Hag** 1:6,10–11

The harvesting of one's crops by others

Lev 26:15–16 " 'and if you reject my decrees and abhor my laws and fail to carry out all my commands and so violate my covenant, then I will do this to you: I will bring upon you sudden terror, wasting diseases and fever that will destroy your sight and drain away your life. You will plant seed in vain, because your enemies will eat it.' " *See also* **Ne** 9:36–37; **Job** 31:7–8; **Jer** 5:17; **Mic** 6:15

Proverbs and poems of sowing and harvest

Pr 10:5; 20:4; **Isa** 28:23–29

Moral and spiritual sowing and reaping

Good and evil

Job 4:8 "As I [Eliphaz] have observed, those who plough evil and those who sow trouble reap it." *See also* **Pr** 11:18; 22:8; **Hos** 8:7; 10:12–13; **Gal** 6:7–8; **Jas** 3:18

Sowing and reaping in the kingdom of God

Mk 4:3–8 "Listen! A farmer went out to sow his seed. As he was scattering the seed, some fell along the path, and the birds came and ate it up. Some fell on rocky places, where it did not have much soil. It sprang up quickly, because the soil was shallow. But when the sun came up, the plants were scorched, and they withered because they had no root. Other seed fell among thorns, which grew up and choked the plants, so that they did not bear grain. Still other seed fell on good soil. It came up, grew and produced a crop, multiplying thirty, sixty, or even a hundred times." pp Mt 13:3–8 pp Lk 8:5–8 *See also* **Mt** 13:18–23 pp Mk 4:14–20 pp Lk 8:11–15; **Mt** 13:24–30,37–39; **Mk** 4:26–29

The certainty of reaping

Ps 126:5–6 Those who sow in tears will reap with songs of joy. Those who go out weeping, carrying seed to sow, will return with songs of joy, carrying sheaves with them.

Gal 6:9 Let us not become weary in doing good, for at the proper time we will reap a harvest if we do not give up.

Reaping where others have sown Jn 4:35–38;

Ro 1:13; **1Co** 3:5–9
Reaping a material harvest from spiritual sowing 1Co 9:9–11

People and nations are reaped for judgment

Joel 3:13 "Swing the sickle, for the harvest is ripe. Come, trample the grapes, for the winepress is full and the vats overflow—so great is their wickedness!" *See also* **Jer** 51:33; **Hos** 6:11; **Rev** 14:15–19

Metaphorical use of sowing and reaping

Isa 5:1–7; 17:4–6; **Jer** 2:3,21; **1Co** 15:35–44; **2Co** 9:6–11 *See also agriculture; feast and festival; harvest; horticulture; ploughing; seed.*

---

stewardship

The careful use, control and management of the possessions of another that have been entrusted to one. The term is also used to refer to the responsible use of wealth and possessions by Christians.

Individuals acting as stewards
Adam in the Garden of Eden
Ge 2:15 The LORD God took the man and put him in the Garden of Eden to work it and take care of it.
Joseph in Potiphar's household
Ge 39:4–6 Joseph found favour in his eyes and became his attendant. Potiphar put him in charge of his household, and he entrusted to his care everything he owned. From the time he put him in charge of his household and of all that he owned, the LORD blessed the household of the Egyptian because of Joseph. The blessing of the LORD was on everything Potiphar had, both in the house and in the field. So he left in Joseph's care everything he had; with Joseph in charge, he did not concern himself with anything except the food he ate . . .
Daniel as administrator in Babylon
Da 6:1–3 It pleased Darius to appoint 120 satraps to rule throughout the kingdom, with three administrators over them, one of whom was Daniel. The satraps were made accountable to them so that the king might not suffer loss. Now Daniel so distinguished himself among the administrators and the satraps by his exceptional qualities that the king planned to set him over the whole kingdom.

Groups acting as stewards
The priests serving in the tabernacle Lev 22:9; **1Sa** 2:15
The seven chosen by the Jerusalem church Ac 6:1–6

Household stewards
Ge 43:16; 44:1–12; **2Sa** 16:1; 19:17; **Est** 1:8

Jesus Christ's teaching on stewardship
Using parables to emphasise accountability
Lk 16:1–12 . . . ". . . Whoever can be trusted with very little can also be trusted with much, and whoever is dishonest with very little will also be dishonest with much. So if you have not been trustworthy in handling worldly wealth, who will trust you with true riches? And if you have not been trustworthy with someone else's property, who will give you property of your own?" *See also* **Mt** 25:14–30; **Lk** 19:12–27
Emphasising each individual's responsibility
Lk 12:48 ". . . From everyone who has been given much, much will be demanded; and from the one who has been entrusted with much, much more will be asked." *See also* **Mt** 12:36

The apostles continued this teaching
Ro 14:12 So then, we will all give an account of ourselves to God. *See also* **1Pe** 4:4–5

To be a good steward is an honourable thing
1Ti 3:13 Those who have served well gain an excellent standing and great assurance in their faith in Christ Jesus. *See also* **Pr** 27:18

Christians are entrusted with the stewardship of the gospel
1Co 4:1-2 So then, you ought to regard us as servants of Christ and as those entrusted with the secret things of God. Now it is required that those who have been given a trust must prove faithful.   *See also* **1Co** 9:17; **2Co** 5:19–21; **Gal** 1:15–16; 2:7; **1Th** 2:4; **1Ti** 1:11; 4:14; 6:20; **2Ti** 1:14; **Tit** 1:3,7

Christians are to be wise stewards of their God-given gifts
1Co 4:7 . . . What do you have that you did not receive? And if you did receive it, why do you boast as though you did not?
They are to use their gifts to benefit others
1Pe 4:10-11 Each of you should use whatever gift you have received to serve others, faithfully administering God's grace in its various forms . . .
They are to develop their gifts 1Ti 4:14–15
They are to care for their bodies
1Co 6:18-20 . . . Do you not know that your bodies are temples of the Holy Spirit, who is in you, whom you have received from God? You are not your own; you were bought at a price. Therefore honour God with your bodies.

Believers are to be wise stewards of their material possessions
Dt 8:17-18 . . . But remember the LORD your God, for it is he who gives you the ability to produce wealth . . .
Jesus Christ's teaching on sharing possessions
Mt 19:21 Jesus answered, "If you want to be perfect, go, sell your possessions and give to the poor, and you will have treasure in heaven. Then come, follow me." pp Mk 10:21 pp Lk 18:22   *See also* **Mt** 6:1–4,19–21; **Lk** 6:38; 21:1–4; **Ac** 20:35
Sharing of possessions among the first Christians
Ac 4:32-35 . . . No-one claimed that any of their possessions was their own, but they shared everything they had . . .   *See also* **2Co** 8:1–5
The apostle Paul's teaching on sharing possessions Ac 20:35; **2Co** 9:6–11   *See also* money, stewardship; property; servants.

stones
Pieces of rock, used extensively for building.

Stones used in building
The temple in Jerusalem
1Ki 5:17-18 At the king's command they [the skilled workers and labourers] removed from the quarry large blocks of quality stone to provide a foundation of dressed stone for the temple . . .   *See also* **1Ki** 6:14–18,36; 7:9–12
King David's preparations for the building of the temple:
1Ch 22:2,14; 29:2
2Ki 22:3–7 pp 2Ch 34:8–11; **Ezr** 6:1–4; **Mt** 24:1–2 pp Mk 13:1–2 pp Lk 21:5–6
Other references to building with stone Ge 11:1–3; **Lev** 14:39–45; **2Ch** 16:6; **Ne** 4:1–3; **Isa** 9:10; **Am** 5:11

Boundary stones
Dt 19:14 Do not move your neighbour's boundary stone set up by your predecessors in the inheritance you receive in the land the LORD your God is giving you to possess.   *See also* **Dt** 27:17; **Job** 24:2; **Pr** 22:28; 23:10–11; **Hos** 5:10

Stones covering openings
Wells
Ge 29:1-10 Then Jacob continued on his journey and came to the land of the eastern peoples. There he saw a well in the field, with three flocks of sheep lying near it because the flocks were watered from that well. The stone over the mouth of the well was large. When all the flocks were gathered there, the shepherds would roll the stone away from the well's mouth and water the sheep. Then they would return the stone to its place over the mouth of the well . . .
The lions' den
Da 6:16-17 . . . A stone was brought and placed over the mouth of the den, and the king sealed it with his own signet ring and with the rings of his nobles, so that Daniel's situation might not be changed.
Tombs
Mk 15:42-46 . . . So Joseph bought some

linen cloth, took down the body, wrapped it in the linen, and placed it in a tomb cut out of rock. Then he rolled a stone against the entrance of the tomb. pp Mt 27:57–60　*See also* **Mt** 27:62—28:4 pp Mk 16:1–5 pp Lk 24:1–3; **Jn** 11:38–44; 20:1

Stone jars
Ex 7:19 The LORD said to Moses, "Tell Aaron, 'Take your staff and stretch out your hand over the waters of Egypt—over the streams and canals, over the ponds and all the reservoirs'—and they will turn to blood. Blood will be everywhere in Egypt, even in the wooden buckets and stone jars."　*See also* **Jn** 2:1–10

Stones as weapons
Jdg 20:16 Among all these soldiers there were seven hundred chosen men who were left-handed, each of whom could sling a stone at a hair and not miss.　*See also* **Nu** 35:17; **1Sa** 17:38–50; **1Ch** 12:2; **2Ch** 26:15

Stones in religious use
Stone altars
Ex 20:24–26 "'. . . If you [Israelites] make an altar of stones for me [the LORD], do not build it with dressed stones, for you will defile it if you use a tool on it . . .'"　*See also* **Dt** 27:1–8; **Jos** 8:30–32; **1Ki** 18:30–38
Memorial stones
1Sa 7:12 Then Samuel took a stone and set it up between Mizpah and Shen. He named it Ebenezer, saying, "Thus far has the LORD helped us."　*See also* **Ge** 28:10–22; 31:43–53; 35:14–15; **Ex** 24:3–4; **Dt** 27:1–8; **Jos** 4:1–24; 24:26–27
Ten Commandments written on stone
Ex 31:18 When the LORD finished speaking to Moses on Mount Sinai, he gave him the two tablets of the Testimony, the tablets of stone inscribed by the finger of God.　*See also* **Ex** 24:12; 34:1–4; **Dt** 4:13; 5:22; 9:9–11; 10:1–3; **1Ki** 8:9; **Heb** 9:3–4
Sacred stones
1Ki 14:22–23 Judah did evil in the eyes of the LORD. By the sins they committed they stirred

up his jealous anger more than those who were before them had done. They also set up for themselves high places, sacred stones and Asherah poles on every high hill and under every spreading tree.
Commands to destroy idolatrous stones in Canaan: **Ex** 23:24; 34:13; **Dt** 7:5; 12:3; 16:22
2Ki 3:2; 10:26–27; 17:10; 18:4; 23:14; **2Ch** 31:1; **Isa** 27:9; **Hos** 3:4; 10:1–2; **Mic** 5:13
Stone idols
Hab 2:19 "Woe to him who says to wood, 'Come to life!' Or to lifeless stone, 'Wake up!' Can it give guidance? It is covered with gold and silver; there is no breath in it."　*See also* **Dt** 4:28; 28:36,64; 29:17; **2Ki** 19:18 pp Isa 37:19; **Ac** 17:29; **Rev** 9:20

Stonecutters and stonemasons
1Ki 5:15 Solomon had seventy thousand carriers and eighty thousand stonecutters in the hills, pp 2Ch 2:2　*See also* **2Sa** 5:11; **2Ki** 12:11–12; **1Ch** 22:2,15; **2Ch** 2:18

Death by stoning
Lev 24:10–16 . . . ". . . Say to the Israelites: 'Anyone who curses their God will be held responsible; anyone who blasphemes the name of the LORD must be put to death. The entire assembly must stone them. Whether an alien or native-born, when they blaspheme the Name, they must be put to death.'"　*See also* **Ex** 19:12–13; 21:28–32; **Lev** 20:2,27; **Nu** 15:32–36; **Dt** 13:6–11; 17:2–5; 21:18–21; **Jos** 7:25; **1Ki** 12:18 pp 2Ch 10:18; **1Ki** 21:1–13
Stoning the prophets: **Mt** 21:33–35; 23:37 pp Lk 13:34
Stoning of Stephen and Paul: **Ac** 7:54–60; 14:19; **2Co** 11:25

Jesus Christ described as a stone
1Pe 2:4–8 As you [believers] come to him [Jesus], the living Stone—rejected by human beings but chosen by God and precious to him—you also, like living stones, are being built into a spiritual house to be a holy priesthood, offering spiritual sacrifices acceptable to God through Jesus Christ. For in Scripture it says: "See, I lay a

stone in Zion, a chosen and precious cornerstone, and the one who trusts in him will never be put to shame." . . .   See also **Ps** 118:22; **Isa** 8:14; 28:16; **Mt** 21:42–44 pp Mk 12:10–11 pp Lk 20:17–18; **Ac** 4:8–12; **Ro** 9:33

Believers described as living stones
1Pe 2:5 you also, like living stones, are being built into a spiritual house . . .

Metaphorical references to stones
Eze 36:26 "'I [the LORD] will give you [Israel] a new heart and put a new spirit in you; I will remove from you your heart of stone and give you a heart of flesh.'"   See also **Ex** 15:5,15–16; **1Ki** 10:27 pp 2Ch 1:15 pp 2Ch 9:27; **Ne** 9:11; **Job** 6:12; 38:29–30; **Eze** 3:9; 11:19
See also altar; building; minerals; tools; weapons.

---

suffering
The experience of pain or distress, both physical and emotional. Scripture is thoroughly realistic about the place of suffering in the world and in the lives of believers. To become a Christian is not to escape from suffering, but to be able to bear suffering with dignity and hope.

---

suffering
Since the fall, human beings have suffered in various ways. Scripture provides insights into the nature and place of suffering both in the world and in the lives of believers.

Suffering began with the fall
Ge 2:17; 3:16–19; **Ro** 5:12

Suffering is universal
Job 5:7; 14:1

Different kinds of suffering
Physical pain and illness
Ge 48:1 . . . Joseph was told, "Your father is ill." . . .   See also **2Ki** 20:1 pp 2Ch 32:24 pp Isa 38:1; **Job** 2:7; **Ps** 42:10; **Mt** 8:6; 17:15; **Lk** 4:38; **Ac** 28:8; **2Ti** 4:20; **Jas** 5:14

Emotional stress
Ps 55:4–5 My heart is in anguish within me; the terrors of death assail me. Fear and trembling have beset me; horror has overwhelmed me.
See also **Ge** 35:18   "Ben-Oni" means "son of my trouble"; **Pr** 12:25; **Jn** 11:32–35; **Php** 2:27
Spiritual suffering
Ps 22:1 My God, my God, why have you forsaken me? Why are you so far from saving me, so far from the words of my groaning?
See also **Mt** 27:46 pp Mk 15:34
The prospect of death
Ge 3:19 ". . . dust you [Adam] are and to dust you will return."   See also **Ecc** 12:7

Major causes of suffering
The disorder in creation
Ge 3:17 . . . ". . . Cursed is the ground because of you [Adam]; through painful toil you will eat of it all the days of your life."   See also **Ge** 12:10; **Joel** 1:4; **Mt** 24:7 pp Lk 21:11; **Ro** 8:22; **Rev** 11:13
Human cruelty
Ps 54:3 Strangers are attacking me; ruthless people seek my life—people without regard for God . . .
Murder: **Ge** 4:8; **Ex** 1:16,22; **1Ki** 21:19; **Mt** 2:16 **Ge** 49:5–7
Oppression: **Ex** 1:11; **Am** 2:6–7; 4:1; **Mal** 3:5 **2Ki** 6:25; 19:17; **2Ch** 10:13–14; **Job** 1:14–15,17; **Am** 1:3,13; **Jas** 5:4–6; **Rev** 6:4
Family troubles
Ps 27:10 Though my father and mother forsake me, the LORD will receive me.   See also **1Sa** 1:7; **2Sa** 16:11; **Job** 19:14–19; **Mal** 2:14; **Mt** 10:36; **Jas** 1:27
Old age
Ps 71:9 Do not cast me away when I am old; do not forsake me when my strength is gone.
See also **Ecc** 12:1–7
Satan's activity
1Jn 5:19 . . . the whole world is under the control of the evil one.   See also **Job** 1:12; 2:6–7; **Lk** 13:16; **2Co** 12:7; **Rev** 2:10; 20:7–8

Aggravations to suffering
Memories Job 29:2

Fears Job 3:25; **Heb** 2:15
Resentment Job 2:9

Sin and suffering
They are not necessarily related
Jn 9:3 "Neither this man [who was born blind] nor his parents sinned," said Jesus, "but this happened so that the work of God might be displayed in his life."   *See also* **Job** 2:3; **Lk** 13:2
They are sometimes closely related
Ro 1:18 The wrath of God is being revealed from heaven against all the godlessness and wickedness of those who suppress the truth by their wickedness,   *See also* **Ge** 6:5–7; **Nu** 14:33; **Dt** 28:15; **Ps** 107:17; **Eze** 23:49; **Ac** 5:5,10; **Ro** 1:27; **1Co** 11:29–30; **Jude** 7; **Rev** 2:22
God's final judgment
Mt 25:41 ". . . 'Depart from me, you who are cursed, into the eternal fire prepared for the devil and his angels.'"   *See also* **Da** 12:2; **Mt** 8:12; **Mk** 9:48; **Isa** 66:24; **Rev** 20:15

Effects of suffering
Hardness of heart
Rev 16:9 . . . they cursed the name of God, who had control over these plagues, but they refused to repent and glorify him.   *See also* **Ex** 7:22; **Rev** 9:20–21
Repentance 2Ch 33:12; **Lk** 15:17–18
Blessing
Ps 119:71 It was good for me to be afflicted so that I might learn your decrees.   *See also* **Isa** 38:17   *See also warfare.*

---

suffering, causes
The ultimate cause of suffering is sin, which has brought violence, disease and death into the world. All suffering, however, is under the sovereign purpose of God, who is able to use it for his glory.

The ultimate cause of suffering is sin
Ge 3:14–19
It need not be the result of particular sins: **Job** 1:1; **Jn** 9:1–3
Job 5:6–7; **Ro** 5:12–14

Suffering as a result of human wickedness
Murder
Ge 4:8 . . . And while they were in the field, Cain attacked his brother Abel and killed him.   *See also* **Ge** 49:5–7; **1Sa** 18:10–11
Injury Mt 26:67
Cruelty
Ps 71:4 Deliver me, O my God, from the hand of the wicked, from the grasp of those who are evil and cruel.   *See also* **Jdg** 1:7; **Ps** 54:3; **Am** 1:13; **Mt** 2:16–18; **Lk** 10:30
Rioting 2Ki 7:17; **Ac** 16:22
Warfare
Jer 50:22 "The noise of battle is in the land, the noise of great destruction!"   *See also* **Ge** 14:1–2,11–12; **Ex** 13:17; **Jos** 6:20–21; 10:22–26; **Jdg** 1:4–7; **1Ki** 22:35; **2Ki** 17:5–6; **Zec** 14:2; **Lk** 21:20–24; **Rev** 6:4
Injustice
Eze 9:9 He [God] answered me [Ezekiel], "The sin of the house of Israel and Judah is exceedingly great; the land is full of bloodshed and the city is full of injustice. They say, 'The LORD has forsaken the land; the LORD does not see.'"   *See also* **Ge** 39:19–20; **1Ki** 21:11–14; **2Ki** 21:16; **Ps** 58:1–2; 64:6
Oppression
Ecc 4:1 Again I looked and saw all the oppression that was taking place under the sun: I saw the tears of the oppressed—and they have no comforter; power was on the side of their oppressors—and they have no comforter.   *See also* **Ex** 1:11; **1Ki** 12:1–4,12–14; **Ps** 12:5; **Jas** 5:1–6
Adultery 2Sa 12:9; **Mal** 2:14
Theft
Mt 6:19 "Do not store up for yourselves treasures on earth, where moth and rust destroy, and where thieves break in and steal."   *See also* **Ge** 31:19; **Job** 1:14–15,17; 24:2
Broken relationships Job 19:14–19; **Ps** 27:10; **Pr** 16:28; **Ac** 15:39
Hatred
Ps 109:3 With words of hatred they [wicked and deceitful people] surround me; they attack me without cause.   *See also* **2Sa** 13:15; **Tit** 3:3

Jealousy

Ge 37:4 When his [Joseph's] brothers saw that their father loved him more than any of them, they hated him and could not speak a kind word to him.   *See also* **Ge** 4:4–5; 16:6; 21:8–10; **1Sa** 18:8–9; **Mt** 27:18

Persecution

Jn 15:20 "Remember the words I spoke to you: 'Servants are not greater than their masters.' If they persecuted me, they will persecute you also . . ."   *See also* **Jer** 38:6; **Da** 3:4–6; 6:7; **Mt** 5:10–12; 10:35–36; **Rev** 6:9–11

Suffering as a result of misfortune

Accidents 2Sa 4:4; **2Ki** 1:2; **Lk** 13:4

Sickness

Ge 48:1 . . . Joseph was told, "Your father is ill." . . .   *See also* **2Ki** 20:1; **Job** 2:7; **Ps** 42:10; **Mt** 8:6; **Ac** 28:8; **Php** 2:27; **2Ti** 4:20; **Jas** 5:14

Hunger and want Ge 12:10; **Job** 30:3; **Isa** 5:13; **Mt** 25:42–43

Natural disasters 1Ki 22:48; **Job** 1:16,18–19; **Isa** 29:6; **Joel** 1:4; **Zec** 14:5; **Mt** 24:7; **Ac** 27:18–20

Suffering through old age and death

Ageing 2Sa 19:34–35; **Ps** 71:9; **Ecc** 12:1

Bereavement Ge 23:1–2; **Job** 1:18–19; **Lk** 7:11–13; **Jn** 11:33–35; **Jas** 1:27

Suffering through anxiety

Pr 12:25 Anxiety weighs down the heart . . .   *See also* **Dt** 28:65–67; **Lk** 21:26

Suffering through foolishness

Ps 107:17 Some became fools through their rebellious ways and suffered affliction because of their iniquities.   *See also* **Jdg** 11:34–36; **Pr** 10:1; 11:15; 14:1; 23:29–30; **Lk** 15:17

Suffering through Satanic activity

The influence of Satan

Ge 3:1 Now the serpent was more crafty than any of the wild animals the LORD God had made. He said to the woman, "Did God really say, 'You must not eat from any tree in the garden'?"   *See also* **Job** 1:12; 2:6–7; **Lk** 13:16; **1Jn** 5:19;

Rev 2:10; 20:7–8

Demon-possession Mt 8:28; 12:22; 15:22

Suffering brought about by God himself

All suffering comes within his will Jn 9:3; **Eph** 1:11

Some suffering is for his immediate glory Jn 21:19

Jesus Christ's suffering produces salvation

Isa 53:10 Yet it was the LORD's will to crush him [the servant] and cause him to suffer, and though the LORD makes his life a guilt offering, he will see his offspring and prolong his days, and the will of the LORD will prosper in his hand.   *See also* **Ac** 2:23

Christian suffering produces good fruits Ro 5:3–4; **2Co** 1:9; **Heb** 12:11; **Jas** 1:2,3

God's people must be disciplined

Heb 12:7 Endure hardship as discipline; God is treating you as children. For what children are not disciplined by their parents?   *See also* **Ex** 32:35; **2Sa** 12:13–14; **Ps** 119:67,71; **Pr** 3:11–12; **Heb** 12:8–11

The wicked must be punished

Ro 6:23 For the wages of sin is death . . .   *See also* **Ge** 6:5–7; **Jn** 5:14; **2Th** 1:8; **Rev** 9:4; 20:15

Suffering accepted voluntarily

By Jesus Christ

1Pe 2:21 To this you were called, because Christ suffered for you, leaving you an example, that you should follow in his steps.   *See also* **Isa** 53:3–5,10; **Lk** 9:22

By his people

2Co 12:15 So I will very gladly spend for you everything I have and expend myself as well . . .   *See also* **2Co** 4:10–12; **Php** 3:10; **Heb** 11:35

For the good of others

Jn 15:13 "Greater love has no-one than this, to lay down one's life for one's friends."   *See also* **Ro** 5:7; **Phm** 18   *See also disease; famine.*

synagogue

A word meaning literally "a gathering together". In the NT it sometimes refers to a group of Jews meeting for worship but most often to the building in which they met.

Synagogue worship may have begun during the exile

Eze 14:1 Some of the elders of Israel came to me and sat down in front of me.   *See also* **Eze** 20:1

A synagogue might be established anywhere

Mk 1:21 They went to Capernaum, and when the Sabbath came, Jesus went into the synagogue and began to teach.   *See also* **Ac** 6:9

Where there were too few male Jews for a synagogue there would sometimes be a place of prayer: **Ac** 16:12–13,16

Ac 17:1,10; 18:19

The role of the synagogue

It was a focus for prayer and the reading of Scripture

Ac 13:15 After the reading from the Law and the Prophets, the synagogue rulers sent word to them [Paul and Barnabas], saying, "Brothers, if you have a message of encouragement for the people, please speak."   *See also* **Ne** 8:2–8; 9:3; **Lk** 4:15–33

It was a centre for community affairs Mt 10:17; **Mk** 13:9; **Lk** 12:11

Exclusion from the synagogue was used as a punishment Jn 9:22; 12:42

The leading of synagogue worship

It was the responsibility of the synagogue ruler Mk 5:22; **Ac** 18:8

Qualified laymen were allowed to teach

Lk 4:16 He [Jesus] went to Nazareth, where he had been brought up, and on the Sabbath day he went into the synagogue, as was his custom. And he stood up to read.   *See also* **Ac** 13:15

Attendance at the synagogue

It was the practice of Jesus Christ

Mt 9:35 Jesus went through all the towns and villages, teaching in their synagogues . . .

See also **Mk** 6:2; **Lk** 4:16; **Jn** 6:59

It was the practice of Paul and other Jewish Christians

Ac 9:19–20 . . . Saul spent several days with the disciples in Damascus. At once he began to preach in the synagogues that Jesus is the Son of God.   *See also* **Ac** 14:1–2; 17:2; 18:8

The first Christians continued to worship in the synagogues Lk 24:53; **Ac** 19:8–9   *See also education; reading.*

tabernacle

The tabernacle (tent) was a portable and temporary shrine used for worship before the temple was built. It denotes the temporary dwelling of God among his people.

tabernacle, in New Testament

The NT sees the tabernacle and its ceremonies as symbolising the saving work of Jesus Christ in his incarnation and death and in the experience of believers.

Jesus Christ as the tabernacle where God dwells

Jn 1:14 The Word became flesh and made his dwelling among us. We have seen his glory . . .

Jn 2:19–21 . . . But the temple he [Jesus] had spoken of was his body.

The tabernacle showed that God was not limited to one place

Ac 7:44–47

The spiritual significance of the tabernacle

Heb 9:1–5

The earthly tabernacle as a copy of the heavenly one

Heb 8:5 They [Jewish high priests] serve at a sanctuary that is a copy and shadow of what is

in heaven . . .   *See also* **Heb** 8:1-2
The altar Rev 6:9-10; 8:3-5
The ark of the covenant Rev 11:19
The atonement cover Ex 25:22; **Heb** 4:16
**The curtain preventing access to the holiest
place Mt** 27:51; **Heb** 6:19-20; 9:8; 10:19-20

Jesus Christ as high priest
Cleansing the earthly tabernacle
Heb 9:21 In the same way, he [Moses]
sprinkled with the blood both the tabernacle and
everything used in its ceremonies.   *See also* **Heb**
9:6-8,25
**Through the blood of the cross, Jesus Christ
enters the heavenly sanctuary**
Heb 9:24 For Christ did not enter a sanctuary
made with human hands that was only a copy of
the true one; he entered heaven itself, now to
appear for us in God's presence.   *See also* **Heb**
9:28   *See also curtain; sanctuary; temple, Herod's.*

---

tabernacle, in Old Testament
A prefabricated portable structure that was used for
worship from the wilderness period until Solomon
built the Jerusalem temple.

The tabernacle was the place of God's
presence
Ex 33:9-10 As Moses went into the tent, the
pillar of cloud would come down and stay at the
entrance, while the LORD spoke with Moses.
Whenever the people saw the pillar of cloud
standing at the entrance to the tent, they all
stood and worshipped, at the entrances to their
tents.   *See also* **Ex** 25:8; 40:34-35

The construction of the tabernacle
It was built at God's command
Ex 25:9 "Make this tabernacle and all its
furnishings exactly like the pattern I [the LORD]
will show you."   *See also* **Ex** 25:40; 39:32,43
The materials used in its construction Ex
25:3-7; 35:21-24
The plan for its construction Ex 26:1,7,14-15,26
The skilled labour employed in its construction
Ex 31:1-6 Then the LORD said to Moses, "See
I have chosen Bezalel son of Uri, the son of Hur,

of the tribe of Judah, and I have filled him with
the Spirit of God, with skill, ability and knowledge
in all kinds of crafts . . . Moreover, I have
appointed Oholiab son of Ahisamach, of the tribe
of Dan, to help him. Also I have given ability to
all the skilled workers to make everything I have
commanded you:" pp Ex 35:30-35   *See also*
Ex 35:10,26; 36:1-2

The tabernacle courtyard and its
contents
Its dimensions and construction Ex 27:9,12,18
The altar of burnt offering Ex 27:1
The laver Ex 30:17-18

The tabernacle's Holy Place and its
contents
Its construction Ex 26:36-37
The incense altar Ex 30:1,5
The lampstand Ex 25:31
**The golden table for the bread of the Presence
Ex** 25:23,30; 26:35

The tabernacle's Most Holy Place and
its contents
**It was separated from the Holy Place by a
curtain Ex** 26:31-33
It contained the ark of the covenant Ex
26:33-34

The Levites were responsible for the
tabernacle
Nu 1:50-51

The non-religious functions of the
tabernacle
**As a reference point for locating the different
tribes in camp**
Nu 2:1-2 The LORD said to Moses and Aaron:
"The Israelites are to camp round the Tent of
Meeting some distance from it, each man under
his standard with the banners of his family."
**The movement of the cloud of glory showed
when it was time to make or break camp Ex**
40:36-38

Places where the tabernacle was sited
The tabernacle was dedicated at Sinai: **Ex**
40:1–2,9–11
Shiloh: **Jos** 18:1; **1Sa** 1:3; **Ps** 78:60
1Sa 21:1; **1Ch** 16:39; **2Ch** 5:2–6   *See also altar;*
ark of the covenant; Atonement, Day of; Feast of
Tabernacles; Most Holy Place; offerings; temple,
Solomon's.

tax collectors

Governments have a right to collect taxes, but
those who collect them have often been
unpopular, not least because they seem to have
demanded more than they were entitled to. Jesus
Christ welcomed such people, as he did other
sinners, and many repented as a result of his
affirming attitude.

Honest tax collectors deserve respect
Ro 13:6–7 This is also why you pay taxes, for
the authorities are God's servants, who give their
full time to governing. Give to everyone what you
owe: If you owe taxes, pay taxes; if revenue,
then revenue; if respect, then respect; if honour,
then honour.
Temple taxes collected by Levites 2Ch 24:6,9
Temple tax paid by Jesus Christ Mt 17:24–26

Tax collectors often unpopular
In NT times
Lk 18:11 "The Pharisee stood up and prayed
about himself: 'God, I thank you that I am not
like other people—robbers, evildoers, adulterers—
or even like this tax collector.'"

**Tax collectors despised as collaborators
with Rome**
Jesus Christ recognises this popular contempt
Mt 5:46; 18:17; **Lk** 18:11

Many tax collectors come to John
Lk 3:12–13 Tax collectors also came to be
baptised. "Teacher," they asked, "what should
we do?" "Don't collect any more than you are
required to," he told them.   *See also* **Mt**
21:31–32; **Lk** 7:29

**Many tax collectors flock around Jesus
Christ**
Lk 15:1 Now the tax collectors and "sinners"
were all gathering round to hear him.   *See also*
Mt 9:10 pp Mk 2:15 pp Lk 5:29
**Jesus Christ criticised for eating with tax
collectors**
Lk 15:2 But the Pharisees and the teachers of
the law muttered, "This man welcomes sinners,
and eats with them."   *See also* **Mt** 9:11 pp Mk
2:16 pp Lk 5:30; **Mt** 11:19 pp Lk 7:34; **Lk** 19:1–7
Jesus Christ defends his concern
Mt 9:12–14 On hearing this, Jesus said, "It is
not the healthy who need a doctor, but the sick.
But go and learn what this means: 'I desire
mercy, not sacrifice.' For I have not come to call
the righteous, but sinners." . . . pp Mk 2:17 pp
Lk 5:31   *See also* **Lk** 15:3–4

Tax collectors converted
In the parable
Lk 18:13–14 "But the tax collector stood at a
distance. He would not even look up to heaven,
but beat his breast and said, 'God, have mercy
on me, a sinner.' I [Jesus Christ] tell you that
this man, rather than the other, went home
justified before God. For all those who exalt
themselves will be humbled, and those who
humble themselves will be exalted."
Matthew Levi
Mt 9:9 As Jesus went on from there, he saw a
man named Matthew sitting at the tax collector's
booth. "Follow me," he told him, and Matthew
got up and followed him. pp Mk 2:13–14 pp Lk
5:27–28

Zacchaeus Lk 19:1–9   *See also taxation.*

taxation

Any form of payment levied on people by a
supervising authority.

Taxation exacted from subject nations
Tribute to Moab Jdg 3:15,17–18
Tribute to David 2Sa 8:2 pp 1Ch 18:2; **2Sa** 8:6
pp 1Ch 18:6
Tribute to Solomon 1Ki 4:21

Tribute to Assyria 2Ki 17:3; **Hos** 10:6
Tribute to Egypt 2Ki 23:33 pp 2Ch 36:3
Tribute to Judah 2Ch 17:11; 26:8; **Isa** 16:1
Tribute to Persia Est 10:1
Universal tribute
Ps 72:10 The kings of Tarshish and of distant
shores will bring tribute to him; the kings of
Sheba and Seba will present him gifts.
**Refusal to pay tribute was a sign of rebellion
2Ki** 17:4; **Ezr** 4:13

Taxation for the support of the state
Land tax
2Ki 23:35 Jehoiakim paid Pharaoh Neco the
silver and gold he demanded. In order to do so,
he taxed the land and exacted the silver and gold
from the people of the land according to their
assessments.   *See also* **Ge** 41:34; **Ne** 5:4

Census tax
Ex 30:11–16; **Lk** 2:1
Trade tax
1Ki 10:14–15 The weight of the gold that
Solomon received yearly was 666 talents, not
including the revenues from merchants and traders
and from all the Arabian kings and the governors
of the land. pp 2Ch 9:13–14
Such levies may be unjustly burdensome
1Sa 8:10–18 . . . He [Samuel] said, "This is
what the king who will reign over you [Israel]
will do . . . He will take the best of your fields
and vineyards and olive groves and give them to
his attendants. He will take a tenth of your grain
and of your vintage and give it to his officials and
attendants. Your male and female servants and
the best of your cattle and donkeys he will take
for his own use. He will take a tenth of your
flocks, and you yourselves will become his
slaves . . ."   *See also* **Da** 11:20

Covenantal taxation: the tithe
Tithing prescribed
Lev 27:30–33 " 'A tithe of everything from
the land, whether grain from the soil or fruit from
the trees, belongs to the LORD; it is holy to the
LORD . . .' "   *See also* **Ge** 14:20
The tithe supported the priests and the poor

Nu 18:21 "I give to the Levites all the tithes
in Israel as their inheritance in return for the work
they do while serving at the Tent of Meeting."
See also **Dt** 14:28–29

The tithe often seems to have been neglected
Mal 3:8–10 "Will a mere mortal rob God? Yet
you rob me. But you ask, 'How do we rob you?'
In tithes and offerings. You are under a curse—
the whole nation of you—because you are
robbing me. Bring the whole tithe into the
storehouse, that there may be food in my
house . . ." . . .   *See also* **2Ch** 31:4

Taxation for the support of the temple
Mt 17:24–26 After Jesus and his disciples
arrived in Capernaum, the collectors of the two-
drachma tax came to Peter and asked, "Doesn't
your teacher pay the temple tax?" . . .
See also **2Ch** 24:4–12 pp 2Ki 12:4–5

Jesus Christ and taxation
**Jesus Christ was falsely accused of opposing
taxation Lk** 23:1–2
He himself paid tax Mt 17:24–27
He commanded others to pay taxes Mt
22:15–22 pp Mk 12:13–17 pp Lk 20:20–26

Believers and taxation
**Paying taxes demonstrates submission to God
Ro** 13:1,5–6; **1Pe** 2:13
Paying taxes should silence unjust criticism Ro
13:3; **1Pe** 2:15
**Paying taxes is reimbursement for services
rendered Mt** 22:15–22; **Ro** 13:7   *See also land;
poverty; tax collectors; tithing.*

temple

A building for the worship of local or national
gods. After settling in the promised land, Israel felt
the need for a permanent building set apart for
worship of the LORD. Three temples were built at
different periods in Jerusalem. In the NT the
individual believer (or the body of the church) is
seen as the true temple or dwelling-place of God.

temple, Herod's

Herod's temple, familiar to Jesus Christ and his disciples and frequented by the first Christians, was destroyed by the Romans in A.D. 70.

The building of Herod the Great's temple
Jn 2:20

Jesus Christ visited the temple and taught in its courts
He was taken there as a baby Lk 2:22,34,36–38

He stayed in the temple courts after his parents had returned home from the Passover Feast Lk 2:41–43,46

He cast out of the temple court those who used it for material profit Mt 21:12–13 pp Mk 11:15–17 pp Lk 19:45–46; **Jn** 2:14–16

He taught in the temple Mk 12:35,41–43 pp Lk 21:1–4; **Jn** 7:14

The temple guards ignored instructions to arrest him because they were impressed by his teaching: **Jn** 7:32,45–46

Jn 8:2–3; 10:22–24

The religious leaders challenged his authority Mt 21:23 pp Mk 11:27–28 pp Lk 20:1–2

He foretold the complete destruction of the temple buildings Mt 24:1–2 pp Mk 13:1–2 pp Lk 21:5–6

The crucifixion and the temple

One of the charges against Jesus Christ was that he had said he would destroy the temple
Mt 26:60–61 . . . Finally two [false witnesses] came forward and declared, "This fellow [Jesus] said, 'I am able to destroy the temple of God and rebuild it in three days.'"

The curtain of the temple was torn in two at Jesus Christ's death

Mt 27:51 At that moment the curtain of the temple was torn in two from top to bottom. The earth shook and the rocks split.

Believers in Jerusalem met in the temple courtyards
Ac 2:46; 5:12

Apostles taught and healed in the temple courtyards
Ac 3:1–26; 5:19–26

Stephen was stoned for allegedly speaking against the temple
Ac 6:12–14
Ac 7:48–49 "However, the Most High does not live in houses made by human hands. As the prophet says: 'Heaven is my throne, and the earth is my footstool. What kind of house will you build for me? says the Lord. Or where will my resting place be?'"

Paul was accused of taking Gentiles into temple courtyards forbidden to them
Ac 21:27–28   *See also curtain; Passover.*

temple, rebuilding

Following the exile Solomon's ruined temple was rebuilt and became the focus of the Jewish faith worldwide.

Preparations for rebuilding the temple
Ezr 1:1–4 pp 2Ch 36:22–23; **Ezr** 1:7

Rebuilding the temple under the leadership of Jeshua and Zerubbabel
Ezr 3:3–6,8–13; 4:1–3

Interruptions to the rebuilding
The Jews' enemies persuaded Artaxerxes to order the work to cease Ezr
4:8,12–15,17,20–21,24
The prophets Haggai and Zechariah called Zerubbabel and the people to restart work
Hag 1:4 "Is it a time for you yourselves to be living in your panelled houses, while this house remains a ruin?"   *See also* **Ezr** 5:1–12; **Hag** 1:5–7,14–15
The rebuilding authorised by King Darius Ezr 5:3,11,13; 6:3–5,7–8

The dedication and worship of the rebuilt temple Ezr 6:16; 7:11–17

The post-exilic temple and its worship was regarded as the spiritual centre for Jews worldwide
Ps 87:1–7; 135:21

The temple is the place where God is to be praised
Ps 100:4 Enter his [the LORD's] gates with thanksgiving and his courts with praise . . .
Ps 134:1–2 Praise the LORD, all you servants [Levites] of the LORD who minister by night in the house of the LORD. Lift up your hands in the sanctuary and praise the LORD. *See also* **Ps** 135:19–20; 138:2

Prophecies of restoration of the temple
Zec 1:16 "Therefore, this is what the LORD says: 'I will return to Jerusalem with mercy, and there my house will be rebuilt. And the measuring line will be stretched out over Jerusalem,' declares the LORD Almighty." *See also* **Jer** 31:6,23; 33:18; **Eze** 40:1—43:27

temple, significance
The temple was both idealised and spiritualised by OT and NT writers.

The OT concept of an ideal temple in the future age of salvation
Isa 2:3 Many peoples will come and say, "Come, let us go up to the mountain of the LORD, to the house of the God of Jacob . . ." . . . pp Mic 4:2 *See also* **Isa** 56:4–7; 66:20; **Jer** 33:11; **Eze** 37:28; 40:2–4; **Hag** 2:6–8; **Zec** 14:16; **Mal** 3:1–3

The superstitious belief that the presence of the temple in Jerusalem safeguarded the city
The origin of such a belief 2Ki 19:32–36; **Ps** 132:13–18
The prophets knew that disobedience to God would be judged in spite of the temple
Mic 3:12 . . . Zion will be ploughed like a field, Jerusalem will become a heap of rubble, the temple hill a mound overgrown with thickets. *See also* **Jer** 7:4,12–14

The link between the earthly temple and heaven
Heaven is described as God's temple
Ps 11:4 The LORD is in his holy temple; the LORD is on his heavenly throne . . . *See also* **Hab** 2:20; **Heb** 8:5; 9:24; **Rev** 11:19; 14:15–17; 15:5–8
The ultimate "city of God" needs no temple, since it is permeated by God's presence
Rev 21:22 I did not see a temple in the city, because the Lord God Almighty and the Lamb are its temple. *See also* **Rev** 21:3

The risen Christ as the temple where God's glory is revealed
Jn 2:19–21 . . . But the temple he [Jesus] had spoken of was his body.

The church as the temple where God's presence dwells
The individual believer as the temple of the Holy Spirit
1Co 6:19 Do you not know that your bodies are temples of the Holy Spirit, who is in you, whom you have received from God? . . .
The local church as God's temple 1Co 3:16–17
The whole church as God's temple
Eph 2:21–22 In him the whole building is joined together and rises to become a holy temple in the Lord. And in him you too are being built together to become a dwelling in which God lives by his Spirit. *See also* **2Co** 6:16; **1Pe** 2:5

temple, Solomon's
From the exodus until the reign of Solomon, the tabernacle located in various places served as Israel's "temple" and the ordained place of sacrifice. Solomon built the first temple in Jerusalem.

Centres for worship and sacrifice before the temple was built
Jos 18:1; **1Sa** 7:2

David's preparations for the building and worship in the first temple
The plan for its construction 2Sa 7:12–13; **1Ch** 17:1 pp 2Sa 7:1; **1Ch** 28:11–12,19
The gifts for its construction 1Ch 29:2–3,6
Arrangements for the temple worship 1Ch 23:3–5

Solomon's construction of the temple
1Ki 5:1–13; 6:7; **2Ch** 2:17–18

The completion of the temple and its furnishings
2Ch 2:5 "The temple I [Solomon] am going to build will be great, because our God is greater than all other gods."   *See also* **1Ki** 6:20–22 pp 2Ch 3:4–9; **1Ki** 6:27 pp 2Ch 3:11–12; **1Ki** 6:38
Not one laver but a huge reservoir and a number of bronze basins: **1Ki** 7:23 pp 2Ch 4:2; **1Ki** 7:26–27 pp 2Ch 4:5; **1Ki** 7:30
1Ki 7:49; **2Ch** 4:8

The dedication of the temple
At the Feast of Tabernacles 1Ki 8:2 pp 2Ch 5:3
The glory of the Lord filled the temple 1Ki 8:6 pp 2Ch 5:7; **1Ki** 8:10–11; **2Ch** 5:11,13–14
The offering of sacrifices 1Ki 8:62–63 pp 2Ch 7:5
Solomon's prayer
1Ki 8:27 "But will God really dwell on earth? The heavens, even the highest heaven, cannot contain you. How much less this temple I have built!" pp 2Ch 6:18

The temple after the division of the kingdom
1Ki 12:26–30; **2Ch** 13:4–12

Later kings of Judah used the temple treasures for political purposes
1Ki 15:18–19 pp 2Ch 16:2–3; **2Ki** 12:17–18; 16:7–8 pp 2Ch 28:21; **2Ki** 18:14–15

Foreign kings pillaged the temple
1Ki 14:25–26 pp 2Ch 12:9; **2Ki** 24:13; **2Ch** 36:18

Under certain kings the temple was cleansed and repaired
Joash: **2Ki** 12:4–5 pp 2Ch 24:5; **2Ch** 24:13–14
2Ki 15:35 pp 2Ch 27:3
Hezekiah: **2Ch** 29:3–5,15–16,18–19,25
2Ki 22:3–7 pp 2Ch 34:8–11

The destruction of the temple by the Babylonians
2Ki 25:13–15 pp Jer 52:17–19; **2Ch** 36:18

The temple and the ministry of the prophets
Isaiah received his call in the temple Isa 6:1–8
Ezekiel had a vision of the glory of God departing Eze 10:18–19
Micah's prophecy concerning the temple's fate Jer 26:18; **Mic** 3:12
Jeremiah's ministry was closely linked to the temple Jer 7:2,4,14; 19:14   *See also altar; Most Holy Place; offerings; sanctuary; tabernacle, in Old Testament.*

tents
A portable structure made of cloth or skins used mainly by nomads or semi-nomads. God's tent or tabernacle is a meeting-place with him.

Tents as portable dwellings used especially by semi-nomadic peoples
They were living quarters for God's people
Ge 4:20 Adah gave birth to Jabal; he was the father of those who live in tents and raise livestock.   *See also* **Ge** 12:8; 13:12; 18:1; 25:27; **Nu** 11:10; **1Sa** 4:10; **2Sa** 20:1; **1Ki** 12:16
Sometimes women of distinction had their own tents
Ge 24:67 Isaac brought her into the tent of his mother Sarah, and he married Rebekah. So she became his wife, and he loved her; and Isaac was comforted after his mother's death.   *See also* **Ge** 31:33; **Jdg** 4:17–18
A tent housed the ark of God
2Sa 6:17 They brought the ark of the Lord and set it in its place inside the tent that David had pitched for it, and David sacrificed burnt offerings

and fellowship offerings before the LORD. pp 1Ch
16:1   *See also* **2Sa** 7:2; **1Ch** 15:1; **2Ch** 1:4

Tents associated with other peoples
Jdg 6:5 They [the Midianites] came up with
their livestock and their tents like swarms of
locusts. It was impossible to count them or their
camels; they invaded the land to ravage it.
See also **Ge** 9:27; **Jdg** 7:13; **Hab** 3:7

Kings and armies camped in tents
Jdg 7:13 Gideon arrived just as a man was
telling a friend his dream. "I had a dream," he
was saying. "A round loaf of barley bread came
tumbling into the Midianite camp. It struck the
tent with such force that the tent overturned and
collapsed." *See also* **Nu** 31:10; **2Ki** 7:7–8

Tents for storage
1Sa 17:54 David took the Philistine's head and
brought it to Jerusalem, and he put the Philistine's
weapons in his own tent. *See also* **Jos** 7:21–23

Tents were illustrative of a nomadic life
Jer 35:7 "'Also you must never build houses,
sow seed or plant vineyards; you must never have
any of these things, but must always live in tents.
Then you will live a long time in the land where
you are nomads.'"

Heb 11:9–10 By faith he [Abraham] made his
home in the promised land like a stranger in a
foreign country; he lived in tents, as did Isaac and
Jacob, who were heirs with him of the same
promise. For he was looking forward to the city
with foundations, whose architect and builder is
God. *See also* **Ge** 12:8; 13:5,18; 18:1–6; 20:13;
Ex 16:16; 33:8,10; **Nu** 1:50

Tents sometimes associated with sin
Job 8:22 "Your [Job's] enemies will be clothed
in shame, and the tents of the wicked will be no
more." *See also* **Ge** 9:21; **Nu** 16:26; **Jos**
7:21–23; **1Ki** 20:16; **Job** 4:21; 11:14; 12:6; 15:34;
18:6; 21:28; 22:23; **Ps** 84:10

The construction of tents
Tentmakers
Ac 18:3 and because he [Paul] was a
tentmaker as they [Aquila and Priscilla] were, he
stayed and worked with them.

The materials used
Ex 26:7 "Make curtains of goat hair for the
tent over the tabernacle—eleven altogether." pp
Ex 36:14   *See also* **Ex** 26:14–29 pp Ex
36:19–34

Tent pegs and ropes
Ex 27:19 "All the other articles used in the
service of the tabernacle, whatever their function,
including all the tent pegs for it and those for the
courtyard, are to be of bronze." *See also* **Ex**
35:18; 38:20,31; 39:40; **Nu** 3:26,37; 4:32; **Jdg**
4:21; **Isa** 22:25; **Zec** 10:4

Colours of tents
SS 1:5 Dark am I, yet lovely, O daughters of
Jerusalem, dark like the tents of Kedar, like the
tent curtains of Solomon. *See also* **Ex** 26:14

Pitching tents
Jer 10:20 My [Jeremiah's] tent is destroyed; all
its ropes are snapped. My children are gone from
me and are no more; no-one is left now to pitch
my tent or to set up my shelter. *See also* **Ge**
26:25; 33:19; **Jdg** 4:11; **2Sa** 16:22

The metaphorical use of tents
As an image of creation
Ps 104:2 He wraps himself in light as with a
garment; he stretches out the heavens like a
tent *See also* **Ps** 19:4

As a metaphor for death 2Co 5:1; **2Pe** 1:13–14

God's tent is a meeting-place with him
The tabernacle
Ex 25:8–9 "Then have them [the Israelites]
make a sanctuary for me [God], and I will dwell
among them. Make this tabernacle and all its
furnishings exactly like the pattern I will show
you." *See also* **Ex** 26:1–37; 39:32

The Tent of Meeting
Ex 27:21 "In the Tent of Meeting, outside the
curtain that is in front of the Testimony, Aaron
and his sons are to keep the lamps burning
before the LORD from evening till morning. This is
to be a lasting ordinance among the Israelites for
the generations to come."

Ex 33:7 Now Moses used to take a tent and
pitch it outside the camp some distance away,

calling it the "tent of meeting". Anyone enquiring of the LORD would go to the tent of meeting outside the camp.   *See also* **Ex** 28:43; 29:10–11,30,44; 33:11; **Lev** 1:1; **Nu** 1:1; **Dt** 31:14–15

God "tenting" with his people
Jn 1:14 The Word became flesh and made his dwelling among us [the human race]. We [disciples] have seen his glory, the glory of the One and Only, who came from the Father, full of grace and truth.   *See also* **Ex** 25:8; 29:45–46; 40:34–38; **Lev** 26:11–12; **Nu** 5:3; **Dt** 12:11; **Eze** 37:27; **2Co** 6:16; **Rev** 21:3   *See also ark of the covenant; curtain; house; nomads; tabernacle, in Old Testament.*

thank-offering
Together with vows and freewill offerings this was one of the three kinds of fellowship offering.

Presenting a thank-offering
An animal sacrifice
Lev 7:15 " 'The meat of their fellowship offering of thanksgiving must be eaten on the day it is offered . . .' "   *See also* **Lev** 22:29
Accompanied by bread, wafers and cakes Lev 7:12–13
The priest shares the meal Lev 7:14; 22:29–30

The occasions for presenting thank-offerings
For deliverance from distress, death or sickness
Ps 50:23 "Those who sacrifice thank-offerings honour me . . ."
Ps 107:21–22 Let them give thanks to the LORD for his unfailing love and his wonderful deeds for human beings. Let them sacrifice thank-offerings and tell of his works with songs of joy.   *See also* **Ps** 56:12–13; 116:17
Following a vow
Ps 7:17 I will give thanks to the LORD because of his righteousness . . .   *See also* **Ps** 66:13–14
At times of religious renewal 2Ch 29:31; 33:15–16

Thank-offerings mark the time of renewal Jeremiah longs for: **Jer** 17:26; 33:11   *See also fellowship offering; freewill offering; offerings; vows.*

tithing
The practice of offering to God a tenth of the harvest of the land and of livestock, as holy to the LORD. The idea is also used in a more general sense, meaning offering one-tenth of one's income to the Lord.

Tithing was practised before the giving of the OT law
Ge 14:18–20 Then Melchizedek king of Salem brought out bread and wine. He was priest of God Most High, and he blessed Abram, saying, "Blessed be Abram by God Most High, Creator of heaven and earth. And blessed be God Most High, who delivered your enemies into your hand." Then Abram gave him a tenth of everything.   *See also* **Ge** 28:22; **Heb** 7:1–3

Tithing under the law
Tithing extends to all kinds of produce and livestock
Lev 27:30–32 " 'A tithe of everything from the land, whether grain from the soil or fruit from the trees, belongs to the LORD; it is holy to the LORD. If redeem any of your tithe, you must add a fifth of the value to it. The entire tithe of the herd and flock—every tenth animal that passes under the shepherd's rod—will be holy to the LORD.' "   *See also* **2Ch** 31:5–6; **Ne** 10:35–38; 13:12
All tithes were paid to the Levites Nu 18:21–24; **Ne** 10:37–38; **Heb** 7:5
Tithes were to be paid in a designated place Dt 12:5–6; 14:22–29; 26:2
Levites offered a tenth to the LORD Nu 18:25–29; **Ne** 10:39

Uses of the tithe
Support of the Levites
Nu 18:21 "I [the LORD] give to the Levites all the tithes in Israel as their inheritance in return for the work they do while serving at the Tent of

Meeting." *See also* **2Ch** 31:4

The tithe meal

Dt 14:23 Eat the tithe of your grain, new wine and oil, and the firstborn of your herds and flocks in the presence of the LORD your God at the place he will choose as a dwelling for his Name, so that you may learn to revere the LORD your God always.

A three-yearly gift to the poor

Dt 14:28–29 At the end of every three years, bring all the tithes of that year's produce and store it in your towns, so that the Levites (who have no allotment or inheritance of their own) and the aliens, the fatherless and the widows who live in your towns may come and eat and be satisfied, and so that the LORD your God may bless you in all the work of your hands.

Tithing of minor items must not lead to neglect of major matters

Mt 23:23 "Woe to you, teachers of the law and Pharisees, you hypocrites! You give a tenth of your spices—mint, dill and cummin. But you have neglected the more important matters of the law—justice, mercy and faithfulness. You should have practised the latter, without neglecting the former." *See also* **Lk** 11:42; 18:9–14

Freewill offerings were made in addition to the tithe

They were given freely

Ex 36:3 They received from Moses all the offerings the Israelites had brought to carry out the work of constructing the sanctuary. And the people continued to bring freewill offerings morning after morning. *See also* **Lev** 7:12–18; **Nu** 15:3; **Ezr** 1:4; **Ps** 54:6; **Eze** 46:12

They were given according to ability

Dt 16:10 Then celebrate the Feast of Weeks to the LORD your God by giving a freewill offering in proportion to the blessings the LORD your God has given you. *See also* **Dt** 16:17; **Ac** 11:29; **1Co** 16:2; **2Co** 8:12 *There is no specific command in the NT for the church to tithe, but many commands to give generously and to support the Lord's work.*

Blessing promised to those who tithe

Mal 3:10 "Bring the whole tithe into the storehouse, that there may be food in my house. Test me in this," says the LORD Almighty, "and see if I will not throw open the floodgates of heaven and pour out so much blessing that you will not have room enough for it." *See also* **Pr** 3:9–10

Failure to tithe and abuses of the tithe

Mal 3:8–10 "Will a mere mortal rob God? Yet you rob me. But you ask, 'How do we rob you?' In tithes and offerings. You are under a curse— the whole nation of you—because you are robbing me. Bring the whole tithe into the storehouse, that there may be food in my house. Test me in this," says the LORD Almighty, "and see if I will not throw open the floodgates of heaven and pour out so much blessing that you will not have room enough for it." *See also* **Lev** 27:33; **1Sa** 8:15,17; **Ne** 13:10 *See also firstfruits; freewill offering; law; money; offerings; poverty; taxation.*

---

tools

Implements used for agricultural or mechanical purposes. Early tools were of wood, flint or stone. The development of ironworking brought iron-bladed tools and farm implements into common use. Axes were used to fell trees; hammers, chisels and saws were used by both carpenters and masons. Assyria and Babylon are depicted as tools in God's hand.

Tools made from iron and bronze

General references

Ge 4:22 Zillah also had a son, Tubal-Cain, who forged all kinds of tools out of bronze and iron . . . *See also* **2Sa** 12:31 pp 1Ch 20:3; **2Sa** 23:7

Iron axe-heads

2Ki 6:4–5 . . . As one of them was cutting down a tree, the iron axe-head fell into the water . . . *See also* **Dt** 19:5

Sharpening iron tools

1Sa 13:19–21 . . . So all Israel went down

to the Philistines to have their ploughshares, mattocks, axes and sickles sharpened . . . *See also* **Ecc** 10:10

Tools used in specific tasks
Axes used for felling trees
Jdg 9:48 . . . He [Abimelech] took an axe and cut off some branches, which he lifted to his shoulders. He ordered the men with him, "Quick! Do what you have seen me do!" *See also* **Dt** 20:19–20; **Ps** 74:5–6

Mt 3:10 "The axe is already at the root of the trees, and every tree that does not produce good fruit will be cut down and thrown into the fire." pp Lk 3:9 *See also* **Jer** 46:22–23

Woodworking tools
Isa 44:13 The carpenter measures with a line and makes an outline with a marker; he roughs it out with chisels and marks it [an idol] with compasses . . . *See also* **Ex** 21:6 pp Dt 15:17; **Jer** 10:3–4

Metalworking tools
Job 19:24 "that they [words] were inscribed with an iron tool on lead, or engraved in rock for ever!" *See also* **Ex** 28:36 pp Ex 39:30; **Jer** 17:1

Isa 41:7 The metal worker encourages the goldsmith, and the one who smooths with the hammer spurs on the one who strikes the anvil. One says of the welding, "It is good." The other nails down the idol so that it will not topple. *See also* **Ex** 32:4; **Isa** 44:12; **Jer** 10:9

Stoneworking tools
1Ki 6:7 In building the temple, only blocks dressed at the quarry were used, and no hammer, chisel or any other iron tool was heard at the temple site while it was being built.

1Ki 7:9 All these structures, from the outside to the great courtyard and from foundation to eaves, were made of blocks of high-grade stone cut to size and trimmed with a saw on their inner and outer faces. *See also* **Ex** 34:1; **Dt** 10:3; **Isa** 22:16; **Jer** 23:29

No tools were to be used on stones for an altar: **Ex** 20:25; **Dt** 27:5; **Jos** 8:31

Agricultural tools
Isa 2:4 . . . They [the nations] will beat their swords into ploughshares and their spears into pruning hooks. Nation will not take up sword against nation, nor will they train for war any more. pp Mic 4:3 *See also* **Joel** 3:10; **Isa** 18:5; 30:24

A winnowing fork is a wooden pitchfork used to toss grain into the wind: **Jer** 15:7; **Mt** 3:12 pp Lk 3:17

The nations as tools in God's hand
Isa 10:15 Does the axe raise itself above the one who swings it, or the saw boast against the one who uses it? As if a rod were to wield the person who lifts it up, or a club brandish one who is not wood! *See also* **Isa** 10:5; **Jer** 50:23 *See also agriculture; arts and crafts.*

---

trade
Fair business transactions are essential to distribute the benefits of God's goodness between individuals and nations. Scripture insists on honesty in trade and warns against abuses.

Trade in ancient Israel
Lev 25:14; **2Ki** 4:7; 7:1; **Ne** 3:31–32

The good wife's trade: **Pr** 31:13–18,24

Zep 1:11; **Mt** 21:12 pp Mk 11:15–16 pp Lk 19:45 pp Jn 2:14–16

International trade
Under Solomon
1Ki 9:26–28 King Solomon also built ships at Ezion Geber, which is near Elath in Edom, on the shore of the Red Sea. And Hiram sent his servants—sailors who knew the sea—to serve in the fleet with Solomon's servants. They sailed to Ophir and brought back 420 talents of gold, which they delivered to King Solomon. pp 2Ch 8:17–18 *See also* **1Ki** 10:14–15 pp 2Ch 9:13–14; **1Ki** 10:28–29 pp 2Ch 1:16–17; **2Ch** 9:21; **SS** 3:6–7

Under Jehoshaphat 1Ki 22:48 pp 2Ch 20:35–37

In the Psalms Ps 107:23

Trade among the nations
Hittites Ge 23:16

Shechemites Ge 34:10,21

Ishmaelites
Ge 37:25 As they [Joseph's brothers] sat down to eat their meal, they looked up and saw a caravan of Ishmaelites coming from Gilead. Their camels were loaded with spices, balm and myrrh, and they were on their way to take them down to Egypt.
Midianites Ge 37:28
Egypt Ge 42:34; **Isa** 45:14
Sheba Job 6:19; **Jer** 6:20
Damascus 1Ki 20:34
Tyre and the surrounding nations
Isa 23:8 . . . Tyre, the bestower of crowns, whose merchants are princes, whose traders are renowned in the earth?   *See also* **Eze** 27:1–36
Tarshish Eze 38:13; **Jnh** 1:3–5
Nineveh Na 3:16
Ancient Babylon Eze 16:29; 17:4
Babylon the Great
Rev 18:9–24 ". . . The merchants of the earth will weep and mourn over her because no-one buys their cargoes any more—cargoes of gold, silver, precious stones and pearls; fine linen, purple, silk and scarlet cloth; every sort of citron wood, and articles of every kind made of ivory, costly wood, bronze, iron and marble; cargoes of cinnamon and spice, of incense, myrrh and frankincense, of wine and olive oil, of fine flour and wheat; cattle and sheep; horses and carriages; and slaves—human beings! . . ." . . .
See also **Rev** 18:2–3

Honesty is essential in trade
Lev 19:35–36 " 'Do not use dishonest standards when measuring length, weight or quantity. Use honest scales and honest weights, an honest ephah and an honest hin. I am the LORD your God, who brought you out of Egypt.' "   *See also* **Dt** 25:13–16; **Pr** 11:1; 16:11; 20:10,23

Warnings against abuses in trade
Dishonesty
Am 8:4–5 Hear this, you who trample the needy and do away with the poor of the land, saying, "When will the New Moon be over that we may sell grain, and the Sabbath be ended

that we may market wheat?"—skimping the measure, boosting the price and cheating with dishonest scales,   *See also* **Eze** 28:18; **Hos** 12:7; **Mic** 6:10–11

Oppression Job 20:18–19; **Eze** 28:16
Overconfidence Jas 4:13–16
Pride
Eze 28:5 " 'By your great skill in trading you have increased your wealth, and because of your wealth your heart has grown proud.' "   *See also* **Isa** 2:12,16; 23:17–18

Sabbath trading Ne 13:15–22; 10:31
The slave trade Ge 37:26–28,36; 39:1; **Am** 2:6; 8:6; **1Ti** 1:10; **Rev** 18:13
Sacrilegious trade Jn 2:14–16
Immoral trade Joel 3:3

The imagery of trade applied to spiritual matters
Mt 13:45–46 ". . . the kingdom of heaven is like a merchant looking for fine pearls. When he found one of great value, he went away and sold everything he had and bought it."   *See also* **Pr** 23:23; **Mt** 25:14–18; **Lk** 19:13; **1Co** 6:20
See also buying and selling; justice, human; market; occupations; Sabbath; scales and balances; seafaring; weights and measures, laws.

treaty

A formal agreement between individuals or nations, promising commitment to each other's interests. Israel was forbidden to enter into such agreements with other nations in the promised land.

Treaties between individuals
1Sa 18:3–4 And Jonathan made a covenant with David because he loved him as himself. Jonathan took off the robe he was wearing and gave it to David, along with his tunic, and even his sword, his bow and his belt.   *See also* **Ge** 21:22–32; 26:26–31; **1Sa** 20:8,16–17; 22:8; 23:18; **2Sa** 3:12–13

Treaties between individuals acting on behalf of their nation
1Ki 5:12–18; 15:18–19; **Isa** 33:8; **Eze** 17:12–14

Treaties between cities or nations
Jos 9:3–16; 10:1; 11:18–19; **1Sa** 11:1–2; **Hos** 12:1

Treaties entered into should be honoured
Eze 17:15–18 " 'But the king [Zedekiah of Judah] rebelled against him [Nebuchadnezzar of Babylon] by sending his envoys to Egypt to get horses and a large army. Will he succeed? Will he who does such things escape? Will he break the treaty and yet escape? As surely as I live, declares the Sovereign LORD, he shall die in Babylon, in the land of the king who put him on the throne, whose oath he despised and whose treaty he broke. Pharaoh with his mighty army and great horde will be of no help to him in war, when ramps are built and siege works erected to destroy many lives. He despised the oath by breaking the covenant. Because he had given his hand in pledge and yet did all these things, he shall not escape.' " *See also* **Jer** 34:8–20; **Da** 11:22–24; **Hos** 10:4; **Am** 1:9–10; **Gal** 3:15

Israel forbidden to enter into treaties with other nations in the promised land
Dt 7:1–2 When the LORD your God brings you into the land you are entering to possess and drives out before you many nations—the Hittites, Girgashites, Amorites, Canaanites, Perizzites, Hivites and Jebusites, seven nations larger and stronger than you—and when the LORD your God has delivered them over to you and you have defeated them, then you must destroy them totally. Make no treaty with them, and show them no mercy. *See also* **Ex** 23:31–32; 34:11–12,15–16; **Dt** 23:6; **1Ki** 20:34,42–43; **Ezr** 9:12 *See also covenant, nature of.*

unleavened bread

Bread baked without yeast, often made because of insufficient time to prepare bread in the conventional manner. It was also eaten at the Passover Feast and was presented with sacrifices and offerings.

Unleavened bread prepared in haste
Ex 12:39 With the dough they [the Israelites] had brought from Egypt, they baked cakes of unleavened bread. The dough was without yeast because they had been driven out of Egypt and did not have time to prepare food for themselves. *See also* **Ge** 19:1–3; **Ex** 12:8–11; **Jdg** 6:17–19; **1Sa** 28:21–25

Unleavened bread eaten to commemorate the Passover
Ex 12:1–20; 13:3–7; 23:15; 34:18; **Lev** 23:5–6 pp Nu 28:16–17; **Nu** 9:9–11; **Dt** 16:1–4,8; **Eze** 45:21

Unleavened bread presented to God as an offering
Lev 2:11 " 'Every grain offering you bring to the LORD must be made without yeast, for you are not to burn any yeast or honey in an offering made to the LORD by fire.' " *See also* **Ex** 29:2–4 pp Lev 8:1–3; **Ex** 29:22–25 pp Lev 8:25–28; **Lev** 2:4–5; 6:14–17; 7:11–12; **Nu** 6:13–20

Symbolism of unleavened bread
1Co 5:6–8 *See also Feast of Unleavened Bread; fellowship offering; food; grain offering; Passover.*

vine

A plant on which grapes grow, cultivated primarily for making wine. Jesus Christ described himself as the true vine, the source of life and growth for all believers.

The vine as an image of peace and security
1Ki 4:25 During Solomon's lifetime Judah and Israel, from Dan to Beersheba, lived in safety, everyone under their own vine and fig-tree. *See also* **2Ki** 18:31 pp Isa 36:16; **Mic** 4:4; **Zec** 3:10

Laws relating to the cultivation of vines
Lev 25:1–5 . . . ". . . '. . . in the seventh
year the land is to have a sabbath of rest, a
sabbath to the LORD. Do not sow your fields or
prune your vineyards. Do not reap what grows of
itself or harvest the grapes of your untended
vines. The land is to have a year of rest.' "
See also **Lev** 25:8–12

Wild vines
Jer 2:21 "I [the LORD] had planted you [Israel]
like a choice vine of sound and reliable stock.
How then did you turn against me into a corrupt,
wild vine?"   *See also* **2Ki** 4:38–40

The destruction of vines as punishment
Jer 8:13 " 'I will take away their harvest,
declares the LORD. There will be no grapes on the
vine. There will be no figs on the tree, and their
leaves will wither. What I have given them [my
people] will be taken from them.' "   *See also*
Ps 78:42–47; 105:27–33; 80:16; **Isa** 7:23; 16:8–9;
17:10–11; 24:5–7; 32:9–13; **Jer** 5:14–17; **Hos**
2:12; **Na** 2:2; **Hag** 2:19

Blessing on vines
Zec 8:12 "The seed will grow well, the vine
will yield its fruit, the ground will produce its
crops, and the heavens will drop their dew. I will
give all these things as an inheritance to the
remnant of this people."   *See also* **Dt** 8:7–8;
Joel 2:22; **Mal** 3:11

Vines in dreams and prophecies
Ge 49:10–12 "The sceptre will not depart
from Judah, nor the ruler's staff from between his
feet, until he comes to whom it belongs and the
obedience of the nations is his. He will tether his
donkey to a vine, his colt to the choicest
branch . . .   *See also* **Ge** 40:9–13

Vines in parables
Jdg 9:12–13 "Then the trees said to the vine,
'Come and be our king.' But the vine answered,
'Should I give up my wine, which cheers both
gods and human beings, to hold sway over the
trees?' "   *See also* **Isa** 5:1–2; **Eze** 17:1–10; **Jnh**
4:5–11

Metaphorical references to vines
Ps 128:3 Your wife will be like a fruitful vine
within your house; your children will be like olive
shoots round your table.   *See also* **Ge** 49:22; **Dt**
32:31–33; **Job** 15:31–34; **SS** 7:8; **Isa** 34:4; **Jer**
48:32; **Eze** 15:1–6; **Hos** 14:7

Israel is described as a vine
Hos 10:1 Israel was a spreading vine; he
brought forth fruit for himself. As his fruit
increased, he built more altars; as his land
prospered, he adorned his sacred stones.
See also **Ps** 80:8–17; **Jer** 2:21; 6:9

Jesus Christ is the true vine
Jn 15:1–8 "I [Jesus] am the true vine, and
my Father is the gardener . . . No branch can
bear fruit by itself; it must remain in the vine.
Neither can you [disciples] bear fruit unless you
remain in me . . ."   *See also drinking; fruit;
vineyard; wine.*

---

vineyard

A cultivated field or garden, sometimes surrounded
by a wall, in which vines and other trees were
grown. Israel is sometimes compared to a
vineyard. Some of Jesus Christ's parables concern
vineyards.

**Vineyards were sometimes surrounded
by walls**
Mt 21:33 ". . . There was a landowner who
planted a vineyard. He put a wall around it, dug
a winepress in it and built a watchtower. Then he
rented the vineyard to some farmers and went
away on a journey." pp Mk 12:1   *See also* **Nu**
22:24

**Vineyards were associated with a
settled, peaceful life**
Isa 65:20–22 ". . . They [God's people] will
build houses and dwell in them; they will plant
vineyards and eat their fruit. No longer will they
build houses and others live in them, or plant and
others eat. For as the days of a tree, so will be
the days of my people; my chosen ones will long

enjoy the works of their hands." *See also* **Ge** 9:20; **Dt** 6:10–11; **2Ki** 18:31–32 pp Isa 36:16–17; **2Ki** 19:29 pp Isa 37:30; **2Ch** 26:10; **Ne** 9:25; **Ps** 107:37–38; **SS** 7:12; **Jer** 31:3–5; 32:15; 35:6–10; **Eze** 28:26; **Am** 9:14

Vineyards were important for agriculture
2Ki 25:11–12 Nebuzaradan the commander of the guard carried into exile the people who remained in the city, along with the rest of the populace and those who had gone over to the king of Babylon. But the commander left behind some of the poorest people of the land to work the vineyards and fields. pp Jer 39:9–10 pp Jer 52:15–16   *See also* **Nu** 20:17; 21:22; **Dt** 20:6; **Jdg** 14:5; 15:4–5; **1Sa** 8:10–14; **1Ch** 27:27; **Ne** 5:1–5,11; **Isa** 61:5

Vineyards were a sign of wealth
1Sa 22:7 Saul said to them, "Listen, men of Benjamin! Will the son of Jesse give all of you fields and vineyards? Will he make all of you commanders of thousands and commanders of hundreds?"   *See also* **2Ki** 5:26; **Pr** 31:16; **Ecc** 2:4

Regulations relating to vineyards
Lev 19:10 " 'Do not go over your vineyard a second time or pick up the grapes that have fallen. Leave them for the poor and the alien. I am the Lord your God.' "   *See also* **Ex** 22:5; 23:11; **Lev** 25:3–4; **Dt** 22:9; 23:24; 24:21

The produce of vineyards not enjoyed by owner
Dt 28:39 You will plant vineyards and cultivate them but you will not drink the wine or gather the grapes, because worms will eat them. *See also* **Dt** 28:30; **Am** 5:11; **Zep** 1:13

Naboth's vineyard
1Ki 21:1–19 Some time later there was an incident involving a vineyard belonging to Naboth the Jezreelite. The vineyard was in Jezreel, close to the palace of Ahab king of Samaria. Ahab said to Naboth, "Let me have your vineyard to use for a vegetable garden, since it is close to my palace. In exchange I will give you a better vineyard or, if you prefer, I will pay you whatever it is worth." But Naboth replied, "The Lord forbid that I should give you the inheritance of my ancestors." . . .

Vineyards in parables
Mt 21:28–32 ". . . There was a man who had two sons. He went to the first and said, 'Son, go and work today in the vineyard.' 'I will not,' he answered, but later he changed his mind and went. Then the father went to the other son and said the same thing. He answered, 'I will, sir,' but he did not go . . ." . . .   *See also* **SS** 8:11–12; **Mt** 20:1–16; 21:33–44 pp Mk 12:1–11 pp Lk 20:9–18; **Lk** 13:6–9; **1Co** 9:7

The metaphorical use of vineyards
Eze 19:10 " 'Your mother was like a vine in your vineyard planted by the water; it was fruitful and full of branches because of abundant water.' "   *See also* **Job** 24:6; **SS** 1:14; 2:15; **Isa** 3:14; 5:1–7; **Jer** 12:10   *See also agriculture; vine; wine.*

VOWS
Promises made to God, usually in the context of worship or religious practice. There was no requirement on any Israelite to make vows, but once made, they were binding and had to be kept.

Vows were binding
Dt 23:21–23 If you make a vow to the Lord your God, do not be slow to pay it, for the Lord your God will certainly demand it of you and you will be guilty of sin. But if you refrain from making a vow, you will not be guilty. Whatever your lips utter you must be sure to do, because you made your vow freely to the Lord your God with your own mouth.   *See also* **Nu** 30:2,9; **Pr** 20:25; **Ecc** 5:4–6; **Mal** 1:14

Exceptions to keeping vows
Nu 30:3–8 "When a young woman still living in her father's household makes a vow to the

LORD or binds herself by a pledge and her father hears about her vow or pledge but says nothing to her, then all her vows and every pledge by which she bound herself will stand. But if her father forbids her when he hears about it, none of her vows or the pledges by which she bound herself will stand; the LORD will release her because her father has forbidden her . . ." *See also* **Nu** 30:10–15

Vows made to God in the context of worship
To offer sacrifices
Lev 22:17–19 The LORD said to Moses, "Speak to Aaron and his sons and to all the Israelites and say to them: 'If any of you—either an Israelite or an alien living in Israel—presents a gift for a burnt offering to the LORD, either to fulfil a vow or as a freewill offering, you must present a male without defect from the cattle, sheep or goats in order that it may be accepted on your behalf.'" *See also* **Lev** 7:16; 22:21; 27:9; **Nu** 15:2–4,8–10; **Dt** 12:6,11; **Ps** 50:14; 66:13; **Pr** 7:14; **Jnh** 2:9
To dedicate people, animals or property to God
Lev 27:1–25 The LORD said to Moses, "Speak to the Israelites and say to them: 'If any of you make a special vow to dedicate persons to the LORD by giving equivalent values, set the value of a male between the ages of twenty and sixty at fifty shekels of silver, according to the sanctuary shekel . . .'"
To give money
2Ki 12:4–5 Joash said to the priests, "Collect all the money that is brought as sacred offerings to the temple of the LORD—the money collected in the census, the money received from personal vows and the money brought voluntarily to the temple . . ." *See also* **Dt** 23:18

Motives for making vows
To elicit God's help
1Sa 1:11 And she [Hannah] made a vow, saying, "O LORD Almighty, if you will only look upon your servant's misery and remember me, and not forget your servant but give her a son,

then I will give him to the LORD for all the days of his life, and no razor will ever be used on his head." *See also* **Ge** 28:20–22; **Nu** 21:2; **Jdg** 11:30–40; **2Sa** 15:7–8; **Ps** 66:13–14
To express thanksgiving
Ps 116:12–14 How can I repay the LORD for all his goodness to me? I will lift up the cup of salvation and call on the name of the LORD. I will fulfil my vows to the LORD in the presence of all his people. *See also* **Ps** 50:14; 56:12; 116:17–18; **Jnh** 1:16; 2:9
To praise God
Ps 22:25 From you [the LORD] comes the theme of my praise in the great assembly; before those who fear you will I fulfil my vows. *See also* **Ps** 61:8; 65:1

Vows of Nazirites
Nu 6:1–21; **Jdg** 13:2–5; **1Sa** 1:11

Examples of vows made to God
By David
Ps 132:2–5 He [David] swore an oath to the LORD and made a vow to the Mighty One of Jacob: "I will not enter my house or go to my bed—I will allow no sleep to my eyes, no slumber to my eyelids, till I find a place for the LORD, a dwelling for the Mighty One of Jacob."
By Paul
Ac 18:18 Paul stayed on in Corinth for some time. Then he left the believers and sailed for Syria, accompanied by Priscilla and Aquila. Before he sailed, he had his hair cut off at Cenchrea because of a vow he had taken. *See also* **Ac** 21:24–26

Abuse of vows
Mt 15:5–6 pp Mk 7:11–13

Vows made to idols
Jer 44:25–28 "This is what the LORD Almighty, the God of Israel, says: You [Judahites living in Egypt] and your wives have shown by your actions what you promised when you said, 'We will certainly carry out the vows we made to burn incense and pour out drink offerings to the Queen of Heaven.' Go ahead then, do what you

promised! Keep your vows! But hear the word of
the LORD . . . .'. . . the Jews in Egypt will perish
by sword and famine until they are all
destroyed . . .'"　*See also idolatry; oaths, human;
pledges.*

wages
Payment by an employer for work done; all
labourers should be paid fairly and regularly.

Laws relating to wages
Payment should be made regularly
Dt 24:14–**15** Do not take advantage of a
hired worker who is poor and needy, whether that
worker is an Israelite or an alien living in one of
your towns. Pay such workers their wages each
day before sunset, because they are poor and are
counting on it. Otherwise they may cry to the
LORD against you, and you will be guilty of
sin.　*See also* **Lev** 19:13
Regular rates of pay Lev 25:50; **Mk** 6:37 pp Jn
6:7; **Mk** 14:5 pp Jn 12:5
Labourers should not be defrauded
Mal 3:5 "So I will come near to you for
judgment. I will be quick to testify against
sorcerers, adulterers and perjurers, against those
who defraud labourers of their wages, who
oppress the widows and the fatherless, and
deprive aliens of justice, but do not fear me,"
says the LORD Almighty.
Jas 5:4 Look! The wages you failed to pay the
workers who mowed your fields are crying
against you. The cries of the harvesters have
reached the ears of the Lord Almighty.　*See also*
Jer 22:13
A fair wage should be paid
Mt 20:2–**4** ". . . He [a landowner] told them
[workers waiting for hire], 'You also go and work
in my vineyard, and I will pay you whatever is
right.'"　*See also* **Col** 4:1
A fair day's work should be done
2Th 3:10–**12** For even when we [Paul and his
companions] were with you, we gave you this
rule: "Anyone who will not work shall not
eat." . . .　*See also* **Eph** 6:7–8; **Col** 3:23

Labourers should be content with a fair wage
Lk 3:14 Then some soldiers asked him [Jesus],
"And what should we do?" He replied, "Don't
extort money and don't accuse people falsely—be
content with your pay."

Wage earners suffer in times of trouble
Egypt under judgment
Isa 19:10 The workers in cloth will be dejected,
and all the wage earners will be sick at heart.
Jerusalem under judgment
Hag 1:6 "You have planted much, but have
harvested little. You eat, but never have enough.
You drink, but never have your fill. You put on
clothes, but are not warm. You earn wages, only
to put them in a purse with holes in it."
See also **Zec** 8:10
The world under judgment Rev 6:6

The example of Jacob as a wage earner
Hos 12:12 . . . Israel served to get a wife,
and to pay for her he tended sheep.　*See also*
Ge 29:15,18,25–27; 30:28–34; 31:6–9,38–42

The wages of God's servants
The Levites Nu 18:30–31; **Ne** 12:44; 13:10–13
Temple workers 1Ki 5:6; **2Ki** 12:11–15; 22:3–7
pp 2Ch 34:8–11; **2Ki** 22:9 pp 2Ch 34:16–17
Zechariah's derisory pay Zec 11:12–13; **Mt**
27:3–10
**Labourers in the parable of the workers in the
vineyard Mt** 20:1–16
Ministers of the gospel
1Ti 5:17–**18** The elders who direct the affairs
of the church well are worthy of double honour,
especially those whose work is preaching and
teaching. For the Scripture says, "Do not muzzle
the ox while it is treading out the grain," and
"Workers deserve their wages."　*See also* **Dt**
25:4; **Lk** 10:7; **Jn** 4:36–38; **1Co** 9:7–14; **Gal** 6:6
The apostle Paul
It was Paul's choice to work freely: **1Co** 9:15; **2Co** 11:7–9
Php 4:18

Spiritual lessons from wages
Life's rewards are hard-earned Job 7:1–3; **Gal**
6:7–10

The wages of sin
Ro 6:21–23 . . . For the wages of sin is death, but the gift of God is eternal life in Christ Jesus our Lord.   *See also* **Job** 15:31–32; **Isa** 65:7; **Jer** 51:6; **2Pe** 2:13
The freeness of God's grace Ro 4:4–5
The generosity of God Mt 20:9–16
The rewards of righteousness Pr 10:16; 11:18; 31:31; **Mt** 10:42 pp Mk 9:41; **1Co** 3:14; **Heb** 6:10; **2Jn** 8

---

warfare
The state of being at war with an opposing nation or people. Scripture neither condemns nor glories in warfare, but recognises it as a continuing aspect of this fallen world.

---

warfare
Warfare is characteristic of a fallen world. Scripture describes how some wars are justified and others are not.

Warfare is characteristic of a fallen world
It is an aspect of life in a fallen world Ex 17:16; **2Sa** 3:1; **1Ki** 14:30
It is caused by sin
Jas 4:1–2 What causes fights and quarrels among you? Don't they come from your desires that battle within you? You want something but don't get it. You kill and covet, but you cannot have what you want. You quarrel and fight. You do not have, because you do not ask God. *See also* **Ps** 140:1–2; **Pr** 10:12; 29:22; **1Co** 3:3
It is horrific in nature
Na 3:3 Charging cavalry, flashing swords and glittering spears! Many casualties, piles of dead, bodies without number, people stumbling over the corpses—   *See also* **2Ch** 25:12; **Zec** 14:2

Warfare as a sign of the end times
Mt 24:6–7 "You will hear of wars and rumours of wars, but see to it that you are not alarmed. Such things must happen, but the end is still to come. Nation will rise against nation, and kingdom against kingdom . . ." pp Mk 13:7–8 pp Lk 21:9–10

Sometimes God forbids war
Dt 1:41–42 . . . But the LORD said to me [Moses], "Tell them, 'Do not go up and fight, because I will not be with you. You will be defeated by your enemies.'"   *See also* **1Ki** 12:24; **1Ch** 22:8; **Ps** 68:30; 120:7

Sometimes God commands war
Jos 8:1 Then the LORD said to Joshua, "Do not be afraid; do not be discouraged. Take the whole army with you, and go up and attack Ai . . ."   *See also* **Nu** 31:7; **Dt** 20:1–4; **Jos** 10:40; **Jdg** 6:16; **Ps** 144:1; **Isa** 13:3–4

Warfare is sometimes a means of judgment
1Sa 15:2 "This is what the LORD Almighty says: 'I will punish the Amalekites for what they did to Israel when they waylaid them as they came up from Egypt.'"   *See also* **2Ki** 21:10–15; 24:2–4; **Isa** 10:12–19; **Jer** 4:14–18

God's will that warfare will finally cease
Ps 46:9; **Isa** 2:4; **Mic** 4:3

---

warfare, examples
From the time of entering the promised land, Israel was obliged to engage in warfare against other nations. Success is attributed to Israel's trust in the LORD and failure to lack of faith and disobedience.

Israel had to engage in warfare to enter Canaan
It was commanded by God
Dt 7:1–2 When the LORD your God brings you into the land you are entering to possess and drives out before you many nations—the Hittites, Girgashites, Amorites, Canaanites, Perizzites, Hivites and Jebusites, seven nations larger and stronger than you—and when the LORD your God has delivered them over to you and you have defeated them, then you must destroy them totally. Make no treaty with them, and show them no mercy.   *See also* **Ex** 23:27–31; **Dt** 9:1–5; 20:16–18

Joshua conquers the land

Jos 11:23 So Joshua took the entire land, just as the LORD had directed Moses, and he gave it as an inheritance to Israel according to their tribal divisions. Then the land had rest from war.
See also **Jos** 6:2; 8:1–2; 10:40–42; **Ne** 9:24; **Ps** 44:1–3

Israel failed to drive out the remaining Canaanites

Jdg 1:19 The LORD was with the men of Judah. They took possession of the hill country, but they were unable to drive the people from the plains, because they had iron chariots.   *See also* **Jdg** 1:28; 2:1–3,14–15

Israel was obliged to engage in warfare to defend the land
When unfaithful they were defeated

Jdg 3:12–14 Once again the Israelites did evil in the eyes of the LORD, and because they did this evil the LORD gave Eglon king of Moab power over Israel. Getting the Ammonites and Amalekites to join him, Eglon came and attacked Israel, and they took possession of the City of Palms. The Israelites were subject to Eglon king of Moab for eighteen years.   *See also* **Lev** 26:14–17,33; **Dt** 28:15,25; **Jdg** 3:7–8; 6:1–3; **2Ch** 12:1–4; 24:23–24

When faithful they were victorious

2Ch 20:20 . . . "Listen to me [Jehoshaphat, king of Judah], Judah and people of Jerusalem! Have faith in the LORD your God and you will be upheld; have faith in his prophets and you will be successful."   *See also* **Dt** 28:1,7; **1Sa** 7:7–14; 11:1–11; **2Ch** 20:15–24

Israel's internal struggles

2Sa 3:1 The war between the house of Saul and the house of David lasted a long time. David grew stronger and stronger, while the house of Saul grew weaker and weaker.

1Ki 12:21 When Rehoboam arrived in Jerusalem, he mustered the whole house of Judah and the tribe of Benjamin—a hundred and eighty thousand fighting men—to make war against the house of Israel and to regain the kingdom for Rehoboam son of Solomon.   *See also*

2Sa 2:8–17; 15:14; **1Ki** 15:6–7,16; **2Ki** 13:12; 14:9–15

Israel's constant unfaithfulness led to the exile

1Ch 5:25–26 But they [Israel] were unfaithful to the God of their ancestors and prostituted themselves to the gods of the peoples of the land, whom God had destroyed before them. So the God of Israel stirred up the spirit of Pul king of Assyria (that is, Tiglath-Pileser king of Assyria), who took the Reubenites, the Gadites and the half-tribe of Manasseh into exile . . .   *See also* **2Ki** 17:5–8,22–23

Judah's constant unfaithfulness led to the Babylonian captivity

2Ch 36:16–17 But they [Judah] mocked God's messengers, despised his words and scoffed at his prophets until the wrath of the LORD was aroused against his people and there was no remedy. He brought up against them the king of the Babylonians, who killed their young men with the sword in the sanctuary, and spared neither young man nor young woman, the elderly or the aged. God handed all of them over to Nebuchadnezzar.   *See also* **2Ki** 25:1 pp Jer 52:4–5; **2Ki** 25:8–11 pp Jer 52:12–15; **2Ki** 25:21 pp Jer 52:27; **Jer** 1:13–16

warfare, strategies

Scripture describes the strategies employed by Israel in warfare. Although recognising the importance of military preparation, Scripture stresses that Israel's trust is to be in God, rather than military might or prowess.

Preparations for warfare
Holding a council of war

Pr 20:18 Make plans by seeking advice; if you wage war, obtain guidance.   *See also* **Pr** 11:14; 24:6; **Lk** 14:31–32

Assembling an army

2Sa 18:1 David mustered the men who were with him and appointed over them commanders of thousands and commanders of hundreds.
See also **Nu** 1:2–3; **1Sa** 11:6–8; **2Ch** 25:5–6;

26:11–14; **Da** 11:10–13
Reconnaissance
Nu 21:32 After Moses had sent spies to Jazer, the Israelites captured its surrounding settlements and drove out the Amorites who were there. *See also* **Dt** 1:22; **Jos** 2:1; 7:2–3; **Jdg** 7:9–11; 18:2,5–10

Avoiding warfare
Making a treaty
Jos 9:15 Then Joshua made a treaty of peace with them [the Gibeonites] to let them live, and the leaders of the assembly ratified it by oath. *See also* **Ge** 26:28–29; **Jos** 10:1; **1Sa** 11:1; **1Ki** 5:12
Representative combat
1Sa 17:8–10 Goliath stood and shouted to the ranks of Israel, ". . . Choose a man and have him come down to me. If he is able to fight and kill me, we will become your subjects; but if I overcome him and kill him, you will become our subjects and serve us." . . . *See also* **2Sa** 2:12–17

Strategies employed in warfare
Dividing into groups
Jdg 9:43–44 So he [Abimelech] took his troops, divided them into three companies and set an ambush in the fields. When he saw the people coming out of the city, he rose to attack them. Abimelech and the companies with him rushed forward to a position at the entrance to the city gate. Then two companies rushed upon those in the fields and struck them down. *See also* **Ge** 14:14–15; 32:7–8; **Jdg** 7:16–21; **1Sa** 11:11; **2Sa** 18:1–2
Attacking by night
Jdg 7:19 Gideon and the hundred men with him reached the edge of the camp at the beginning of the middle watch, just after they had changed the guard. They blew their trumpets and broke the jars that were in their hands. *See also* **Ge** 14:14–15; **1Sa** 14:36; **Jer** 6:5
Setting an ambush
2Ch 13:13–14 Now Jeroboam had sent troops round to the rear, so that while he was in front of Judah the ambush was behind them. Judah

turned and saw that they were being attacked at both front and rear . . . *See also* **Jos** 8:4–7; **Jdg** 9:34,42–44; 20:29–44
Swiftness of action
Jos 8:19 As soon as he [Joshua] did this [held out his javelin], the men in the ambush rose quickly from their position and rushed forward. They entered the city and captured it and quickly set it on fire. *See also* **Jos** 10:6–9; 11:7; **2Sa** 5:22–25

Trusting in God in warfare
Of greater importance than military might or prowess
Dt 20:1 When you go to war against your enemies and see horses and chariots and an army greater than yours, do not be afraid of them, because the LORD your God, who brought you up out of Egypt, will be with you.
Ps 20:7 Some trust in chariots and some in horses, but we trust in the name of the LORD our God. *See also* **1Sa** 17:45–47; **Ps** 33:16–17; 147:10–11; **Zec** 4:6
Demonstrated by seeking God before a battle
Jdg 1:1 After the death of Joshua, the Israelites asked the LORD, "Who will be the first to go up and fight for us against the Canaanites?" *See also* **Jdg** 20:27–28; **2Sa** 5:18–19,22–25
Strengthened by seeing God fighting for Israel
Ex 14:29–31; **Jos** 10:10–14; **2Ki** 19:35 *See also armies; armour; treaty.*

washing
The physical or ritual cleansing of part or all of a person's body, a person's clothing or certain vessels. Washing can be symbolic of purification from defilement or cleansing from sin. It can also be part of preparation for a special act of religious service.

Washing as the cleansing of the body, clothing or certain vessels
Ex 30:17–21 Then the LORD said to Moses, "Make a bronze basin, with its bronze stand, for washing. Place it between the Tent of Meeting and the altar, and put water in it. Aaron and his

sons are to wash their hands and feet with water from it. Whenever they enter the Tent of Meeting, they shall wash with water so that they will not die. Also, when they approach the altar to minister by presenting an offering made to the LORD by fire, they shall wash their hands and feet so that they will not die. This is to be a lasting ordinance for Aaron and his descendants for the generations to come."

Lev 13:53–54 "But if, when the priest examines it, the mildew has not spread in the clothing, or the woven or knitted material, or the leather article, he shall order that the contaminated article be washed . . ."   *See also* **Ex** 40:30–32; **Lev** 6:27; 14:8–9; 15:2–13; 16:24,26–28; **Nu** 31:24; **2Ch** 4:6 pp 1Ki 7:38; **Jn** 2:6

Jesus Christ taught that inner purity was more important than ritual washing

Mt 15:17–20 ". . . For out of the heart come evil thoughts, murder, adultery, sexual immorality, theft, false testimony, slander. These are what make you 'unclean'; but eating with unwashed hands does not make you 'unclean'." pp **Mk** 7:20–23   *See also* **Mk** 7:1–9 pp Mt 15:1–3; **Mk** 7:14–15 pp Mt 15:10–11; **Lk** 11:37–41

Washing as a symbolic act
Of purification from defilement

Lev 11:24–25 "'. . . Those who pick up one of their [unclean animals'] carcasses must wash their clothes, and they will be unclean till evening.'"   *See also* **Lev** 11:28,40; 13:6,34; 15:4–8; 17:15–16; **Dt** 23:10–11; **2Ki** 5:10

Of cleansing from sin

1Co 6:9–11 Do you not know that the wicked will not inherit the kingdom of God? . . . And that is what some of you were. But you were washed, you were sanctified, you were justified in the name of the Lord Jesus Christ and by the Spirit of our God.

Eph 5:25–27 Husbands, love your wives, just as Christ loved the church and gave himself up for her to make her holy, cleansing her by the washing with water through the word, and to

present her to himself as a radiant church, without stain or wrinkle or any other blemish, but holy and blameless.   *See also* **Ps** 51:2,7; **Isa** 1:16; 4:4; **Jer** 4:14; **Ac** 22:16; **Tit** 3:5; **Heb** 10:22; **Jas** 4:8; **Rev** 7:14; 22:14

Of personal cleansing before a special act of religious service

Lev 16:24 "He [Aaron] shall bathe himself with water in a holy place and put on his regular garments. Then he shall come out and sacrifice the burnt offering for himself and the burnt offering for the people, to make atonement for himself and for the people."   *See also* **Ex** 19:10–11; 29:4; 40:12–13,30–32; **Lev** 8:6; **Nu** 8:6–7,21

Washing one's hands was used as a symbolic declaration of innocence

Dt 21:6–7 Then all the elders of the town nearest the body shall wash their hands over the heifer whose neck was broken in the valley, and they shall declare: "Our hands did not shed this blood, nor did our eyes see it done."   *See also* **Ps** 26:6; 73:13; **Mt** 27:24   *See also clean and unclean; ritual washing; water.*

water

The colourless, odourless liquid that is essential for sustenance of life in human beings and animals. God is described as the spring of living water, being the source of life and salvation to those who come to him.

Water for drinking
For human beings

2Sa 23:15–16 David longed for water and said, "Oh, that someone would get me a drink of water from the well near the gate of Bethlehem!" . . . pp 1Ch 11:17–18   *See also* **Ge** 21:14–19; **Ex** 15:22–27; 17:1–3; **Nu** 20:1–11; **Dt** 2:28; **Jdg** 4:19; 5:25; **1Sa** 30:11–12; **1Ki** 17:10; **2Ki** 6:22; **2Ch** 18:25–26; **Ne** 9:20; **Job** 6:19; **Isa** 33:16; **Da** 1:8–16; **Hos** 2:5; **Mt** 10:42 pp Mk 9:41; **Jn** 4:7; **1Ti** 5:23

For animals

2Ki 3:9 So the king of Israel set out with the king of Judah and the king of Edom. After a roundabout march of seven days, the army had no more water for themselves or for the animals with them.   *See also* **Ge** 24:13–19; 29:1–10; **Ex** 2:15–16; 17:3; **2Ki** 3:17; **Ps** 104:10–11; **Isa** 43:20; **Lk** 13:15

Water as a general descriptive term for liquid
Ex 23:25 "Worship the LORD your God, and his blessing will be on your food and water . . ."
See also **1Sa** 25:11; **1Ki** 13:6–22; 18:4; **Job** 22:7; **Pr** 25:21

Abstention from water during fasting
Dt 9:9 When I [Moses] went up on the mountain to receive the tablets of stone, the tablets of the covenant that the LORD had made with you, I stayed on the mountain forty days and forty nights; I ate no bread and drank no water.   *See also* **Ex** 34:28; **Dt** 9:18; **Ezr** 10:6

Water for washing
For general hygiene
Ge 18:4 "Let a little water be brought, and then you [Abraham's visitors] may all wash your feet and rest under this tree."   *See also* **Ge** 24:32; 43:24; **Lk** 7:44; **Jn** 13:1–17
For ritual cleansing
Lev 17:15 " 'Anyone, whether native-born or alien, who eats anything found dead or torn by wild animals must wash their clothes and bathe with water, and they will be ceremonially unclean till evening; then they will be clean.' "   *See also* **Ex** 30:17–21; **Lev** 1:3–9; 16:20–24; **Nu** 19:7–9; **Jn** 2:6; **Heb** 10:22

Water for cooking
Ex 12:9–10 "Do not eat the meat raw or cooked in water, but roast it over the fire—head, legs and inner parts . . ."   *See also* **Eze** 24:3–5

Rainwater
Jdg 5:4 "O LORD, when you went out from Seir, when you marched from the land of Edom, the earth shook, the heavens poured, the clouds poured down water."   *See also* **Ge** 7:11–12; **Job** 5:10; 37:13; 38:25–28,37; **Ps** 77:17; **Ecc** 11:3; **Hos** 6:3

Sources and stores of water
Wells
Ge 26:19–20 Isaac's servants dug in the valley and discovered a well of fresh water there . . .   *See also* **Ge** 21:19; 24:11; **Isa** 37:25; **Jn** 4:6
Springs
Jas 3:11–12 Can both fresh water and salt water flow from the same spring? My brothers and sisters, can a fig-tree bear olives, or a grapevine bear figs? Neither can a salt spring produce fresh water.   *See also* **Jos** 15:15–19 pp Jdg 1:11–15; **Rev** 8:10–11; 14:7; 16:4
Cisterns
Jer 2:13 "My [the LORD's] people have committed two sins: They have forsaken me, the spring of living water, and have dug their own cisterns, broken cisterns that cannot hold water."   *See also* **Lev** 11:36; **2Ki** 18:31 pp Isa 36:16; **Pr** 5:15–16; **Jer** 14:3; 38:6

Abundance of water as a sign of blessing
Dt 8:7 For the LORD your God is bringing you [Israel] into a good land—a land with streams and pools of water, with springs flowing in the valleys and hills;   *See also* **Nu** 24:7; **Dt** 10:7; **Ps** 1:1–3; **Jer** 17:7–8; **Eze** 17:5–6; 19:10–11

Baptism in water
Mt 3:11 "I [John] baptise you with water for repentance. But after me will come one who is more powerful than I, whose sandals I am not fit to carry. He will baptise you with the Holy Spirit and with fire." pp Mk 1:8 pp Lk 3:16   *See also* **Mt** 3:13–17 pp Mk 1:9–11 pp Lk 3:21–22 pp Jn 1:31–34; **Jn** 1:26–27; 3:23; **Ac** 1:5; 8:36–39; 10:47; 11:16; **1Pe** 3:20–22

Living water
Jer 17:13 O LORD, the hope of Israel, all who forsake you will be put to shame. Those who turn away from you will be written in the dust because they have forsaken the LORD, the spring of living water.   *See also* **Zec** 14:8–9; **Jn** 4:4–26; 7:37–39; **Rev** 7:13–17; 21:6–8; 22:1–2,17

Metaphorical references to water

As a symbol of affliction 2Sa 22:17; **Ps** 69:1; **Isa** 30:20; 43:2

As a symbol of salvation Isa 12:3; 49:10; 55:1; **Eze** 36:25; **Jn** 7:38

As a symbol of life Jn 4:14; 7:37–39; **Rev** 21:6; 22:17

Other metaphorical references SS 4:15; **Isa** 30:20; 35:6; 44:12; **Jer** 9:1; **Eph** 5:25–26; **2Pe** 2:17   *See also rain; washing; wells.*

---

wave offering

A gift specially dedicated to God. The term itself may not be intended to convey a particular action.

The wave offering was part of every fellowship offering

Lev 7:34 " 'From the fellowship offerings of the Israelites, I have taken the breast that is waved and the thigh that is presented and have given them to Aaron the priest and his sons as their regular share from the Israelites.' "   *See also* **Lev** 7:28–32; 9:21

The wave offering was eaten by the priests

Ex 29:26–28; **Lev** 10:15; **Nu** 18:11,18

Occasions for making a wave offering

As a cereal offering when priests were consecrated Ex 29:23–24; **Lev** 8:27–29

As a guilt offering sacrificed at a ceremonial cleansing Lev 14:12,21,24

As part of the ritual when a woman was accused of adultery Nu 5:25

When celebrating harvest Lev 23:10–11

At the Feast of Weeks: **Lev** 23:15–17,20

When presenting a gift to God

Materials given for constructing the tabernacle: **Ex** 35:22; 38:24,29

When dedicating the Levites to God

Nu 8:11 "Aaron is to present the Levites before the LORD as a wave offering from the Israelites, so that they may be ready to do the work of the LORD."   *See also* **Nu** 8:13,15,21   *See also Feast of Firstfruits; Feast of Weeks; fellowship offering; firstfruits; guilt offering; priesthood.*

weapons

Instruments of warfare. God's people are to trust in him rather than in weapons. Scripture speaks of a day when weapons will become instruments of peace. The term is also used metaphorically.

Weapons of warfare

1Ch 12:23 These are the numbers of the men armed for battle who came to David at Hebron . . .

1Ch 12:33 from Zebulun, experienced soldiers prepared for battle with every type of weapon, to help David with undivided loyalty—50,000;

Ne 4:16–18 From that day on, half of my men did the work, while the other half were equipped with spears, shields, bows and armour. The officers posted themselves behind all the people of Judah who were building the wall. Those who carried materials did their work with one hand and held a weapon in the other, and each of the builders wore his sword at his side as he worked . . .   *See also* **Ge** 49:5; **1Sa** 8:12; 17:45,54; 21:8; **2Sa** 1:27; **2Ki** 11:8 pp 2Ch 23:7; **2Ki** 11:11 pp 2Ch 23:10; **1Ch** 12:34–37; **2Ch** 32:5; **Ne** 4:23; **Eze** 26:7–11; 32:27; **Jn** 18:3

Trust in God rather than in weapons

Ps 20:7–8 Some trust in chariots and some in horses, but we trust in the name of the LORD our God. They are brought to their knees and fall, but we rise up and stand firm.

Isa 31:1 Woe to those who go down to Egypt for help, who rely on horses, who trust in the multitude of their chariots and in the great strength of their horsemen, but do not look to the Holy One of Israel, or seek help from the LORD.   *See also* **Dt** 1:41–44; 20:1; **1Sa** 17:45–47; **2Ch** 20:20–24; 32:7–8; **Ps** 33:16–19; 76:3; 147:10–11; **Pr** 21:31; **Ecc** 9:18; **Isa** 22:8–11; 54:16–17; **Zec** 4:6

A day when weapons of war will become instruments of peace

Isa 2:4 . . . They [the nations] will beat their swords into ploughshares and their spears into pruning hooks. Nation will not take up sword against nation, nor will they train for war any more. pp Mic 4:3   *See also* **Ps** 46:9; **Isa** 9:5; **Eze** 39:7–10; **Hos** 2:18; **Zec** 9:10

Weapons used metaphorically by God

Isa 59:15–18 . . . The Lord looked and was displeased that there was no justice. He saw that there was no-one, he was appalled that there was no-one to intervene; so his own arm worked salvation for him, and his own righteousness sustained him. He put on righteousness as his breastplate, and the helmet of salvation on his head; he put on the garments of vengeance and wrapped himself in zeal as in a cloak. According to what they have done, so will he repay wrath to his enemies and retribution to his foes; he will repay the islands their due.

Jer 50:25 "The Lord has opened his arsenal and brought out the weapons of his wrath, for the Sovereign Lord Almighty has work to do in the land of the Babylonians."   *See also* **Ps** 7:11–13; **Isa** 13:5; **Jer** 51:20; **Eze** 9:1–8

Weapons used metaphorically by Christians

2Co 10:4 The weapons we fight with are not the weapons of the world. On the contrary, they have divine power to demolish strongholds.

Eph 6:11–17 Put on the full armour of God so that you can take your stand against the devil's schemes . . .   *See also* **Ro** 13:12; **2Co** 6:7; **1Th** 5:8   *See also armour; stones.*

---

weather

Patterns of climatic conditions, such as wind and rain, which were of major importance to the rural economies of the Near East. Scripture stresses the sovereignty of God over the weather and sees it as a possible means of judgment or reward.

---

weather, God's judgment

The weather can be seen as an expression of God's judgment and grace, as well as providing insights concerning human nature.

The weather as an expression of God's judgment
Judgment in battle

Jos 10:11 As they [Israel's enemies] fled before Israel on the road down from Beth Horon to Azekah, the Lord hurled large hailstones down on them from the sky, and more of them died from the hailstones than were killed by the swords of the Israelites.   *See also* **2Sa** 22:10–15; **Isa** 30:30; **Eze** 38:22

Judgment in general

1Ki 17:1 Now Elijah the Tishbite, from Tishbe in Gilead, said to Ahab, "As the Lord, the God of Israel, lives, whom I serve, there will be neither dew nor rain in the next few years except at my word."

Hag 1:10–11 "Therefore, because of you the heavens have withheld their dew and the earth its crops. I [the Lord Almighty] called for a drought on the fields and the mountains, on the grain, the new wine, the oil and whatever the ground produces, on people and animals, and on the labour of your hands."   *See also* **Ge** 7:11–12; **Ex** 9:22–26; **Lev** 26:18–19; **Dt** 11:17; 28:22–24; **Jer** 3:3; 14:1–6; **Eze** 22:24; **Am** 4:7; **Zec** 14:17–19

The weather as a source of spiritual insight
About the shortness of life

Jas 4:14 Why, you do not even know what will happen tomorrow. What is your life? You are a mist that appears for a little while and then vanishes.   *See also* **Job** 7:9; 24:19; 30:15; **Hos** 13:3; **Jas** 1:11

About empty profession

Hos 6:4 "What can I do with you, Ephraim? What can I do with you, Judah? Your love is like the morning mist, like the early dew that disappears."   *See also* **Job** 6:15–17; **Pr** 25:14; **2Pe** 2:17

About God's judgment

Jer 23:19 See, the storm of the Lord will burst out in wrath, a whirlwind swirling down on the heads of the wicked.   *See also* **Jer** 4:11; **Hos** 8:7

About God's salvation
Isa 55:10–11 "As the rain and the snow come down from heaven, and do not return to it without watering the earth and making it bud and flourish, so that it yields seed for the sower and bread for the eater, so is my word that goes out from my mouth: It will not return to me empty, but will accomplish what I desire and achieve the purpose for which I sent it." *See also* **Isa** 44:22; 45:8

About righteous rule
2Sa 23:3–4 "The God of Israel spoke, the Rock of Israel said to me [David]: 'When one rules over people in righteousness, when he rules in the fear of God, he is like the light of morning at sunrise on a cloudless morning, like the brightness after rain that brings the grass from the earth.'" *See also* **Ps** 72:6; **Pr** 16:15; **Isa** 25:4–5

About wholesome teaching
Dt 32:2 Let my [Moses'] teaching fall like rain and my words descend like dew, like showers on new grass, like abundant rain on tender plants. *See also* **Job** 29:23

About the troubles of life **Mt** 7:24–27

About the signs of the times
Mt 16:2–3 He [Jesus] replied, "When evening comes, you say, 'It will be fair weather, for the sky is red,' and in the morning, 'Today it will be stormy, for the sky is red and overcast.' You know how to interpret the appearance of the sky, but you cannot interpret the signs of the times." *See also* **Lk** 12:54–56

weather, God's sovereignty

The weather is under the control of God, who alone is able to direct it.

The weather is under God's control
Job 28:25–27 "When he [God] established the force of the wind and measured out the waters, when he made a decree for the rain and a path for the thunderstorm, then he looked at wisdom and appraised it; he confirmed it and tested it."

Mt 8:26–27 He [Jesus] replied, "You of little faith, why are you so afraid?" Then he got up

and rebuked the winds and the waves, and it was completely calm. The disciples were amazed and asked, "What kind of man is this? Even the winds and the waves obey him!" pp Mk 4:39–41 pp Lk 8:24–25 *See also* **Job** 5:10; 26:8–9,13; 37:1–18; **Ps** 135:7; 147:8,16–18; 148:8; **Jer** 10:13

God alone understands the mysteries of the weather
Pr 3:19–20 By wisdom the LORD laid the earth's foundations, by understanding he set the heavens in place; by his knowledge the deeps were divided, and the clouds let drop the dew.
Jn 3:8 "The wind blows wherever it pleases. You hear its sound, but you cannot tell where it comes from or where it is going. So it is with everyone born of the Spirit." *See also* **Job** 36:26–33; 38:22–30,34–35,37; **Ecc** 11:3–5

Israel's economy was dependent on the weather
Lev 26:4 "'I [the LORD] will send you rain in its season, and the ground will yield its crops and the trees of the field their fruit.'" *See also* **Dt** 11:10–15; 28:12; **Jer** 5:24; **Hos** 6:3

The weather demonstrates God's goodness and mercy
Ge 8:22 "As long as the earth endures, seedtime and harvest, cold and heat, summer and winter, day and night will never cease."
Mt 5:45 ". . . He [your Father in heaven] causes his sun to rise on the evil and the good, and sends rain on the righteous and the unrighteous."
Ac 14:17 "Yet he [God] has not left himself without testimony: He has shown kindness by giving you rain from heaven and crops in their seasons; he provides you with plenty of food and fills your hearts with joy." *See also* **Ge** 9:14–16; **Dt** 33:13–14; **Ps** 68:7–9; **Isa** 30:23; 49:10; **Joel** 2:23; **Zec** 10:1

The weather as a demonstration of God's direct intervention
Jnh 1:4 Then the LORD sent a great wind on the

sea, and such a violent storm arose that the ship threatened to break up.   *See also* **Ex** 14:21; **Nu** 11:31; **Ps** 78:26; **Jnh** 4:8

The weather as an answer to prayer
Jas 5:17–18 Elijah was human just as we are. He prayed earnestly that it would not rain, and it did not rain on the land for three and a half years. Again he prayed, and the heavens gave rain, and the earth produced its crops.   *See also* **1Sa** 12:17–18; **1Ki** 8:35–36 pp 2Ch 6:26–27; **1Ki** 18:41–44

The weather can cause suffering
Ge 31:40 "This was my [Jacob's] situation: The heat consumed me in the daytime and the cold at night, and sleep fled from my eyes."
Ac 28:2 The islanders showed us [Paul and his companions] unusual kindness. They built a fire and welcomed us all because it was raining and cold.   *See also* **Ezr** 10:9; **Job** 1:16,18–19; **Mt** 20:12; **Jn** 18:18; **Ac** 27:15   *See also rain.*

wedding
The public acknowledgment and celebration of a couple's marriage. The wedding followed betrothal and was a preliminary to sexual union. The occasion was marked by feasting, singing and rejoicing. The bride wore a wedding dress, jewellery and ornaments and both she and the groom were waited on by attendants.

Wedding garments
The bride's wedding dress
Ps 45:13 All glorious is the princess within ˌher chamberˌ; her gown is interwoven with gold. *See also* **Ge** 24:65; **Eze** 16:10; **Rev** 19:7–8; 21:2
The bride's jewellery and ornaments
Isa 49:18 "Lift up your eyes and look around; all your children gather and come to you. As surely as I live," declares the Lᴏʀᴅ, "you [Zion] will wear them all as ornaments; you will put them on, like a bride."   *See also* **Isa** 61:10; **Jer** 2:32; **Eze** 16:11–12

Wedding festivities
Weddings were occasions for rejoicing
Jer 33:11 " 'the sounds of joy and gladness, the voices of bride and bridegroom, and the voices of those who bring thank-offerings to the house of the Lᴏʀᴅ . . .' "
Wedding festivities might last for a week or two: **Ge** 29:27–28; **Jdg** 14:12
SS 3:11; **Isa** 62:5; **Jer** 7:34
Wedding songs Ps 45 Title; 78:63
The wedding banquet
Jdg 14:10 Now his father went down to see the woman. And Samson made a feast there, as was customary for bridegrooms.   *See also* **Ge** 29:21–22; **Mt** 22:2; **Jn** 2:3–10; **Rev** 19:9

Guests and attendants at weddings
Wedding guests
Jn 2:1–2 On the third day a wedding took place at Cana in Galilee. Jesus' mother was there, and Jesus and his disciples had also been invited to the wedding.   *See also* **Mt** 22:3–10,11–12; **Lk** 14:8–10
Attendants on the groom
Jn 3:29 "The bride belongs to the bridegroom. The friend who attends the bridegroom waits and listens for him, and is full of joy when he hears the bridegroom's voice . . ."   *See also* **Jdg** 14:11,20; **Mt** 9:15 pp Mk 2:19 pp Lk 5:34
Bridesmaids
Ps 45:14 In embroidered garments she [the bride] is led to the king; her virgin companions follow her and are brought to you.   *See also* **Mt** 25:1–10

Wedding gifts
1Ki 9:16 (Pharaoh king of Egypt had attacked and captured Gezer. He had set it on fire. He killed its Canaanite inhabitants, and then gave it as a wedding gift to his daughter, Solomon's wife.)   *See also* **Ge** 24:59; 29:24,29; **Jdg** 1:14–15

Elements in the wedding ceremony
Covering the bride
Sometimes the groom would cover the bride with his cloak as a symbol of protection: **Ru** 3:9; **Eze** 16:8

A covenanted commitment Pr 2:17; **Mal** 2:14

Blessing the couple Ge 24:60; **Ru** 4:11

Consummating the marriage

Joel 2:16 . . . Let the bridegroom leave his room and the bride her chamber.   *See also* **Ge** 29:23; **Ps** 19:5   *See also banquets; betrothal; bride; bridegroom; clothing; marriage; ornaments.*

---

weights

Ancient weights were usually made of stone or metal, often inscribed with their weight and standard, the shekel being the basic weight of all Semitic nations. Weights of gold and silver served as currency, since coinage was not invented until the seventh century B.C. Weights are given in ascending order, with their approximate imperial and metric equivalents.

Gerah (1/20 shekel): about 1/50 ounce (about 0.6 gram)

Lev 27:25 " 'Every value is to be set according to the sanctuary shekel, twenty gerahs to the shekel.' "   *See also* **Ex** 30:13; **Nu** 3:47; 18:16; **Eze** 45:12

Beka (10 gerahs): about 1/5 ounce (about 5.8 grams)

2Ch 9:15–16 King Solomon made two hundred large shields of hammered gold; six hundred bekas of hammered gold went into each shield. He also made three hundred small shields of hammered gold, with three hundred bekas of gold in each shield . . . pp **1Ki** 10:16–17   *See also* **Ge** 24:22; **Ex** 38:25–26

Pim (2/3 shekel): about 1/4 ounce (about 7.7 grams)

1Sa 13:21 The price was two thirds of a shekel for sharpening ploughshares and mattocks, and a third of a shekel for sharpening forks and axes and for repointing goads.   *The Hebrew word translated "two thirds of a shekel" is "pim", its only mention in Scripture.*

Shekel (2 bekas): about 2/5 ounce (about 11.5 grams)

The shekel in relation to other weights

Eze 45:12 " 'The shekel is to consist of twenty gerahs. Twenty shekels plus twenty-five shekels plus fifteen shekels equal one mina.' "

The shekel as a weight of metal objects

1Sa 17:5 He [Goliath] had a bronze helmet on his head and wore a coat of scale armour of bronze weighing five thousand shekels;   *See also* **1Sa** 17:7; **2Sa** 21:16

The shekel as a weight of food

Eze 4:10 "Weigh out twenty shekels of food to eat each day and eat it at set times."

The shekel as a weight of gold or silver objects

2Ch 3:9 The gold nails weighed fifty shekels . . .   *See also* **Ge** 24:22; **Nu** 7:13–14; **Jdg** 8:26

The shekel as a weight of gold or silver

Ge 23:14–16 . . . Abraham agreed to Ephron's terms and weighed out for him the price he had named in the hearing of the Hittites: four hundred shekels of silver, according to the weight current among the merchants.   *See also* **Ge** 37:28; **Dt** 22:28–29; **Jos** 7:20–21; **Jdg** 17:1–4; **2Sa** 18:11–12; **1Ki** 10:29 pp 2Ch 1:17; **2Ki** 5:4–5; **Ne** 5:15; **Jer** 32:9; **Da** 5:25–27   *"Tekel" can mean "weighed" or "shekel".*

The royal shekel

2Sa 14:26 Whenever he [Absalom] cut the hair of his head—he used to cut his hair from time to time when it became too heavy for him—he would weigh it, and its weight was two hundred shekels by the royal standard.

The sanctuary shekel

Nu 18:15–16 "The first offspring of every womb, both human and animal, that is offered to the Lᴏʀᴅ is yours. But you must redeem every firstborn son and every firstborn male of unclean animals. When they are a month old, you must redeem them at the redemption price set at five shekels of silver, according to the sanctuary shekel, which weighs twenty gerahs."   *See also* **Ex** 30:13–15,22–25; 38:24–26; **Lev** 5:15; 27:1–7; **Nu** 3:46–50

Mina (50 shekels): about 1 1/4 pounds (about 0.6 kilogram)
Eze 45:12 " 'The shekel is to consist of twenty gerahs. Twenty shekels plus twenty-five shekels plus fifteen shekels equal one mina.' " *See also* **1Ki** 10:17; **Ezr** 2:69; **Ne** 7:71–72; **Da** 5:25–26 *"Mene" can mean both "numbered" and "mina";* **Lk** *19:11–27 By NT times the mina had become coinage rather than simply a weight of silver, and was worth about three months' wages.*

Talent (3,000 shekels, 60 minas): about 75 pounds (about 34 kilograms)
1Ch 29:7 They gave towards the work on the temple of God five thousand talents and ten thousand darics of gold, ten thousand talents of silver, eighteen thousand talents of bronze and a hundred thousand talents of iron. *See also* **Ex** 25:39; **2Sa** 12:30 pp 1Ch 20:2; **1Ki** 10:14 pp 2Ch 9:13; **1Ki** 16:24; **2Ki** 18:14; **Ezr** 8:26; **Est** 3:9; **Mt** 18:24–25 *By NT times the talent had become coinage, and ten thousand talents would have been the equivalent of millions of pounds sterling;* **Mt** 25:14–30

Other minor weights
Kesitah Ge 33:19 *The price in the original Hebrew is "one hundred kesitahs", a unit of unknown weight and value.*
Litra
The word translated "pint" in Jn 12:3 and "pound" in 19:39 is "litra", a loanword from the Latin "libra", meaning "pound" and weighing 12 ounces (327 grams): **Jn** 12:3; 19:39
Peres Da 5:28 *"Peres" means "division" and denotes a half-shekel. See also coinage; metals; money.*

weights and measures, laws
God expects his people to use accurate weights and measures, and to use just balances. This is underlined in the Law, the Prophets and the wisdom literature.

The law demanded honesty in using weights and measures
Lev 19:35–36 " 'Do not use dishonest standards when measuring length, weight or quantity. Use honest scales and honest weights, an honest ephah and an honest hin. I am the LORD your God, who brought you out of Egypt.' " *See also* **Dt** 25:13–16

The prophets called for the right use of weights and measures
A call for honesty
Eze 45:9–10 " 'This is what the Sovereign LORD says: You have gone far enough, O princes of Israel! Give up your violence and oppression and do what is just and right. Stop dispossessing my people, declares the Sovereign LORD. You are to use accurate scales, an accurate ephah and an accurate bath.' "
Condemnation of dishonesty
Am 8:4–6 Hear this, you who trample the needy and do away with the poor of the land, saying, "When will the New Moon be over that we may sell grain, and the Sabbath be ended that we may market wheat?"—skimping the measure, boosting the price and cheating with dishonest scales, buying the poor with silver and the needy for a pair of sandals, selling even the sweepings with the wheat. *See also* **Hos** 12:7–8; **Mic** 6:10–14

Instruction from Proverbs on weights and measures
Pr 20:10 Differing weights and differing measures—the LORD detests them both. *See also* **Pr** 11:1; 16:11; 20:23; 22:28 *See also buying and selling; measures, dry; scales and balances.*

wells
Artificial openings to tap underground water supplies. They were very important for life in a settled urban society and this is reflected in their symbolical use in Scripture.

The importance of wells in urban life
Ne 9:25 "They [the Israelites] captured fortified cities and fertile land; they took possession of houses filled with all kinds of good things, wells already dug, vineyards, olive groves and fruit trees in abundance. They ate to the full and were well-

nourished; they revelled in your great
goodness."   *See also* **Dt** 6:10–11

Women drew water for domestic use
Ge 24:11–20 He [Abraham's servant] made
the camels kneel down near the well outside the
town; it was towards evening, the time the
women go out to draw water . . .   *See also*
1Sa 9:11; **Jn** 4:7–9

Livestock were watered at wells
Ge 29:2–3 There he saw a well in the field,
with three flocks of sheep lying near it because
the flocks were watered from that well. The stone
over the mouth of the well was large. When all
the flocks were gathered there, the shepherds
would roll the stone away from the well's mouth
and water the sheep. Then they would return the
stone to its place over the mouth of the well.
See also **Ge** 29:7–10; **Ex** 2:15–17

Wells were sometimes a source of contention
Ge 21:25 Then Abraham complained to
Abimelech about a well of water that Abimelech's
servants had seized.   *See also* **Ge** 26:12–22; **Nu**
20:17; 21:22

Wells as landmarks
Ge 16:7 The angel of the Lord found Hagar
near a spring in the desert; it was the spring that
is beside the road to Shur.   *See also* **Ge** 16:14;
21:31   *"Beersheba" means either "well of seven" or*
"well of the oath"; **Ge** 26:20–22; **Jn** 4:6

Figurative use of wells
Associated with God and his goodness
Isa 12:3 With joy you will draw water from the
wells of salvation.
Jer 17:13 O Lord, the hope of Israel, all who
forsake you will be put to shame. Those who turn
away from you will be written in the dust because
they have forsaken the Lord, the spring of living
water.   *See also* **Jer** 2:13; **Jn** 4:14; **Rev** 7:17
Associated with human love Pr 5:15
In warnings against and judgment of sin
Jer 6:7 "As a well pours out its water, so she

[Jerusalem] pours out her wickedness . . ."
See also **Pr** 23:27; **Jer** 51:36   *See also water.*

---

widows

God's tender concern for bereaved wives is
declared throughout the whole of Scripture. He
defends their rights and expects his people to do
the same.

God is the protector of widows
Ps 68:5 A father to the fatherless, a defender
of widows, is God in his holy dwelling.   *See also*
Dt 10:18; **Ps** 146:9; **Pr** 15:25; **Jer** 49:11

Jesus Christ's concern for widows
Mk 12:41–44 pp Lk 21:1–4; **Lk** 7:11–15;
18:1–5

Widows are to be treated justly
Dt 27:19 "Cursed is anyone who withholds
justice from the alien, the fatherless or the
widow." . . .   *See also* **Ex** 22:22–24; **Job**
24:21–22; **Ps** 94:6; **Isa** 10:1–4; **Jer** 22:3–5; **Eze**
22:25

Widows are not to be exploited
Ex 22:22 "Do not take advantage of a widow
or an orphan."   *See also* **Isa** 10:1–2; **Eze** 22:7;
Mal 3:5; **Mk** 12:38–40 pp Lk 20:45–47

The law requires God's people to provide for widows
Dt 24:19 When you are harvesting in your field
and you overlook a sheaf, do not go back to get
it. Leave it for the alien, the fatherless and the
widow . . .   *See also* **Dt** 14:28–29; 16:11;
24:17,20–21; 26:12; **Isa** 1:17

The Christian community are to care for widows
1Ti 5:3 Give proper recognition to those widows
who are really in need.   *See also* **1Ti** 5:4–16;
1Co 7:8–9; **Jas** 1:27

Examples of widows and their treatment
Dt 16:14; **Ru** 1:16–17; **1Ki** 17:13–14; **Job** 24:3; 29:13; **Lk** 2:36–38; 4:25–26; 7:11–17; **Ac** 6:1; 9:36–41

Women widowed because of God's judgment
Ex 22:22–24 ". . . My anger will be aroused, and I will kill you with the sword; your wives will become widows and your children fatherless." *See also* **Ps** 109:9; **Isa** 9:17; **Jer** 15:8; **La** 5:3

Laws governing the remarriage of widows
The people generally
Dt 25:5–10 If brothers are living together and one of them dies without a son, his widow must not marry outside the family. Her husband's brother shall take her and marry her and fulfil the duty of a brother-in-law to her . . . *See also* **Ge** 38:8; **Ru** 3:12; 4:10; **Mk** 12:19 pp Lk 20:28
The priests
Lev 21:13–14 " 'The woman he [the high priest] marries must be a virgin. He must not marry a widow . . .' " *See also* **Eze** 44:22

Widowhood as the personification of a city
La 1:1 How deserted lies the city, once so full of people! How like a widow is she, who once was great among the nations! . . . *See also* **Isa** 54:4–5; **Rev** 18:7 *See also justice; marriage, restrictions; mourning; poverty; queen; wife.*

---

wife
The female partner in a marriage relationship. The origin of this God-ordained institution is traced back in the Bible to the Garden of Eden. Scripture stresses that marriage is a God-ordained institution, within which the husband should love and care for his wife, just as the wife should obey, honour and care for her husband. A good wife is portrayed as a great blessing, but a bad wife influences her husband for evil. In the OT, Israel is sometimes portrayed as God's wife; in the NT, the church is described as Christ's bride.

God's pattern for marriage
Husband and wife are one flesh
Ge 1:27 So God created human beings in his own image, in the image of God he created them; male and female he created them. *See also* **Ge** 2:23–24; **Mal** 2:15; **Mt** 19:4–6 pp Mk 10:6–9
The wife as helper and companion
Ge 2:18 The LORD God said, "It is not good for the man to be alone. I will make a helper suitable for him." *See also* **Ge** 2:20–22
The husband is head of the wife
Eph 5:23 For the husband is the head of the wife as Christ is the head of the church, his body, of which he is the Saviour. *See also* **1Co** 11:3
The wife is the weaker partner
1Pe 3:7 Husbands, in the same way be considerate as you live with your wives, and treat them with respect as the weaker partner and as heirs with you of the gracious gift of life, so that nothing will hinder your prayers. *See also* **Ge** 3:16

The Israelites were forbidden to take foreign wives
Dt 7:3–4 Do not intermarry with them [foreigners]. Do not give your daughters to their sons or take their daughters for your sons, for they will turn your children away from following me to serve other gods, and the LORD's anger will burn against you and will quickly destroy you. *See also* **Ex** 34:16; **Jos** 23:12–13

Duties of a wife
To submit to and respect her husband
Col 3:18 Wives, submit to your husbands, as is fitting in the Lord. *See also* **Eph** 5:22–24,33; **1Pe** 3:1–6
To care for her husband and household
Pr 31:10–31 . . . Her husband has full confidence in her and lacks nothing of value . . . She [the wife of noble character] watches over the affairs of her household and does not eat the bread of idleness . . . *See also* **Tit** 2:4–5
To be faithful to her husband
Ex 20:14 "You shall not commit adultery." pp Dt 5:18 *See also* **Nu** 5:11–31; **Pr** 23:27;

Mt 14:3–4 pp Mk 6:17–18; **Mk** 10:12; **Lk** 3:19

Advice on widows remarrying
1Co 7:39–40 A woman is bound to her husband as long as he lives. But if her husband dies, she is free to marry anyone she wishes, but he must belong to the Lord . . . *See also* **1Co** 7:8–9

Childless wives
Ge 25:21 Isaac prayed to the Lord on behalf of his wife, because she was barren. The Lord answered his prayer, and his wife Rebekah became pregnant. *See also* **Ge** 18:9–15; **Jdg** 13:2–5; **1Sa** 1:9–20; **Lk** 1:5–25

Good wives
Pr 31:10–31 A wife of noble character who can find? She is worth far more than rubies. Her husband has full confidence in her and lacks nothing of value. She brings him good, not harm, all the days of her life . . . *See also* **1Sa** 19:11–17; 25:14–35; **Pr** 12:4; 18:22; 19:14; **Tit** 2:3–5; **1Pe** 3:1–6

Wives giving good counsel
Mt 27:19 While Pilate was sitting on the judge's seat, his wife sent him this message: "Don't have anything to do with that innocent man, for I have suffered a great deal today in a dream because of him." *See also* **Jdg** 13:22–23; **Da** 5:10–12

Bad wives
Pr 12:4 A wife of noble character is her husband's crown, but a disgraceful wife is like decay in his bones. *See also* **Pr** 19:13; 21:19; 25:24

Wives influencing their husbands for evil
Ge 3:8–12 . . . The man said, "The woman you put here with me—she gave me some fruit from the tree, and I ate it." *See also* **1Ki** 11:3–4; 21:20–26; **Est** 5:9–14; **Job** 2:9

Israel as the wife of God
Jer 3:20 "But like a woman unfaithful to her husband, so you have been unfaithful to me, O house of Israel," declares the Lord.
Eze 16:8 " 'Later I [the Lord] passed by, and when I looked at you [Israel] and saw that you were old enough for love, I spread the corner of my garment over you and covered your nakedness. I gave you my solemn oath and entered into a covenant with you, declares the Sovereign Lord, and you became mine.' "
See also **Isa** 62:5; **Jer** 2:2; **Eze** 16:32; **Hos** 1:2; 2:2

The church as the bride of Christ
Rev 21:2 I [John] saw the Holy City, the new Jerusalem, coming down out of heaven from God, prepared as a bride beautifully dressed for her husband. *See also* **Eph** 5:25–27; **Rev** 19:7
See also bride; divorce; husband; marriage; widows.

---

wine
Drink made from fermented grape juice, often drunk instead of water in biblical times. Scripture recognises the richness of wine and its value in bringing joy to people; however, it condemns the excessive drinking of wine, and recommends total abstinence in some situations.

Offerings of wine
Nu 15:5 " 'With each lamb for the burnt offering or the sacrifice, prepare a quarter of a hin of wine as a drink offering.' " *See also* **Ex** 29:40; **Lev** 23:12–13; **Nu** 28:14; **Dt** 32:37–38; **1Sa** 1:24; **Ezr** 6:8–10

Tithes and firstfruits of wine
Ne 13:12 All Judah brought the tithes of grain, new wine and oil into the storerooms. *See also* **Nu** 18:11–12; **Dt** 12:17; 14:23–26; 18:4–5; **2Ch** 31:4–5

Wine as a sign of blessing
Ge 27:28 "May God give you [Jacob] of heaven's dew and of earth's richness—an abundance of grain and new wine." *See also*

Dt 7:13; 11:13–14; 33:28; **2Ki** 18:31–32; **1Ch** 12:40; **Ps** 4:7; **Pr** 3:9–10; **Jer** 31:12; **Joel** 2:18–24; 3:18; **Am** 9:13–14

Lack of wine as a sign of God's displeasure

Jer 48:33 "Joy and gladness are gone from the orchards and fields of Moab. I [the LORD] have stopped the flow of wine from the presses; no-one treads them with shouts of joy. Although there are shouts, they are not shouts of joy." *See also* **Dt** 28:38–51; **Isa** 24:7–9; **Joel** 1:10; **Hag** 2:14–16

Wine as an alternative to water

1Ti 5:23 Stop drinking only water, and use a little wine because of your [Timothy's] stomach and your frequent illnesses. *See also* **Ge** 14:17–18; **Jdg** 19:19; **La** 2:12; **Mt** 27:48 pp Mk 15:36 pp Lk 23:36 pp Jn 19:28–29

Wine with meals

Ge 27:25 Then he [Isaac] said, "My son, bring me some of your game to eat, so that I may give me my blessing." Jacob brought it to him and he ate; and he brought some wine and he drank. *See also* **Ru** 2:14; **Job** 1:18–19; **Pr** 9:1–6; **Isa** 22:13

The pleasant taste and effects of wine

Isa 25:6 On this mountain the LORD Almighty will prepare a feast of rich food for all peoples, a banquet of aged wine—the best of meats and the finest of wines. *See also* **Jdg** 9:12–13; **Ps** 104:14–15; **Ecc** 9:7; 10:19; **SS** 1:2–4; 4:10; 7:8–9

The dangers of drinking wine

Pr 20:1 Wine is a mocker and beer a brawler; whoever is led astray by them is not wise. *See also* **Ge** 9:20–27; 19:30–38; **1Sa** 1:13–15; **2Sa** 13:28; **Est** 1:10–12; **Isa** 28:1,7; **Hos** 7:3–5; **Joel** 1:5; **Na** 1:9–10; **Ac** 2:1–21; **Eph** 5:18

The irresponsibility of wine drinkers

Pr 21:17 Whoever loves pleasure will become poor; whoever loves wine and oil will never be rich. *See also* **Pr** 23:19–21,29–35; 31:4–7;

Ecc 2:3; **Isa** 5:11–12,22–23; 22:13; 56:12; **Mic** 2:11

Abstinence from wine

Lev 10:9 "You [Aaron] and your sons are not to drink wine or other fermented drink whenever you go into the Tent of Meeting, or you will die. This is a lasting ordinance for the generations to come." *See also* **Nu** 6:1–21; **Jdg** 13:2–7; **Jer** 35:1–19; **Eze** 44:21; **Da** 1:3–16; 10:1–3; **Am** 2:11–12; **Lk** 1:11–17; 7:33

Stores of wine

2Ch 32:28 He [Hezekiah] also made buildings to store the harvest of grain, new wine and oil; and he made stalls for various kinds of cattle, and pens for the flocks. *See also* **1Ch** 9:29; 27:27; **2Ch** 11:11–12; **Ne** 10:37–39

Wine stewards

Est 1:7–8 Wine was served in goblets of gold, each one different from the other, and the royal wine was abundant, in keeping with the king's liberality. By the king's command each guest was allowed to drink in his own way, for the king instructed all the wine stewards to serve each man what he wished. *See also* **Ge** 40:1–13; **Ne** 1:11—2:1

Trade in wine

Joel 3:3 "They cast lots for my [the LORD's] people and traded boys for prostitutes; they sold girls for wine that they might drink." *See also* **Rev** 18:11–13

Jesus Christ's miracle of water turned into wine

Jn 2:1–11

Drugged wine

Mt 27:34 There they offered Jesus wine to drink, mixed with gall; but after tasting it, he refused to drink it. pp Mk 15:23

Metaphorical use of wine

Ps 75:8 In the hand of the LORD is a cup full of foaming wine mixed with spices; he pours it out, and all the wicked of the earth drink it down to its very dregs.   *See also* **Ge** 49:11–12; **Job** 32:19; **Ps** 60:3; 78:65; **Pr** 4:17; **Isa** 55:1; **Jer** 23:9; 25:15; 48:11; 51:7; **Rev** 14:8–10; 16:19; 17:1–2; 18:3

Wine as a symbol of the suffering and death of Jesus Christ

Lk 22:20 In the same way, after the supper he [Jesus] took the cup, saying, "This cup is the new covenant in my blood, which is poured out for you." pp Mt 26:27–28 pp Mk 14:23–24 pp 1Co 11:25–26   *See also banquets; drink offering; drinking; vine; vineyard.*

work, ordained by God

God ordained work as the normal routine of living. Every legitimate human task, therefore, is of intrinsic worth, however menial it may seem, and is potentially a means of glorifying God.

Work is ordained by God

Ge 1:27–28 . . . God created human beings . . . male and female he created them. God blessed them and said to them, "Be fruitful and increase in number; fill the earth and subdue it. Rule over the fish of the sea and the birds of the air and over every living creature that moves on the ground."   *See also* **Ex** 20:9 pp Dt 5:13; **Ps** 104:23

God's purposes in ordaining work

That people should be self-supporting

Ge 3:19 "By the sweat of your brow you will eat your food . . ."   *See also* **Ps** 128:2; **1Th** 4:12

That people should find self-fulfilment

Ecc 2:24 People can do nothing better than to eat and drink and find satisfaction in their work. This too, I see, is from the hand of God,   *See also* **Pr** 14:23; **Ecc** 3:22; 5:19

That people should serve others

Eph 4:28 Those who have been stealing must steal no longer, but must work, doing something useful with their own hands, that they may have something to share with those in need.   *See also* **Pr** 31:15; **1Th** 2:9; **1Ti** 5:8

That people should glorify God

Col 3:17 And whatever you [Colossian Christians] do, whether in word or deed, do it all in the name of the Lord Jesus, giving thanks to God the Father through him.   *See also* **1Co** 10:31; **Eph** 6:5–8 pp Col 3:22–24

Consequences of viewing work as God's ordinance

Work is seen as a moral duty

Tit 3:14 Our people must learn to devote themselves to doing what is good, in order that they may provide for daily necessities and not live unproductive lives.   *See also* **Pr** 6:6; **Ecc** 9:10; **1Th** 4:11; **2Th** 3:7–12

Any legitimate work may be seen as God's calling

Ge 2:15 The Lord God took the man and put him in the Garden of Eden to work it and take care of it.   *See also* **Ex** 31:1–6; 35:30–35; **Ps** 78:70–71; **Mt** 13:55 pp Mk 6:3; **Ro** 13:6; **1Co** 7:17,20–24

Work is seen as a stewardship from God himself

Col 3:23–24 Whatever you [Colossian Christians] do, work at it with all your heart, as working for the Lord, not for human masters, since you know that you will receive an inheritance from the Lord as a reward. It is the Lord Christ you are serving.   *See also* **Mt** 25:14–30 pp Lk 19:12–27; **Eph** 6:5–8

Criticism of those who will not work

2Th 3:10–11 For even when we were with you, we gave you this rule: "Anyone who will not work shall not eat." We hear that some among you are idle. They are not busy; they are busybodies.   *See also occupations; servants; wages.*

writing

A form of communication, including the writing of books, letters and scrolls. Many kinds of materials have been written on. Figuratively speaking, the heart can be written on.

Uses of writing
Books
Jer 30:2 "This is what the Lord, the God of Israel, says: 'Write in a book all the words I have spoken to you.'" *See also* **Lk** 1:3

The law
Dt 31:24 . . . Moses finished writing in a book the words of this law from beginning to end, *See also* **Jos** 24:26; **2Ki** 23:21

Annals and records
1Ki 11:41 As for the other events of Solomon's reign—all he did and the wisdom he displayed—are they not written in the book of the annals of Solomon? *See also* **2Ki** 12:19; **1Ch** 29:29; **2Ch** 35:25

Agreements **Ne** 9:38

Legal documents **Dt** 24:1; **Mk** 10:4

Letters
2Sa 11:14 In the morning David wrote a letter to Joab and sent it with Uriah.

Ro 16:22 I, Tertius, who wrote down this letter, greet you in the Lord.

Col 4:18 I, Paul, write this greeting in my own hand . . . *See also* **1Ki** 21:8–11; **Est** 3:12; **Gal** 6:11; **2Pe** 3:1

Writing materials
Stone
Ex 32:15–16 Moses turned and went down the mountain with the two tablets of the Testimony in his hands. They were inscribed on both sides, front and back. The tablets were the work of God; the writing was the writing of God, engraved on the tablets. *See also* **Dt** 27:2–3; **Job** 19:24

Wood **Nu** 17:2–3; **Dt** 6:9

Metal **Zec** 14:20

Walls **Da** 5:5–8

Writing tablets **Hab** 2:2; **Lk** 1:63

Scrolls
Dt 17:18 When he [the king] takes the throne of his kingdom, he is to write for himself on a scroll a copy of this law, taken from that of the priests, who are Levites.

Rev 1:11 . . . "Write on a scroll what you see

and send it to the seven churches: to Ephesus, Smyrna, Pergamum, Thyatira, Sardis, Philadelphia and Laodicea." *See also* **Ex** 17:14; **Nu** 5:23; **Job** 19:23; **Isa** 8:1; **Jer** 36:18; 51:60

Writing kits
Eze 9:2–3 And I saw six men coming from the direction of the upper gate, which faces north, each with a deadly weapon in his hand. With them was a man clothed in linen who had a writing kit at his side. They came in and stood beside the bronze altar . . . Then the Lord called to the man clothed in linen who had the writing kit at his side . . . *See also* **Eze** 9:11; **2Jn** 12; **3Jn** 13

God writes
The law **Ex** 31:18; 32:15–16; 34:1
Figurative writing of God
Ps 139:16 . . . All the days ordained for me were written in your book before one of them came to be. *See also* **Ps** 87:6; **Lk** 10:20

Jesus Christ writes
Jn 8:6 . . . Jesus bent down and started to write on the ground with his finger.

Writing on the heart
Jer 31:33 "This is the covenant that I will make with the house of Israel after that time," declares the Lord. "I will put my law in their minds and write it on their hearts. I will be their God, and they will be my people." *See also* **Heb** 8:10; 10:16

Ro 2:15 (. . . they [the Gentiles] show that the requirements of the law are written on their hearts, their consciences also bearing witness, and their thoughts now accusing, now even defending them.) *See also* **Pr** 3:3; 7:3; **Jer** 17:1; **2Co** 3:2

General references to writing
Ge 5:1; **Dt** 31:19; **Jos** 18:4; **2Ch** 35:4; **Ps** 102:18 *See also book; law, Ten Commandments; reading.*

Index